Law & American Society

Samuel D. Hodge, Jr.

Temple University

 **Learning Solutions**

Boston Burr Ridge, IL Dubuque, IA New York San Francisco St. Louis
Bangkok Bogotá Caracas Lisbon London Madrid
Mexico City Milan New Delhi Seoul Singapore Sydney Taipei Toronto

The *McGraw-Hill* Companies

Law & American Society

890 DIG DIG 0 9 8 7

ISBN-13: 978-0-07-354432-8
ISBN-10: 0-07-354432-9

Custom Publishing Specialist: Ann Hayes
Production Editor: Nicole Baumgartner
Cover Design: Paul L. Illian
Printer/Binder: Digital Impressions

ACKNOWLEDGMENTS

The author gratefully acknowledges the editorial assistance
of Geri St. Joseph, Esquire and Rhonda Hodge.

Special thanks is also extended to
Jakarta M. Eckhart of NiteOwl Creations for her
assistance with the layout and design.

DEDICATION

This book is dedicated to Samuel Tyler Roseman,
a special little boy who won his battle with adversity while
putting smiles on the faces of those around him.

TABLE OF CONTENTS

CHAPTER 9 ALTERNATIVE DISPUTE RESOLUTION

PART ONE

THE SUBSTANTATIVE LAW

Chapter 1

Law in American Society, An Overview

Section 1.1
Introduction

Law is a dynamic force that is not capable of a single or simple definition. For instance, the Greek philosopher *Aristotle* believed that "law is a pledge that citizens of a state will do justice to one another." *Black's Law Dictionary* defines the term as "that which must be obeyed and followed by citizens, subject to sanctions or legal consequences." Regardless of how the term is defined, the law affects all aspects of life and establishes the parameters of acceptable conduct within our society. These rules can be created by the legislature, administrative regulations, or be imposed by court decree. While one may not always agree with the law, deviations from these mandates may result in both criminal and civil liabilities.

In the face of expanding government regulations and a litigation-oriented society, individuals and businesses must be cognizant of the legal implications of their actions. Seemingly minor violations of the law may have significant financial and emotional consequences. Million-dollar verdicts occur with some frequency in the United States, and the courts continually recognize new or expanded theories of liability.

Law books tend to be theoretical and discuss the economic, sociological, and political framework within which the law operates. This text will examine the forces that shape the law in American Society and will provide the reader with the opportunity to observe the legal system in action. As the semester unfolds, the reader will be introduced to several families in a neighborhood who become involved in a variety of squabbles. Minor disturbances become major confrontations and the neighbors are soon embroiled in various civil and criminal proceedings. Students will learn of these legal controversies through a series of problems that the reader will be requested to help solve.

Great care has been used in the selection of the cases for this text. Some decisions will involve the legal exploits of well-known personalities. Others will focus on some of the more unusual judicial opinions concerning particular principles of law or cutting edge legal issues.

The text itself is broken down into three segments. Part One will examine some of the basic laws that govern this country and maintain order among members of society. Part Two of the text will expose the reader to legal procedure. These are the so-called "technicalities" that govern lawsuits. Part Three will look at ethical issues in American society.

SECTION 1.2
THE STUDY OF LAW

The rules, regulations and judicial edicts that make up the American legal system can be difficult to understand. The law is not perfect, but it does establish a system of order and justice. What would automobile traffic be like if we didn't have a motor vehicle code to establish rules of the road? How could we be secure in our homes if we didn't have the threat of imprisonment for those who violate the sanctuary of those residences?

Unlike any other facet of life, the law operates in an adversarial setting. There are two sides to every dispute and one party must lose. Who is to obtain custody of the children in a divorce proceeding? If the court awards custody to the mother, does that mean the father loves the children any less?

Judges make difficult decisions which are not always popular with all members of society. The rulings by various courts on the constitutionality of a ban on same-sex marriages are an example which rulings will be highlighted in this text. However, it is clearly superior to the alternative; uncontrolled behavior, military rule, or dictatorship where the people have no rights or say in the operation of the government.

The law can be complicated because legal documents are not easy to understand and seem to be filled with Latin phrases. Instead of simply saying a person has filed an appeal to the United States Supreme Court, this procedure is labeled a *Writ of Certiorari*. Precedent becomes *stare decisis* and legal papers are filled with wherefore's and hereinafter's.

Change is occurring, but reform takes time. More and more contracts are required to be written in easy-to-understand language. For instance, we now have "plain language" leases and authors of contracts are penalized by the court who construe ambiguities in a document against the drafter.

This text will attempt to simplify the law by explaining how the law affects members of American Society in both theory and practice. Legal terms will be translated into common English and a variety of contemporary legal issues will be explored. It is only through this type of learning process that one may gain a better appreciation of the American system of jurisprudence.

Section 1.3
The Courtroom

Judges are the final arbiters of legal disputes and the courtroom is like a stage filled with drama and suspense. It is through this forum that stories unfold with people's futures hanging in the balance. Did the suspect really kill his wife to collect the proceeds of a million dollar life insurance policy, or was his car forced off the road by an unknown assailant who robbed the couple at gunpoint and killed the woman because she started to scream? The outcome is never certain until the verdict is announced.

There is no better place to start this educational experience than to introduce the players in the courtroom.

The master of ceremonies is the judge who sits facing the parties on an elevated platform. All are bound by the judge's rulings and the jurist oversees everything that occurs within the courtroom. The starting and concluding times of the hearing and legal determinations are within the province of the judge.

The directors in the drama are the attorneys. They orchestrate the presentation of evidence and determine the sequence of witnesses to maximize the impact of their testimony.

The parties to the suit are the plaintiff and the defendant. The plaintiff initiates the case, and the defendant is the one being sued. The easiest way to remember the difference is to look at the word "defendant." Note that the term contains "defend" in its spelling.

The positions of the parties in the courtroom is predetermined by custom. The party with the burden of proof, sits closest to the jury. In a civil case, the plaintiff has the burden of proof and in a criminal case, the government must prove that the accused is guilty of the crime. The other side of the courtroom is reserved for the defense or the party being sued.

The jury sits to the side of the judge and is segregated from all others in the courtroom. This is done to guard against tampering and undue influence. Jurors are instructed not to discuss the case with anyone and to refrain from contact with those involved in the dispute. Jurors are brought into and leave the courtroom separately from all the other parties. While the judge makes all decisions concerning the applicable law, the jury resolves the factual issues. For instance, the judge will decide whether it is improper for a motorist to enter an intersection after the traffic light has turned yellow, while the jury will make the factual determination as to whether the defendant actually entered the intersection on a yellow light.

As for the actual litigation, cases are tried by the presentation of evidence. Witnesses testify as to the facts and occasionally act as character witnesses. The witness stand is located next to the judge, and is in close proximity to the jury because of the importance of the stories being told..

COURTROOM

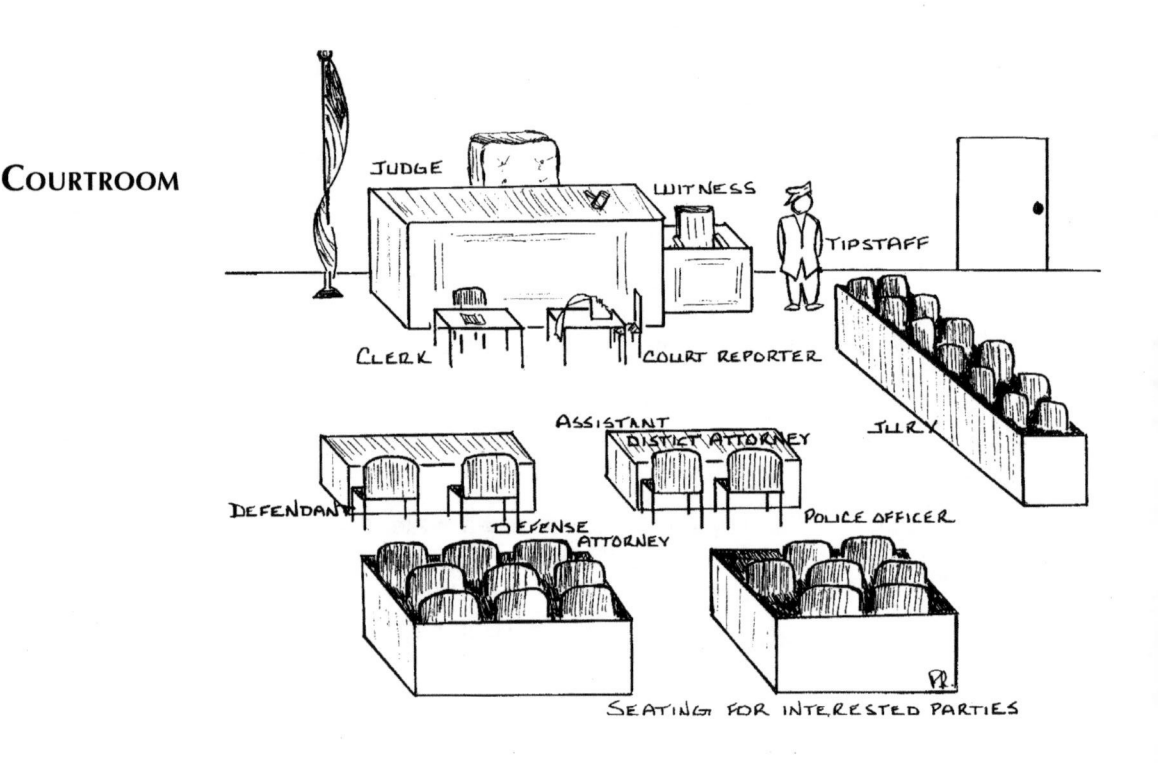

SEATING FOR INTERESTED PARTIES

All dramas need an audience and trials are no different. Courtrooms are generally open to the public and spectators are seated in the back of the room.

As a theater needs a production crew, a courtroom needs a staff. A stenographer records everything that is said for appellate review. A court clerk keeps track of the exhibits, administers the oath to all who testify, and oversees the jury. Each judge has a court officer who helps run the courtroom and assists the judge in the daily operation of the office.

SECTION 1.4
THE EVOLUTION OF
THE JURY TRIAL

The right to be judged by one's peers is so basic to a fair hearing that a trial by jury is constitutionally guaranteed. In turn, the power of a jury is immense. Did Scott Peterson murder his wife and unborn baby? Did Martha Stewart lie to the federal authorities when they investigated her sale of ImClone Systems' stock just before the value of the stock plummeted? The jury decides these types of factual questions, and their answers determine the outcome of the case.

This right to a trial by one's peer is so engrained in the American system that it is part of the United States Constitution. In most cases, parties to a trial are entitled to have their fate decided by a collective group of people chosen from the county in which the case is being heard.

The evolution of the jury system is presented in the following article prepared by the **American Association for Justice:**

The U.S. jury system has its origin in English history. Before juries, there were three general methods of "trial" in England. The first, the **wager of law**, simply required the accused person to take an oath, swearing to a fact. In those days, a person's oath carried great weight. In fact, the word "jury" derives from the term "jurare" which means to swear, to take an oath. Those with good reputations who were accused of a crime had only to swear that they were innocent to be acquitted.

If others swore against the accused, however—in effect challenging the truth of the accused's oath—a **compurgation** was necessary. The accused had to bring in 11 supporters called **compurgators**, making 12 people in all who would be willing to take an oath on behalf of the accused. The **compurgators** did not swear that what the accused said was true. They served more as character witnesses, swearing that the accused was considered a credible person. If the accused was found guilty, the compurgators might also be punished because they were then implicated in the defendant's guilt.

An accused who was a repeat offender, or who was unable to find enough compurgators willing to swear to his good character, would be subjected to a **trial by ordeal**, some sort of physical test, the results of which were supposed to indicate guilt or innocence. Unfortunately, the trials were usually designed so that, in proving innocence, the physical ordeal often resulted in bodily harm or even death to the accused.

For instance, in a **trial by hot water**, a ring might be suspended by a string in a cauldron of boiling water, either wrist-deep or elbow-deep, depending upon the severity of the crime. The accused was first "cleansed" by prayer and fasting and then was instructed to reach into the boiling water to grab the ring. If the accused's hand and arm were burned, that was considered a sign of guilt. If not burned, the obvious miracle was treated as a sign of innocence.

In a **trial by cold water**, used in the American colonies at the time of the Salem witch trials, the accused was bound and placed in a body of water that had been purified by prayer. An accused who sank was considered innocent because the water would "accept" one who was pure; floating indicated that the accused's body was polluted by sin and the water was rejecting it. Apparently the object of this ordeal was not always to drown the innocent or the guilty—the accused might be removed from the water after sinking or floating for awhile.

There were various types of **trial by fire**. Some entailed having the accused show innocence by either walking across hot coals or holding a white-hot iron rod. In these trials, the accused was guilty if burned or innocent if not burned. Sometimes the test was not whether the person was burned, but how the burn healed after a certain period of time. For instance, if the burn healed well after a few days, it was a sign of innocence because the body was "clean." But if the wound showed signs of infection, it was considered a sign that the body was defiled by evil.

Not all trials by ordeal were so dramatic. For example, one trial consisted only of taking a large piece of bread from an altar and eating it. An accused who could eat the bread without difficulty was considered innocent; choking or gagging was thought to show an evil presence in the body rejecting the bread. Another less dramatic trial required the accused to wear a blindfold and choose between two pieces of wood, one of which had a cross drawn on it. If an accused selected the one with the cross it was considered that divine intervention had proved innocence.

One common aspect of all of the trials by ordeal was that the outcomes were often a matter of chance or placed the accused in a "no-win" situation. To prove innocence, an accused had to risk death or serious bodily injury. Yet, since survival was often considered a sign of guilt, an accused lucky enough to survive the ordeal was often immediately judged guilty and put to death.

Most of these trials had a religious context and were conducted by clergymen or other church officials. Most were preceded by a purifying prayer for either the accused or the object used in the trial—water, bread, etc. If the trial required purification of the body before the ordeal, the accused was often sequestered and forced to fast and pray for up to three days prior to the trial.

These kinds of trials had no juries, and often citizens did not want to be chosen for "jury duty" as compurgators because they faced the possibility of punishment for "incorrect" verdicts. As trial by jury began to develop, the situation for the jurors did not improve much. When the courts were under royal control, the jurors were often punished if they decided against the king. Often, "incorrect" jurors had their property seized, were imprisoned, or were separated from their families as punishment for not "properly" fulfilling their duties as jurors. And since the jurors were still considered witnesses, they were also subject to punishment for perjury.

Trial by jury did not fully come into being until the trial by ordeal was abolished. The move to jury trial took longer for criminal matters than for civil cases, since trials by ordeal were used mainly to resolve common crimes or offenses against the king, the state, or the church. Corrupt rulers were known to "plant" witnesses or jurors to manipulate the outcomes of trials. In order to guard against this, the church began to support the principle that jurors should have no interest in the case at issue. With the church's influence, the courts began to insist on impartiality in jurors. The separation of the roles of witness and juror, and the desire for protection against royal manipulation, combined to spark the evolution of the system of trial with an impartial and unbiased jury.

New developments brought additional changes to the nature of the jury. For instance, when attorneys began to bring in witnesses to corroborate facts in a case, it was no longer necessary for the jurors to know the accused. And witnesses began to testify before the judge as well as the jury, not before the jury alone. Since both the judge and the jury were to hear the facts, it became more desirable for all persons to be at the same place, hear the same facts, and base their decisions solely upon the information presented in open court, instead of having some persons on the jury who knew more about the case than others. Gradually, juries came to decide only questions of fact, while judges ruled on questions of law.

By the time the colonists were settled in America, the right to **trial by jury** was considered essential. British rulers attempted to deny the colonists this right but were met by strong resistance. The importance and value the colonists placed on this right was clearly evidenced in the Declaration of Independence, and in the Sixth and Seventh Amendments to the U.S. Constitution. Today, the jury is a mainstay of the American legal system.[1]

<table>
<tr><td>

SECTION 1.5
THE PLAYERS

</td><td>

PARK, BROWN & SMITH, P.C.
ATTORNEYS AT LAW
MEMORANDUM

</td></tr>
</table>

To: All Law Clerks

FROM: Peter Smith, Esquire

RE: Biographical Sketches

My name is Peter Smith, and I am the managing partner of the law firm of *Park, Brown & Smith, P.C.* We are a multi-faceted firm which provides representation in all types of cases. We have been retained by Joseph Roberts to represent him in several disputes that have arisen with his neighbors. I am providing you with brief biographical sketches of the people whose legal problems you will hear about during the next few months.

Estelle Worthington Roberts

Estelle Worthington met Joe Roberts when they were sixteen, and they married shortly after graduating from high school. Within a year of their marriage, Estelle became pregnant and gave birth to a son, Anthony. Over the ensuing years, the couple had three more children: Kathy, Brad, and Greg.

In addition to being a full-time mother, Estelle is very involved in community service and has developed a reputation as a tenacious consumer advocate. Her causes have included lobbying for warning labels on sexually explicit music and advocating for the rights of children with learning disabilities.

Joseph Roberts

Because Joseph Roberts became a father shortly after graduating from high school, he was unable to attend college and had to obtain work with a construction firm as a bulldozer operator. As the pressures of married life mounted, Joe developed a drinking problem that caused numerous conflicts at home and work. Events climaxed when Joe accidently hit his supervisor's new car with a piece of construction equipment while inebriated. Joe was fired and was unable to pay his mounting bills. His creditors eventually sold Joe's house at Sheriff's sale.

With his last bit of money, Joe jumped on a bus and headed to the casinos in Atlantic City. Much to his disbelief, Joe hit the jackpot and won a million dollars while playing a progressive slot machine. With his new found wealth, Joe purchased the construction company that had fired him. He renamed the entity, Joro Construction Company, and assumed the title of President and CEO. Joe quickly doubled his wealth and made two unusual purchases: He purchased a baby bear from a bankrupt circus which he named "Harry," and a yacht that he called *ONLY IN AMERICA;* to reflect his life story.

Anthony Roberts

Joe and Estelle's son, Tony, is 23 years old. Throughout high school, Tony excelled in athletics and was the goalie on the soccer team.

During his junior year, Tony took up football. His soccer background enabled him to become an outstanding place kicker, and his high school team went on to win a state championship.

Tony was offered a full-paid scholarship to play college football. During his last year at college, he set a number of school records for points and field goal accuracy. The various scouting combines rated him as one of the top kickers in collegiate football. He subsequently tried out for the Stallions, the latest professional football expansion team and was signed to a three-year contract.

Kathleen Roberts

Kathy is 16 years old and spends hours talking on the phone or surfing the internet. One might assume that she is a normal teenager, but Kathy has a serious problem.

Ever since she started experimenting with drugs, her grades have gone from A's to F's and she has detached herself from the day-to-day life of her family. Whenever her parents try to communicate with her, Kathy reacts with great hostility. Since her parents increasingly avoid any sort of confrontation with her, Kathy's decline accelerates.

Peter Christopher

Peter Christopher was born one of a pair of identical twins. Since no one was able to tell them apart, their father gave each boy an identical tattoo of a shark on opposite shoulders. The Christopher brothers enlisted in the military after graduating from high school and specialized in military intelligence and photographic analysis. They spent their army days in the Middle East and Afganistan where they conducted undercover surveillance for the government.

After leaving the military, they started a private investigation service specializing in undercover surveillance and industrial espionage. However, Peter relocated to the Philadelphia area after he had a falling out with his brother over the allocation of profits from their business and moved next door to the Roberts family.

Donald Jones, M.D.   Donald Jones always wanted to be a physician, and studied diligently to achieve this lofty goal. Upon graduating from medical school, he became a surgical resident at a hospital in Chicago. Following several years in a clinical rotation, he relocated to Philadelphia and is now a successful surgeon. Dr. Jones is Joe's other neighbor.

Officer John O'Brien   John O'Brien is the oldest of five children. Both his father and grandfather were members of the police force, and it has always been John's ambition to follow in their footsteps. He graduated from college with a degree in criminal justice and secured a job as a police officer with a suburban police department. He is presently assigned to patrol the neighborhood in which Joe Roberts lives.

SECTION 1.6
CASE ANALYSIS

COMMON LAW AND STATUTORY LAW

The laws of the United States originate primarily by legislative enactment or by judicial decree. The creation of statutory law is the primary function of the legislature, whether it is on the federal, state, or municipal levels. These laws are designed to address specific problems in our society and to set forth rules to regulate the areas of concern. This process is so important to the governance of this country that this lawmaking function is found in Article One of the United States Constitution.

The Constitution also empowers the judiciary with the authority to interpret the laws and to establish standards of care. This process is known as common law or judge-made law. The court is empowered to pass judgment on what type of conduct is proper and valued in our society. These pronouncements are based upon the judge's perception of what is in the best interest of the people given the political, sociological, and economic climate of the time. The court even has the power to review a law passed by the legislature to ensure its constitutionality or to ascertain whether certain conduct falls within the contemplation of the statute.

These judicial pronouncements are rendered in the form of written explanations called **opinions** so that the parties to the litigation and the general public may understand the basis for the court's resolution of the dispute.

The study of law requires a review of these court decisions in order to gain an appreciation as to how legal determinations are made, to learn the rules that govern our conduct, and to understand the factors that a judge weighs in rendering a decision.

Reading and understanding court decisions is an acquired skill that takes time to learn. This skill, however, is extremely important to master, as judicial decisions affect every aspect of our lives.

Chapter One will introduce students to this judicial decision-making process. Initially, the reader will examine two unrelated decisions. The first case, **Ganey v. New York Jets,** provides an example of the common law process and will demonstrate how the court resolves competing interests between a professional football organization and a season-ticket holder who lost his game tickets. The second case, **Washington v. Glas,** provides an illustration of statutory law and the difficulties that arise in applying an existing statute to problems that surface with new technology, the cell phone camera, that were never contemplated when the law was first enacted.

The second step in this learning process will involve the examination of one particular legal issue over a period of time: same-sex marriage. The reader will be exposed to both a common law and statutory response to this issue.

This educational process starts with **Ganey v. New York Jets Football Club**. The case involves the rights of a season ticketholder who lost his game tickets. The football franchise merely allowed the season ticketholder to re-purchase the lost tickets for the same designated seats. The team would not provide free replacement tickets. This policy was implemented because of fans who fraudulently notified the team that their tickets were misplaced in order to obtain a second set of game passes which were given to others. An honest fan, however, who could not find the game tickets was forced to pay for the same seats a second time, claiming that this payment provided the team with a windfall profit. Which party should succeed in this dispute, and is there any public policy that would be advanced by the court's siding with one of the litigants?

MICHAEL GANEY v. NEW YORK JETS FOOTBALL CLUB
550 N.Y.S. 2D 566 (CIV. CT. N.Y. 1990)

The issue raised in this action is what recourse does a holder of season tickets for a professional football team have when the tickets are lost?

Ganey purchased season tickets for the New York Jets football team. Shortly after the football season began, the claimant notified the Jets organization that the tickets were lost and requested replacement tickets. Ganey was informed that the Jets' policy regarding ticket holders who have lost or misplaced their tickets is to allow the ticket holder an opportunity to purchase a new season ticket subscription for the same designated seats.

Ganey then purchased two of his three season tickets and commenced this action for double billing and unjust enrichment. The causes of action for double billing and unjust enrichment are based on the theory that the two sales transactions represented one single contract, and that defendant charged Ganey twice for the same designated seats.

This argument cannot prevail since the two sales transactions made between the parties constituted separate and distinct contracts. Ganey originally purchased three season tickets for the New York Jets. The season tickets gave claimant the privilege to view home games of the New York Jets from the designated seats. The condition precedent in the contract provides that the ticket holder must present the ticket at the gate for admission. Ganey could not meet this condition and by his own conduct has caused his own inability to reap the benefit of the agreement. The New York Jets have fulfilled its end of the bargain between the parties. It is printed clearly on the ticket that, "Tickets cannot be replaced if lost, stolen or destroyed."

The subsequent sale and purchase of season tickets between the parties constituted a new and separate contract. Although the Jets' organization sold tickets twice to Ganey for the same seats, the second sale was made at the request of Ganey who could not fulfill his contractual obligation for admission under the first contract with the team. The Jets were under no obligation to sell Ganey new tickets for the same seats. However, the second set of tickets were offered for sale to him as an option which would permit him to attend the Jets' games. Ganey accepted the option by purchasing the new tickets. The football club has also offered claimant a refund if the original tickets are found.

The football organization argues that the Jets' policy of no refund or replacement and the opportunity to purchase a new ticket subscription was made to balance two competing interests. On the one hand, the Jets do not want to deprive ticket holders who have actually lost or misplaced their tickets of the opportunity to attend and view Jets' games in their contracted seats. On the other hand, the Jets' organization had to devise a procedure by which individuals who did not purchase Jets' tickets are prevented from entering the stadium which can cause serious security problems.

The Jets' policy concerning claims of lost and misplaced tickets has been implemented for approximately nine years. Prior to this policy, the Jets' organization learned that many season ticket holders would falsely claim to have lost or misplaced their tickets in order to obtain a new and free set of season tickets. The ticket holder would then give a set of tickets to friends, or ticket scalpers who would use or sell them to gain improper entry into the stadium. This not only caused theft of services but also created a security problem which affected the safety and welfare of the other attendants. Often the intruders would sit in the seats of other fans which created arguments and altercations. This situation resulted in a security nightmare for the Jets' organization. They argue that since the implementation of this policy, the claims of lost Jets' tickets have decreased by thirty percent.

The Court finds that the present policy of the Jets is not only sound but is a necessary precaution to insure the general safety and welfare of those who attend Jets' games.

Since the two ticket sales transactions made between the parties represented separate contracts, the Jets could not be held liable for double billing or unjust enrichment as urged by claimant. The recourse of obtaining a free duplicate set of tickets from the club for those bona fide ticket holders who actually lost or misplaced their tickets has been extinguished by the action of those unscrupulous fans who have abused the Jets' earlier policy of free replacement tickets to gain improper entry by others into the stadium.

Based on the foregoing, Ganey's causes of action against the New York Jets Football Club is dismissed.

Advances in computer technology allow a product to contain a bar code which is unique to that item. Most merchants utilize this system and scan the product's bar code to check the price or to keep track of inventory. Does this new technology negate the concerns by the New York Jets about a second fan entering the stadium with a replacement ticket? Would embedding a bar code on each ticket solve the problem of misplaced tickets to the mutual satisfaction of both the team and ticket holder? Tickets presented at an event would merely have to be scanned by security to see if someone else has already presented the same bar code for admission to the stadium. If the sports team refuses to invest in the bar code technology, should the court punish the franchise by requiring the team to issue free replacement tickets?

The second case for review involves the cell phone camera, an engineering marvel that is gaining in popularity. As more and more of these mobile devices are purchased, a number of novel legal issues have surfaced involving such things as voyeurism, invasion of privacy, child security, and workplace espionage. Camera phones and small video cameras make it easy to take pictures or video of an unsuspecting person, or to transmit images of workplace secrets across the internet. Some facilities, such as fitness centers, schools, and military installations have even barred these devices from their premises. In most cases, however, precautions have not been put into place so citizens must resort to existing laws for a remedy.

In **State of Washington v. Sean Tyler Glas,** the court had to ascertain whether the criminal laws of Washington on invasion of privacy could be used to prosecute an individual who utilized a camera phone to take inappropriate pictures of unsuspecting women. This case is an example of statutory law.

STATE OF WASHINGTON V. SEAN TYLER GLAS
54 P.3D 147 (WASH. 2002)

Sean Glas and Richard Sorrells were each found guilty of voyeurism for taking pictures underneath women's skirts ("upskirt" voyeurism). Glas and Sorrells contend that Washington's voyeurism statute does not apply to their actions because it does not criminalize upskirt photography in a public place.

On April 26, 1999, Glas took pictures up the skirts of two women working at the Valley Mall. Mosier was working in the ladies' department at Sears when Glas caught her attention. Glas was lurking near her and acting suspiciously. Mosier saw a flash out of the corner of her eye and turned around to discover Glas squatting on the floor a few feet behind her. She later noticed a small, silver camera in his hand. Police confiscated the film, revealing pictures of Mosier's undergarments.

On July 21, 2000, Sorrells attended the Bite of Seattle at the Seattle Center with a video camera. Jang was standing in line to buy ice cream when she noticed Sorrells behind her. Jang thought that Sorrells had his hand on her purse so she reacted and Sorrells fled from the line. A witness later informed police that she had observed Sorrells videotaping underneath little girls' dresses. Police viewed a copy of the videotape from Sorrells' camcorder and discovered images of children and adults, including Jang. Many of the images were taken from ground level, recording up the females' skirts.

Under **RCW 9A.44.115**, does a person have a reasonable expectation of privacy in a public place? Washington's voyeurism statute provides:

> A person commits the crime of voyeurism if, for the purpose of arousing or gratifying the sexual desire of any person, he or she knowingly views, photographs, or films another person, without that person's knowledge and consent, *while the person* being viewed, photographed, or filmed *is in a place where he or she would have a reasonable expectation of privacy.*

The statute defines a place where a person "would have a reasonable expectation of privacy" as either "a place where a reasonable person would believe that he or she could disrobe in privacy, without being concerned that his or her undressing was being photographed or filmed by another," or "a place where one may reasonably expect to be safe from casual or hostile intrusion or surveillance." Both Glas and Sorrells contend that the voyeurism statute was misapplied because the victims were in *public* places and therefore did not possess a reasonable expectation of privacy.

The voyeurism statute protects an individual "while the person… is in a *place* where he or she would have a reasonable expectation of privacy." **RCW 9A.44115(2)**. Thus, it is the physical location of the person that is ultimately at issue, not the part of the person's body.

California draws the closest parallel to the case presented here. In 1998, citizens in Orange County were subjected to three incidents of video voyeurism, including one case where the perpetrator followed several dozen women while he attempted to position a gym bag containing a hidden video camera between the woman's legs while she stood in line or shopped in a crowded store. Prosecutors determined that California's voyeurism statute was inadequate to cover these incidents. The statute provided:

> Any person who looks through a hole or opening, into, or otherwise views, by means of any instrumentality, including, but not limited to, a periscope, telescope, binoculars, camera, motion picture camera, or camcorder, the interior of a bathroom, changing room, fitting room, dressing room, or tanning booth, or the interior of any other area in which the occupant has a reasonable expectation of privacy, with the intent to invade the privacy of a person or persons inside.

Significantly, the statute focused on the location of the incident and did not cover public places. In response, the California Legislature amended its statute, adding a subsection that focused on the nature of the invasion itself, rather than where the crime was committed. The supplemental subsection stated:

> Any person who uses a concealed camcorder, motion picture camera, or photographic camera of any type, to secretly videotape, film, photograph, or record by electronic means, another, identifiable person under or through the clothing being worn by that person, for the purpose of viewing the body of, or the undergarments worn by, that other person, without the consent or knowledge of that other person, with the intent to arouse, appeal to, or gratify the lust, passions, or sexual desires of that person and invade the privacy of that other person, under circumstances in which the other person has a reasonable expectation of privacy.

The key language "under circumstances in which the other person has a reasonable expectation of privacy" differs from the first subsection, which named the place where this privacy is expected, thus leaving the option open to include public places.

Both Glas and Sorrells engaged in disgusting and reprehensible behavior. Nevertheless, we hold that Washington's voyeurism statute does not apply to actions taken in purely public places and hence does not prohibit the "upskirt" photographs they took.

Pennsylvania's Invasion of Privacy statute is set forth in **18 Pa.C. S.§7507.1(a)** and provides:

> A person commits the offense of invasion of privacy if he knowingly views, photographs or films another person without that person's knowledge and consent while the person being viewed, photographed or filmed is in a state of full or partial nudity and is in a place where the person would have a reasonable expectation of privacy.

What would be the outcome of a criminal prosecution in Pennsylvania for "upskirt" voyeurism if the facts are identical to those presented in **State of Washington v. Sean Tyler Glas?**

The Pennsylvania House of Representatives has introduced an amendment to that state's invasion of privacy law. Would the following proposed amendment change your answer in an upskirt voyeurism case?

A person commits the offense of invasion of privacy if he, for the purpose of arousing or gratifying the sexual desire of any person, knowingly does any of the following:

(1) Views, photographs, electronically depicts, films or otherwise records another person without that person's knowledge and consent while that person viewed, photographed or filmed is in a state of full or partial nudity and is in a place where the person would have a reasonable expectation of privacy.

(2) Views, photographs, videotapes, electronically depicts, films or otherwise records the intimate parts of another person, whether or not covered by clothing or undergarments, which that person does not intend to be visible by normal public observation without that person's knowledge and consent.

SECTION 1.7
ELEMENTS OF A
JUDICIAL OPINION

It is important to be familiar with the elements of a judicial opinion so one may better understand the law that the court has established. These concepts will be illustrated by examining judicial pronouncements on same-sex marriages. The firestorm concerning this controversial issue erupted in November 2003 when the Massachusetts Supreme Judicial Court ruled that a statute barring same-sex couples from marrying was unconstitutional. Not only will the reader learn the parts of a juridical decision, but he or she will also read the trial court's decision on this issue which reached the opposite result.

The full name of the case is **Goodridge v. Department of Public Health;** this is known as the caption of a case since it identifies the parties to the lawsuit. In other words, Goodridge sued the Department of Public Health so she is known as the plaintiff. The Department of Public Health is the defendant since it has been sued. When a case is appealed to a higher court, the names of the parties change. The person who appeals the lower court's decision is the **"appellant."** The party against whom the appeal is filed is the **"appellee."**

The **citation** tells a person how to locate the case. In this instance, the citation of the trial court decision is 14 Mass. L. Rptr. 591 (Mass. Super. 2002). "Mass. L. Rptr." refers to the book that contains this decision or the Massachusetts Law Reporter. The number "14" refers to the volume of the book that contains the decision, and "59" is the page number on which the case is published. Goodridge was initially decided by the trial court. In Massachusetts, the trial court is known as the Superior Court. By way of comparison, the Superior Court in Pennsylvania refers to an intermediate appellate court. If a federal court decided the case, the initials F. or F. Supp. would appear. Finally, "2002" is the year in which the case was decided.

Goodridge v. Department of Public Health was appealed and assigned a new number to reflect that fact. The appellate decision is located at 798 N. E. 2d 941 (Mass. 2003). The abbreviation "N.E. 2d" refers to the Northeast Reporter, Second Series. The Northeast Reporter contains appellate court decisions in Massachusetts, Illinois, Indiana, New York and Ohio. By comparison, California decisions are published in the Pacific Reporter, and Pennsylvania cases are set forth in the Atlantic Reporter.

The next item that appears after the caption is the name of the judge who authored the opinion. On appeal, one judge writes the opinion or body of the case for the "majority" of the court. Because an appellate court consists of a panel of three or more judges, a decision reached by more than half of the judges constitutes the **"majority opinion."** A decision rendered by the majority is the law. A judge authors a **"dissenting opinion"** when he or she disagrees with the result reached by the majority—however, the dissent has no value as precedent. A judge may also write a **"concurring opinion"** when the jurist agrees with the outcome of the case but wants to note a difference in logic for reaching the decision.

SECTION 1.8
BRIEFING OF A CASE

Breaking a case down into its component parts simplifies a person's understanding of the opinion. An opinion has four main parts:

1. The Action;
2. The Facts;
3. The Issue; and
4. The Opinion of the Court.

The Action — What kind of case is it? What remedy is being sought? For instance, does the case involve a criminal prosecution or a civil lawsuit for money damages?

The Facts — What happened? The reader should be concerned with the three *W's*: specifically, *Who* did *What* to *Whom?* The facts of a case are discussed in a narrative form.

The Issue — What question is presented to the court for it to decide?

The Opinion of the Court — First, the reader must ascertain what the court decided. In other words, how did the court answer the question posed in the Issue section? Second, and more importantly, what justification does the court provide for coming up with its answer? For example, what sociological, economic or political policies does the court use to justify its decision? Any dissenting or concurring opinions should also be noted in this section, but the discussion will be less detailed than that of the majority opinion.

An appellate court can affirm, reverse or remand the decision of a lower court. When a decision is **affirmed**, the appellate court determines that the lower court reached the correct decision. The appellate court **reverses** a decision when it finds that the lower court's decision was incorrect. A case may also be **remanded** to the trial court. This occurs when the appellate court finds that the trial judge committed an error in deciding the case, additional evidence must be obtained, or the lower court's decision must be clarified.

The reader should now examine the two opinions in **Goodridge v. Department of Public Health** and break the cases down into their component parts.

Marriage is part of the basic fabric of Western civilization that is created and regulated by state law. More than 100 years ago, the Supreme Court in **Maynard v. Hill** acknowledged the connection between marriage and a free society when it pronounced marriage as "the foundation of the family and society, without which there would be neither civilization nor progress." Other courts have followed this principle by stating that "the structure of society itself largely depends upon the institution of marriage... The joining of the man and woman in marriage is the most socially productive and individually fulfilling relationship that one can enjoy in the course of a lifetime." **Marvin v. Marvin, 557 P. 2d 106 (Cal. 1976).**

Over the years, however, the institution of marriage has not been without its controversies. For instance, interracial couples were prohibited from marrying until 1967 when the United States Supreme Court found the following Virginia statute unconstitutional:

> All marriages between a white person and a colored person shall be absolutely void without any decree of divorce or other legal process.

In announcing its decisions, the court noted that "marriage is one of the 'basic civil rights of man,' fundamental to our very existence and survival. To deny this fundamental freedom on so unsupportable a basis as racial classifications... is surely to deprive all the State's of liberty without due process of law."

The last few years has witnessed a new controversy—same-sex marriages. Countries around the world are being asked to recognize these unions in increased frequency. Massachusetts, however, is the first state in this country to recognize same-sex marriages in **Goodridge v. Department of Public Health.** The case was initially heard by a trial judge who refused to recognize the union on the theory that history, statutory construction and the need to procreate only recognizes marriage as a union between a man and a woman. This decision was reversed by the Massachusetts Supreme Judicial Court which ruled that marriage is a voluntary union between two individuals as spouses and that any prohibition against same-sex marriages would be constitutionally invalid. These decisions are presented so that the reader may gain an appreciation of how the courts arrive at a decision when there is no precedent in the jurisdiction.

HILLARY GOODRIDGE V. DEPARTMENT OF PUBLIC HEALTH
14 MASS. L. RPTR. 591 (MASS. SUPER. 2002)

Thomas Connolly, Justice

This case concerns the most fundamental institution: marriage. The plaintiffs are seven same-sex couples who want the state and society to recognize their commitment to each other through marriage. Plaintiffs argue that the Commonwealth's marriage statute should be interpreted gender-neutrally so as not to restrict marriage to a man and a woman.

The Supreme Judicial Court defines marriage as follows:

> Marriage is…a civil contract, founded in the social nature of man, and intended to regulate, chasten, and refine the intercourse between the sexes; and to multiply, preserve, and improve the species. It is an engagement by which a single man and single woman, of sufficient discretion, take each other as husband and wife. From the nature of the contract, it exists during the lives of the two parties, unless dissolved for causes which defeat the object of marriage…

The Supreme Judicial Court has interpreted "marriage," within Massachusetts' statutes, "as the union of one man and one woman." Likewise, other jurisdictions' courts have interpreted their marriage statutes to apply only to one man and one woman.

Second, the statutory construction of the marriage statutes demonstrates the Legislature's intent to limit marriage to a man and a woman. Because marriage is not defined in the statue itself, the term must be construed as it is "commonly understood." Accordingly, Black's Law Dictionary defines "marriage" as "[t]he legal union of a man and woman as husband and wife." Similarly, Webster's Third New International Dictionary defines marriage as "the state of being united to a person of the opposite-sex as husband or wife."

The history of marriage further illuminates the purpose of the modern marriage statutes. Marriage emphasized the unity of husband and wife. Within that unity, the man and woman divided gender-specific responsibilities with the husband responsible first for farming and later for financial support and the wife responsible for domestic work, childbearing, and child rearing.

Based on the legal application of the word "marriage," the construction of the marriage statutes and the history of marriage, Massachusetts' marriage statutes cannot support same-sex marriage.

Plaintiffs assert that the right to marry the person of their choice is a fundamental right. Therefore, to construe the state marriage statutes to exclude same-sex couples is unconstitutional.

Massachusetts has recognized as fundamental those rights that are deeply rooted in the Commonwealth's history and tradition. Restricting marriage to the union of one man and one woman is deeply rooted in the Commonwealth's legal tradition and practice.

No state legislature has enacted laws permitting same-sex marriage; and a large majority of states, as well as the United States Congress, have affirmatively prohibited the recognizing of same-sex marriage. Thus, this court cannot conclude that "a right to same-sex marriage is so rooted in the traditions and collective conscience of our people that failure to recognize it would violate the fundamental principles of liberty and justice that lie at the base of all our civil and political institutions."

This court acknowledges the inherent contradiction that the Commonwealth allows same-sex couples to establish legal relationships with their children but not with each other. Furthermore, the Legislature amended the adoption laws to allow adoption of children by same-sex couples. Commonwealth's elected representatives, not the courts, should resolve this paradox. While this court understands the plaintiffs' efforts to be married, they should pursue their quest on Beacon Hill.

For the foregoing reasons, it is ORDERED that plaintiffs' motion for summary judgment be DENIED.

This trial court decision was immediately appealed by the plaintiffs to the Supreme Judicial Court of Massachusetts which reached the opposite result. This state's highest court found that a ban on same-sex marriage would be a violation of its constitution.

HILLARY GOODRIDGE V. DEPARTMENT OF PUBLIC HEALTH
798 N.E. 2D 941 (MASS. SUPREME. 2003)

The plaintiffs are fourteen individuals from Massachusetts. In March and April, 2001, each of the plaintiff couples attempted to obtain a marriage license from a city clerk's office. In each case, the clerk either refused to accept the notice of intention to marry or denied a marriage license on the ground that Massachusetts does not recognize same-sex marriage. Because obtaining a marriage license is a necessary prerequisite to civil marriage in Massachusetts, denying marriage licenses to the plaintiffs was tantamount to denying them access to civil marriage itself, with its social and legal protections, benefits, and obligations.

We interpret statutes to carry out the Legislature's intent. The everyday meaning of "marriage" is "[t]he legal union of a man and woman as husband and wife," Black's Law Dictionary. The plaintiffs do not argue that the term "marriage" has ever had a different meaning.

The larger question is whether, government action that bars same-sex couples from civil marriage constitutes a legitimate exercise of the State's authority to regulate conduct, or whether this categorical marriage exclusion violates the Massachusetts Constitution.

We begin by considering the nature of civil marriage itself. Simply put, the government creates civil marriage. In a real sense, there are three partners to every civil marriage: two willing spouses and an approving State. While only the parties can mutually assent to marriage, their terms of the marriage—who may marry and what obligations, benefits, and liabilities attach to civil marriage—are set by the Commonwealth.

The plaintiffs challenge the marriage statute on both equal protection and due process grounds. The department posits three legislative rationales for prohibiting same-sex couples from marrying: (1) providing a "favorable setting for procreation;" (2) ensuring the optimal setting for child rearing, which the department defines as "a two-parent family with one parent of each sex;" and (3) preserving scarce State and private financial resources. We consider each in turn.

Our laws of civil marriage do not privilege procreative heterosexual intercourse between married people above every other form of adult intimacy and every other means of creating a family. Fertility is not a condition of marriage, nor is it grounds for divorce. It is the exclusive and permanent commitment of the marriage partners to one another, not the begetting of children, that is the sine qua non of civil marriage.

The department's first state rationale, equating marriage with unassisted heterosexual procreation, shades imperceptibly into its second: that confining marriage to opposite-sex couples ensures that children are raised in the "optimal" setting. Protecting the welfare of children is a paramount State policy. Restricting marriage to opposite-sex couples, however, cannot plausibly further this policy.

The third rational advanced by the department is that limiting marriage to opposite-sex couples furthers the Legislature's interest in conserving scarce State and private financial resources. An absolute statutory ban on same-sex marriage bears no rational relationship to the goal of economy. The department's generalization, that same-sex couples are less financially dependent on each other than opposite-sex couples, ignores that many same-sex couples, such as many of the plaintiffs in this case, have children and other dependents (here, aged parents) in their care.

We declare that barring an individual from the protections, benefits, and obligations of civil marriage solely because that person would marry a person of the same sex violates the Massachusetts Constitution. Entry of judgement shall be stayed for 180 days to permit the Legislature to take such action as it may deem appropriate in light of this opinion.

The Massachusetts legislature responded to this controversial appellate court decision recognizing same-sex marriages by introducing a constitutional amendment that would ban these types of unions. The legislature's solution to the problem is to create a new category of domestic partnerships as opposed to civil unions. The following amendment has been proposed:

PROPOSAL for a legislative amendment to the Constitution to define marriage as the union of one man and one woman.

It being the public policy of this Commonwealth to protect the unique relationship of marriage, in order to promote, among other goals, the stability and welfare of society and the best interests of children, only the union of one man and one woman shall be valid or recognized as a marriage in Massachusetts. Any other relationship shall not be recognized as a marriage or its legal equivalent, nor shall it receive the benefits or incidents exclusive to marriage from the Commonwealth, its agencies, departments, authorities, commissions, offices, officials and political subdivisions.

QUESTIONS FOR DISCUSSION:

1. Does this proposed constitutional amendment satisfy the concerns raised by the Massachusetts Supreme Judicial Court?

2. Will people of a civil union enjoy the same benefits as a married couple?

Several countries have validated same-sex marriages including Holland, Belgium, Denmark, the Netherlands, and several provinces in Canada. In the United States, however, the results have been mixed with most courts upholding the ban on same-sex marriages. Congress has even weighed in on the issue by passing the Defense of Marriage Act which defines marriage as a union between a man and a woman thereby prohibiting federal recognition of same-sex marriages. The legislation also gives states the right to refuse to honor same-sex marriages obtained in another state. At least 38 states have followed the lead of the federal government, and have banned same-sex marriages. As of January 2004, New Jersey agreed to recognize civil unions. Some members of Congress are attempting to regulate same-sex marriages by a constitutional amendment which provides:

Marriage in the United States shall consist only of the union of a man and a woman. Neither this Constitution, nor the constitution of any State, nor State or Federal law, shall be construed to require that marital status or the legal incidents thereof be conferred upon unmarried couples or groups.

SECTION 1.9
STATUS AND PROCESS

Status and process is a concept that makes judicial decisions a little easier to understand. The principle is quite simple. If one is able to ascertain who enjoys favored status with the law, it is often possible to predict the outcome of a case without even knowing the law.

Status and process requires an examination of the parties to the litigation. The outcome of the case will depend on whom the courts want to protect and what goals society wants to achieve.

For example, consider the institution of marriage. Does the law favor or frown upon marriage? Historically, the laws supported marriage and the outcome of a case was frequently decided to uphold that institution. From a sociological point of view, marriage serves three functions:

1. It is a way of regulating the struggle between men and women. This is amply reinforced during the marriage vows when one takes a spouse for better or for worse, and through sickness and in health.

2. The law recognizes marriage as the accepted way of producing children, albeit not the only way. A child born out of wedlock is frowned upon and labeled "illegitimate."

3. Marriage is favored since it offers a logical way of transferring assets from generation to generation. Assets are passed down to children and spouses rather than being given to the first person that arrives at the home of the decedent.

To prove that the law historically favored the institution of marriage, one merely has to think of how easy it is to become married and how difficult it is to obtain a divorce. Everyone is aware that a marital union can be created through a religious or civil ceremony. The law, however, went out of its way to establish marital relationships and had created the fiction of a common law marriage.

In **Hall v. Duster, 727 So. 2d 834 (Ala. Civ. App. 1999)**, the court outlined three general requirements for a common law marriage. First, the parties must have the capacity to marry. Next, they must agree to enter into a marital relationship, but no particular words are necessary to show a present agreement to marry. This is demonstrated in **In re Estate of Garges, 378 A. 2d 307 (Pa. 1977),** where the court stated:

> A marriage contract does not require any specific form of words. In particular, words of taking or explicit utterances, such as "I take you to be my wife" or "I hereby marry you" are unnecessary. All that is essential is proof of an agreement to enter into a legal relationship of marriage at the present time. For example,

a marriage contract was found where a man gave a woman a ring and said, "Now you have the right and you are my wife," whereupon she replied, "That is fine, I love it."

Finally, the parties must consummate the marriage; that is, they must live in such a way as to gain public recognition that they are living as husband and wife. For instance, the fact that a man "made no comment" when introduced as a woman's husband was taken as an objective manifestation of an intent to be married. Sexual relations between the parties is also not an indispensable element of co-habitation.

The implications of these informal arrangements are dramatic. A common law marriage is just as valid as a religious or civil ceremony and requires a formal divorce decree to dissolve.

What other institutions enjoy favor with the law? These groups would include children, incompetents, the government, and religious organizations. For instance, the government, its agencies, and high ranking officials enjoy immunity from suit in most cases.

Status and process, however, requires that one analyze the institution as it existed at the time of the court decision. As times change, so do the institutions that the law protects. With regard to marriage, women were traditionally viewed as the weaker of the sexes. Therefore, women in the past were automatically awarded one-third to one-half of the husband's net income in a support proceeding. Following the Equal Rights movement, and the shifting of public opinion, the role of women in today's society has vastly changed. They are considered equal to men and have made significant inroads in the market place. It is now common to see a female doctor, lawyer, construction worker, police officer or soldier. This equality of the sexes has resulted in change in the support laws. The courts now examine the earning capacity of each person instead of making an automatic award to the wife. This has resulted in court decisions requiring wives to pay support to husbands and giving husbands custody of the children.

Traditional notions of marriage are also being reexamined in view of the number of people who choose to cohabitate instead of becoming married. The U.S. Census Bureau estimates that unmarried couples make up about 5.5 million households with about 40 percent of those households having children. New terms are being coined to identify this growing group such as domestic partners who seek the same benefits afforded to their married counterparts. For example, a number of employers now offer benefits to this group with increasing frequency similar to those provided to a married couple. In view of this trend, has the concept of a common law marriage outgrown its usefulness?

Common law marriage was created because of the difficulties in obtaining a marriage license during the early years of this nation. Women were also considered the weaker partner and needed to be protected at all costs. In view of the current ease in obtaining a marriage license and the economic power of women, the continued validity of common law marriage is the issue in **PNC Bank Corporation v. Workers Compensation Appeal Board.**

PNC Bank Corporation v. Workers' Compensation Appeal Board
831 A. 2d 1269 (Pa. Cmwlth. 2002)

In this appeal, we are called upon to address the issue of the continued viability of common law marriages.

In 1997, Kretz filed a fatal claim petition alleging that he was the common law spouse of Stamos, who died in an airplane crash in 1994 while working for her employer. The nature of Kretz's relationship with Stamos was the subject of the hearings that followed before the Worker's Compensation Judge.

The doctrine of common law marriage was recognized by the United States Supreme Court as early as 1877. As settlement in America moved westward, common law marriages existed due to necessity. The country was sparsely populated, and travel difficult such that it was often difficult to have access to officials or clergy.

The vast majority of cases pondering the validity and desirability of common law marriage shared a common sociological backdrop: female economic dependency. Almost all common law marriage cases involved women in need of financial support, and most were initiated by female plaintiffs.

Common law marriage provided judges with a way to privatize the financial dependency of economically unstable women plaintiffs. By declaring a woman to be a man's wife or widow at common law, courts shielded the public from the potential claims of needy women, effectively deflecting those claims inward to a particular private, family unit.

Because claims for the existence of a marriage in the absence of a certified ceremonial marriage present a "fruitful source of perjury and fraud," Pennsylvania courts have long viewed such claims with hostility. Common law marriages are tolerated, but not encouraged.

Many sound reasons exist to abandon a system that allows the determination of important rights to rest on evidence fraught with inconsistencies, ambiguities and vagaries. The circumstances creating a need for the doctrine are not present in today's society. A woman without dependent children is no longer thought to pose a danger of burdening the state with her support and maintenance simply because she is single, and the right of a single parent to obtain child support is no longer dependent upon his or her marital status.

The fact that in today's world many couples choose to cohabit without any intention of being presently married only adds to the potential difficulties generated by common lack of public understanding as to what separates a common law marriage from mere cohabitation. Some persons may mistakenly believe they are common law spouses if they have lived with another for an extended period of time, particularly if they have children together. Others may assume that they can never be deemed married unless they have gone through the statutory formalities. When their understanding is challenged by dispute with their partners, third parties or government authorities, they may discover too late that they have forgone rights or undertaken responsibilities contrary to their intentions.

Moreover, uncertainty as to marital status has a far greater detrimental impact on third parties today than when the doctrine was created. At that time, persons contemplating business transactions with couples relied predominantly upon the creditworthiness and earning capac-

ity of the husband. In twenty-first century commerce, third parties are entitled to know whether the men, women and couples with whom they contract are married or single, for that may significantly affect their rights. Statutory marriage provides a certain record if third parties chose to investigate; common law marriage may be impossible to ascertain or verify until some dispute brings about court proceedings.

This conclusion seems inescapable that recognizing as married only those who have duly recorded their union pursuant to the Marriage Law will greatly reduce the need for litigation to determine marital status. We must conclude that this court can no longer place its imprimatur on a rule which seems to be a breeding ground for such conduct and its attendant disrespect for the law itself.

SECTION 1.10
CHRISTOPHER V. ROBERTS

PROBLEM ONE—A

PARK, BROWN & SMITH, P.C.
ATTORNEYS AT LAW
MEMORANDUM

TO: All Law Clerks

FROM: Peter Smith, Esquire

RE: Kathy Roberts and the Purchase of Her Car

Kathy Roberts, a 16 year-old, related the following story to me.

Immediately after passing her driving test, Kathy decided she must have a car. Unfortunately, she and her father, Joe Roberts, disagreed as to whether she was ready for what her father considered an "unnecessary extravagance." Joe had called his insurance agent and learned that the annual premium for insuring the car was more than what the automobile was worth.

Despite her father's objections, Kathy decided to secretly purchase a vehicle on her own. While walking home from school, she noticed that her next-door neighbor, Peter Christopher, had a *For Sale* sign in the window of a car parked in his driveway. The vehicle seemed perfect for Kathy's needs. The Honda was in good mechanical condition and

Kathy was certain that her father would be favorably impressed with her choice of transportation. Kathy contacted the neighbor and purchased the vehicle for $5,000.

When Kathy's father learned of the purchase, he exploded. "How dare you buy a car after I told you no." Kathy had never seen her father more outraged. Even her sweetest smile couldn't calm him down. Not only did he suspend her driving privileges, he even attempted to return the car to Christopher but the neighbor refused to take the car back, claiming that a "deal is a deal." Two days later, Kathy figured that her father had calmed down enough for her to start driving the vehicle. Unfortunately, Kathy was unable to negotiate a sharp turn a block from home and demolished the Honda. As she sat on the curb crying, the hubcap of the vehicle rolled by her. Since this was the only thing left of the car, she picked it up and walked home.

Kathy spent the rest of the day calling friends for advice. One girl-friend told Kathy that she could obtain the return of her money from Christopher since she was only sixteen. The girlfriend had her money refunded from a record club that she had joined when she was fifteen. Relying on this advice, Kathy approached her neighbor and demanded her money back. She even offered Christopher the return of the hubcap. After all, that was all that was left of the car. Christopher laughed and said that Kathy had entered into a valid contract and she had destroyed the car.

Please read **Swalberg v. Hannegan** and apply the case to Kathy's problem. You must decide the following:

1. Should Kathy be able to rescind the contract and get her money back from Christopher?

2. Does it matter that the only thing she can return to Christopher is the hubcap, or must she pay to have the car repaired before she can disaffirm the contract?

3. Did status and process play any part in the Swalberg decision? Explain your answer.

Larry Swalberg v. Todd Hannegan
883 P. 2d 931 (Ct. App. Utah 1994)

In 1990, Hannegan contracted with Swalberg to purchase plaintiff's 1974 Ford truck for $2,500. Defendant's minority was apparently not discussed when the parties entered into the contract, and there is no allegation that defendant made any misrepresentation as to his age. Defendant paid plaintiff $640 and agreed to pay the balance three months later. Rather than paying the balance, however, defendant disaffirmed the contract on the basis of his minority. Plaintiff filed a complaint asking that the contract be enforced, or in the alternative, that the truck be returned and that defendant be held responsible for the reasonable value of his use of the truck or for the amount it depreciated while in defendant's possession.

Plaintiff argued that when defendant disaffirmed the contract, defendant did not properly "restore" the truck since he purchased it for $2,500 and returned it in a condition worth only $700. The court awarded $1,160, which was the remaining balance minus the value placed upon the truck in its returned condition.

The dispositive issue on appeal is whether a minor who disaffirms a contract is required to restore the full value of the property received under the contract. Defendant argues that the law does not require a disaffirming minor to restore the other party to his or her precontractual status. We agree.

Utah Code Ann. § 15-2-2 (1986) provides:

A minor is bound not only for the reasonable value of necessities but also for his contracts, unless he disaffirms them before or within a reasonable time after he obtains his majority and restores to the other party all money or prop-

erty received by him and remaining within his control at any time after attaining his majority.

This statute requires only that the property remaining within the minor's control be returned to the other party. The trial court held, however, that defendant was required to return the property in its original condition or be liable for the difference in value. This holding is clearly contrary to the provisions of this statute and case law.

In **Blake v. Harding, 54 Utah 158 (1919),** a minor sold a pony, harness, and buggy to an adult at an agreed value of $150, for which the adult delivered 3,000 shares of stock in a mining company. The minor later disaffirmed the contract and returned the stock to the adult. The minor sued to recover $150 since the adult had sold the pony, harness, and buggy. The jury was instructed that "if you believe that the contract was reasonable, and if you further find that the mining stock traded to the minor by the adult is now worthless, the minor is not entitled to recover in this action." A jury returned a verdict in favor of the adult. The Utah Supreme Court reversed the verdict and held that the jury instruction was in "direct conflict with our statute." The Supreme Court stated that this jury instruction would require the minor to place the adult in his precontractual status, which would "disregard and misapply the purpose of the law. The law is intended for the benefit and protection of the minor; and hence an adult, in dealing with a minor, assumes all the risk of loss."

Further, in **Harvey v. Hadfield, 13 Utah 2d 258 (1962),** a minor contracted with an adult to buy a house trailer. The minor paid $1,000 as a down payment without selecting a trailer. The minor later disaffirmed the contract, requesting the return of his money. When the adult refused to return the money, the minor brought an action against the adult. The trial court returned a judgment in favor of the adult. The Utah Supreme Court reversed the trial court, holding that the minor could recover the down payment without compensating the adult for the loss of a sale.

Section 15-2-2 requires that a disaffirming minor must only return the property remaining within his or her control. The court has interpreted this statute to allow a minor to effectively disaffirm the underlying contract without restoring the full value of the property received under the contract.

We find in favor of the defendant.

PROBLEM ONE—A
ANSWER SHEET

Name   **Please Print Clearly**

1. Should Kathy be able to rescind the contract and get her money back from Christopher? (Support your answer with case law.)

2. Does it matter that the only thing Kathy can return to Christopher is the hubcap, or must she pay to have the car repaired before she can disaffirm the contract?

_____

_____

_____

_____

_____

_____

_____

_____

_____

3. Do you think that the concept of status and process played any part in the **Swalberg** decision? Explain your answer.

_____

_____

_____

_____

_____

_____

_____

_____

_____

_____

SECTION **1.11**
PRECEDENT:
THE BACKBONE OF
AMERICAN
JURISPRUDENCE

Precedent is the process whereby judges apply the decisions and rules of prior cases to the case over which they are currently presiding. The correct legal term for this concept is **stare decisis**. This doctrine forms the backbone of the American legal system and offers litigants certainty and uniformity in the application of the law. As noted in **In re Larry A. Deboer,** 1999 WL 33486710 (Bankr. D. Idaho), stare decisis provides that when the court has once laid down a principle of law as applicable to a given state of facts, it will adhere to that principle and apply it in future cases where the facts are substantially the same. This principle has long been a cornerstone of common law.

Judges will generally follow precedent but are not bound to do so in every situation. A legal principle may be changed by the legislature and the court has the discretion to change the law as the social, political, or economic conditions change. Changes are also observed as members of the court, especially the United States Supreme Court, are replaced by jurists with different judicial or political philosophies.

A change in precedent may occur for a number of reasons including: (1) when the court is convinced that prior decisions are irreconcilable; (2) the application of a rule or principle has created confusion; (3) a rule of law has been inconsistently applied; (4) to correct a misconception in a decision; or (5) where the court believes that the reason for the law no longer exists, justice requires a change, and no vested property interests will be injured by the change. **Niederman v. Brodsky, 261 A. 2d 84 (Pa. 1970).**

Conway v. Town of Wilton involves the doctrine of stare decisis, and offers an illustration of when the court will depart from established precedent. As the reader will note, the litigation provides an example of a court admitting that it made a mistake in a prior ruling.

AMY CONWAY v. TOWN OF WILTON
680 A. 2D 242 (CONN. 1996)

In **Manning v. Barenz, 603 A. 2d 399 (Conn. 1992),** this court held that municipalities and their employees are "owners" under *General Statutes §52-557* and entitled to immunity from liability for injuries sustained on land available to the public for recreational purposes. Today, we reconsider **Manning,** conclude that it was not properly decided and, overrule it.

Conway brought this action against the town of Wilton for personal injuries sustained while participating in a state high school tennis tournament on premises owned by the town. The plaintiff alleged that the Interscholastic Athletic Conference held a championship tennis tournament for high school girls at the Wilton High

School tennis courts and she fell as a result of a defect and sustained serious injuries.

General Statutes §52-557 provides that an owner of land who makes any part of the land available to the public without charge for recreational purposes owes no duty of care to keep the land safe.

This court has repeatedly acknowledged the significance of stare decisis to our system of jurisprudence because it gives stability and continuity to our case law. State decisis is a formidable obstacle to any court seeking to change its own law. It is the most important application of a theory of decision make consistency in our legal culture and it is an obvious manifestation of the notion that decision making consistency itself has normative value.

Moreover, we have deemed it appropriate to depart from common law precedents where we have found compelling reasons and logic for doing so. In short, consistency must not be the only reason for deciding a case in a particular way, if to do so would be unjust.

At first glance, the term "owner," as defined in the statute is "the possessor of a fee interest in land, a tenant, lessee, occupant or person in control of the premises," is not opaque. Indeed, we have concluded that the clear and unambiguous meaning of that term encompassed municipal property owners. Nevertheless, upon closer scrutiny of this issue, we conclude that an ambiguity arises in the application of the statute to municipalities.

Connecticut passed the Recreational Land Use Act in 1971. The philosophy behind the legislation was to make the option of opening private land for public recreational use more attractive. For many types of outdoor activities such as hiking, hunting, and fishing, we have long depended upon the generosity of private owners of land to open their property to the use and enjoyment of their property to the public.

The landowner owes no duty of care to keep the land so made available, safe for entry or use by others for recreational purposes, or to give any warning of a dangerous condition, use, structure or activity on the land to persons entering for recreational purposes.

There are compelling reasons why, in the absence of explicit direction from the legislature, this court should not read the term "owner" to include municipalities.

The legislature was not contemplating immunity for governmental entities. At the time the Recreational Land Use Act was enacted, the legislature was interested in increasing the availability of land for public recreational use. Consequently, municipalities would have had to pay large sums to purchase and maintain land in order to accomplish that goal had the legislation not succeeded. The legislature's sole motive was to encourage private citizens to donate their land as an alternative to this costly enterprise. There is no indication that the legislature was seeking to permit a municipality to have immunity for responsibilities arising out of property that it already owned.

In conclusion, there is nothing in the legislative history to suggest that the legislature intended or even contemplated that the act would provide immunity for governmental entities that owned land. The judgment of the Appellate Court is reversed.

SECTION 1.12
COMMONWEALTH
OF PENNSYLVANIA
V. JOSEPH ROBERTS

PROBLEM ONE—B

PARK, BROWN & SMITH, P.C.
ATTORNEYS AT LAW
MEMORANDUM

To: All Law Clerks

FROM: Peter Smith, Esquire

RE: The Skateboarding Accident

Joe Roberts is an avid skateboarder and is so proficient that he often skateboards many miles to work. During one particularly hot and humid day, Joe suffered heat exhaustion after practicing for several hours. Therefore, he consumed several cans of beer to quench his thirst and skateboarded to a nearby park that had several mountain trails to build up his endurance.

As Joe was skateboarding down the street, he waved to a neighbor. Unfortunately, Joe was going so fast that he lost his balance and crashed into Officer John O'Brien who was crossing the street. As Officer O'Brien helped Joe to his feet, the police officer smelled alcohol on Joe's breath. A breathalyzer revealed a blood-alcohol level of .09, so Joe was arrested for driving under the influence of alcohol. Joe is shocked by the absurdity of the situation and has come to our office for advice. He cannot understand how a person can be arrested for driving under the influence when he is using a skateboard and not an automobile. Joe is particularly distressed since he will lose his driver's license if found guilty of the charge.

Pennsylvania has lowered the legal requirements to convict a person for driving under the influence of alcohol from a blood-alcohol level of .10 to the lower level of .08. This change was made in order to receive federal highway construction funds. That new law is as follows:

§ 3802. Driving under the influence of alcohol or controlled substance

(a) General impairment.—

> **(1)** An individual may not drive, operate or be in actual physical control of the movement of a vehicle after imbibing a sufficient amount of alcohol such that the individual is rendered incapable of safely driving, operating or being in actual physical control of the movement of the vehicle.

(2) An individual may not drive, operate or be in actual physical control of the movement of a vehicle after imbibing a sufficient amount of alcohol such that the alcohol concentration in the individual's blood or breath is at least 0.08% but less than 0.10% within two hours after the individual has driven, operated or been in actual physical control of the movement of the vehicle.

I told Joe that you would do a fine research job. Please read **Commonwealth v. Brown** and apply the holding to Joe's case. You will need to answer the following questions:

1. Does new *Section 3802 of the Motor Vehicle Code* apply to an individual riding a skateboard while under the influence of alcohol?

2. According to the case, what factors should the Court consider in determining the legislature's intention in enacting a statute?

3. Is there enough evidence to convict Joe of driving under the influence? Support your answer with case law.

COMMONWEALTH OF PENNSYLVANIA V. LEE BROWN
620 A. 2D 1213 (PA. SUPER. 1993)

On September 20, 1990, Brown was riding her bicycle in the wrong lane of Miller Avenue, Clairton, Pennsylvania, and traveling in the wrong direction. As the bicycle weaved down the street, Brown struck an automobile whose driver had attempted to avoid her by swerving his vehicle. After the accident, a state police officer observed a strong odor of alcohol on Brown's breath. She consented to a blood alcohol test which revealed a blood alcohol content of 0.29%. She also admitted to the police officer that she had been consuming beer.

Based on this incident, the Commonwealth charged Brown with two counts of driving under the influence of alcohol or controlled substances, and with riding on the wrong side of the roadway, a summary offense. The Commonwealth raises the following issue: Whether the trial court erred in holding that bicycles are not "vehicles" for purposes of *75 Pa.C.S.A. Section 3731,* and therefore, that a person cannot be convicted of driving under the influence for operating a bicycle on a public highway while under the influence of alcohol or controlled substances?

Because this case presents a question of the proper interpretation of a legislative enactment, we will review the relevant rules of statutory construction. The cardinal principle in interpreting legislative enactments is "to ascertain and effectuate the intent of the General Assembly." When the words of a statute are clear and free from all ambiguity, the letter of the law is not to be disregarded under the pretext of pursuing its spirit. A court interpreting a statute must ascertain and effectuate the intention of the legislature and give full effect to each provision of the statute if at all possible. **Fireman's Fund Insurance Company v. Nationwide Mutual Insurance Company, 317 Pa. Super. 497, 464 A.2d 431 (1983).** "When the words of a statute are not explicit, the intention of the General Assembly may be ascertained by considering, among other factors:"

1. The occasion and necessity for the statute.

2. The circumstances under which it was enacted.

3. The mischief to be remedied.

4. The object to be attained.

5. The former law, if any, including other statutes upon the same or similar subjects.

6. The consequences of a particular interpretation.

7. The contemporaneous legislative history.

8. Legislative and administrative interpretations of such statute.

The statute which requires interpretation herein is *Section 3731 of the Motor Vehicle Code*, which provides:

a. Offense defined. A person shall not drive, operate or be in actual physical control of the movement of any vehicle while:

   1. under the influence of alcohol to a degree which renders the person incapable of safe driving;

   2. under the influence of any controlled substance, to a degree which renders the person incapable of safe driving;

   3. under the combined influence of alcohol and any controlled substance to a degree which renders the person incapable of safe driving; or

   4. the amount of alcohol by weight in the blood of the person is 0.10 percent or greater.

The issue presented by this case is whether *Section 3731* applies to an individual operating a bicycle, as opposed to a motor vehicle.

Keeping in mind the principle that a statute must be construed to give effect to all of its parts, we note the definitions of "vehicle" and "motor vehicle" as set forth in the Vehicle Code. A "**vehicle**" is defined as **"[e]very device in, upon or by which any person or property is or may be transported or drawn upon a highway, except devices used exclusively upon rails or tracks."** 75 Pa. C.S.A.§102. "Motor vehicle" is defined as **"a vehicle which is self-propelled except one which is propelled solely by human power or by electric power obtained from overhead trolley wires, but not operated upon rails."** *Section 3731* prohibits the driving or operating of a "vehicle"—while under the influence of alcohol. A bicycle clearly falls within the confines of that definition. It is a "device" upon which a person or property may be "transported or drawn upon a highway," and it is not a device which is "used exclusively upon rails or tracks." See *Section 102*, supra ("vehicle"). A bicycle is clearly not a motor vehicle as it is a vehicle "which is propelled solely by human power." However, it is the operators of vehicles, not the operators of motor vehicles, who are regulated under *Section 3731*. Since *Section 3731* applies to the operators of vehicles, and since the bicycle which appellee was riding falls within the definition of that term, the lower court erred in holding that appellee could not be prosecuted under *Section 3731* for operating her bicycle while purportedly under the influence of alcohol.

For these reasons, we hold that the lower court abused its discretion in dismissing the charges against appellee under *Section 3731*.

Order reversed; case remanded for further proceedings in accordance with this memorandum.

DEL SOLE, J., concurring.

I join the opinion of my distinguished colleague, Judge Cercone. I only wish to point out that the Vehicle Code evidences the Legislature's understanding that the word "vehicle" does include bicycles. At **Pa. C.S.A. Section 1101,** all vehicles are required to be titled except those exempted in *Section 1102.* There, in subparagraph 7, vehicles "moved solely by human or animal power" are excluded from this requirement. This same limitation also applies to the registration requirements of *Section 1301* at. seq. These sections demonstrate to me that the members of the General Assembly fully understood that bicycles were included in the definition of "vehicle" when used in *Section 3731.*

PROBLEM ONE—B
ANSWER SHEET

Name   **Please Print Clearly**

1. Does the amended **Section 3802 of the Motor Vehicle Code** apply to an individual riding a skateboard while under the influence of alcohol?

_____

_____

_____

_____

_____

_____

_____

2. According to **Commonwealth of Pennsylvania v. Brown,** what factors does the court indicate should be examined in order to ascertain the intention of the legislature when the words of a statute are not specific?

_____

_____

_____

_____

_____

_____

_____

_____

3. Is there enough evidence to convict Joe of driving under the influence? Please explain.

_____

_____

_____

_____

_____

_____

_____

_____

_____

_____

_____

_____

_____

_____

_____

_____

_____

_____

_____

**SECTION 1.13
LEGAL RESEARCH
AND THE INTERNET**

The Internet has become a major source of information, communication, and even entertainment for people all over the world. Materials on a variety of subjects can be accessed at the touch of a key, including law-related topics. Court decisions, law review articles, and legislation are now instantly accessible.

A good start for legal research on the Internet is to visit a law-oriented directory or search engine. These resources can help you find subjects from different types of law to specific cases, legal news, and even U.S. Government sites. Several specific legal research sites are:

- **www.lawcrawler.com**
  Lawcrawler is a legal search engine that is powered by Alta Vista and allows for a comprehensive legal search on the topic of your choice.

- **www.findlaw.com**
  Findlaw is a legal subject index.

- **www.hg.org**
  Hieros Games has information on legal organizations, including every government in the world. This is a good research tool for those interested in practicing law.

- **www.ilrg.com**
  Internet Legal Resource Guide is a categorized index of over 3100 select websites in 238 nations, islands, and territories.

- **www.nolo.com**
  Legal Encyclopedia is a self-help center on the Internet.

- **www.lawguru.com**
  This useful tool contains answers to frequently asked legal questions and has many interesting links.

- **www.lectlaw.com**
  The *Lectric Law Library* contains practical links such as "Legal help for the poor" and "How to fight your traffic ticket."

- **www.legis.state.pa.us**
  This website allows access to information from the Pennsylvania legislature, including the text of bills and the history of the legislation.

- **www.fedworld.gov**
  This site provides access to the search engine of the federal government.

- **www.lawoffice.com**
  West Publications has created this link to allow the public to gain access to the profiles of law firms and attorneys around the country.

- **www.aclu.org**
  This is the official site for the American Civil Liberties Union and offers information on civil liberty controversies, such as lesbian and gay rights and women's rights.

- **www.uslaw.com**
  This comprehensive site covers all aspects of the legal field, including articles, current events, and chat rooms where you can submit questions to be answered by attorneys.

- **www.megalaw.com**
  This site discusses recent legal developments in the news and provides access to information in different legal fields, as well as information on state and federal court decisions.

- **www.itslegal.com**
  This site provides links to different legal topics, including real estate law, personal injury, credit and debt issues, family law, and employment law.

- **www.law.indiana.edu/v-lib**
  Indiana University School of Law-Bloomington's virtual law library allows searches about the legal field and will provide links relating to the search.

- **www.law.com**
  The law.com connection features law-related articles and stories, summaries from local, state, and federal court decisions, law links, and other legal information.

- **www.prairielaw.com**
  Through articles, columns, and online discussions, this site offers information about the law including consumer concerns, crime, immigration and work related issues.

Now it's time to try one of these legal research tools. The Steven Spielberg movie, *Amistad,* is based upon a United States Supreme Court decision that decided the fate of African slaves who staged a shipboard revolt off the cost of Cuba in an attempt to gain their freedom. The slaves ended up in America, but Spain demanded their return in order to face criminal prosecution for the uprising. American abolitionists became involved in the frey and the matter ended up in the courts. In a landmark decision, our highest court established the principle that all people are "presumptively free" and entitled to the protections of American law. This holding granted the African slaves the freedom they desired in order to return to their homeland. ***The Amistad, 40 U.S. 518 (1841).*** If you wish to read the case or learn more about the story, you merely have to access the Internet. If you submit the term *Amistad* to a search engine, it will take you to a variety of stories and references on the topic. You can also access **www.findlaw.com** which will take you to the home page of **Find Law,** whose research engine scans court cases and other legal information on most legal topics. Go to the box marked Supreme Court and click on it. The Supreme Court decision in the *Amistad* case should be visible when the page opens. You may also gain access to the case by typing *40 U.S. 518* in the appropriate box.

More and more courts are placing their dockets and other court related information on the Internet. For instance, a person can access the records of the Philadelphia Court of Common Pleas by going to **http://courts.phila.gov**. Depending on the search, one may check the dockets of a specific case, conduct a judgment search involving a specific person, or conduct a litigation search involving a person's name.

FOR GENERAL INFORMATION ON THE INTERNET

- **http://info.isoc.org/guest/zakon/Internet/History/HIT.html**
  Hobbs' Internet Timeline provides information about the Internet, the people who use it, and on-line culture.

- **www.columbia.edu/~hauben/netbook**
  Netizens: On the history and Impact of Usenet and the Internet— this site contains a collection of essays about the history, nature, and impact of the Internet.

- **http://home.netscape.com/eng/mozilla/3.0/handbook**
  The *Navigator Handbook Online* provides detailed information on how to use netscape navigator.

SECTION **1.14**
INTERNET RESEARCH
ON MALPRACTICE

PROBLEM ONE—C

PARK, BROWN & SMITH, P.C.
ATTORNEYS AT LAW
MEMORANDUM

To: All Law Clerks

FROM: Peter Smith, Esquire

RE: Internet Research on Medical Malpractice

It has become very expensive to maintain a law library, so I am interested in learning how to conduct legal research on the internet. I have been told that many courts have posted their decisions on the web and a number of excellent search engines and websites provide answers to a variety of legal problems.

Park, Brown & Smith, P.C. has been consulted by a client who suffered a tragic loss as the result of the amputation of her foot due to the negligence of Dr. Jones. The client had a cancerous tumor on the right foot that required amputation. However, in the operating room, Dr. Jones became confused and mistakenly amputated the left foot. I believe this is a clear case of medical malpractice, and we should recover millions.

Please research the issue of medical malpractice on the internet. I want to learn if there are any legal resources on this topic. Let me know the results of your internet research and provide me with an explanation on how you uncovered the information. Print out two of these resources and attach the first page of each site to this assignment. Your research should not be confined to cases involving the amputation of a leg or foot.

PROBLEM ONE—C
ANSWER SHEET

Name   **Please Print Clearly**

1. Does the Internet have legal resources on the topic of medical malpractice? If so, please list and describe five of these resources.

2. Please explain how you found these resources. How many resources were there?

3. Please print out two of these references and attach the first printed page of each site to this assignment.

_____

_____

_____

_____

_____

_____

_____

_____

_____

_____

_____

_____

_____

_____

_____

_____

_____

_____

_____

_____

_____

Section 1.15 Review Cases

1. A 16-year-old went to a local car dealer in order to purchase an automobile. When the salesman learned of the customer's age, he refused to sell the car unless the purchase was made by an adult. A few hours later, the minor returned with an adult that the child had just met. The salesman sold the car to the adult and then assisted the buyer in having the title transferred to the youth. A few days later, the 16-year-old returned with his father and attempted to rescind the contract. Will the car dealer be required to take the automobile back and return the money? **Quality Motors, Inc. v. Johnny Hayes, 225 S. W. 2d 326 (Ark. 1949).**

2. The mother of a mentally challenged female was concerned that her 15-year-old daughter would become pregnant without understanding the consequences. The mother filed a "Petition To Have A Tubaligation Performed On A Minor" with the court. Although there was no legal authority for the court to order the sterilization, the judge felt that the procedure would be in the best interest of the child in order "to prevent unfortunate circumstances..." The child was taken to the hospital under the pretext of having her appendix removed, and the tubaligation was performed. Several years later, the child married and attempted to become pregnant. At this time, she learned that she had been sterilized. As a result of her inability to have children, she sued the judge, claiming that he violated her constitutional rights. Under the concept of status and process, will the judge be immuned from suit for his actions? **Judge Harold Strump v. Linda Sparkman, 435 U.S. 349 (1978).**

3. The parties to a lawsuit attended a settlement conference before the trial judge. During a break, the judge confronted the plaintiff in the hallway, and in a loud, angry voice, yelled at the plaintiff that his settlement demand was "Bull - - - -", and if he thought that there was money in the case, the plaintiff had "s - - - for brains!" The judge then told counsel for the plaintiff that the client "had to deal with him and now he was their enemy." Sometime later, the judge was interviewed by a reporter about the incident and denied that he had acted improperly as the plaintiff was alleging. This made it appear as though the plaintiff was lying. Subsequently, the plaintiff filed suit against Judge Williams for his improper conduct. Will the judge enjoy immunity for his actions, or should he be held responsible for the outbursts? Do you see a difference between the statements that the judge made during the settlement conference as opposed to those he made to the reporter? **Robert Soliz v. Alexander Williams, III, 74 Cal. App. 4th 577 (1999).**

4. Charles Kuralt, the former "On The Road" correspondent with CBS, maintained a longtime and intimate relationship with Elizabeth Shannon. This relationship was kept secret because Kuralt was married;

Kuralt was the primary source of financial support for Shannon at the time. In 1989, the television personality sent Ms. Shannon a letter indicating that in the event of his death, he wanted her to own the property in Montana which was used as their retreat. In 1994, Kuralt executed a will naming his wife and children as the beneficiaries of his Estate. The will said nothing about the Montana property. In 1997, Kuralt decided to transfer the property to Shannon. The transaction was disguised as a sale, but it was Kuralt's intention to give Shannon the money for the transfer. Prior to the completion of the sale, Kuralt become critically ill. While in the hospital, he wrote a letter to Shannon and enclosed a check to complete the transfer with a notation that it was his intent for her to inherit the Montana property. Before the transfer could take place, Kuralt died. Subsequently, conflicting claims were made against the Montana property by both Kuralt's family and Ms. Shannon. Who do you believe is entitled to the property? Does status and process play any part in your decision? **In re: The Estate of Charles Kuralt, 2000 Mont. LEXIS 375 (2000).**

Footnote: 1. Reprinted with permission from **"When Justice Is Up To You,"** 1992, by the American Association for Justice and the National Institute for Citizen Education in the Law.

KEY TERMS

Affirmed

Appellant

Appellee

Article One of the Constitution

Briefing of a Case

Burden of Proof

Caption

Citation

Common Law

Common Law Marriage

Compurgation

Concurring Opinion

Court Clerk

Defendant

Defense of Marriage Act

Dissenting Opinion

Domestic Partnership

Internet Research

Judge

Jury

Judicial Decree

Judicial Opinion

Legislative Enactment

Majority Opinion

Plaintiff

Precedent

Questions of Fact and Law

Remanded

Reversed

Same-Sex Marriage

Stare Decisis

Status and Process

Statutory Law

Trial by Ordeal

Trial by Water and Fire

Voyeurism

Wager of Law

Witness

CHAPTER 2

CLASSIFICATIONS OF LAW

**SECTION 2.1
PUBLIC LAW V.
PRIVATE LAW**

The major classifications of law are public law and private law. **Public law** involves the rights of society, and those rights are usually represented by a governmental agency. An example of a public law is the crime of murder. This criminal offense affects the rights of all members of society to be safe and secure. The categories of public law are criminal law, constitutional law and administrative law.

Private law, on the other hand, involves matters between individuals, such as the leasing of an apartment, a claim against a doctor for making a mistake during surgery, or the purchasing of a new car. These matters are personal between the parties to the transaction or incident. The major classifications of private law are contract law, tort law, property law, and family law.

**SECTION 2.2
CRIMINAL LAW**

A **crime** is a violation of those duties that an individual owes to his or her community and the breach of which requires the offender to make satisfaction to the public. As a result, a crime is a violation of the rights of society and not of the individual victim. This distinction is immediately apparent when the victim of a crime does not want to prosecute the suspect. While the prosecutor will usually follow the victim's wishes, a district attorney can force a victim to testify against the accused if there is a compelling societal interest, such as in cases of child or spousal abuse or rape. Since the government is responsible for taking action against a criminal defendant on behalf of society, the caption of the case contains the name of the governmental unit, such as the "United States," "The State," or "The People" versus the defendant.

According to the United States Department of Justice, twenty-four million crimes were committed in 2003, and 15% of all households were victimized. Statistically, 77% of those crimes were classified as property crimes, 22% involved crimes of violence, and 1% related to crimes of theft. Men were more likely to be violently attacked by a stranger while women were more likely to be victimized by a friend, or acquaintance.

Criminal laws are established by the legislature and are broken down into different categories based upon one thing—the penalty for the offense. While each jurisdiction will differ on what crimes go into a specific category, these classifications are treason, felonies, misdemeanors, and summary offenses. **Treason** is defined in the United States Constitution because it is considered the most serious offense against the country. **Article III, Section 3** states: "Treason against the United States shall consist only in levying war against them or in adhering to their enemies, giving them aid and comfort." A person cannot be convicted of treason unless two witnesses testify to the commission of the same overt act done to betray the United States, or if the accused confesses in open court. Because this burden of proof is so high, the government has prosecuted less than 100 cases involving treason in its history. Examples of people accused of being traitors include Benedict Arnold, Aaron Burr, Julius and Ethel Rosenberg, Anthony Cramer, and John Walker Lindh, the 20-year-old American who was captured while fighting for the Taliban. The penalty for treason can range from death to a minimum of five years in prison along with a fine of $10,000.

Although penalties for most crimes vary from state to state, a felony is a crime generally punishable by more than one year in jail. Examples include such offenses as murder, rape, burglary, and arson. A **misdemeanor** is usually punishable by less than one year in jail and includes such matters as assault, criminal trespass, and harassment. A defendant accused of a **summary offense** will generally be responsible for the payment of a fine, such as that which occurs with a traffic ticket.

The government has the burden of proving a defendant guilty **beyond a reasonable doubt**. This phrase has been interpreted to mean "fully satisfied," "entirely convinced," or "satisfied to a moral certainty." This is a very strict standard requiring the prosecutor to prove that the defendant actually committed the crime or **actus reus,** and that he or she had the necessary state of mind to commit the crime. This requisite state of mind, or criminal intent, is called **mens rea**. The legal system is concerned with what the defendant intended, knew, or should have known when he or she committed the crime.

There are various ways of proving mens rea. Criminal intent may be proved through an intentional, knowing, reckless, or negligent act. For example, in **Commonwealth of Pennsylvania v. Cheatham, 615 A. 2d 802 (Pa. Super. 1992),** the court had to decide whether a seizure-induced-black-out caused by epilepsy was an involuntary act which relieved the driver of a car of criminal responsibility for a fatal motor vehicle accident. The driver was found guilty because he possessed the necessary mens rea to commit the offense. The court concluded that the driver clearly knew that he suffered from unannounced seizures and was ordered not to operate a car. By choosing to drive a motor vehicle, the motorist exhibited recklessness under the circumstances. A different resolution would occur, however, if a person causes an accident by suffering an unexpected heart attack. Mens rea would be lacking since the act would be involuntary and the accident unforeseeable.

Criminal intent may also be inferred by the circumstances and actions of the accused. For instance, the actress Gwyneth Paltrow was the recipient of unwarranted advances by an overzealous fan who appeared at her parents' doorstep and sent the actress letters and packages on a daily basis. The man was charged with stalking under the California Penal Code; this statute requires the defendant's intent to place a person in fear for his or her safety in order to sustain a conviction. The defendant argued that his behavior was motivated by a desire to have a romantic relationship with the actress rather than the intent to cause her fear. The court disagreed and found that mens rea was present because the stalker did not stop his unwelcomed advances after he was informed that Ms. Paltrow and her family were fearful of his actions.

PEOPLE v. DANTE SOIU
2002 WL 222570 (CAL. APP. 2D DIST.)

Dante Soiu appeals his conviction for stalking. Defendant argues there was insufficient evidence to prove he intended to cause the victim fear.

Gwyneth Paltrow stayed with her parents when she was in the Los Angeles area. In March 1999, defendant began communicating with Ms. Paltrow at her parents' address. Defendant mailed a letter to Ms. Paltrow at her parents' home. The tone of defendant's letter made Ms. Paltrow unsettled and concerned. Defendant stated in the letter that God had ordained he and Ms. Paltrow to be together. Thereafter, Ms. Paltrow received letters and packages from defendant on an almost daily basis. Ms. Paltrow, testified as to the content of the letters, which ranged from religiously based letters that God had empowered [defendant] to contact her, that they were joined and that she shouldn't resist it, and then they would range from letters that were angrier in tone and more frustrated that she wasn't making contact with him, and they started to be sexual in nature.

Defendant began sending explicit pornographic pictures to Ms. Paltrow. Defendant wrote his name over the man in the picture and Ms. Paltrow's over the woman. Defendant's letters described in detail what kind of sexual acts he planned to perform with her. Defendant sent sexual objects to Ms. Paltrow.

Defendant went to the home of Ms. Paltrow's parents in May 1999. Defendant approached Ms. Paltrow's mother. When defendant identified himself, Ms. Paltrow's mother became terrified. Because defendant had sent threatening letters, Ms. Paltrow's mother believed defendant was going to take out a gun and shoot her.

Defendant returned to the home of Ms. Paltrow's family on May 13, 2000, at which time he was arrested. Defendant continued to send Ms. Paltrow letters after he was arrested.

Defendant argues there was insufficient evidence to demonstrate he had the specific intent to cause fear to Ms. Paltrow or her family. He further argues, "Appellant's behavior... was motivated by a twisted desire to have a romantic relationship with Ms. Paltrow rather than the desire to cause her fear." **Section 646.9,** subdivision (a), defines stalking: "Any person who willfully, maliciously, and repeatedly follows or harasses another person and who makes a credible threat with the intent to place that person in reasonable fear for his or her safety, or the safety of his or her immediate family, is guilty of the crime of stalking...."

There is substantial evidence that defendant intended to evoke fear in both Ms. Paltrow and her parents. For 18 months, defendant repeatedly sent letters to their home, which referenced his belief: God ordained that he and Ms. Paltrow be together and suggestions she should not resist his desires to engage in various sexual acts, including violent ones; and his desire to take God's scalpel and cut out Ms. Paltrow's cancer-like sin. In addition, defendant sent Ms. Paltrow numerous packages containing various sexual implements. Defendant was warned by federal agents that he should discontinue his contact with Ms. Paltrow and her family because they were fearful. In spite of these repeated warnings, defendant continued to send letters and packages. He also appeared at Ms. Paltrow's home on two occasions. Finally, after admitting he knew Ms. Paltrow was frightened by his conduct, defendant continued to contact her. His admission that he knew his conduct was frightening her, coupled with his subsequent continuation of his harassment of Ms. Paltrow is substantial evidence of the requisite mens rea to support the trial court's findings. There is no merit to defendant's sufficiency of the evidence contentions.

(Judgment affirmed.)

SECTION 2.3
CONSTITUTIONAL LAW

The idea of a constitution to govern and protect the citizens of a country is not a novel idea. Ancient Rome was formed as a republic that granted certain fundamental freedoms to its citizens. King John of England approved the Magna Carta in 1297. This historic document provided that the people of England had certain fundamental rights that could not be abridged and the threads of this document are found in this country's Bill of Rights.

Following the Revolutionary War, the states decided to create a lasting document to govern the people of America. In the summer of 1787, fifty-five men gathered in secret session in Philadelphia to amend the Articles of Confederation, a document that joined 13 independent colonies into a loose confederation of states with a weak central government. An infirmed Ben Franklin was the oldest delegate at 81 and Jonathan Douglas was the youngest at 26. George Washington presided over the meetings, but Thomas Jefferson and John Adams were unable to attend. Rhode Island refused to send a delegation.

After much debate, the delegates agreed upon the United States Constitution, which document created a strong centralized government whose primary purpose is to serve its citizens.

The document was then forwarded to the thirteen original states for ratification. One year later, the United States Constitution became the law of the land, and no federal or state law may conflict with that document. Today, the Constitution is the oldest written national constitution in effect. For instance, Italy did not become a democratic republic until 1948 at which time its constitution was enacted. Likewise, Japan did not create its constitution until after World War Two.

The Constitution is the most important legal document in American jurisprudence. It establishes the branches of the government, creates the fundamental rights of the people and protects them from unlawful governmental interference.

The Constitution is purposely written in broad and often vague terms so that it can adapt to changing times. This concept is called **constitutional relativity** and insures that this legal document will maintain its vitality. How does this occur? The courts continually interpret and apply the Constitution to current issues. This power of the judiciary was established by John Marshall, Chief Justice of the United States Supreme Court, in the landmark decision of **Marbury v. Madison, 1 Cranch 137 (1803).**

The application of constitutional relativity is demonstrated by the evolution of the **Fourth Amendment**. This Amendment provides:

> The right of the people to be secure in their persons, houses, papers, and effects, against unreasonable searches and seizures, shall not be violated, and no warrants shall issue, but upon probable cause.

How could this Amendment, which was adopted more than 220 years ago, have application to a police search of a computer hard drive when this technology was clearly not within the contemplation of the drafters of the Constitution? Quite simply, the Fourth Amendment does not identify what is to be searched but merely specifies that warrants must be issued upon probable cause. This allows the court to decide what is and is not subject to police searches over the course of time.

The Constitution of the United States starts with the following Preamble:

> We the people of the United States, in order to form a more perfect Union, establish justice, insure domestic tranquility, provide for the common defense, promote the general welfare, and secure the blessings of liberty to ourselves and our posterity, do ordain and establish this Constitution for the United States of America.

This introductory sentence provides the framework for the origins, purpose and beneficiaries of this historical document. The Preamble clearly reflects that the Constitution originates with the citizens and not with the states and its purpose is to form a better government that will insure fairness and protection of the people over time.

The body of the Constitution consists of seven **Articles** and twenty-seven **Amendments**. The framework of the document creates an intentional distribution of power. The framers realized the need for a Federal or National system rather than a loose confederation of states. They also realized the need to prevent a concentration of power in a single branch of the government. With this in mind, the drafters created a framework of limited government power through the concept of the separation of powers. The first three Articles of the Constitution apportion the power to run the country among the legislative, executive, and judicial branches of the government. Article I empowers the legislature to make the laws which the executive branch enforces pursuant to the authority granted to the President in Article II. Article III designates the judiciary as that branch of the government that interprets the Constitution.

Ratification of the Constitution by the original states was not a certainty because of the lingering doubt that a strong central government would infringe upon the individual rights of its citizens. In fact, some states ratified the Constitution only after noting that the document had to be amended to include a list of individual protections that people would enjoy from governmental interference.

This concern was addressed by James Madison two years after the ratification of the Constitution when he drafted the Bill of Rights. Twelve Amendments were proposed but only ten were adopted. These personal safeguards include the right to freedom of speech, protection of religion, and right to assemble. The Amendments also guarantee that people will be secure in their person, the government will not conduct unreasonable search and seizures, and no person shall be forced in a criminal case to testify against himself. Citizens are also guaranteed the right to a speedy and public trial by an impartial jury.

Over the years, these protections have generated a number of lawsuits that have tested the limits of what is meant by these personal freedoms. For instance, does the First Amendment protect the burning of the American Flag or hate speech that has the ability to incite a riot? Does the First Amendment protect religious groups from holding anti-gay protests at military funerals? Does the law against unlawful search and seizures prohibit the government from conducting warrant-less searches of computer hard drives and does a prohibition against cruel and unusual punishment prohibit the state from executing a defendant?

While many people think that the last Amendment to the Constitution was the 26th, which granted 18-year-olds the right to vote, the last Amendment was passed in 1992. This 27th Amendment provides:

> No law, varying the compensation for the services of the Senators and Representatives, shall take effect, until an election of Representatives shall have intervened.

In other words, the Constitution prohibits the legislature from granting itself a pay raise that is effective before those representatives run for re-election.

Passing an amendment to the Constitution is a very difficult task. This is amply demonstrated by the fact that over 11,000 amendments have been proposed since the Constitution's inception but only 27 have been adopted. Article V of the Constitution requires that an amendment be passed by two-thirds of each House and by three-fourths of the State Legislatures. The framers did not want the Constitution to be amended every time the population was impassioned by a controversial court decision or legal issue.

The call for an amendment to protect the American flag from desecration is a prime example of such constitutional politics. Whether an amendment to prevent the burning of a flag is necessary or appropriate has become the source of great debate. To put the matter in the proper context, should an amendment be passed to protect the American flag when the country could not agree on the passage of the Equal Rights Amendment which guaranteed equal rights for men and women? It is possible that a constitutional amendment to prevent flag burning may be adopted by appealing to the emotional support of the population. This, however, is the type of issue the framers hoped to avoid by making the amendatory process so difficult to fulfill.

Another proposed amendment that has sparked much discussion is an amendment to limit the terms of those in Congress. This proposal stems from disgruntled voters who believe that career politicians have lost touch with the American people and should not be allowed to stay in office for an indefinite period. The United States Supreme Court in **U.S. Term Limits Inc. v. Thronton** decided that a state cannot limit service in Congress without amending the Constitution. The Court stated that any change in term limits must not come by legislation adopted by Congress or an individual state, but through amendment procedures. The passage of such a constitutional amendment would require a two-thirds vote in the House of Representatives and the Senate, as well as ratification by thirty-eight states.

The Constitution in Everyday Language

To better understand the rights guaranteed to citizens of the United States, it is important to review briefly the Constitution and its Amendments. The archaic language of this more than 220-year-old document is often difficult to understand, so the following summary is written in simplified language.

We the People of the United States establish this Constitution for the United States of America.

Article I	The power to make the laws of the United States will be given to Congress, which will consist of a Senate and House of Representatives.
Article II	All power to enforce and execute the laws of the United States will be given to an elected President and Vice President.
Article III	The power to interpret the laws of the United States will be given to the Supreme Court and other federal courts.
Article IV	Each state will enforce and recognize the laws, legal records, and results of lawsuits from every other state. No state shall discriminate against citizens from another state.
Article V	Congress may propose Amendments to the Constitution based upon a two-thirds vote of both Houses of Congress or two-thirds of the states can call a convention to propose Amendments. Three-fourths of the states must ratify the proposed change before it may become an Amendment to the Constitution.
Article VI	This Constitution, and the laws and treaties made under it, are the supreme law of the land.
Article VII	The Constitution became effective on September 17, 1787.

Amendments to the Constitution of the United States of America

Amendment I	Citizens have the right to freedom of religion, speech, press, and to assemble peaceably.

AMENDMENT II	Citizens have the right to bear arms.
AMENDMENT III	Citizens cannot be required to house soldiers in their homes during peace time.
AMENDMENT IV	Citizens are protected against unreasonable searches and seizures of both their person and property.
AMENDMENT V	No person can be tried twice for the same crime or be forced to testify against himself. A person's life, liberty, or property cannot be taken away by the government without going through the proper and fair legal procedures.
AMENDMENT VI	A defendant in a criminal trial is entitled to legal representation and must be provided with a speedy and public trial by an impartial jury.
AMENDMENT VII	Citizens are entitled to jury trials in civil cases involving more than twenty dollars.
AMENDMENT VIII	A court cannot impose cruel and unusual punishment or excessive bail on defendants.
AMENDMENT IX	Rights that are not specifically mentioned within the Constitution are held by the citizens.
AMENDMENT X	Rights that are not delegated to the federal government are reserved for the states and the citizens.
AMENDMENT XI	Citizens are not permitted to sue states where they are not residents.
AMENDMENT XII	The Electoral College will select the President and Vice President.
AMENDMENT XIII	Slavery and involuntary servitude is abolished.
AMENDMENT XIV	No state can make or enforce any law which will take away the privileges and immunities of citizens; nor deprive any person of life, liberty or property, without due process of law; nor deny any person within its borders the equal protection of its laws.

AMENDMENT **XV**	Citizens of all races and colors have the right to vote.
AMENDMENT **XVI**	Congress may tax income.
AMENDMENT **XVII**	When a Senator is required to leave office before his or her term in Congress expires, the governor of the Senator's state can appoint another to fill the position until the citizens of the state elect a new Senator.
AMENDMENT **XVIII**	The manufacture, sale, or transportation of intoxicating liquors is prohibited. [REPEALED]
AMENDMENT **XIX**	Both male and female citizens have the right to vote.
AMENDMENT **XX**	The President and Vice President begin their terms January 20; Senators and Representatives January 3. If the President-Elect dies before being sworn in, the Vice-President-Elect becomes President.
AMENDMENT **XXI**	The Eighteenth Amendment enforcing the prohibition of intoxicating liquors is repealed.
AMENDMENT **XXII**	The President may not be elected more than twice.
AMENDMENT **XXIII**	The District of Columbia is entitled to representation at the Electoral College.
AMENDMENT **XXIV**	Citizens cannot be charged a fee in order to vote.
AMENDMENT **XXV**	When the President cannot perform his official duties, the Vice President will assume the duties of the President. The President can be impeached upon a two-thirds vote of Congress.
AMENDMENT **XXVI**	Citizens who are eighteen (18) years of age and older have the right to vote.
AMENDMENT **XXVII**	Members of Congress cannot raise their pay while in office. Any law that provides for a pay raise for Congress cannot take effect until after the election, which follows the vote, granting the raise.

SECTION 2.4
JOE ROBERTS'
CONSTITUTIONAL
LAW PROBLEMS

PROBLEM TWO—A

PARK, BROWN & SMITH, P.C.
ATTORNEYS AT LAW
M E M O R A N D U M

TO: All Law Clerks

FROM: Peter Smith, Esquire

RE: Joe Roberts' Constitutional Law Problems

Joe Robert and his family are again in trouble. This particular incident occurred on Election Day.

Joe started brewing beer in the basement of his summer home at the New Jersey shore. He calls it "Jersey Joe's Home Brew," and he transported the liquor into Pennsylvania on Election Day to sell to his neighbors. Joe has a bar in the basement of his house and enough neon signs to light up a street. Unfortunately for Joe, Pennsylvania doesn't allow anyone to bring liquor into the state to sell to customers on Election Day. The state wants to make sure people are sober when they vote.

As Joe was unloading the last of the beer, Officer O'Brien showed up with the FBI. Even though they had no search warrant, these law enforcement officials stormed past Joe, went into his basement and confiscated the beer, taps and the neon signs. They then began loading the contraband into their cars.

"Hey, Tony," Joe yelled, calling to his son, who was asleep on the living room couch. "Help me; I'm being robbed." Tony ran to his father's aid, carrying a 9-mm pistol. An FBI agent grabbed the gun and confiscated the weapon. "Only law enforcement officials are allowed to have these types of guns," O'Brien told them.

Joe protested, claiming that he had the right to keep guns in his house. It was the American way, he said, but O'Brien ignored him. I have since learned that there is a law in Pennsylvania that prohibits citizens from having semi-automatic weapons.

Suddenly, two men walked out of the house. Joe told O'Brien they worked for him. "For how much?" O'Brien asked. "For nothing," Joe said. "They work when I tell them to, and they don't go anywhere else. They live here in the basement." Indeed, the men told Officer O'Brien, they owed Joe several thousand dollars in gambling debts, and Joe was forcing them to pay it back by working for him.

Officer O'Brien took Joe to the police station and tossed him into a holding cell. "Hey, how come you're doing this to me?" Joe asked. "I don't have to tell you anything," O'Brien replied. "You'll stay in there until you tell us where you obtained the ingredients for the beer. Or you can pay a million dollar's bail, and then we'll let you out."

Meanwhile, New Jersey state officials read about Joe's arrest and used the opportunity to seize Joe's summer home. The state has a law that provides for the confiscation of property used in the commission of a crime. Joe doesn't buy it. The state has been after his land for years to use it for a public parking lot for one of the nearby casinos. Joe swears this is a scheme by the state to take his property without paying for it. In addition, the state wants Pennsylvania to return Joe to New Jersey, since Joe made the mistake of starting his brewery in a "liquor-free town." But Pennsylvania refuses to honor New Jersey's wishes.

The Internal Revenue Service has also informed Joe he owes the government back taxes for the money he made on selling his beer. And, to make matters worse, the National Guard has decided that the shore home would make a great barracks, so they moved a couple of soldiers from an Air Force base into Joe's living room.

Estelle got into the act, too. She put on her most patriotic shirt—the one she stitched together from an American flag—and went to the police station. Estelle then started to yell insults at Officer O'Brien. A crowd started to form around her. "She's right," said a woman in the crowd, "O'Brien was mean to me, too. Let's go to the mayor's office and complain." Just as Estelle was building momentum, several police officers grabbed her microphone and threatened to arrest Ms. Roberts for inciting a riot and defacing the American flag.

Joe and Estelle want to sue the states of Pennsylvania and New Jersey, but we're not sure they can do it. Read the Constitution and answer the following questions so that we can advise our clients on how to proceed.

QUESTIONS FOR DISCUSSION:

1. Which provisions in the Constitution support the actions of Joe and Estelle; which provisions prohibit what they did?

2. Is there anything in the Constitution that shows that O'Brien, the township police, the FBI, and the election officials were wrong in their actions?

3. How does someone propose a new amendment to the Constitution?

4. What other amendments do you believe should be included in the Constitution?

**ANSWER SHEET
PROBLEM TWO—A**

Name **Please Print Clearly**

1. Which provisions in the Constitution support the actions of Joe and Estelle; which provisions prohibit what they did?

_____

_____

_____

_____

_____

_____

_____

_____

2. Is there anything in the Constitution that shows that O'Brien, the township police, the FBI, and the election officials were wrong in their actions?

_____

_____

_____

_____

_____

_____

_____

_____

3. How does someone propose a new amendment to the Constitution?

_____

_____

_____

_____

_____

_____

_____

_____

_____

4. What new amendments would you propose to the Constitution?

_____

_____

_____

_____

_____

_____

_____

_____

_____

SECTION 2.5
ADMINISTRATIVE LAW

As the United States has grown in population and complexity, the task of running the country has become extremely difficult, and the needs of the population too great for the legislative branch to handle on its own. In an effort to ease its burden, Congress has created administrative agencies to deal with specialized areas and has staffed the agencies with experts who know how to deal with the particular problems encountered in each area.

An **administrative agency** is a "governmental body charged with administering and implementing particular legislation." Administrative agencies have greatly increased in number over the past several decades in order to effectuate general policy mandates of the legislative and executive branches of the government at the national, state, and local levels. Administrative agencies are created through congressional action called *Enabling Acts.*

Administrative or regulatory law, therefore, is concerned with the legal rules and principles that regulate governmental agencies. These agencies are unique because they enjoy legislative, executive and judicial powers. As public agencies, they protect a public interest or sector instead of a private right or person.

Administrative agencies can exist at any level of the government including the federal, state and local levels. The following are examples of federal administrative agencies:

- *Environmental Protection Agency* (**EPA**). This agency is designed to protect human health and to safeguard the environment, including the air, water, and land upon which life depends. The **EPA** has been responsible for environmental safeguards such as the banning of DDT, which is used in pesticides and has been found to be a cancer-causing agent. They have also banned the use of lead in gasoline, limited discharges by factories of pollution into waterways, and established fuel economy standards for motor vehicles. The **EPA's** website is: **www.epa.gov**.

- *Securities and Exchange Commission* (**SEC**). This regulatory body is designed to protect investors and maintain the integrity of the securities market. This agency was created following the economic collapse in the 1930s. The **SEC** oversees the various stock exchanges, mutual fund markets, broker/dealers, and public utility-holding companies. The **SEC** is aggressive in its enforcement function and brings between 400 to 500 enforcement actions each year against individuals and companies that break the security laws. Examples of infractions include insider trading and providing false or misleading information about securities or the companies that issue them. The website for the **Securities and Exchanges Commission** can be found at: **www.sec.gov**.

- *Occupational Safety and Health Administration* **(OSHA)**. The bureau is designed to reduce the number of safety and health hazards at work. **OSHA** regulates work environments to ensure that they are free from recognized hazards that are likely to cause death or serious physical harm to workers. This goal is accomplished through work place inspections and by establishing protective standards. Since this agency was created in 1970, the overall workplace death rate has been cut in half. The website for this agency is: **www.osha.gov.**

- *Food and Drug Administration* **(FDA)**. This agency protects the health of the public by monitoring products for safety, and helps safe and effective products reach the marketplace in a timely fashion. The *FDA* regulates the sale of food, drugs, medical devices, and radiation-emitting products such as cell phones, lasers, and microwaves. The agency's website is: **www.fda.gov**.

- *Federal Trade Commission* **(FTC)**. The **FTC** enforces anti-trust and consumer protection laws. The bureau investigates and prosecutes unfair or deceptive business practices, seeks monetary damages for conduct detrimental to consumers, is responsible for the labeling of cigarettes with health-related warning labels, requires the labeling of ingredients for food, drugs, and cosmetics products, and regulates automatic teller machines. The agency's website is: **www.ftc.gov.**

- *Federal Communications Commission* **(FCC)**. This agency was created in 1934 and is responsible for regulating communications by radio, television, satellite, wire, and cable. It also oversees the nation's emergency alert system, which notifies the public about a local or national emergency. The **FCC's** website is: **www.fcc.gov.**

The functions of all of these administrative agencies include the imposition of sanctions; licensing and other regulatory decisions; environmental and safety decisions; awards of benefits, loans, grants and other subsidies; inspections, audits, and approvals; and planning and policy-making.

Administrative agencies are unique because they are created with legislative, executive and judicial powers. An agency acts as a legislative body in the sense that it can issue rules and regulations. Its regulations are promulgated through a daily publication called the **Federal Register**. This power allows the agency to investigate alleged violations of the Act.

Administrative agencies also possess a judicial power called agency adjudication. Administrative hearings are very similar to court proceedings. Witnesses are heard, and evidence is presented so that an administrative law judge can decide the case. Because agencies possess rule-making, adjudicating and investigative powers, they have been considered by some to be a fourth branch of government.

The theory behind the creation of administrative agencies is that the administrator's expertise allows them to resolve problems within a particular area or industry quickly and effectively. The administrator's expertise should lead to proper decisions in the problem areas, as opposed to improper decisions that might be handed down by Congress or the courts due to good intentions but inadequate knowledge.

Because administrative agencies are empowered to regulate and develop the law for a specific area, the scope of review of an agency's adverse determination is very limited. The courts often feel that agencies possess the expertise in their field. Thus, their decisions are rarely overturned unless they are arbitrary, capricious, or an abuse of discretion. Factual findings, however, are conclusive so long as they are supported by "**substantial evidence**." Under this standard, a finding will not be changed on appeal if it is supported by relevant evidence that a reasonable mind might accept as adequate to support a conclusion. This is a very difficult burden for an aggrieved party to overcome.

Martha Stewart gained notoriety as a "domestic diva" whose cooking, sewing, and home remodeling talents seemed endless. She was very successful in promoting her ideas and turned her talents into a multi-million dollar enterprise. In 2003, however, her world was turned upside down because of a stock scandal involving ImClone Systems, Inc. The Food and Drug Administration informed that corporation that its cancer drug, Erbitux, was not going to obtain FDA approval. Shortly before this news was released to the public, Stewart sold almost 4,000 shares of ImClone stock. By selling the stock one day before the news was made public, Stewart avoided losses of more than $45,000.

Following an investigation, the Securities Exchange Commission charged Ms. Stewart both civilly and criminally for violating the Security Act of 1933 dealing with insider trading. The court's disposition of the Motion to have the criminal charges dismissed follows:

UNITED STATES V. MARTHA STEWART
NO. 03 CR. 717 (S.D. NEW YORK 2004)

Defendant Martha Stewart has moved for a judgment of acquittal. The motion is granted with respect to Count Nine.

The criminal charges against Stewart arose from Stewart's December 27, 2001 sale of 3,928 shares of stock in ImClone Systems, Inc. ("ImClone"). ImClone's then-chief executive officer, Samuel Waksal, was a friend of Stewart's and a client of Stewart's stockbroker at Merrill Lynch, defendant Bacanovic. On December 28, 2001, the day after Stewart sold her shares, ImClone announced that the Food and Drug Administration had rejected the company's application for approval of Erbitux, a cancer-fighting drug that ImClone had previously described as its lead product.

The Indictment alleges that on the morning of December 27, 2001, Bacanovic learned that Waksal and several of his family members were selling their ImClone shares. Bacanovic allegedly instructed his assistant to inform Stewart of the Waksal's trading activity, and she sold her shares in response to that information. According to the Indictment, the defendants then lied about the real reason for Stewart's sale in order to cover up what was possibly an illegal trade. The defendants claimed that they had a standing agreement that Stewart would sell her position in ImClone if the stock fell to $60 per share.

The Indictment charges the defendants with conspiracy, obstruction of an agency proceeding, and making false statements to government officials. Count Nine of the Indictment charges Stewart, the CEO of Martha Stewart Omnimedia, Inc., ("MSLO") with fraud in connection with the purchase and sale of MSLO securities.

Stewart held approximately sixty percent of the shares of stock in MSLO. The jury could reasonably infer from this evidence that Stewart had a significant financial stake in MSLO. Stewart was also aware that certain activities could send a negative message to the market.

The prospectus for MSLO states that: "Our success depends on our brands and their value. Our business would be adversely affected if Martha Stewart's public image or reputation was tarnished. Our continued success and the value of our brand name depend, to a large degree, on the reputation of Martha Stewart."

A reasonable jury could infer from this evidence that Stewart was aware of the importance of her reputation to the continued health of MSLO. With respect to Stewart's state of mind, a jury could infer, based on the falling stock price and the news reports that Stewart believed that the price of MSLO was falling in response to the negative publicity about the SEC investigations.

The Government introduced evidence of the timing, context, and substance of allegedly false public statements which appeared in *The Wall Street Journal*.

Included in an article entitled "Martha Stewart Sold ImClone Stock," is the following paragraph: According to her attorney, Ms. Stewart's sale, involving about 3,000 shares of ImClone, occurred on December 26 or 27. The sale was executed, he said, because Ms. Stewart had a predetermined price at which she planned to sell the stock. That determination, made more than a month before that trade, was to sell if the stock ever went below $60, he said. At the time, the stock was trading at about $60.

The Government contends that a reasonable jury could draw inferences from the evidence that would permit it to find beyond a reasonable doubt that Stewart intended to deceive investors with her statement. Specifically, the Government argues that the evidence supports the inferences that Stewart was aware of the impact of the negative publicity about her ImClone trade on the market value of MSLO securities and on her personal wealth, and that Stewart deliberately directed her statements to investors in MSLO securities.

In viewing the evidence in the light most favorable to the Government, I hold that a reasonable juror could not find beyond a reasonable doubt that Stewart's purpose was to influence the market in MSLO securities.

The Government contends that intent can be drawn from the fact that *The Wall Street Journal*

is "the most widely read financial publication in the nation." Specifically, by making the statement to that newspaper, Stewart intended to influence investors with her statement. The Government presented no evidence that Stewart or her lawyer reached out to *The Wall Street Journal* as opposed to other publications. Thus, there is no evidence that Stewart chose the forum for the statement. The fact that *The Wall Street Journal*, as a financial publication, had an interest in an investigation into a stock trade by the well-known CEO of a public company does not evidence Stewart's intent.

For the foregoing reasons, defendant Stewart's motion for a judgment of acquittal on Count Nine of the Indictment is granted.

SECTION 2.6
CONTRACT LAW

We enter into a variety of contracts every day. However, because of their informal nature we rarely think of these agreements as contracts. Buying gas, getting lunch, taking public transportation, or buying a newspaper are all examples of agreements entered into by the parties that represent valid contracts. Merely walk out of a restaurant without paying for lunch, and the legal significance of your actions will be quickly realized.

The courts face a dilemma, however, when asked to enforce a promise that seems social in nature. For instance, how should a court decide a case where a high school student sues her prom date who never showed up for the prom? Suppose the student bought a prom dress and had her hair done. Should a court allow her to collect damages from her date in the form of payment for her dress and beauty treatment? Is this the type of agreement that will give rise to an enforceable contract, or is it merely a social agreement?

A **contract** is the exchange of promises voluntarily made by the parties, which agreement is enforceable in court. While the terms may vary from bargain to bargain, five essential elements must be present. They are:

1. an offer
2. acceptance
3. consideration
4. capacity
5. legality

An offer is a proposal by one party (offeror) to the other (offeree) manifesting a willingness to enter into a valid contract. An offer has three requirements. It must be: (1) definite, (2) made with the intent to contract, and (3) be communicated to the party for whom the offer is intended.

An acceptance is the unconditional promise by a party to be bound by the terms of the offer. For example, the words "I accept your offer to purchase my car for $15,000" shows intent to be bound by the offer. Until this occurs, there has been no meeting of the minds. Also, a change in the proposal by the offeree constitutes a rejection of the offer and becomes a counter-offer. If the buyer responds to an offer to sell a car for $15,000 by saying, "I really like your car but I can only pay $13,500." This statement constitutes a counter-offer. The acceptance must also follow the same format as the offer, and: (1) be made with the intent to contract, (2) be communicated to the offeror, and (3) be unconditional.

Consideration is the third element of a contract and refers to what each party gives up in return for the act or promise of the other. This is called the quid pro quo, or "bargained for exchange." Two elements must be present to satisfy the requirements of consideration. It must appear that the parties intended to incur legal rights and liabilities, and the bargain for exchange must have legal value. For example, if a person purchases a slice of pizza from a vendor for two dollars, what is the consideration? The vendor is giving up a slice of pizza in exchange for two dollars. The consumer is giving up two dollars but is receiving a slice of pizza in return. This bargain for exchange is supported by consideration from both parties. If the merchant only has one slice of pizza left, and the customer offers the vendor $20.00 in order to outbid three other customers, is the contract valid since the consideration offered by the buyer is so much more than what the slice of pizza is worth? The value of a bargain does not have to be equal as long as fraud or undue influence is not present.

The courts will not usually disturb a contract freely entered into by the parties of similar bargaining power. Nevertheless, when one of the individuals does not have the capacity to fully understand the ramifications of the contractual obligation, mutual consent to bargain is lacking. The law provides protection to certain groups deemed to lack the capacity to contract. These include children, insane people, and intoxicated individuals.

The contracts of a minor are voidable at the child's election. This means that the child may disaffirm the contract but the adult is still bound by the agreement. In order to disaffirm, the child does not have to return the adult to the status quo or return the adult to the same position as the adult was in before the contract was formed. The minor merely has to return what is left of that purchased or received. In addition, a minor may ratify a contract upon reaching majority. Ratification occurs when a child reaches maturity and expresses an intention to be bound by the agreement or fails to disaffirm the contract. For instance, a child who purchases a car while a minor but continues to drive a car that he purchased as a minor after reaching majority will be found to have ratified the contract.

The last element of a contract requires the purpose and subject matter of the agreement be legal. A contract is illegal if its performance is criminal, tortuous or against public policy. For instance, a contract to purchase drugs or the agreement to reward a person for assaulting another are illegal contracts and void as a matter of law. In other words, neither party may seek court intervention to enforce the obligations even when one party has performed the act or promise specified in the agreement. Courts will simply leave the parties where it finds them. For example, the court will not enforce a gambling debt between two friends over a college football game. The court takes the position that the enforcement of an illegal transaction makes the judiciary an indirect participant in the wrongful conduct.

On the rare occasion that a party does enter into a formal written contract, each term must be carefully analyzed and understood. An Agreement of Sale to purchase a home, an employment contract, an apartment lease, or the loan documentation from a bank are complex written documents containing many provisions, each paragraph of which has legal significance.

Nothing is more frustrating than when a client seeks legal advice about a contract that has already been signed without review by the attorney. This is reinforced over and over again when a distraught client calls about the purchase of a home. A buyer will eagerly sign an Agreement of Sale without the advice of counsel. Disputes over the perfect house soon arise when the buyer fails to qualify for the mortgage or learns that the refrigerator is not included in the purchase. There is little an attorney can do at this time to overcome the deficiencies in the legal document.

When a party breaches a contract, the consequences are almost always a question of damages. The penalty can vary from nothing to forfeiting the down payment or losing a substantial amount of money. A written contract will frequently dictate the penalty for the breach of the agreement. In fact, the contract can even specify how the dispute is to be resolved. Do the parties resort to the traditional remedies of court, or does the contract provide for an alternative dispute resolution process such as binding arbitration? Only a review of the document will provide an answer to a party's legal rights and obligations.

The following is a sample motion picture contract so that one may appreciate the individual elements of a contract.

MOTION PICTURE CONTRACT

THIS AGREEMENT made by and between **Five Star Motion Pictures**, hereinafter referred to as "Employer" and **Jason Versace** (hereinafter **"Actor"**) .

1. **Employer** agrees to employ the **Actor**, and **Actor** agrees to render services exclusively to the **Employer** during the duration of the filming of the motion picture *"Hot Ice,"* in the parts of such characters or roles and in such plays or subjects as the **Employer** may select.

2. The **Actor** agrees that he will, during the term of this contract, devote his services exclusively to the **Employer** and will not engage in any other occupation.

3. The **Actor** grants the right to the **Employer** to use his name and photograph in any way **Employer** deems fit in connection with the advertising of said motion picture film.

4. The **Employer** agrees to pay the **Actor** for his services, the sum of $100,000.00 payable at the end of the filming of the Motion picture.

5. It is agreed that the services of said **Actor** are extraordinary and unique, and there is no adequate remedy at law for breach of contract by the **Actor**, and that in the case of such a breach, the **Employer** shall be entitled to equitable relief by way of injunction or otherwise.

6. The **Employer** is to supply the **Actor** with all of the costumes required for the assignment under the terms of this contract.

IN WITNESS WHEREOF, we hereto set our hands and seals.

Jason Versace	*Ira Jones*
JASON VERSACE	FIVE STAR MOTION PICTURES

Not all transactions and relationships give rise to a contract. This is demonstrated in **Yarde Metals, Inc. v. New England Patriots** where a season ticket holder's privileges were revoked because of the actions of a business associate who had been given one of the tickets to a Patriots game and misbehaved during the event.

YARDE METALS, INC. V. NEW ENGLAND PATRIOTS
834 N.E.2D 1233 (MASS. APP. CT. 2005)

After twenty years as a season ticket holder of the New England Patriots (Patriots), Yarde Metals, Inc. (Yarde), received a letter from the Patriots' front office advising that Yarde's season ticket privileges had been terminated, "effective immediately." As the reason, the Patriots stated that on October 13, 2002, an individual named Mikel LaCroix, using a ticket from Yarde's account, was "ejected from Gillette Stadium for throwing bottles in the seating section." The letter requested return of Yarde's remaining season tickets and offered a refund of their value. Yarde admitted that LaCroix, a business associate, had been given a ticket for the October 13, 2002, game. Yarde denied that LaCroix had thrown any bottles and offered the following account. Gillette Stadium had an insufficient number of men's restrooms in use for football games. On the date in question, LaCroix, along with others, used available women's restrooms to answer the call of nature. These patrons were unimpeded by security guards, but for some unexplained reason, as he left the women's restroom, LaCroix was arrested, removed from the stadium, and charged with the crime of disorderly conduct.

Yarde argues that its twenty-year relationship with the Patriots created a contractual right to renew its season tickets annually. That such a right was part of the bargain between it and the Patriots, Yarde maintains, is evidenced by the Patriots' annual offer of the opportunity to purchase season tickets for the upcoming football season to Yarde because of Yarde's status as a season ticket holder. Yarde claims that by revoking its tickets for the actions of its guest, a course the Patriots originally took believing he had been ejected for throwing bottles rather than for using the women's room, the Patriots breached that contractual obligation. Specifically, Yarde argues that the process the Patriots followed in terminating Yarde's season tickets constituted a violation of the covenant of good faith and fair dealing that would be implied in any contractual right to renew annually.

The purchase of a ticket to a sports or entertainment event typically creates nothing more than a revocable license. No Massachusetts cases, however, address the nature of the relationship between season ticket holders and ticket issuers, and the cases do not preclude parties from contracting for such things as renewal or transfer rights. Picking up on that fact, Yarde suggests we should follow cases from other jurisdictions where it has been concluded

that season ticket holders have some protected expectations regarding their season ticket accounts.

In particular, Yarde urges us to extrapolate from two bankruptcy court decisions that ruled that the opportunity to transfer renewal rights to season tickets was an asset of the bankrupt season ticket holder's estate. The contractual right Yarde asks this court to imply here would substantially expand the reasoning of the decisions that it cites for support. The bankruptcy decisions focus on the nature of the season ticket as an asset of the bankrupt ticket holder's estate. In those cases, the teams did not attempt to revoke season tickets, but rather intervened only when the estate tried to transfer season ticket accounts, a practice both teams typically allowed. Therefore, they provide little support for the proposition that a court can enforce a contractual right to renew that trumps a ticket issuer's decision to cancel a specific season ticket on account of the behavior of the ticket holder.

Despite the fact that the parties themselves are not precluded from contracting for renewal rights, Yarde's allegations would not justify implying a contractual right that would contradict the explicit language on the ticket. The annual "automatic and unsolicited" offer from the Patriots to purchase season tickets may not thwart the Patriots' right to revoke ticket privileges for cause that the ticket holder agreed to as part of the season ticket package. Where there is a seemingly clear transaction-Yarde purchased six tickets to ten games at $100 each-we cannot infer an annual renewal right, the value of which would dwarf the value of the otherwise clear commercial exchange. More importantly, such a theory would disregard the Patriots' express disclaimers of any right of the purchaser to renew in subsequent years printed on game tickets and informational material provided to season ticket holders. The ticket specifically stated that "[p]urchase of season tickets does not entitle purchaser to renewal in a subsequent year." Yarde has articulated no basis on which we can ignore the language on the ticket.

In sum, Yarde's complaint did not plead a justifiable cause of action. The judge did not err in dismissing the complaint.

SECTION 2.7
TORT LAW

A **tort** is a private or civil wrong against an individual for which the court will award money damages. The word "tort" is derived from the Latin term "torquer," meaning "to twist." Torts are classified into the categories of negligence or intentional torts. **Negligence** arises when one fails to act as a reasonable person under the circumstances. Four elements must be established to make out a case of negligence: (1) the defendant must owe a duty, (2) there must be a breach of that duty, (3) that negligence must be the proximate cause of the harm, and (4) damages must flow from the wrongful conduct. For example, a motorist is negligent when the driver loses concentration and unintentionally runs into another car. The motorist did not intentionally try to injure the driver of the second car, however, he will be responsible for money damages in causing the accident.

The plaintiff has the burden of proving all of these elements by the preponderance of the evidence. Suppose Joe Roberts is stopped at a traffic light when Peter Christopher loses control of his vehicle and rams the rear of Joe's car. The force of the impact propels Joe forward and he sustains a whiplash type injury. Is Christopher negligent? Christopher owed a duty to drive his car carefully and avoid hitting another vehicle. Christopher breached that duty by striking the rear of the Roberts' vehicle. Finally, the negligence of Christopher in the operation of the car was the proximate cause of Joe's neck injury causing him to incur medical expenses and conscious pain and suffering. Not all cases are as easy to prove and a more detailed examination of each element of negligence is required.

Duty of care establishes the type of behavior a person must exhibit in a given situation. The basic rule is that a person must conform to the standard of care of a reasonable person under the circumstances. This duty can vary from case to case depending upon the age of the person, and his or her expertise in the specific situation. Generally, the law does not make a distinction concerning the standard of care between adults of different ages. A 65 year-old-man will be held to the same standard of care as a person 18 years of age in driving a car. That standard of care is simply the "average driver." A professional, however, is held to a higher standard of care when he or she is engaged in that professional capacity. This type of claim is called malpractice and the defendant is held to the standard of care of the average professional in that discipline. For example, a neurosurgeon who makes a mistake during surgery is held to the standard of care of the average neurosurgeon and not to the standard of care of the average person performing surgery – or even the average physician. The neurosurgeon has been selected because of this individual's specialized skill so the doctor must possess the skill and expertise of the average neurosurgeon.

Children develop differently each year of their lives. There is a vast difference in the motor and intellectual skills of a child of six years of age and a child of twelve. Therefore, minors are held to a different standard of care than the average adult. A minor is held to the standard of care of a child of similar age, intelligence, and experience. The exception to this rule is when the child engages in adult activity, such as the driving of a car or the flying of an airplane. In those cases, children are held to the standard of care of the average person engaged in those activities.

The second element of a negligence action is quite simple. If a duty is owed, and a person fails to fulfill that obligation, a breach of duty has occurred. For example, a property owner owes a duty to a business visitor to make the property safe. This includes the obligation to inspect the premises on a reasonable basis. If a department store does not inspect its facility, and a business visitor is injured because a broken bottle is not picked up from the floor, the merchant has breached the duty of care.

Proximate cause is the third element of a negligence action and requires there be a reasonable connection between the negligence of a defendant and the harm suffered by the plaintiff. The fact that a party is careless and another suffers an injury is not by itself enough to impose liability. Rather, the negligent conduct must be a substantial factor in causing the harm. For instance, a surgeon who leaves an instrument in a patient's abdomen following surgery has obviously breached the duty of exercising reasonable medical care. The patient's need for additional surgery to remove the medical instrument would be directly related to the doctor's malpractice.

The last element of a negligence claim is damages. This is the amount of money awarded to an injured person as the result of the wrongful or improper conduct of the defendant. This recovery may take the form of compensatory and punitive damages.

The purpose of compensatory damages is to make an injured party whole by providing a sum of money that would return the aggrieved party to the same position as though nothing had happened. These damages must always have a reasonable relationship to the negligent act of the defendant and cannot be speculative. In a tort action, the damages should place an injured party in substantially as good of a position as that occupied before the injury. Those damages, however, are not always easy to quantify. While one may quantify the amount of lost wages, how much is a broken arm worth? Would it matter if the injured party is a painter and could no longer use his arm?

Reasonable people differ on the value of the case but the following elements must be considered when arriving at a dollar figure: medical expenses, lost wages, property damage, and pain and suffering.

Pain and suffering is the most controversial element of recoverable damages because it is subjective and cannot be calculated with mathematical certainty. The value of each case will also change depending upon the circumstances. For instance, if the victim of a broken arm makes a good recovery after six weeks, the case will have one value. If the injury, however, results in permanent impairment of a person's range of motion of the arm, it is worth a much greater sum of money.

Even though a defendant is negligent, the injured party's own conduct may preclude recovery. There are two basic defenses to a negligence action—contributory negligence and assumption of the risk.

Contributory negligence is the failure of the plaintiff to act as a reasonable person under the circumstances. For instance, a driver who fails to stop for a red light is negligent. While the operator of the other vehicle with the green light has the right of way, that driver may not blindly proceed through the intersection without first looking to the left and right. If the two vehicles collide, and neither driver looked for the other, they are both negligent. Since the individual who went through the red light bears the bulk of the liability, can the motorist with the green light collect damages? The answer is no. A plaintiff may not recover if he or she has any degree of contributory negligence even if that fault is 1% of the responsibility for the accident.

Most jurisdictions find this principle too harsh and have adopted a modified concept called, **comparative negligence.** Basically, as along as the plaintiff's negligence is not greater than the defendant's misdeeds, the plaintiff may recover damages, but the verdict will be reduced by the percentage of the plaintiff's negligence. In other words, if the plaintiff is found to be 30% of fault and the verdict is $10,000, the award will be reduced to $7,000. Pennsylvania and New Jersey follow this approach while Maryland and the District of Columbia use the more rigid contributory negligence standard.

The second defense to a negligence action is **assumption of the risk.** If the plaintiff knows of the danger, but voluntarily exposes himself to the harm, the plaintiff will be barred from recovery. For example, if a person jumps over an open manhole instead of walking around it, he will have assumed the risk of injury if he falls into the hole.

When the wrongdoer purposely sets out to harm another, that conduct gives rise to an **intentional tort** and may result in the imposition of money damages. Theories of liability include actions for a battery, assault, defamation, false imprisonment, and infliction of emotional distress.

Intentional torts are treated more seriously by the courts and verdicts frequently include an award of **punitive damages,** which sum is to punish the wrongdoer for his actions. These types of claims are generally not covered by insurance.

One must always be mindful, however, that the mere fact someone suffers a loss does not mean that he or she is entitled to recover money. The claimant must prove that another person was at fault in causing the harm and that the law recognizes a theory of liability.

For instance, in **Ali v. Gates, 1998 WL 317584 (W.D. N.Y.),** an individual instituted suit against Bill Gates and a number of others alleging that his constitutional rights were being violated by the defendants, who were trying to murder him through a Windows 95 program hooked to his mind. This case was dismissed by the court because Mr. Ali failed to establish a recognized cause of action under the various theories he asserted in his lawsuit.

Winder v. Franck deals with a situation where the driver of a car suffered a fatal heart attack causing his vehicle to strike another automobile. The court had to decide if the innocent plaintiffs could recover compensation for the accident.

James L. Winder v. Barbara J. Franck, Administratrix
669 N.W. 2d 262 (Iowa App. 2003)

Everett Franck had a family history of heart disease. He suffered his first heart attack in June, 1998. After this attack, his doctors recommended he exercise, lose weight, lower his blood pressure, and cholesterol. Everett complied with his doctors' recommendations. His doctors gave him medical clearance to drive.

Everett was driving a vehicle on February 9, 1999 when he suffered another heart attack. He crossed the center line of the highway and struck a vehicle being driven by Winder. Kerr was a passenger in Winder's vehicle. According to an autopsy report, Everett died from the heart attack prior to the accident. The medical examiner concluded Everett "was dead when the car swerved before the collision occurred."

Winder and Kerr sued the defendants for negligence, claiming that Everett was negligent in the operation of his vehicle. They also alleged Everett was negligent in operating his vehicle when he knew or should have known doing so posed a danger to the motoring public, including the plaintiffs.

Everett suffered a heart attack on February 9, 1999, which caused the accident injuring the plaintiffs. There is no evidence whatsoever that Everett's heart attack was foreseeable or that it was not sudden. He had been asymptomatic since his prior heart attack eight months earlier. He had followed his doctors' instructions to reduce his risk factors, and he had taken medication as directed. His doctors allowed him to drive.

Everett was seen before noon on February 9, 1999, at the country courthouse. The attendant who served him stated he was not in any distress, he was fully coherent and seemed fine, he did not say he felt poorly nor did he act like he felt poorly.

Furthermore, a passenger in a vehicle behind the plaintiffs at the time of the accident saw Everett. This witness stated, "Maroon car swerved quickly into the white van and hit it head on. It looked like the driver of the maroon car either fell asleep or became incapacitated in some way."

We note that the inference the plaintiffs want us to deduce from the evidence, that Everett was suffering a heart attack and knew it while operating his vehicle, is based on mere speculation and conjecture. We conclude there is no genuine issue concerning the fact that Everett suffered a sudden heart attack which caused him to cross the centerline of the highway and resulted in the accident.

It is well-established that in order to prove a case of negligence, the plaintiff must establish that the defendant owed him a duty of care, the defendant breached that duty, defendant's breach was the actual and proximate cause of plaintiff's injuries, and the plaintiff suffered damages.

We conclude that the trial court correctly determined there was no genuine issue of material fact concerning whether Everett's February 9 heart attack was foreseeable or whether he acted reasonably in driving on that date. We refer to the unrefuted evidence, namely that Everett had not only been asymptomatic since his June 1988 heart attack, but also that as of his February 9, 1999 heart attack, he had fully complied with his doctors' orders to reduce risk factors, his doctors had months earlier cleared him to drive, and his doctors believed his February 9 heart attack was unpredictable. Everett did not act unreasonably in driving, nor was his heart attack foreseeable.

QUESTIONS FOR DISCUSSION:

1. Do you think the court would have reached the same conclusion if the operator of the car was experiencing chest pains as he was driving, and did not pull his car over to the side of the road?

2. Should a person with a heart condition not be allowed to operate a motor vehicle?

SECTION 2.8
SHOOTING OF
PETER CHRISTOPHER

PROBLEM TWO—B

PARK, BROWN & SMITH, P.C.
ATTORNEYS AT LAW
MEMORANDUM

To: All Law Clerks

FROM: Peter Smith, Esquire

RE: Shooting of Peter Christopher

Tony Roberts' has been arrested for aggravated assault. My investigation reveals that the football player shot his neighbor, Peter Christopher, to prevent Christopher from stealing his car. Tony claims he was merely defending his property and questions the fairness of prosecuting him for shooting a thief. The following story emerged after I spoke to Tony at the police station.

Tony came home from football practice around 4 p.m. Just as Tony was about to watch TV, he heard rattling noises coming from outside. Tony peered out his bedroom window and saw Peter Christopher standing by the Corvette in the driveway. Christopher was trespassing, and Tony was aware of the recent encounter the neighbor had had with Kathy over the Honda that she damaged in the accident. Tony also knew that Christopher was furious over what happened to the Honda.

When Tony's requests that Christopher get away from the car went unheeded, he ran into his father's study. From there he had access to the deck overlooking the driveway. Tony thought that from this vantage point, he would be able to scare his neighbor away.

Tony again warned Christopher to get away from the car. When it became apparent that the neighbor was determined to steal the vehicle, Tony decided to make his request a little more threatening. He ran back into the study and grabbed a gun from his father's collection. He warned Christopher that he would shoot if the neighbor didn't leave immediately. Christopher responded with obscene words and gestures while continuing to break into the car.

Tony really hadn't expected any trouble. He didn't want to shoot Christopher, but he refused to stand there helplessly while Peter drove away with his most prized possession. So Tony fired a single shot, which pierced the neighbor's left arm.

Having apprehended the neighbor, Tony called the police to report the attempted theft. He also called Dr. Jones to provide medical attention to Christopher. Officer O'Brien arrived almost immediately. Tony greeted the policeman with a big smile but was shocked when O'Brien drew his service revolver and handcuffed him. Tony thought O'Brien was joking. In fact, he expected O'Brien to pat him on the back. Tony continued to smile. After all, Tony had just caught a thief. But there was no mistake. O'Brien took the football player to headquarters, where Tony was fingerprinted, booked, and thrown in jail.

An important decision on the topic is **Katko v. Briney, 183 N.W.2d 657 (Iowa 1971).** According to the rules set forth in that case, decide whether Tony can escape liability. You must answer the following:

1. Is Tony allowed to use force to protect his property? As Tony said, "I warned him to get away from the car. He made an obscene gesture, so I shot him in the arm in self-defense."

2. Was this a reasonable degree of force under the circumstances?

3. Does it matter that Tony warned his neighbor before he shot him?

4. Can Tony be criminally prosecuted and sued civilly for the shooting?

5. Do you agree with the law?

Your decision should include an analysis of these questions along with any other facts or arguments you believe are relevant in deciding Tony's culpability.

MARVIN KATKO v. EDWARD BRINEY
183 N.W.2D 657 (IOWA 1971)

The primary issue presented here is whether an owner may protect personal property in an unoccupied boarded-up farm house against trespassers and thieves by a spring gun capable of inflicting death or serious injury.

At defendants' request plaintiff's action was tried to a jury consisting of residents of the community where defendants' property was located. The jury returned a verdict for plaintiff and against defendants for $20,000 actual and $10,000 punitive damages.

Most of the facts are not disputed. In 1957 defendant, Bertha L. Briney inherited her parents' farmland. Included was an 80-acre tract in southwest Mahaska County where her grandparents and parents had lived. No one occupied the house thereafter.

There occurred a series of trespassing and housebreaking events with loss of some household items, the breaking of windows and "messing up of the property in general."

Defendants boarded up the windows and doors in an attempt to stop the intrusions. They had posted "no trespass" signs on the land. The nearest one was 35 feet from the house. Defendants set a "shot-gun trap" in the north bedroom where they secured it to an iron bed with the barrel pointed at the bedroom door. It was rigged with wire from the doorknob to the gun's trigger so it would fire when the door was ópened. Briney first pointed the gun's trigger so an intruder would be hit in the stomach but at Mrs. Briney's suggestion it was lowered to hit the legs. Tin was nailed over the bedroom window. The spring gun could not be seen from the outside. No warning of its presence was posted.

Plaintiff worked regularly as a gasoline station attendant seven miles from the old house and considered it as being abandoned. He knew it had long been uninhabited. Plaintiff and McDonough had been to the premises and found several old bottles and fruit jars which they took and added to their collection of antiques. About 9:30 p.m. they made a second trip to the Briney property. They entered the old house by removing a board from a porch window which was without glass. While McDonough was looking around the kitchen area plaintiff went to another part of the house. As he started to open the north bedroom door the shotgun went off striking him in the right leg above the ankle bone. Much of his leg, including part of the tibia, was blown away.

Plaintiff testified he knew he had no right to break and enter the house with intent to steal bottles and fruit jars therefrom. He further testified he had entered a plea of guilty to larceny in the nighttime of property of less than $20 value from a private building. He stated he had been fined $50 and costs and paroled during good behavior from a 60-day jail sentence.

The main thrust of defendant's defense in the trial court and on this appeal is that "the law permits use of a spring gun in a dwelling or warehouse for the purpose of preventing the unlawful entry of a burglar or thief."

The overwhelming weight of authority, both textbook and case law, supports the trial court's statement of the applicable principles of law.

Prosser on Torts, Third Edition, pages 116-118, states:

> The law has always placed a higher value upon human safety than upon mere rights in property, it is the accepted rule that there is no privilege to use any force calculated to cause death or serious bodily injury to repel the threat to land or chattels unless there is also such a threat to the defendant's personal safety as to justify a self-defense… Spring guns and other man-killing devices are not justifiable against a mere trespasser, or even a petty thief. They are privileged only against those upon whom the landowner, if he were present in person would be free to inflict injury of the same kind.

Restatement of Torts, section 85, page 180 states: "The value of human life and limb, not only to the individual concerned but also to society, so outweighs the interest of a possessor of land in excluding from it those whom he is not willing to admit thereto that a possessor of land has no privilege to use force intended or likely to cause death or serious harm against another whom the possessor see about to enter his premises or meddle with his chattel, unless the intrusion threatens death or serious bodily harm to the occupiers or users of the premises.

The facts in **Allison v. Fiscus, 156 Ohio 120, 100 N.E.2d 237, 44 A.L.R.2d 369,** decided in 1951, are very similar to the case at the bar. There plaintiff's right to damages was recognized for injuries received when he feloniously broke a door latch and started to enter defendant's warehouse with intent to steal. As he entered a trap of two sticks of dynamite buried under the doorway by defendant owner was set off and plaintiff seriously injured. The court held the question whether a particular trap was justified as a use of reasonable and necessary force against the trespasser engaged in the commission of a felony should have been submitted to the jury. The Ohio Supreme Court recognized plaintiff's right to punitive or exemplary damages in addition to compensation damages. The jury's findings of fact including a finding defendants acted with malice and with wanton and reckless disregard, as required for an allowance of punitive or exemplary damages, are supported by substantial evidence. We are bound thereby.

Affirmed.

ANSWER SHEET
PROBLEM TWO—B

Name   **Please Print Clearly**

1. Is Tony allowed to use force to protect his property?

_____

_____

_____

_____

_____

_____

_____

_____

_____

2. Was this a reasonable degree of force under the circumstances?

_____

_____

_____

_____

_____

_____

_____

_____

_____

3. Does it matter that Tony warned his neighbor before he shot him in the arm?

_____

_____

_____

_____

_____

_____

_____

_____

_____

4. Can Tony be criminally prosecuted and sued civilly for the shooting? Do you agree with the law?

_____

_____

_____

_____

_____

_____

_____

_____

_____

_____

Katko v. Briney addressed the issue of how a person can protect personal property against an intruder. What happens, however, when the issue becomes how much force a person can use against a home intruder in self-defense? The following case answers that question.

COMMONWEALTH OF PENNSYLVANIA V. EARL JOHNSTON
263 A.2D 376 (PA. 1970)

Earl F. Johnston was tried for the murder of Charles Pittman, and found guilty of voluntary manslaughter. We reverse.

On October 8, 1966, a group gathered for social purposes on the business property of defendant Johnston. Among others, the group included Johnston, Pittman, Mrs. Pittman and Mrs. Wolfe. Strong ill feeling existed between Mrs. Pittman and Mrs. Wolfe, and an argument started between them which culminated in a physical tussle. When the pair were separated, Mrs. Wolfe began to berate Pittman and called him obscene names. Pittman became angry, drew a knife and threatened to kill her. He chased her from the building and inflicted two knife wounds on her arm as she fled.

Johnston separated the two, led Pittman to his automobile and asked him to leave. Pittman and his wife got in the car. Mrs. Wolfe then threw a brick through the rear window of the Pittman automobile. Pittman jumped from his automobile and chased Mrs. Wolfe into the building with the knife in his hand, saying, *"I'm going to kill you."*

Johnston tried to stop Pittman from entering his building, and when this effort failed, he went to his automobile, parked nearby, and secured a loaded .45 automatic revolver. He then followed Pittman into the building, grabbed him by the left arm (Pittman had the knife in his right hand) and pulled him back several feet from the area where Mrs. Wolfe was standing.

Pittman then approached Johnston with the knife in an upraised hand, saying he was going to kill Mrs. Wolfe and what was that to Johnston. Johnston retreated 10 to 15 feet, then stood his ground and drew his gun, saying to Pittman: "Charles, don't come any closer. I don't want to hurt you." Despite this, Pittman kept approaching Johnston with the knife held in a menacing position. When Pittman was about 11 feet away from him, Johnston fired one shot at his feet. When Pittman was about 6 feet away, Johnston fired two shots into Pittman's body, one of which entered his heart causing instant death.

The killing of another human being without justification or excuse is felonious homicide. However, a killing is excusable if it is committed in self-defense. At trial, Johnston did not deny killing Pittman, but maintained that he did so in defense of his own life.

The following conditions must be satisfied before one can successfully invoke the defense of self-defense:

1. The slayer must have been free from fault in provoking or continuing the difficulty which resulted in the killing.

2. The slayer must have reasonably believed that he was in imminent danger of death, great bodily harm, or some felony, and that there was a necessity to kill in order to save himself therefrom.

3. The slayer must not have violated any duty to retreat or avoid the danger.

Even though a person has entered the business premises of another, at the invitation of the owner, his subsequent conduct may be such as to justify the revocation of the invitation to remain as a guest. As owner of the business premises, defendant Johnston had the right to order the deceased, Pittman, from the premises, and in case of refusal had the right to remove him by force, if necessary. Since the difficulty ensued in the exercise of Johnston's legal right of ejection, Johnston is without fault in provoking the controversy within the meaning of the first element of self-defense.

In view of Pittman's actions immediately prior to and at the time of the killing involved, Johnston had reasonable grounds to believe that he was in imminent danger of his life or great bodily harm from his attacker.

But, it is argued by the Commonwealth that Johnston could have retreated from the building through a nearby door and escaped harm without resorting to shooting Pittman. In a long line of decisions, we have held that the right to take life in self-defense does not arise while there are means of escape open to the person attacked. Life is sacred and if it is merely a question of whether one man should flee or another should die, then certainly the taking of life should be avoided and the person under attack should flee.

There is an exception to this rule, however. Where a man is dangerously assaulted or attacked in his own dwelling house, he need not retreat, but may stand his ground and meet deadly force with deadly force to save his own life or protect himself from great bodily harm.

Since, in this case, defendant Johnston was in his own place of business and was in imminent danger of serious personal harm or death from an unjustified attack, he was not required to retreat and will not be denied the right of self-defense.

Judgment is reversed.

Katko v. Briney clearly demonstrates that a person cannot use force that will inflict death or serious bodily injury in the protection of property. Human life is simply more important than property. In **Commonwealth v. Johnston,** however, the court was confronted with the issue as to whether a person can use deadly force in order to protect human life. While the killing of another without justification is illegal, a killing is excusable if it is committed in self-defense. This will occur when **(1)** the slayer reasonably believes that he is in imminent danger of great bodily harm, **(2)** he has attempted to flee the harm, and **(3)** deadly force is the only way to protect human life.

While the use of a shotgun in the protection of property is clearly excessive force, is the owner of a store liable for an attack by a vicious dog that is allowed to roam the store at night in order to stop trespassers? Based upon the reasoning in **Katko v. Briney,** the store owner will be liable for the attack. The dog has been kept on the premises for the sole purpose of protecting property by inflicting serious harm to the intruder. Will liability, however, be imposed on a homeowner whose pet dog attacks a burglar that enters a home when no one is present? The answer is no. The dog is not kept at the family dwelling for the sole purpose of attacking people. Dogs are territorial and they will protect their master's home against an intruder.

Will the owner of a dog be liable if the animal bites a guest or if a large playful dog, that has a habit of jumping on people, knocks someone down? The law is well settled that a dog's owner will be liable for the actions of the pet if the owner knows or has good reason to know of the dog's dangerous or vicious propensities and fails to take reasonable measures to protect the guest from the pet's actions. The saying that "every dog is entitled to one bite" is not true. If a dog has displayed a vicious propensity in the past, the owner will be liable to another for a dog bite even if the animal has not bitten anyone previously. Likewise, the law imposes a duty of restraint on the owner of a dog when the owner knows of the animal's playful but dangerous propensity of jumping on people and knocking them down.

THOMAS ROWE V. TROY GONGWER
30 S.W. 3D 922 (CT. APP. MO. 2000)

Thomas Rowe appeals the judgment of the court in favor of Troy Gongwer, arising out of an incident which occurred, when Gongwer's dog, "Guiness" bit him. We affirm.

Rowe and Gongwer were neighbors. They both owned dogs who occasionally fought. There was no evidence that Guiness ever attacked or threatened a person. On June 13, 1998, Guiness escaped from his home, ran up the street and began fighting with Rowe's dog. Rowe attempted to break up the fight, and Guiness bit him.

Gongwer moved for summary judgment asserting, Rowe cannot show that Guiness exhibited any dangerous and/or vicious propensities prior to the incident in which Rowe was bitten. Under the law, a dog owner is liable for injuries the dog inflicts only if the owner harbors the dog with actual or constructive knowledge that the dog has vicious or dangerous propensities. **Crimmins v. Mirly, 675 S.W. 2d 663, (Mo. App. E.D. 1984).**

In order to establish a submissible case, Rowe must show that: (1) the dog has vicious or dangerous propensities, and (2) Gongwer had knowledge of such propensities. Rowe believes he met this standard in that Guiness fought with his dog and one other dog, and Rowe complained to Gongwer after Guiness injured his dog while fighting.

Rowe claims the trial court failed to consider two cases which are factually analogous to the instant case. The first case is **Boosman v. Moudy, 488 S.W. 2d 917 (Mo. App. 1972).** In that case, the plaintiffs submitted sufficient evidence to show that the defendants knew of the dog's dangerous propensities in that the dog acquired the persistent menacing habit of growling, bristling, and snapping at people and the defendants were aware of the ill-natured changes in the dog toward the family and other people. Similarly, Rowe claims his complaints to Gongwer regarding Guiness's behavior toward his dog gave Gongwer the requisite knowledge that Guiness had dangerous propensities. Yet, Rowe failed to notice, the court in Boosman stated that an owner knowing of a dog's dangerous propensity is liable when the dog displays these tendencies in injuring "persons."

The second case Rowe relies on is **Dansker v. Gelb, 352 S.W. 2d 12 (Mo. 1961).** In Dansker, the plaintiff recovered damages following her visit to defendant's home when the family dog lunged at plaintiff, causing her to fall down a flight of stairs. The dog owner's testimony showed knowledge of the dog's viciousness toward other persons. The court held that propensities to jump and lunge at people show a tendency that the dog's actions potentially were injurious to people. Rowe misplaces his reliance; the Dansker dog owner had knowledge of the dog's viciousness toward people, and was liable for the plaintiff's injuries.

In the instant case, there was no evidence that Guiness had any propensity to harm another person. The case law is clear that an owner must know of an animal's propensity to act viciously against people. Rowe failed to present a genuine issue of material fact to defeat the motion for summary judgment. The judgment of the trial court is affirmed.

SECTION 2.9
PROPERTY LAW

Property law deals with the rights and duties that arise out of the ownership or possession of real property and personal property. **Real property** includes land and everything attached to the land. For instance, a building, a tree, or ground are all considered part of the realty. **Personal property** consists of all other property and would include a book, a car, money, or even a folding chair. In other words, personal property includes everything not attached to the land.

Personal property is further sub-divided into tangible and intangible property. **Tangible property** is a physical object, such as this textbook. **Intangible property**, on the other hand, is personal property that is not a physical object. The ownership of intangible property is usually evidenced by a legal document. Examples of such property include a patent or invention, a copyright for published material, or a trademark to identify a manufacturer or merchant's product.

The purchase of a home has certain inherent problems. Disputes frequently arise as to what was included in the sale. When the buyer inspected the home, a crystal chandelier hung in the foyer. At the time of settlement, a plastic fixture has replaced the chandelier. The seller refuses to give the buyer the chandelier, claiming that it is a family heirloom worth several thousand dollars. The buyer maintains that the fixture was part of the realty since it was on display at the time the home was inspected. Who is correct? The answer will depend upon whether the item is real or personal property.

In **O'Donnell v. Schneeweis, 73 D. & C. 2d 400 (Chester County Ct. of Common Pleas, Pa. 1975),** the court offered guidelines as to what constitutes a fixture that would be included in the sale of real estate. A **fixture** is an item of personal property which, by reason of its being attached to a building, becomes part of the real estate. In reaching this conclusion, the court noted that personal property used in connection with real estate falls into one of three classes.

First, furniture, such as a couch or table, always remains personal property; second, fixtures, or those things so affixed to the property that they cannot be removed without material injury to the real estate are considered real property; and third, those things which, although physically connected to the real estate, are affixed in such a manner that they may be removed without destroying or materially injuring the item to be removed. This third category of property becomes part of the realty or remains personal property, depending upon the intention of the parties at the time of annexation.

For example, wall-to-wall carpeting remains as a fixture, but a mirror or picture attached to a wall by a wire is considered personal property. If the mirror was affixed in such a way that it provided the impression that it was meant to be permanent, it would be considered a fixture that remained with the house. Such an example would include a mirror that was glued to the wall and could not be removed without causing damage to the wall.

Dogs are known as "man's best friend" for their loyalty and companionship. But in a custody battle where the dog is the proper subject of the dispute, is it a canine whose time may be split between the couple or is the dog merely a piece of personal property. This is the subject of **Desanctis v. Pritchard.**

Anthony Desanctis v. Lynda Pritchard
2002 WL 14445389 (Pa. Super.2002)

Desanctis and Pritchard were married in 1991 and divorced in October, 2000. During their marriage Pritchard purchased a dog, Barney, from the SPCA. In August, 2000, pursuant to their divorce, the parties entered into an "Agreement" that purported to be a property settlement but dealt primarily with Barney's future. The Agreement states "Barney is [Pritchard's] property and she will have full custody." Further, the Agreement provided for an arrangement allowing Desanctis to visit Barney. In March of 2000, Pritchard moved to Bucks County, Pennsylvania and no longer made Barney available for Desanctis' visits.

Desanctis filed a Complaint requesting the trial court to mandate "shared custody" of Barney. In seeking "shared custody" and a "visitation" arrangement, Desanctis appears to treat Barney, a dog, as a child. Despite the status owners bestow on their pets, Pennsylvania law considers dogs to be personal property. The Agreement explicitly awarded this property to the wife. Desanctis argues that **23 Pa.C.S.A. § 3105(a),** allows the court to enforce a supplementary agreement to a divorce decree. Desanctis, however, overlooks the fact that any terms set forth in the Agreement are void to the extent that they attempt to award custodial visitation with or shared custody of personal property. As the trial court noted, Desanctis is seeking an arrangement analogous, in law, to a visitation schedule for a table or a lamp. This result is clearly not contemplated by the statute. Indeed, §3504 governs this issue:

§ 3504 Disposition of property after termination of marriage

Unless provided otherwise by the court, whenever a decree of divorce or annulment is entered by a court of competent jurisdiction, both parties whose marriage is terminated or affected shall have complete freedom of disposition as to their separate real and personal property and may mortgage, sell, grant, convey or otherwise encumber or dispose of their separate property, whether the property was acquired before, during or after coverture, and neither need join in, consent to or acknowledge a deed, mortgage or instrument of the other.

By the clear and unambiguous terms of the Agreement, Barney and his social schedule belong exclusively to Pritchard. This claim is meritless.

Ownership of property is viewed as consisting of a bundle of rights. Owners have specific rights with their respect to their property; they may use it, prevent others from using it, lend it to someone else, sell it, give it away or destroy it.

It is also common for people to join their own assets with others. The law calls it **concurrent or joint ownership** and it occurs when the title to property is shared by two or more people who hold title to the asset. The most common form of concurrent ownership is **tenancy in common,** and **joint tenants with the right of survivorship.** Both forms of joint ownership give the owners essentially equal rights to the property. Each owner, however, has given up the right to exclusivity; meaning one owner cannot prevent his co-owner from using the property.

The difference between tenancy in common and joint tenancy with the right of survivorship occurs when one co-owner dies. In tenancy in common, if one co-owner dies, his or her share will pass to that person's heirs. In a joint tenancy with the right of survivorship, when one co-owner dies, the decedent's share will pass to the surviving co-owner. Thus, if Joe Roberts and Peter Christopher have a joint bank account as tenants in common, either one of them may make deposits or withdraw funds. If Joe dies, however, his share will pass to his heirs, usually the family, and Peter will retain his one-half share. If, on the other hand, Joe and Peter are joint tenants with the right of survivorship, and Joe dies, his share will automatically pass to Christopher who becomes the sole owner of the bank account. When property is owned as joint tenants with the right of survivorship, the co-owners forfeit their individual rights to dispose of the property as they wish at the time of death. The property is automatically transferred to the survivor.

Married people enjoy a special form of co-ownership designed to protect the marital assets from creditors and to ensure an easy transition of the property to the surviving spouse upon a tenant's death. Most states recognize **tenancy by the entirety,** which is similar to a joint tenancy with the right of survivorship. It differs from a joint tenancy, however, in that neither spouse can convey his or her interest in the property without the other. In other words, each spouse owns 100% interest in the property and cannot dispose of the asset without the consent of the other. Because each spouse owns 100% of the property, the creditor of one spouse is unable to seize the joint asset. Sophisticated creditors, such as banks and mortgage companies, are aware of this rule and require both spouses to sign the loan documentation even though only one spouse may receive the money.

Several states including California, Arizona, Texas and Nevada have adopted **community property rights.** As with a tenancy by the entirety, neither spouse can convey separately his or her interest during life. In these states, community property will pass to the surviving spouse if one dies unless it is given by will to another. Both the tenancy by entireties and community property rights will be severed by a divorce. The property is then automatically converted to a tenancy in common with each owning a one-half interest. These forms of co-ownership apply to both real and personal property.

SECTION 2.10
FAMILY LAW

The institution of marriage no longer enjoys the same favor that it did historically, and more and more couples are establishing family units without much formality or binding commitment. Regardless of how the family unit is created, issues regarding children, assets and benefits arise. **Family law** encompasses the rights, duties, and obligations involving marriages, civil unions, domestic partnerships, divorce, custody, child support, paternity, and other family related issues.

This category of private law is exclusively regulated by state law whose rules and regulations vary from jurisdiction to jurisdiction. There are, however, a number of basic concepts that remain constant.

A **marriage** is a contract between a man and a woman whereby they take each other to be husband and wife for life. Massachusetts is the only state that varies this definition by allowing people of the same sex to marry and New Jersey has held that same-sex couples must be afforded the same rights as married individuals. A handful of other jurisdictions recognize **domestic partnerships** in which an unwed couple, including those of the same sex, can acquire legal rights and protections. Usually this arrangement can only have legal standing if the parties register with the state by filing a Declaration of Domestic Partnership or similar document. While registration does not create a marriage, it does secure a number of rights such as the ability to collect insurance benefits from a partner's employer.

Marriages have a 50% failure rate and the legal dissolution of a marriage is called a **divorce.** Historically, this dissolution could only be accomplished by an innocent spouse who had to prove that his or her partner was at fault in causing the termination of the marriage by engaging in cruel and barbarous treatment, desertion, indignities, adultery or some other type of conduct that caused the marriage to fail. This rigid requirement has changed and partners are now allowed to obtain no-fault divorces, For instance, Pennsylvania allows a couple to file for divorce if the marriage is irretrievably broken.

An **annulment** occurs when there is a legal impediment to a marriage so that the union is declared null and void from its inception. For example, this occurs when one of the parties is still married to another at the time of the subsequent marriage, impotence, insanity or fraud.

SECTION 2.11 VIOLATIONS OF PUBLIC AND PRIVATE LAW

Can one incident give rise to a violation of both public and private law? The answer is yes. This is a frequent occurrence in situations involving criminal misconduct. For instance, an intoxicated person who is involved in an accident may be criminally prosecuted for drunken driving and sued civilly by the aggrieved party for personal injury. An election of remedies between public and private law need not be made, since both forms of action may be pursued. The government prosecutes the criminal case in the name of the State, and the aggrieved party is merely a witness. A civil lawsuit may be instituted for the same misconduct by the individual harmed to seek monetary compensation. Each suit is independent of the other.

This distinction is demonstrated by the O.J. Simpson criminal and civil trials. The former football player was criminally prosecuted for the murder of his ex-wife and Ronald Goldman. Simpson was found not guilty following a highly publicized criminal trial that was filled with dramatic and theatrical moments, such as when the late Johnnie

Cochran uttered his famous line, *"If the glove doesn't fit, you must acquit."* Everyone has an opinion on Simpson's guilt or innocence. Nevertheless, the jury did not believe that the government satisfied its burden of proof "beyond a reasonable doubt." Following the acquittal, the families of Nicole Simpson and Ronald Goldman filed civil lawsuits against Simpson to recover money for the wrongful death of the two murder victims. Much of the same evidence used during the criminal prosecution was presented in the civil trial. However, the lower burden of proof for a civil trial, allowed the jury to find the former football player responsible for the two murders and awarded the families $8.5 million dollars in compensatory damages and $25 million dollars in punitive damages. Simpson appealed that finding.

RONALD GOLDMAN V. O.J. SIMPSON
CASE #B112612 (CAL. CT. APP. 2001)

These civil actions arise from the murders of Nicole Simpson and Ronald Goldman. In a prior criminal trial, Simpson was acquitted of these murders. In the present civil trial, the jury concluded that Simpson killed Nicole and Ronald. Simpson does not contend on appeal that the evidence is legally insufficient to support the jury's verdict. He contends that the judgments should be reversed on the grounds that the evidence was erroneously admitted and the award of damages is excessive.

Nicole and Ronald were stabbed to death on June 12, 1994, in front of Nicole's home in Los Angeles. Plaintiffs contended that Nicole's ex-husband had the motive to kill Nicole in a rage. On several prior occasions during their marriage, Simpson had physically abused Nicole. On June 7, 1994, Nicole telephoned a battered women's shelter hotline and stated she was frightened because her ex-husband was stalking her. On June 12, 1994, Simpson's and Nicole's young daughter performed in a dance recital. Simpson was in a foul mood that day. At the dance recital, Simpson and Nicole sat

apart and did not interact. When the recital ended, Nicole excluded Simpson from a post-recital family dinner.

Ronald was a waiter at the restaurant where the dinner occurred. Afterwards, Nicole telephoned the restaurant about a pair of eyeglasses left at the dinner. Ronald may have been killed because he encountered the murder of Nicole while delivering the eyeglasses to her home. Shortly after the killings, Nicole and Ronald's bodies were found in front of her residence.

Simpson contends the court erred in admitting evidence that Simpson previously abused Nicole. This evidence showed: **(1)** outside a veterinary clinic around the spring of 1983, Simpson approached Nicole's car, tried to pull off Nicole's fur coat, and hit Nicole in the face, saying he "didn't buy this fur coat for you to go f--- somebody else;" **(2)** in 1984, Simpson lost his temper and struck Nicole's Mercedes with a baseball bat; **(3)** at a public beach in July 1986, Simpson slapped Nicole and she fell to the sand; **(4)** on New Years Day 1989, Simpson and Nicole had a violent argument during which he pulled her hair and struck her on the face or head, for which Simpson pleaded nolo contendere to spousal abuse; and **(5)** during a rage in October 1993, Simpson broke a door of Nicole's residence.

Simpson contends that prior instances of abuse did not establish a motive for these killings and were not similar to these killings. The courts have concluded that evidence of prior quarrels between the same parties is relevant on the issue whether the accused committed the charged acts. Where a defendant is charged with a violent crime and has or had a previous relationship with a victim, prior assaults upon the same victim, when offered on disputed issues, e.g., identity, intent, motive are admissible based solely upon the consideration of identical perpetrator and victim.

Here the trial court correctly concluded the evidence of Simpson's prior abuse of Nicole was relevant to motive, intent, and identity.

Sharon Rufo and Fredric Goldman, the parents of Ronald, were awarded compensatory damages of $8.5 million dollars. The jury rendered this award under instructions that for death, the heirs are entitled to reasonable compensation for the loss of love, companionship, comfort, affection, society, solace, or moral support suffered as a result of the death. Simpson contends the amount is excessive.

The appellate court will interfere with the jury's determination only when the award is so disproportionate to the injuries suffered that it shocks the conscience and compels the conclusion the award is attributable to passion or prejudice. Here, Fredric Goldman testified about his close and affectionate relationship with Ronald, which continued to the time of the death. As Simpson points out, Sharon Rufo's relationship with Ronald was much less close and regular. The jury award, however, was in the aggregate with no allocation between the father and mother. Although the verdict is very

large, this alone does not compel the conclusion the award was attributable to passion or prejudice. "That result which requires reversal, should clearly appear from the record. We are unable to say, as a matter of law, that the judgment in this case is so excessive as to warrant us in interfering with the finding of the jury." **DiRosario v. Havens, supra, 196 Cal.App.3d 1224.**

The jury also awarded punitive damages of $12.5 million to Ronald's estate and $12.5 million to Nicole's estate. Punitive damages are awardable based on the cause of action the decedent would have had if he or she had survived. Simpson contends that, even taking his projected income into account, the amount of punitive damages awarded was excessive as a matter of law. There is no merit to this contention.

Mark Roesler is chairman of CMG Worldwide, which is engaged in marketing and licensing for sports and entertainment personalities. Roesler prepared a financial estimate of the income Simpson could earn for the rest of his life from his name and likeness. Roesler opined that Simpson could earn $2 million to $3 million a year for the rest of his life. In Roesler's opinion, $25 million was a reasonable amount that a person in Roesler's business would pay in present dollars for the exclusive right to use Simpson's name and likeness for the rest of Simpson's life.

Simpson's business manager testified Simpson's net worth at the time of trial was a negative $856,000. He testified that since the murders, Simpson had basically been selling assets to pay expenses. Over the past year, he had vigorously attempted to market Simpson memorabilia and autographs, to secure personal appearance contracts, to secure a book deal based on the criminal trial, and to market a video, all without significant commercial success.

Simpson contends the trial court should not have admitted Roesler's testimony into evidence. Simpson contends that his ability to earn income in the future is irrelevant as a factor to be considered by the jury in assessing punitive damages.

The simple answer is that the evidence at trial contradicts it. Roesler testified the right to exploit Simpson's name and likeness had a present market value, for which a person in Roesler's business would pay. The conflict between this evidence and the defense evidence that the market for Simpson memorabilia and services had dried up, was for the jury to resolve. In denying the motion for new trial, the trial court called plaintiffs' evidence credible.

Simpson contends the verdict totaling $25 million in punitive damages is excessive. An appellate court will not reverse the jury's determination unless the award, as a matter of law, is excessive or appears so grossly disproportionate that it raises a presumption it was the result of passion or prejudice.

In this case, the reprehensibility of the defendant's conduct and the severity of harm to the victims, have the greatest weight legally possible. In effect, the jury found that Simpson committed two deliberate, vicious murders. This is the most reprehensible conduct that society condemns. The harm suffered by the victims was the maximum possible; they were intentionally killed. Considering the outrageousness of Simpson's conduct and the enormity of its consequences, the amount of $25 million is not offensive and does not raise a presumption that the verdict resulted from passion or prejudice. Considering all these factors, the punitive damages award, "in light of the defendant's wealth and the gravity of the particular act," does not exceed "the level necessary to properly punish and deter." **Neal v. Farmers Ins. Exchange, 21 Cal. 3d at 928.**

The judgments are affirmed.

SECTION 2.12 REVIEW CASES

1. Lawmakers from Virginia have approved specialty license plates for a number of organizations for many years. However, the state legislature refused to allow the Sons of Confederate Veterans to obtain license plates that contained a rebel flag logo because it might offend African-Americans. Does this action by the lawmakers violate the Sons of the Confederate Veterans' First Amendment freedom of speech rights?

2. Morris released a computer program known as a "worm" on the internet which spread and multiplied, eventually causing computers at various educational institutions to crash or cease functioning. Morris was charged with violating the *Computer Fraud and Abuse Act* which punishes anyone who intentionally accesses, without authorization, a category of computers known as "federal interest computers," or prevents authorized use of information in such computers. Morris argues that the government did not prove that he had the necessary mens rea to have committed the computer crime since it was necessary for the government to show not only that (1) he intended the unauthorized access of a federal interest computer, but also (2) that he intended to prevent others from using it. The government argued that the criminal intent requirement required

then to prove only one part of the crime. Which side do you believe is correct? **United States v. Robert Morris, 928 F.2d 504 (1991).**

3. Following the entry of a civil judgment against O.J. Simpson, Fred Goldman attempted to seize a grand piano at Simpson's home in order to help satisfy the multi-million dollar judgment. O.J. Simpson's mother testified that the piano was given to her as a gift in 1984. Although the grand piano was still in the football player's house, Simpson claimed that it belonged to his mother, and that she was the only one who could play the musical instrument. Who do you think should obtain possession of this item of personal property? **Ronald Goldman v. O.J. Simpson, Los Angles Superior Court (Sept. 1997).**

4. Bernard Getz boarded a New York subway and sat down on a bench. Four individuals surrounded Getz and asked him for five dollars. Getz stood up and fired four shots striking the individuals that surrounded him. Getz told the police that two youths stood to his left and two stood to his right. After he was asked for the money, Getz said the four had smiles on their faces and they wanted to "play with me." While he did not think that any of the people had a gun, Getz had a fear of harm based upon prior experiences of being "maimed." Will Getz have any liability for using deadly force in either a criminal or civil context? **People of New York v. Bernard Getz, 68 N.Y. 2d 96 (Ct. App. N.Y. 1986).**

5. Clark owned a fifty pound puppy named Rocky that had a habit of jumping on people. In fact, Rocky had a talent for playing football, and striking people with his body just as a tackler would do. Clark asked a friend to watch the dog while he was out of town. He did not, however, inform her of the dog's playful habits. When the Good Samaritan let the puppy out in the back yard, Rocky ran up behind the woman and struck her forcibly at the back of the knees. The friend fell and fractured her left hip. Is Clark liable for the actions of the playful puppy? **Alice Clark v. Kenneth Clark, 215 A.2d 293 (Pa. Super. 1965).**

SECTION 2.13
INTERNET REFERENCES

For more information on public and private law, see the following internet sites:

A. *Criminal Law*

- **www.fbi.gov/homepage.htm**
  The Federal Bureau of Investigation's website provides information on major criminal investigations, their most wanted-list, and crime reports.

- **www.thebestdefense.com**
  This criminal law firm's website provides information about various crimes and the judicial process.

- **www.talkjustice.com**
  At this site, a person can post notes on message boards about the criminal justice system and access "Cybrary," an online library which provides 12,000 links to different websites relating to criminal law.

- **www.law.indiana.edu/law/crimlaw.html**
  Indiana University School of Law at Bloomington provides downloads of short lectures on different aspects of criminal law, such as double jeopardy and being called as a witness in a criminal trial.

B. *Constitutional Law*

- **www.usconstitution.net/index.html**
  This site focuses on the U.S. Constitution and provides a general overview of this historic document, its history, and other related information.

- **www.supremecourtus.gov**
  The Supreme Court's official site is located at this address. It provides access to court opinions, rules, and other general information about the Supreme Court.

C. *Administrative law*

- **www.law.fsu.edu/library/admin.com**
  The American Bar Association's Administrative Procedure Database is located at this address. The site provides information about the organization, federal and state resources, and other related links.

D. *Contract Law*

- **www.ira-wg.com/library/contract.html**
  This site is devoted to issues involving contract law.

E. Tort Law

- **www.itslegal.com/infonet/injury/injurymain.html**
  This link provides answers to frequently asked questions about tort issues, specifically involving transportation accidents, injury to property, medical malpractice, and defamation.

- **www.prairielaw.com**
  This web address provides a general overview of personal injury claims and the law of torts. Information is provided about the statute of limitations, airline liability, products liability, and wrongful death.

F. Property Law

- **http://propertymart.net**
  Advertisements and other related links dealing with real estate may be accessed through this site

KEY TERMS

Acceptance
Administrative Agencies
Administrative Law
Annulment
Article
Articles of Confederation
Assumption of the Risk
Beyond a Reasonable Doubt
Bill of Rights
Burden of Proof
Capacity
Comparative Negligence
Compensatory Damages
Community Property
Concurrent Ownership
Consideration
Constitutional Amendment
Constitutional Law
Constitutional Relativity
Contract
Contributory Negligence
Crime
Criminal Intent
Criminal Law
Damages
Divorce
Domestic Partnership
Duty of Case
Family Law

Federal Register
Felony
Fixture
Intangible Property
Intentional Tort
Legality
Marriage
Mens Rea
Misdemeanor
Negligence
Offer
Ownership of Property
Pain and Suffering
Personal Property
Private Law
Proximate Cause
Public Law
Real Property
Self-Defense
Substantial Evidence
Summary Offense
Tangible Property
Tenancy in Common
Tenancy by the Entirety
Tenancy with Right of
    Ownership
Tort
Treason

CHAPTER 3

DUE PROCESS

"No law perfectly suits the convenience of every member of the community; the only consideration is, whether upon the whole it be profitable to the greater part."

Levi
"History of Rome," c.10 B.C.
"The Quotable Lawyer" Facts on File, 1986

Due Process is synonymous with fundamental fairness and the concept is deeply rooted in history. For instance, ancient Egyptians required judges to hear both sides of a dispute before issuing a ruling. The Romans and Greeks provided for juries. Even Jesus Christ was allowed to confront his accusers and to present evidence during his trial.[1]

Citizens of the world have always expected their governments to establish a system of rules to maintain law and order. However, the actual balance between individual freedoms and government regulation differs from society to society.

In 1215, the **Magna Carta** provided the people of England with a degree of protection against the unchecked power of the King. The "due process" clause in this historic document provided that "no freeman shall be taken or imprisoned or exiled…except by the lawful judgment of his peers or by the law of the land." This Great Charter was not the result of a magnanimous act on the part of King John but stemmed from a bitter conflict between the King and the Barons over finances and royal governance. Events came to a head on the hills of Runnymede when the Barons confronted the unpopular ruler and forced him to sign this historic document guaranteeing that no one is above the law including the King.

The founders of this country did not include a due process clause in the original Constitution. Instead, James Madison drafted this protection as part of the **Bill of Rights** a few years later. More specifically, part of the **Fifth Amendment** provides that no person shall be deprived of life, liberty, or property without **due process** of law. This guarantee is designed to insure that the government acts fairly with members of society. The meaning of this clause, however, is not defined in the Constitution. The drafters wanted the protections to be determined in light of the times so that the Constitution would remain a living and contemporary document. As Justice Cardoza noted, "Due Process guarantees those personal immunities which are so rooted in the traditions and conscience of our people as to be ranked as fundamental... or are implicit in the concept of ordered liberty."[2]

Surprisingly, the Fifth Amendment only extended the protection of the due process clause to the actions of the federal government. This flaw was rectified in 1868 when a second due process clause was written into the United States Constitution through the **Fourteenth Amendment.** This latter clause made due process applicable to the states by providing that "nor shall any State deprive any person of life, liberty, or property without due process of law." Known as the **Reconstruction Amendment,** this clause was originally drafted to protect the recently freed slaves. Not surprisingly, its ratification was rejected by many of the Southern states but the rest of the country voted in favor of the proposal. Over the years, the Fourteenth Amendment has become a cornerstone for the civil rights movement. For instance, it is the basis for overturning laws preventing African Americans from serving on juries.

The original purpose of the Fourteenth Amendment, however, has dramatically changed over the years because of the **Doctrine of Incorporation.** Basically, the courts have used the Fourteenth Amendment to incorporate many of the other protections afforded by the Bill of Rights so that they may have applicability to the states governments.

Due process consists of two parts:

1. **Substantive due process;** and
2. **Procedural due process.**

In order to understand these two concepts, one must first ascertain the meaning of substantive law and procedural law.

Substantive law is the "actual law." It defines the duties and rights of members of society. The Motor Vehicle Code is an example of substantive law. It provides for the proper operation of motor vehicles and prohibits such conduct as speeding, reckless driving, or proceeding through a red light. It is only by the enforcement of the Motor Vehicle Code that the roads are made safer for the public to transverse.

Procedural law is the way that the substantive law is made, enforced, and administered. For example, the Motor Vehicle Code is enforced by issuing an errant driver a traffic ticket and requiring the offender to appear in court to answer the charges.

This Chapter will present an overview of the due process guarantee with an emphasis on legislation and the elements of a fair hearing.

SECTION 3.2
LEGISLATION

The power to make laws on the federal level is vested in **Congress** and is contained in the first Article of the Constitution. Article I, Section 1 of the United States Constitution provides that "All legislative powers herein granted shall be vested in a Congress of the United States, which shall consist of a Senate and House of Representatives."

The **United States Senate** is composed of 100 members. Two senators are elected from each state for six-year terms. On the other hand, the **House of Representatives** consists of 435 members, elected every two years from the 50 states according to population. Together, these chambers make up the U.S. Congress, which is composed of two-year periods when the legislature meets.

The chief function of Congress is to make the laws that govern the people of the United States. In addition, the Senate has the function of consenting to treaties and to certain nominations by the President such as the individuals who serve as judges in the federal court. The House has the power to pass laws raising revenue.

The work of Congress is initiated by the introduction of a proposal in one of four principle forms. These are: the bill; the joint resolution; the concurrent resolution; and the simple resolution. A **bill** is the form used for most legislation. Bills may originate in either the House of Representatives or the Senate. A bill originating in the House of Representatives is designated by the letters "H.R." followed by a number. A Senate bill is designated by the letter "S." followed by its number.

Any member of the legislature may introduce a bill while Congress is in session by simply placing it in the **hopper**, or basket located at the side of the clerk's desk in the House Chamber. The individual who introduces a bill is referred to as the **sponsor** and more than one legislator can co-sponsor a bill. The bill is then assigned to the committee that has jurisdiction over the subject matter of the proposed law. For instance, the House Committee on Armed Services deals with matters involving military installations, service personnel and military readiness. The Select Committee on Intelligence analyzes issues involving terrorism, homeland security, counterintelligence and espionage.

One of the most important phases of the congressional process is the action taken by the Committee. It is at the Committee level that the most intense consideration is given to the proposed measures and where citizens are given an opportunity to be heard.

If a bill is of sufficient importance, and particularly if it is controversial, the committee will usually set a date for public hearings. Each committee is required to publically announce the date, place, and subject matter of any hearing to be conducted by the committee. Witnesses may testify at the hearing either voluntarily or at the request of the committee. A vote of the committee is taken to determine whether it will issue a favorable report or "table" the bill. Committee reports are a valuable element of the legislative history of a law. They are used by courts, executive departments, agencies, and the public, as a source of information regarding the purpose and meaning of the legislation.

When a committee gives a bill a favorable report, the chamber in which the proposed legislation originated votes on the bill. If that chamber passes the bill, the other house then considers it. A bill that is agreed to by both bodies becomes the law if the President signs it. A bill also becomes law when the President fails to return it within ten days with objections to the chamber in which it originated. However, a **pocket veto** may occur if the President receives the legislation within ten days of adjournment by Congress and the Chief Executive fails to sign the bill into law. The President may **veto** a bill that he does not want to enact into law. However, two-thirds of the members in each house can vote to override the veto. In that event, the bill becomes law.

There is not a large difference between a joint resolution and a bill. The **joint resolution** is not proposed simultaneously in Congress but originates in either House and generally goes through the same review process as a bill. Their use is usually restricted to advancing a proposed amendment to the Constitution or for emergency appropriations.

The reader may remember Congress providing authorization to President Bush to invade Iraq in 2002 because of the fear that Saddam Hussein was accumulating weapons of mass destruction. This declaration was done through a joint resolution.

Another joint resolution was passed by Congress following 9/11 to allow the President to use the Armed Forces to protect this country:

> Whereas, on September 11, 2001, acts of treacherous violence were committed against the United States and its citizens; and

> Whereas, such acts render it both necessary and appropriate that the United States exercise its rights to self-defense and to protect United States citizens both at home and abroad; and

> Whereas, in light of the threat to the national security and foreign policy of the United States posed by these grave acts of violence; and

> Whereas, such acts continue to pose an unusual and extraordinary threat to the national security and foreign policy of the United States; and

Whereas, the President has authority under the Constitution to take action to deter and prevent acts of international terrorism against the United States: Now, therefore, be it

Resolved by the Senate and House of Representatives of the United States of America in Congress assembled,

To authorize the use of United States Armed Forces against those responsible for the recent attacks launched against the United States.

A **concurrent resolution** is an informal pronouncement by Congress that does not have the effect of a law and does not require the signature of the President. For instance, it can be used to extend congratulations to someone over a special event.

State and Federal laws are called **statutes**. Local laws are called **ordinances**[3]. To learn more about the activities of Congress, visit the official web sites of the House of Representatives and the Senate. Those addresses are: **www.house.gov** and **www.senate.gov**.

SECTION 3.3
SUBSTANTIVE
DUE PROCESS

If **substance law** is the actual law and **due process** means fundamental fairness, substantive due process can only mean that the law itself must be fundamentally fair. This mandate is directed to the legislative branch of government and requires that (1) the legislation be capable of serving a legitimate public interest; (2) the law may not be broader than is necessary to meet the public program; and (3) the statute cannot be vague. One who does not believe a law satisfies these three conditions may challenge the constitutionality of the legislation in court.

Examine the following case in order to ascertain whether the law is valid from a substantive due process point of view and satisfies the requirements for constitutionality.

A state legislator is unhappy with the damage to property that is taking place on college campuses, especially in the dorms. He believes that the majority of trouble-makers are students with long hair who drink alcohol and deface school property. To curb the transgressions of these disruptive youths, the legislator introduces a bill requiring "any student with long hair who attends a state related institution to pay an additional $250 in tuition." The state representative believes that this assessment will help defray the cost of damage done to college property by the responsible parties. A student with long hair refuses to pay the extra tuition and claims that his substantive due process rights are being violated. The issue presented is whether the law is capable of serving a legitimate public interest. Just because an individual has long hair does not mean that he will be disruptive. The legislation is also vague since the statute is silent as to what constitutes "long hair." Also, does the law apply unequally to women? The standard to be applied in ascertaining the constitutionality of the legislation is not what the individual who introduced the bill thinks but whether the average person would believe that the law is sensible and capable of serving a legitimate public interest. This statute is clearly unconstitutional.

Cellular telephones have become a way of life. People use these mobile devices in restaurants, while walking down the street, or in shopping malls. While some may find these habits annoying, these phone uses do not pose any harm to the public. There is a growing debate, however, about the safety of using a cell phone while driving a motor vehicle. According to the National Highway Safety Administration, eighty five percent of cellular telephone subscribers talk on the phone while driving. Farmers Insurance Group discovered that people overwhelming agree that using a phone while driving impairs the person's ability to safely operate a motor vehicle. An article in *The New England Journal of Medicine* concluded that the risk of being in an automobile accident while talking on a cell phone is increased four times. In fact, the danger has been equated with driving a car while intoxicated.

Most states are considering legislation to regulate cell phone use while driving. For instance, Connecticut, New York, New Jersey and the District of Columbia have banned cell phone use while operating a motor vehicle. Arizona, California, Florida, Illinois and Massachusetts have laws on the subject but their statutes merely require car rental agencies to provide written instructions on the safe operation of cellular phones or mandate drivers to keep at least one hand on the steering wheel while talking on a mobile device. Maine bans drivers under eighteen and those with learner permits from using a cell phone while operating a motor vehicle.

According to a study by the National Conference of State Legislatures, twenty four countries prohibit or restrict cell phone use while driving including Australia, Germany, Greece, Italy, Japan and Spain. As more and more people obtain cell phones, increased pressure will be placed on various legislative bodies to find an acceptable solution to the problem of cell phone use and safety. Whether Congress will step in and regulate the subject on a national basis or additional states will adopt the strict approach taken by New York and New Jersey remains to be seen.

Regardless of the legislative path taken, those opposed to this remedial measure will advance arguments similar to those raised when the mandatory use of seats belts was first advocated—the law is unenforceable, adequate research does not support the need for the legislation or the law would invade a person's privacy and personal freedoms.

New York was the first state to pass legislation to ban the use of cell phones while driving. The constitutionality of that law is discussed in **People of New York v. Victoria Neville.**

PEOPLE OF NEW YORK V. VICTORIA NEVILLE
737 N.Y.S. 2D 251 (NASSAU COUNTY, N.Y. 2002)

Victoria Neville is charged with the use of a mobile telephone (cell phone) while operating a motor vehicle on a public street or highway.

The New York "Cell Phone Law" is perhaps the first in the nation to govern this new area of legislation. Accordingly, the constitutional aspects of the new statute should be addressed as early as possible.

On June 28, 2001, New York enacted a law prohibiting use of hand held cell phones while operating a motor vehicle.

The first question for consideration is if the law is so vague or overly broad to the point where a reasonable person of ordinary intelligence would be unable to ascertain what conduct is prohibited. Under **VTL 1225-C(2)(a),** it is stated "No person shall operate a motor vehicle upon a public highway using a mobile telephone to engage in a call while such vehicle is in motion." The statute distinguishes between prohibited "mobile telephones" and the permitted "hands free mobile telephone" where the operator of the motor vehicle can maintain "both hands" on the applicable steering device. This language is clear and indisputable to the ordinary citizen.

As a general rule, the police powers of the government concern the delicate balancing act between the regulating authority of the state and the rights of the individuals whose freedoms may be somewhat curtailed.

It is the opinion of this Court that a law prohibiting the use of hand held cell phones satisfies the state's interest in protecting the health, safety and welfare of its citizens and a proper use of its police power. The legislative intent sets forth the need to protect its citizens from the numerous motor vehicle accidents and serious physical injuries that result from the use of hand held cell phones. In the case at bar, the only impediment placed upon the public is to refrain from using a hand held cell phone while the car is in motion. The citizen can speak after the car has stopped or may operate a "hands free" cell phone. This limited inconvenience is no greater than requiring the use of seat belts or motorcycle helmets, or prohibiting cigarette smoking in public buildings.

Moreover, the statute mandates that a Court must waive the fine if a defendant provides the Court with proof of purchase of a hands free device. Accordingly, the state's regulation is reasonable in its intentions and is a valid use of the legislature's police authority.

Driving while intoxicated is a major problem in our society. For instance, the American Automobile Association reports that there is an alcohol-related motor vehicle fatality every thirty-three minutes and nearly 40% of all motor vehicle related deaths involve alcohol. There are countless horror stories of innocent people who are seriously injured or killed as the result of individuals who get behind the wheel of a car while intoxicated. Society has become intolerant of these irresponsible drivers, and judges are imposing stiffer penalties for these infractions. In fact, a number of state legislatures have imposed mandatory sentencing for "driving under the influence of drugs or alcohol." The city of New York has taken a radical step in their efforts to penalize those individuals who drink and drive. Known as the New York **Vehicle Forefeiture Initiative,** the city has adopted a tough policy that provides for the forfeiture of one's motor vehicle upon arrest by the police for drunk driving. This law has been challenged as violating due process because it authorizes the police to take and retain a vehicle without a hearing before the person is even convicted of driving while intoxicated. The constitutionality of this law is the subject of the following case.

GRINBERG V. POLICE COMMISSIONER SAFIR
694 N.Y.S.2D 316 (N.Y. 1999)

On February 20, 1999, Police Commissioner Safir announced that the City would apply the Property Clerk Forfeiture Law to vehicles operated by individuals arrested for Driving While Intoxicated. On February 21, 1999, the police stopped and arrested petitioner for DWI. The arresting officer concluded that petitioner was intoxicated based on the strong smell of alcohol, watery and bloodshot eyes, and coordination tests. A breathalyzer indicated 0.11 per cent blood alcohol content, over the 0.10 per cent intoxication threshold. Officers took petitioner's 1988 Acura for forfeiture.

New York City Administrative Code Section 14-140 directs that certain property, including that "suspected of being used as a means of committing crime or employed in or furtherance of crime...shall be given...into the custody"

of the Police Department property clerk. The City's forfeiture procedures permit the property clerk to decline to return property if there is "reasonable cause to believe that [it]....was the instrumentality of a crime...." The property clerk then must "cause a civil forfeiture proceeding or other similar civil proceeding to be initiated" within 25 days of a claimant's demand.

Petitioner alleges that the new City policy violates the Due Process clause of the constitution because it authorizes the police to take and retain a vehicle without a seizure hearing.

The Due Process Clause guarantees that, absent extraordinary circumstances, "individuals must receive notice and an opportunity to be heard before the Government deprives them of their property." **U.S. v. James Daniel Good Real property, 510 U.S. 43.** Forfeiture actions inherently may present such extraordinary circumstances. A pre-hearing seizure of an instrumentality for forfeiture comports with due process when:

> the seizure has been necessary to secure an important governmental or general public interest. Second, there has been a special need for very prompt action.

Immediate seizure of a drunk driver's automobile upon arrest is necessary because the arrestee is legally and physically incapable of driving. A car is property that could be removed to another jurisdiction, destroyed, or concealed, if advance warning of confiscation was given.

The seizure is simultaneous with a DWI arrest for which the police must have probable cause.

While the City's DWI policy prevents accused drunk drivers from using property before a determination in the criminal action, the City's interest in deterring drunk driving and ensuring enforceability of a subsequent forfeiture order, clearly outweighs the private interest affected.

Retention prevents the vehicle from being used for repeated illegal activity. An automobile is an integral part of DWI; it poses the threat of being used as an "instrumentality of death" should the crime be repeated. Just as there is a strong public interest in withholding a non-contraband murder weapon from a homicide defendant, there is a strong public interest in withholding a car from a DWI defendant.

Petitioner has not met his burden of demonstrating that the City DWI forfeiture policy is unconstitutional. Accordingly it is ADJUDGED that the petition is denied and the proceeding is dismissed.

The constitutionality of the seizure of a motor vehicle before conviction for driving under the influence of alcohol has been litigated extensively in New York with multiple appeals. The United States Court of Appeals for the Second Circuit noted in 2006 that in considering whether the demands of the Due Process Clause have been satisfied when the government seeks to maintain possession of property before a final hearing, three factors must be weighed: (1) the private interest affected; (2) the risk of erroneous deprivation through the procedures used; and (3) the government's interest. While this test does not require a full hearing in which the defendant can test the sufficiency of the arrest, the court found that the district attorney must request ex-parte permission from a judge to keep the vehicle as evidence.

One case has been reported in New York in which a trial judge returned a confiscated car to its innocent owner. In **County of Nassau v. Pereira,** an owner's Mercedes was borrowed by his son with the admonition that no one else was to use the vehicle. The son then visited a bar and thought that he had too much to drink so he asked a friend to drive the vehicle home. Unfortunately, the friend was also intoxicated, and ending up getting arrested for DUI. While the car was confiscated by the police, the owner was successful in obtaining its return after he testified that he did not know the driver and had not given him permission to use the vehicle.[4]

Compare this ruling, however, with the Supreme Court decision in **Bennis v. Michigan,** 516 U.S. 442 (1996) in which an automobile was seized by the police because a man had used the vehicle to solicit a prostitute. The car was declared a public nuisance under Michigan law that allowed the confiscation of a building, vehicle, boat or airplane that is used for prostitution or gambling. The man's innocent spouse and co-owner of the vehicle argued that when she entrusted the car to her husband, she did not know he was going to use it to solicit a prostitute so that its confiscation violated her due process rights. The Supreme Court upheld the car's confiscation by ruling that there is a 75-year history of cases that hold that an owner's interest in property may be forfeited by reason of the use to which the property is put even though the owner did not know that it was to be put to such use.

Employers are rightfully concerned about workplace safety and the negative effects of substance abuse. As a result, employers have implemented procedures to reduce these risks, the most controversial of which is drug testing at work. Forty percent of the working population is subjected to **drug-testing,** and marijuana is the illegal substance that surfaces in the majority of positive test results. Employers are in favor of drug-testing because of the financial implications of absenteeism, low productivity, injuries, and theft. Workers are concerned about the accuracy of the test results. For instance, a false positive test result can occur with something as simple as a person eating a poppy seed bagel, which can suggest opium use.

When drug-testing is part of the collective bargaining agreement, employee concerns can be minimized though the negotiation process. Ardent criticism of drug-testing is more apt to occur when the test is unilaterally imposed on members of the workforce. This can happen when the legislature mandates drug-testing of a particular work group. Such legislation usually triggers a constitutional challenge to the drug-testing program on a variety of grounds such as invasion of privacy, due process, and unlawful search and seizure.

The earliest legislative-mandated, drug-testing program focused on railroad employees, who were involved in train accidents. The courts have upheld that legislation because of the need to protect the public against alcohol and drug abuse among transit workers. Random drug-testing of student athletes has also been upheld in order to protect the welfare of children who might be susceptible to the physical, emotional, and social damage of drug abuse.

Drug testing of professional athletes has taken place for years. These programs are implemented through collective bargaining agreements between the players' union and management and may result in the team member's suspension from the sport. Olympic and college athletics have also established rigorous drug testing programs with Olympic medals being forfeited by those who test positive. The justification for this testing is to promote the long-term health of athletes and to level the playing field among the participants in the sport. While drug testing of high school athletes occurs with some frequency, secondary schools are expanding their interest in testing other members of the student population. This ambitious goal to deter the use of illicit drugs among children has generated much debate and controversy over the merits of this approach. Critics maintain that it destroys the element of trust between student and teacher and constitutes an invasion of privacy. The Supreme Court, however, has given its tacit approval for high schools to conduct random drug testing of all those who wish to participate in extracurricular activities. The rational for this important decision is set forth in **Board of Education v. Earls.**

BOARD OF EDUCATION v. LINDSEY EARLS
122 S. CT. 2559 (2002)

Tecumseh, Oklahoma, is approximately 40 miles southeast of Oklahoma City. In the fall of 1998, the School District adopted the **Student Activities Drug Testing Policy (Policy)**, which requires all middle and high school students to consent to drug testing in order to participate in extracurricular activity. Under the Policy, students are required to take a drug test before participating in extracurricular activity, must submit to random drug testing while participating in that activity, and must agree to be tested at any time upon reasonable suspicion.

Plaintiffs argue that the School District failed to identify a special need for testing students who participate in extracurricular activities, and that the Policy neither addresses a proven problem nor promises to bring any benefit to students or the school.

We first consider the nature of the privacy interest allegedly compromised by the drug testing. A student's privacy interest is limited in a public school environment where the State is responsible for maintaining discipline, health, and safety. School children are routinely required to submit to physical examinations and vaccinations against disease. Securing order in the school environment sometimes requires that students be subjected to greater controls than those appropriate for adults.

Students who participate in extracurricular activities voluntarily subject themselves to many of the same intrusions on their privacy as do athletes. Some of these clubs and activities require occasional off-campus travel and communal undress. All of them have their own rules and requirements for participating students that do not apply to the student body as a whole. This regulation of extracurricular activities further diminishes the expectation of privacy among school children.

Next, we consider the character of the intrusion imposed by the Policy. But the "degree of intrusion" on one's privacy caused by collecting a urine sample depends upon the manner in which production of the urine sample is monitored.

Under the Policy, a faculty monitor waits outside the closed restroom stall for the student to produce a sample and must listen for the normal sounds of urination in order to guard against tampered specimens and to insure an accurate chain of custody. This procedure protects privacy by allowing male students to produce their samples behind a closed stall.

Moreover, the test results are not turned over to any law enforcement authority. Nor do the test results here lead to the imposition of discipline or have any academic consequences. The only consequence of a failed drug test is to limit the student's privilege of participating in extracurricular activities.

Given the minimally intrusive nature of the sample collection and the limited uses to which the test results are put, we conclude that the invasion of students' privacy is not significant.

This Court must consider the nature and immediacy of the government's concerns and the efficacy of the Policy in meeting them. This Court has already articulated in detail the importance of the governmental concern in preventing drug use by school children. The drug abuse problem among our Nation's youth has hardly abated. In fact, evidence suggests that it has only grown worse. The necessity for the State to act is magnified by the fact that this evil is being visited not just upon individuals at large, but upon children for whom it has undertaken a special responsibility of care and direction.

Finally, we find that testing students who participate in extracurricular activities is a reasonably effective means of addressing the School District's legitimate concerns in preventing, deterring, and detecting drug use. We conclude that the drug testing of Tecumseh students who participate in extracurricular activities effectively serves the School District's interest in protecting the safety and health of its students.

Citizens of the United States cherish their individual freedoms. This tenet is reinforced throughout the first Ten Amendments of the Constitution, commonly known as the **Bill of Rights**. For instance, the government may not conduct improper searches of homes or personal property, people have the right to peacefully assemble and to practice their religion without interference from the state. Also, individuals may not be forced to provide incriminating testimony and they have the right to express their opinions without unwarranted governmental interference. Because of these types of constitutional guarantees, legislation must be narrowly tailored to further a legitimate and compelling government interest.

The death of Dale Earnhardt in a racing accident at the Daytona 500 triggered off a court challenge as to whether a law that prohibited the production of his autopsy photographs was overly broad and unconstitutional.

CAMPUS COMMUNICATIONS INC. V. ESTATE OF DALE EARNHARDT
821 SO. 2D 388 (CT. APP. FLA. 2002)

Mr. Earnhardt was a car driver who became involved in a fatal crash during the Daytona 500 race on February 18, 2001. An autopsy was performed in accordance with Florida law governing accidental deaths. In performing the autopsy, photographs were taken solely as a back-up to the dictation system utilized by the medical examiner to record his findings.

The written autopsy report, post-crash photographs of Mr. Earnhardt's car, a toxicology report and a sketch showing the markings on Mr. Earnhardt's body were promptly made available to the public. The autopsy photographs, however, were not released because Mrs. Earnhardt sought and obtained an ex parte injunction precluding the medical examiner from releasing them.

On March 29, 2001, the Florida Legislature enacted **Section 406.135 of the Public Records Act**. Campus seeks an order requiring the medical examiner to allow inspection and copying of the photographs.

The issue we are confronted with whether **Section 406.135** is overly broad and therefore unconstitutional.

Both the Florida Constitution and the Public Records Act allow for the creation of exemptions to the Act by the Legislature, provided the exemption 1) serves an identifiable public purpose and 2) is no broader than necessary to meet

that public purpose. In order to fulfill these requirements, the Legislature made the following findings:

> The Legislature finds that photographs, video and audio recordings of an autopsy be made confidential. Photographs or video or audio recordings of an autopsy depict or describe the deceased in graphic and often disturbing fashion. As such, photographs, video or audio recordings of an autopsy are highly sensitive depictions or descriptions of the deceased which, if heard, viewed, copied or publicized, could result in trauma, sorrow, humiliation, or emotional injury to the immediate family of the deceased.

As to the requirement that the exemption serve an identifiable public purpose, the Legislature must state with specificity the public necessity justifying the exemption. We find that (the legislature's explanation) clearly satisfies this requirement. The legislative findings detail the graphic and often gruesome nature of such autopsy photographs and the trauma and emotional injury the immediate family of the deceased would likely suffer if these records were disclosed and disseminated to the public.

Campus contends that **Section 406.135** is unconstitutional because it is broader than necessary to meet the statute's public purpose.

Specifically, Campus argues that the finding made by the Legislature that some photographs "may" show gruesome scenes and that trauma "could" result from publication of the autopsy photographs is explicit recognition that photographs are not always gruesome and that trauma does not always result from their viewing.

We find the statute to be specific and narrow: it applies only to autopsy photographs and audio and video recordings of the autopsy. It does not apply to other records of the autopsy such as the written autopsy report and, therefore, those materials remain unrestricted public records.

We find that **Section 406.135** serves an identifiable public purpose, is no broader than necessary to meet that public purpose and was enacted in accordance with the constitutional and legislative requirements we have previously discussed. We affirm the judgment under review.

QUESTIONS FOR DISCUSSION:

Are the following laws constitutional?

1. In order to prevent the sexual harassment of women walking past construction sites, a city passes an "anti-ogling" law for its employees. Looking at someone in a leering manner is considered "ogling" and illegal. First time violators face verbal warnings and repeat offenders can be fired.

2. A beach town enacts an ordinance that prohibits a person who is not physically fit from wearing a bikini on a public beach. The penalty is removal from the beach and a $200.00 fine.

3. A city passes a parental responsibility ordinance that makes parents liable for offenses committed by their children under 18. The law makes the failure to supervise a minor a civil offense. First-time offenders receive a warning. Repeat offenders may be fined as much as $1,000 and be compelled to attend eight-week "parenting courses" approved by the court. In addition, parents must pay for property damage caused by their children.

4. In order to slow down Chicago's increasing murder rate among gang members, the city enacts a law that allows police officers to order the dispersal of individuals whom the officers reasonably believe are street gang members remaining in a public place with no apparent purpose. Those who do not promptly obey the order to move can be arrested.

5. California has enacted a statue that prohibits college athletes at state institutions from participating in team sports if the athlete has been convicted of a crime of violence and he or she has not yet completed the terms of the sentence.

The drafting of a statute is not an easy task. The problems of society are complex, and the legislature must deal with issues ranging from trash collection to nuclear energy. It is unrealistic to expect that each member of the legislature is an expert in every field of proposed legislation. They must rely upon others for guidance and are subjected to pressures from their peers, constituents, and special interest groups. This requires a constant balancing of personal beliefs against the wishes of others when considering proposed legislation.

In drafting a law, it is a primary goal to avoid using ambiguous words and to make the statute as clear as possible. Unfortunately, this cannot always be done. It is impossible to envision every problem or predict how future events will affect the legislation. For instance, definitions that once seemed obvious become subject to attack as technology changes.

One example is the word "motor vehicle." As automobiles became the favored mode of transportation, statutes were adopted requiring "motor vehicles" used for the transportation of people to be registered with the state. Cars, buses, and trucks are obviously within the contemplation of the legislation, but would airplanes, jet skis, or mopeds be covered?

The following problem will allow the reader to experience the unique issues that arise in trying to properly draft remedial legislation that regulates the conduct in question but is narrowly tailored to prevent an unjustified intrusion into the rights of the citizens.

SECTION 3.4

PARK, BROWN & SMITH, P.C.
ATTORNEYS AT LAW
MEMORANDUM

PROBLEM THREE—A

TO: All Law Clerks

FROM: Peter Smith, Esquire

RE: Legislation to Prohibit Stalking by Photographers

Congress is considering the adoption of a bill to prohibit paparazzi from stalking famous people in order to sell the pictures to the tabloid magazines. Many support the legislation in light of the general annoyance of movie stars, athletes, and national celebrities by these photographers.

Estelle Roberts is assisting in the lobbying efforts to pass this type of remedial legislation. While Mrs. Roberts understands the desire of fans to learn more about their favorite stars, she believes that celebrities should be able to have some private moments, especially when they take reasonable steps to protect their privacy. After all, famous people should not be prisoners in their own homes. They should have access to public facilities in much the same way that the general public does.

Our firm has been asked to draft the proposed legislation so I have looked into the issue and have spoken to various legislators about the matter. One Senator told me that she was troubled by the constitutionality of this proposed laws. For instance, the Senator thought the bill could criminalize routine news gathering. The Senator also wanted to know who would be covered under the law and how the phrase "reasonable expectation of privacy" would be defined, since that is the term that concerned citizens keep mentioning during their lobbying efforts.

A number of celebrities wrote letters in support of the legislation. Governor Schwarzenegger, George Clooney, Sean Penn, and Madonna have had problems with the press. One female celebrity complained about an incident in which a photographer tried to bungy-jump into her backyard in order to take a picture of her infant son. Another celebrity complained about a group of photographers who followed him into the restroom in order to take his picture while in a compromising position.

The tabloids are concerned about this proposed legislation. The media explained that they have the right to take pictures of celebrities because the stars are public figures. They further explained that the general public wants to know anything and everything about their favorite celebrities. Fans' interest ranges from learning about a star's favorite color to learning what flavor ice cream he or she likes. In light of the public's curiosity, the paparazzi believe they are doing a public service whenever they take "candid" pictures of famous people—when they least expect a photographer. Besides, the photographers assert that celebrities know that being famous entails an encroachment into their private lives.

The paparazzi also claim that the proposed bill is unconstitutional because it is overly vague. For instance, the lobbyist want to target photographers who take pictures for profit and would exempt from prosecution a lunatic fan who follows a celebrity. They claim that this distinction makes no sense. After all, the paparazzi do not want to hurt the celebrities, while lunatic fans have actually stalked their favorite stars and can represent an actual and real danger to the celebrities.

The task of drafting the bill has been assigned to you, but you should keep several goals in mind. The proponents of the bill maintain that people have a constitutional guarantee to be left alone, especially when one takes extra steps in order to protect his or her privacy. A professional lobbyist hired by the movie industry also mentioned that the law should target photographers who sell pictures to tabloid magazines.

Please write a draft of the proposed law and focus on the following three aspects:

1. Definitions. Who should be covered under the legislation and how should the phrase "reasonable expectation of privacy" be defined? This section needs careful attention to detail in order to prevent a constitutional challenge on the basis of vagueness.

2. Define what conduct is prohibited. As I mentioned before, the proponents of the legislation believe that photographers should be prevented from taking pictures of an individual when he or she has a reasonable expectation of privacy.

3. What penalties should be imposed for violating the statute? Should the penalty be criminal in nature, or should the remedy be civil in which case the aggrieved person can collect money damages?

I have prepared the following outline for your use in drafting the legislation:

1. Definitions

2. Prohibited Conduct

3. Penalty

ANSWER SHEET
PROBLEM THREE—A

Name   **Please Print Clearly**

Section 5005. Regulation of Stalking

1. Definitions

2. Prohibited Conduct

3. Penalty

SECTION 3.5
PROCEDURAL
DUE PROCESS

Q. What do Scott Peterson, Jeffrey Dahmer, and the officers in the Rodney King beating trial have in common?

A. Their prosecution all raised issues as to whether they could obtain a fair and impartial hearing as guaranteed by the Constitution.

Procedural due process guarantees that before a person's rights can be determined, he or she must be given a fair hearing. A fair hearing consists of three elements:

1. Notice of the proceeding;

2. Opportunity to be heard; and

3. An impartial tribunal.

The first element necessary to insure a fair hearing is proper notice. Just imagine if you went home and found a certified letter from the court informing you for the first time that you were tried and convicted of burglary the week before. To insure that this does not occur, a party must receive some type of notification of the pending litigation.

In a civil action, the defendant is given a copy of the lawsuit. In a criminal case, the defendant is arrested and informed of the charges against him.

Each party must also be given the opportunity to be heard. This is accomplished by allowing the litigants to be present at trial and to participate in the proceeding. They may sit with counsel during all phases of the trial and assist in presenting or attacking the evidence. It is not uncommon to see a litigant pass a note to counsel during the trial or to speak to the attorney in whispered tones about the case.

Can a party be denied the right to be present during the trial without violating the tenets of due process? The answer is yes. The court has the superior right to make sure that the trial progresses in an orderly fashion. Unruly parties can be excluded from the courtroom. A number of famous cases can be cited which involved disruptive behavior by litigants, attorneys, or spectators. One such case involved the Chicago Seven. This criminal proceeding dealt with the prosecution of seven flamboyant individuals who were charged with conspiring to incite a riot during the 1968 Democratic National Convention. The defendants disrupted the proceedings by shouting vulgarities, singing songs from the witness stand, eating jelly beans, reading comic books, reciting Hari Krishna Mantra, and showing up for one court session wearing judicial robes. The court held the defendants in contempt and ordered them to be restrained and gagged for portions of the proceedings.

The trial of Charles Manson for the murder of actress Sharon Tate also involved disruptive behavior, which resulted in the defendants being removed from the courtroom. Manson threatened the judge during the trial several times and on one occasion leaped toward the judge wielding a pencil. At another point, Manson and three co-defendants disrupted the trial by singing and chanting. To avoid a mistrial, the judge removed the defendants from the courtroom and placed them in a separate room where they were permitted to listen to the testimony through a sound system.

Finally, a fair hearing requires the right to be tried by an impartial tribunal. Because of the extensive media coverage focused on unusual or notorious cases, the defendant's right to a fair trial is frequently an issue. How can a defendant receive a fair trial when most of the prospective jurors have already heard about the case and have formed an opinion as to the defendant's innocence or guilt?

The Court must exercise great care to minimize outside influences that may improperly affect the verdict. Measures to insure a fair trial range from issuing a gag order to control the dissemination of information to moving the trial to another location where the case is not so well known.

The "Fugitive," was a movie loosely based upon the murder trial of Dr. Sam Shepard, who was convicted of the bludgeoned death of his pregnant wife in the upstairs bedroom of their home. The case went before the United States Supreme Court on the issue of whether Dr. Shepard received a fair trial because of the massive, pervasive and prejudicial publicity that attended his prosecution.

During the murder investigation, the news media published a number of stories that emphasized the evidence that appeared to incriminate Shepard and they pointed out discrepancies in the doctor's statements to the authorities. One editorial asked: "Why don't police quiz top suspect," with a demand that Dr. Shepard be taken to police headquarters. Another editorial stated: "Why isn't Sam Shepard in jail?" During the trial, which took place two weeks before the general election, the chief prosecutor was a candidate for Common Pleas Court judge, and the trial judge was a candidate to succeed himself. The newspapers published the names and addresses of all potential jurors, and a radio station was permitted to set up broadcasting facilities next to the jury room. When Dr. Shepard was brought into the courtroom before each session, he was surrounded by reporters and extensively photographed for the newspapers and television. During deliberations, the sequestered jury was allowed to make telephone calls without any type of supervision.

In considering whether Dr. Shepard's procedural due process rights were violated, the Supreme Court noted that the extensive newspaper, radio, and television coverage of the criminal trial, together with the physical arrangements in the courtroom for the news media, deprived Shepard of the judicial serenity and calm to which he was entitled. The Justices noted that our legal system requires that the verdict be reached only according to the evidence and arguments in open court, and not by any outside influences, whether by private talk or public print. The carnival atmosphere could have been avoided because the courtroom and courthouse were subject to the control of the trial judge. The court should have adopted stricter rules governing the use of the courtroom by reporters, and efforts should have been initiated to control the release of leads, information and gossip to the press. The Supreme Court concluded that the trial court did not protect Dr. Shepard from the inherently prejudicial publicity which saturated the community, and the jurist failed to control the disruptive influences in the courtroom. Due process requires that the accused receive a trial by an impartial jury free from outside influences. This did not occur in the Sam Shepard criminal trial.

In Philadelphia, the trial of Gary Heidnik for the brutal murders and torture of several mentally handicapped women could not proceed until an impartial jury was empaneled. The case was so gruesome and shocking in detail that it received daily press coverage. Very few citizens in Philadelphia were unaware of the killings.

Of the 180 potential jurors called, all had heard about Mr. Heidnik, and 124 had already predetermined his guilt or innocence based upon the press coverage. The presiding judge agreed with the defense about the prejudicial affect of the pre-trial publicity and noted: "It was impossible to get a fair and impartial jury in Philadelphia because this case was turned into nothing short of a freak show." The judge considered moving the trial to Pittsburgh. Instead, a panel of jurors from Pittsburgh were selected and brought to Philadelphia for the trial. In this way, the court balanced the right of the public to know what was going on in the Gary Heidnik case with the defendant's right to have a fair and impartial tribunal.

In Jeffrey Dahmer's murder trial, defense lawyers questioned whether their client could obtain a fair trial given the widespread publicity surrounding the gruesome nature of the murders. Dahmer was accused of killing 17 people and storing their remains in his apartment. His lawyers asked that jurors be selected from outside Milwaukee, where the media focus would be less intense. The court denied this request, citing the worldwide publicity given to the case.

A controversy in jury selection involves the racial makeup of the jury. Nowhere was this more prominent than in the trial of four white Los Angeles police officers accused of beating Rodney King, an African American. At the request of the defendants, the trial was moved from Los Angeles, which has a 13 percent African-American population, to suburban Simi Valley, where the black population is 2 percent. The officers were then acquitted of all but one of 11 criminal charges by a jury in a California State court. The jury was composed of 10 whites, one Hispanic, and one Asian American. The outcry after the verdict led to angry mob violence. The officers were later tried in federal court, and two were convicted of violating King's civil rights. As a result of the rioting in Los Angeles, Florida nervously sought to move the trial of a Miami police officer accused of fatally shooting an African-American motorcyclist and his passenger. The first trial of Officer William Lozano ended in a conviction on manslaughter charges, but an appeals court reversed the verdict, saying that the jurors may have feared that an acquittal would spark rioting in Miami, just as it did in Los Angeles in the King case.

MATTHEW MUSLADIN v. ANTHONY LAMARQUE
403 F.3D 1072 (CAL. 2005)

Musladin was charged with first degree murder for the killing of Tom Studer, the fiancé of his estranged wife Pamela. Musladin came to the house where Pamela, Studer, and Pamela's brother Michael Albaugh lived in order to pick up his son for a scheduled weekend visit. Pamela testified that she and Musladin had an argument, and that Musladin pushed her to the ground. According to Pamela, when Studer and Albaugh came out of the house to assist her, Musladin reached into his car to grab a gun and fired two shots at Studer, killing him. Musladin contends, however, that after Pamela fell to the ground, Studer and Albaugh appeared, holding a gun and a machete respectively, and threatened him. Musladin asserted that, after seeing the weapons, he shot in the general direction of Studer out of fear for his own life. At trial Musladin argued self-defense. There is no dispute that Musladin fired the shot that killed

Studer, although experts for both sides agree that the fatal shot was the result of a ricochet rather than a direct hit. Under Musladin's theory of defense, there was no crime and, thus, no "victim."

During the 14-day trial, Studer's family sat in the front row of the gallery. On each of those 14 days, at least three members of the family wore buttons on their shirts with the deceased's photograph on them. According to declarations submitted by the defendant, the buttons were several inches in diameter and "very noticeable." Furthermore, the family members were seated in the row directly behind the prosecution and in clear view of the jury. Before opening statements, counsel for Musladin requested that the trial judge instruct the family members to refrain from wearing the buttons in court, out of fear that the button's expressive content would influence the jury and prejudice Musladin's defense. The trial judge denied the request. Musladin was convicted of first degree murder.

Musladin alleged, among other things, that the court unreasonably applied established law in determining that his right to a fair trial was not violated by the family members' wearing of the buttons depicting the deceased.

Due process requires that the accused receive a fair trial by an impartial jury free from outside influences. The Supreme Court has held that when the consequence of a courtroom practice is that an "unacceptable risk is presented of impermissible factors coming into play," there is "inherent prejudice" to a defendant's constitutional right to a fair trial and reversal is required. **Holbrook v. Flynn, 475 U.S. 560 (1986).** In order to determine whether Musladin is entitled to relief, we must assess whether the buttons depicting Studer worn by spectators at the trial posed a risk of impermissible factors coming into play that is similar to those previously found to exist in other circumstances, such as in compelling a criminal defendant to wear prison garb and shackles before the jury, and in permitting spectators at a rape trial to wear anti-rape buttons. We hold that the court unreasonably applied established Supreme Court law in denying Musladin relief.

The underlying federal law in this case-that certain practices attendant to the conduct of a trial can create such an "unacceptable risk of impermissible factors coming into play," as to be "inherently prejudicial" to a criminal defendant-was clearly established in **Estelle v. Williams, 425 U.S. 501(1976)**. In **Williams**, the Court considered whether compelling a criminal defendant to appear at his jury trial dressed in prison clothing violated his right to a fair trial. The Court found that the compelled wearing of prison clothing constitutes a continuous impermissible reminder to the jury of the de-

fendant's condition: an accused in custody who is unable to post bail. The Court held that the influence of prison clothing, and the message it conveyed to the jurors, impaired a defendant's presumption of innocence. Because "[t]he defendant's clothing is so likely to be a continuing influence throughout the trial, an unacceptable risk is presented of impermissible factors coming into play."

This court's decision in **Norris v. Risley, 918 F.2d 828 (9th Cir.1990)**, has persuasive value in an assessment of the meaning of the law that was clearly-established by **Williams** and whether the court's application of that law in the case before us is objectively unreasonable. Like the present case, **Norris** involved the application of the Supreme Court's "inherent prejudice" rule in assessing whether buttons worn by audience members during a trial created an "unacceptable risk of impermissible factors coming into play." In **Norris**, the defendant was facing a criminal charge of rape. During the trial, several women sat in the spectator's gallery wearing buttons that read "Women Against Rape." We noted that at any given time, approximately three women in the audience would be wearing the anti-rape buttons. Faced with these facts, we applied **Williams** and concluded that "[j]ust as the compelled wearing of prison garb during trial can create an impermissible influence on the jury, throughout trial the buttons' message constituted a continuing reminder that various spectators believed Norris's guilt before it was proven, eroding the presumption of innocence." As we explained, because of the button's clear communicative purpose, its impermissible message was far more clear and direct than that deemed unlawful in **Williams**.

Thus, though far more subtle than a direct accusation, the buttons' message was all the more dangerous precisely because it was not a formal accusation. Unlike the state's direct evidence, which could have been refuted by any manner of contrary testimony to be judged ultimately on the basis of each declarant's credibility, the buttons' informal accusation was not susceptible to traditional methods of refutation. Instead, the accusation stood unchallenged, lending credibility and weight to the state's case without being subject to the constitutional protections to which such evidence is ordinarily subjected.

In both **Norris** and the case before us, the law requires the courts to look beyond the general sentiment a button reflects and to determine the specific message that the button conveys in light of the particular facts and issues before the jury. Doing so here, a reasonable jurist would be compelled to conclude that the buttons worn by Studer's family members conveyed the message that the defendant was guilty, just as the buttons worn by spectators in **Norris** did in that case.

Reversed and Remanded.

Due process issues arise in a variety of contexts in the academic environment. From a faculty member's denial of tenure to a student's expulsion from school for academic dishonesty or an act of violence, due process requires a fair and orderly determination of the dispute. In application, this constitutional guarantee presents its own set of problems since determinations are made by individuals who do not possess legal training. Decision making, therefore, is less formal and is usually administered expeditiously. A court's review of an academic decision is very narrow and judges show great respect for the judgment of the academic institution.

A 1999 study by the ERIC Clearinghouse on Higher Education indicates that before 1960, the courts rarely reviewed a college's academic decision making process. Schools were thought to stand in place of parents and were believed to be acting in the best interest of the students. While the court's standard of review has broadened, modern tribunals merely require that the decision making process not interfere with established constitutional rights of faculty and students. The judiciary continues to grant colleges and universities considerable latitude in deciding how to apply due process protections and will only interfere with academic and disciplinary decisions when constitutional protections are clearly violated.

Brent Wheeler v. Texas Woman's College
168 F. 3d 241 (5th Cir. 2001)

Brent Wheeler was a graduate student at Texas Woman's University (TWU). After failing to obtain a Ph.D. in psychology, he sued the university and two professors. The district court granted summary judgment in favor of TWU. We affirm.

Wheeler claimed that he was falsely accused of cheating, resulting in unfair treatment. Specifically, he claimed that false accusations of cheating resulted to inadequate grades, a punitive remediation plan, denial of participation in an internship program, and his ultimate dismissal from the program. He also complained that TWU never gave him a hearing on the cheating allegations.

In his first year of study, several faculty members expressed dissatisfaction with the plaintiff's performance on one rotation. On the recommendation of the evaluation council, the student advanced to his second year on a probationary basis. Faculty dissatisfaction continued. The council concluded that the student not be considered for graduation in June, and recommended that, absent radical improvement, the student be dropped from the school. The student was allowed to take a set of oral and practical examinations as an appeal of the decision not to permit him to graduate. As part of this procedure, the student spent time with several practicing physicians. After receipt of recommendations from these physicians, the council reaffirmed its prior position. After later reviewing reports of his rotations, the council recommended that the student be dropped from the school. The coordinating committee and the dean approved the recommendation. Following the school's procedures, the student appealed the decision to the provost, who sustained the school's actions.

The Court, assuming (as do we) that the student had a property or liberty interest subject to procedural due process protection, held that constitutional due process requirements had been met. Noting that the school had fully informed the student of the faculty's dissatisfaction with his clinical progress and that "[t]he ultimate decision to dismiss respondent was careful and deliberate," the Court found the procedures not only sufficient, but beyond the constitutional requirements of procedural due process.

By this minimal standard, TWU afforded Wheeler procedural due process. The school's decision to terminate him from the doctoral program was careful and deliberate, following a protracted series of steps to rate Wheeler's academic performance, identify and inform him of his weak performance, and provide Wheeler with a specially tailored remedial program in light of his poor performance.

In addition to procedural due process rights, the Supreme Court recognized, in **Regents of University of Michigan v. Ewing**, that decisions in the academic setting are subject to "a narrow avenue for judicial review" under a substantive due process standard. Under this narrow standard:

> When judges are asked to review the substance of a genuinely academic decision … they should show great respect for the faculty's professional judgment. Plainly, they may not override it unless it is such a substantial departure from accepted academic norms as to demonstrate that the person or committee responsible did not actually exercise professional judgment.

Courts must accept, as consistent with due process, "an academic decision that is not beyond the pale of reasoned academic decision-making when viewed against the background of [the student's] entire career at the University...."

Under this standard, Wheeler does not come close to showing that TWU did not exercise professional judgment. On this record a rational trier of fact could not find that TWU's treatment of Wheeler and ultimate decision not to award him a doctorate fell beyond the pale of reasoned academic decision-making in light of Wheeler's entire academic career.

QUESTIONS FOR DISCUSSION:

1. How important is the racial makeup of a jury? If it is important, what should the justice system do to make sure a defendant receives a fair trial by an "impartial" jury?

2. It is often said that a defendant must be tried by a jury of peers, but there is nothing in the Constitution that requires it. Should there be? What is a "peer?"

3. Should individuals not be allowed to be excused from jury duty regardless of the reason, so that the litigants obtain a cross section of the population?

4. What is the best way to handle a disruptive party in the courtroom so that due process is not violated?

5. Should the government be required to buy the defendant clothes for a trial so that the jury does not see the defendant in prison garb?

SECTION 3.6
KATHY ROBERTS
AND HER UNFAIR
CRIMINAL TRIAL

PROBLEM THREE—B

PARK, BROWN & SMITH, P.C.
ATTORNEYS AT LAW
MEMORANDUM

To: All Law Clerks

From: Peter Smith, Esquire

Re: Kathy Roberts and her Criminal trial

Kathy Roberts has been arrested and convicted for drug possession. This sixteen year old believes her conviction should be reversed on the basis of a violation of her procedural due process rights. My investigation has uncovered the following information.

Kathy was arrested for possession of drugs after running a stop sign. Officer O'Brien had been keeping his eye on Kathy, so he was right on the scene when she failed to stop. Needless to say, Kathy was quite annoyed. She had a baggy filled with marijuana on the seat beside her and cocaine hidden in the gym bag in her trunk. Somehow O'Brien caught a glimpse of the baggy when he peered through her window while examining her license. His subsequent search of the car uncovered an ounce of marijuana and a kilo of cocaine.

Kathy was arrested for possession of marijuana and cocaine. Following Ms. Roberts' trial, she was convicted of all charges and is awaiting sentencing. Not surprisingly, the trial was a nightmare. From the moment of her arrest, Kathy was belligerent, disruptive, and uncontrollable. On the way into the courtroom, she attempted to run away from the police escorts. When they recaptured her, a struggle ensued with Kathy biting and kicking the officers. It took four men to eventually contain her. They then had to drag her into the courtroom with her arms handcuffed behind her back and her feet manacled together.

What follows is an excerpt from the courtroom transcript:

THE COURT:	*Ladies and Gentlemen of the jury, you should know that the defendant has been escorted into this courtroom in handcuffs and manacles because she refused to enter peacefully and of her own volition. You must not look upon these restraints as indicating in any way that she is guilty of the crime charged. I remind you that you must presume the defendant is innocent until the government proves otherwise. Ms. Roberts, the restraints will be removed if you agree to remain peaceably within the courtroom.*
ROBERTS:	I will cooperate, Your Honor.
THE COURT:	*Remove the restraints.*

Kathy was cooperative for the initial stages of the trial and made no further trouble until she took the stand. The defendant became uncontrollable when the judge granted an objection raised by the prosecution. Kathy grabbed a book from the witness box and hurled it at the judge. The court had Kathy removed from the witness stand and handcuffed to her chair.

THE COURT:	*Ms. Roberts, you will remain handcuffed to your seat until I have adequate assurances that you will control yourself.*
ROBERTS:	You're not giving me a fair trial.
THE COURT:	*Ladies and Gentlemen of the jury, please pay no attention to the defendant.*

ROBERTS:	Pay attention to everything that's prejudicial. I can't get a fair trial. You're not giving my attorney half a chance.
THE COURT:	*You will be bound and gagged if you continue. Now be quiet!*
ROBERTS:	I will not sit here quietly while you railroad me into jail!
THE COURT:	*You will be bound and gagged with one more outburst. Be quiet or you will be very sorry you ever set foot in this courtroom!*

At that point, Kathy proclaimed her constitutional right to freedom of speech and started to recite the Pledge of Allegiance. She was finally quieted when the bailiff taped her mouth shut. The gag was removed after Kathy promised to contain herself. It was only used for a few minutes.

Ms. Roberts claims that gagging, handcuffing, and manacling her in court in the presence of the jury offended her procedural due process right to a fair and impartial tribunal. The client believes that having a jury see her in restraints was so prejudicial that she was not able to receive a fair trial. Please review the cases of **Commonwealth v. Cruise and State v. Lee** and answer the following questions:

1. According to rules set forth in **State v. Lee,** is it permissible for the judge to merely gag Kathy rather than have her removed from the courtroom as the judge did in **State v. Lee?**

2. What are the pros and cons of the alternative disciplinary measures enumerated in **State v. Lee?** What considerations do you think should be made in determining which approach is the best to use against a disruptive defendant?

3. How does the approach taken to control Kathy compare with the approaches taken in **Lee** and **Cruz?**

4. Even if you do not agree with the approach used by the court, did Kathy's trial comply with the requirements of due process?

COMMONWEALTH OF PENNSYLVANIA V. CRUZ
311 A.2D 692 (PA. 1973)

Cruz contends he is entitled to a new trial because of the prejudicial effect of being seen handcuffed in the courtroom by members of the jury.

Appellant was tried with a co-defendant on the charge of possession of marijuana. The jury found the appellant guilty and the co-defendant not guilty.

The record reveals that appellant was handcuffed when the court recessed for the day while a portion of the jury was still in the jury box and on the following morning he was brought into the courtroom while handcuffed.

The early Common Law recognized that a defendant in a criminal trial had the right to appear in a court free of restraint. "The prisoner must be brought to the bar without irons and all matter of shackles or bonds unless there be danger of escape…" 2 **Hale's Pleas of the Crown,** 219 (1678). Such has been the rule in this country from the time that issue was first discussed.

Under ordinary circumstances a defendant's freedom from handcuffs, shackles or manacles is an important component of a fair and impartial trial, and restraints should not be employed except to prevent him from escaping or injuring others, and to maintain a quiet and peaceable trial.

In **State v. Roberts, 86 N.J. Super. 159, 206 A.2d 200, 205 (1965),** defendant was compelled to appear before the jury with his feet and hands shackled, the court stated: "In any case where the trial judge, in the exercise of sound discretion, determines that the defendant must be handcuffed or shackled, it is of the essence that he instruct the jury in the clearest and most emphatic terms [which the Judge did not do in the instant case] that it give such restraint no consideration whatever in assessing the proofs and determining guilt. This is the least that can be done toward insuring a fair trial. It may be doubted whether any jury, even with the best of cautionary instructions, can ever dismiss from its mind that the accused has appeared before it in handcuffs or chains. His being restrained must carry obvious implications even to the most fair-minded of juries. Unless the situation is so exceptional as to call for shackles, the trial court should instead arrange for additional guard in the courtroom for the protection of all present and the prevention of any disorder or escape."

Furthermore, the ABA Project on Standards for Criminal Justice, trial by Jury, Approved Draft (1968) suggests:

"[A]s confusion or embarrassment of the person and jury prejudice can result from wearing the clothing of a convict or prisoner just as it can from the wearing of shackles." (In Eaddy, the defendant was brought into court wearing coveralls with the words "County Jail" in large letters across the back).

In **Commonwealth v. Keeler, 216 Pa.Super. 193 at 195-196, 264 A.2d 407 at 409 (1970) we held:** "A defendant in prison garb gives the appearance of one whom the state regards as deserving to be so attired. It brands him as convicted in the state's eyes It insinuates that the defendant has been arrested not only on the charge being tried but also on other charges for which he is being incarcerated." A clear analogy can be drawn to the appellant being handcuffed in front of the jury and the "prison garb" cases.

The Commonwealth cites **Commonwealth v. Carter, 219 Pa.Super. 280, 281 A.2d 75 (1971)** in support of its position that a mistrial need not be granted in such a case. That case is inapposite to the appeal. In *Carter,* supra, our court upheld the action of the trial judge in dismissing two jurors who had witnessed the appellant being placed in handcuffs, during a trial recess. The trial judge determined that the dismissed jurors had not discussed the observed event with the other jurors.

Prejudice could have easily been created in the minds of the jurors due to the disparity between the co-defendant and the appellant in that co-defendant appeared in court free of restraints. Furthermore, the record does not indicate appellant was violent while in court, that he conducted himself in an unruly manner, or that he threatened to escape.

For the aforementioned reasons, the judgment of sentence is reversed and the case remanded for a new trial.

STATE OF LOUISIANA V. JAMES LEE
395 SO.2D 700 (LA. 1980)

On July 15, 1977, James Allen Lee was indicted for First Degree Murder. A twelve person jury found the defendant guilty as charged on June 29, 1979. The trial court sentenced the defendant to life imprisonment and the defendant appealed.

The facts incident to the murder are not at issue. The defendant was convicted of shooting Jerry Dennis, the owner of the Shady Oaks Cafe, following an altercation over missing car keys. The defendant turned himself in to police several hours later.

During trial, the defendant persistently interrupted the proceedings by pseudo-Biblical rhetoric and singing the Star Spangled Banner. After numerous warnings by the trial judge, Lee was removed to an adjoining room where he could hear the trial proceedings. After continued outbursts and interruptions from the next room, the defendant was bound and gagged. The jury found him guilty of First Degree Murder.

The defendant urges that the trial court erred in removing the defendant from the courtroom during trial, in overruling defense counsel's

objection regarding an alleged inability to communicate effectively with his client, and in having the defendant handcuffed, shackled and gagged. The defendant argues that these measures effectively deprived him of the right to be present during trial, and to confront the witnesses against him.

The selection of prospective juror as well as the trial proceedings were repeatedly interrupted by defendant's disruptive behavior. He began singing the Star Spangled Banner in front of the prospective jurors. Despite a reprimand and warning from the judge the defendant continued by reciting scripture. The judge initially ordered the defendant removed from the courtroom, but reconsidered and warned both defendant and counsel that he would give Lee another chance but remove him if the behavior continued. After additional outbursts and warnings the defendant was ordered removed to an adjoining room, with the understanding that he would be allowed to return once he agreed to act in an acceptable manner. Arrangements were made for the proceedings to be piped into the adjoining room and an attorney was appointed to sit with the defendant. Jury selection continued and the defendant again began singing the National Anthem, and speaking in a ministerial fashion. Though these outbursts were in the adjoining room, they were loud enough to disrupt proceedings in the courtroom. The defendant at this point had been handcuffed and shackled following an altercation with deputies. The trial judge stated that he had no alternative but to consider gagging the defendant. After some discussion, however, the judge proceeded without having defendant Lee gagged. At some point the defendant was returned to the courtroom only to interrupt the proceedings again by singing the National Anthem. Again the judge warned him that he would be removed and gagged unless he controlled himself. The defendant's disruptive behavior continued throughout the proceedings, and included a prolonged interruption of the state's closing argument. In light of the innumerable interruptions at all stages of the court proceedings it appears that the defendant's arguments objecting to the measures taken by the court are without merit.

In **Illinois v. Allen, 397 U.S. 337, 90 S.Ct. 1057, 25 L.Ed.2d 353 (1970)** the United States Supreme Court held that "a defendant can lose his right to be present at trial if, after he has been warned by the judge that he will be removed if he continues his disruptive behavior, he nevertheless insists on conducting himself in a manner so disorderly, disruptive, and disrespectful of the court that his trial cannot be carried on with him in the courtroom.

The Court concluded that "trial judges confronted with disruptive, contumacious, stubbornly defiant defendants must be given sufficient discretion to meet the circumstances of each case." Noting also the absence of a panacea for dealing with disruptive defendant, the court further observed that at least three constitutionally acceptable avenues exist for dealing with a defiant defendant:

(1) bind and gag him, thereby keeping him present;

(2) cite him for contempt;

(3) take him out of the courtroom until he promises to conduct himself properly.

The defendant was given every opportunity to remain in the courtroom without restraint if he conducted himself properly. The handcuffs and shackles were utilized only after the defendant struggled with deputies. The judge saw further outbursts as a security risk and only then allowed the restraints. Considering the incessant outbursts it appears the judge acted with considerable restraint. When the defendant was held in an adjoining room he was able to hear the trial proceedings and was accompanied by a second attorney to relay any messages to lead counsel in the courtroom. This Court has stated that: "We recognize that the use of restraining devices, including manacles, is within the sound discretion of the trial judge. In the absence of a clear showing of abuse of discretion on the part of he trial judge, a conviction will not be disturbed on appeal because of restraint imposed upon defendant." **State v. Burnett, 337 So.2d 1096 at 1099 (La. 176).** There was no such abuse of discretion here.

We find these assignments to be without merit.

Name   **Please Print Clearly**

1. Is it permissible for the judge to merely gag Kathy rather than have her removed from the courtroom?

_____

_____

_____

_____

_____

_____

_____

_____

_____

2. What are the pros and cons of the alternative disciplinary measures discussed in **State v. Lee**? What considerations do you think should be used in determining which approach is the best to use against a disruptive defendant?

_____

_____

_____

_____

_____

_____

_____

_____

3. How does the approach taken to control Kathy compare with the approaches taken in **Lee** and **Cruz**?

_____

_____

_____

_____

_____

_____

_____

_____

_____

4. Even if you do not agree with the approach used by the court, did Kathy's trial comply with he demands of Due Process?

_____

_____

_____

_____

_____

_____

_____

_____

_____

_____

SECTION 3.7
PROBLEM CASES

1. A city passed an ordinance limiting the number of dogs that can be kept at a residential premise to two dogs over the age of six months. A person who wishes to keep three or four adult dogs at home must obtain a permit. Holt runs a "stud service" from her house and rescues Newfoundland dogs until homes can be found for them. When the law went into effect, she had twelve adult dogs at her residence. Is this ordinance constitutional? **Mary Holt v. City of Sauk Rapids, 559 N.W. 2d 444 (Minn. Ct. App. 1997).**

2. A city passed an ordinance prohibiting the maintenance of a "nuisance." The storage of abandoned or junked motor vehicles is automatically considered a nuisance. A city inspector found a stove, water heater, and car parts on the property owned by Kadash. This individual was then convicted of violating the ordinance. Do the actions of Kadash constitute a nuisance? Is the ordinance constitutional? **George Kadash v. City of Williamsport, 340 A.2d 617 (a. Cmwlth. 1975).**

3. During Tribblett's criminal trial for robbery, a spectator stood up and began screaming: "He threatened my life. He's going to jail." The individual continued her ravings while she was physically removed from the courtroom. The court admonished the jurors to eliminate the outburst from their minds and to base their verdict solely on the evidence. The attorney for Tribblett moved for mistrial and claimed that his client's procedural due process rights to a fair trial were violated. Do you agree? **Commonwealth of Pennsylvania v. Tribblett, 363 A.2d 12123 (Pa. Super. 1976).**

4. Davis was charged with the brutal beating and shooting death of a woman and her two children. The case was the subject of enormous pre-trial publicity, including the fact that Davis had failed a lie detector test and had a history of violent crime. During the jury selection process, ten out of forty jurors admitted to having prior knowledge about the case. The trial judge, however, refused to allow these jurors to be questioned individually by defense counsel. As a result, the defense was precluded from learning the specific information that the potential jurors had heard or read . Was the right of Davis to a fair and impartial jury violated by the trial court's action? **Allen Davis v. State of Florida, 473 U.S. 913 (1985).**

5. Dixon was convicted of attempted robbery. During the course of the crime, he brandished a gun, so he was sentenced to an automatic five-year imprisonment for the weapon's offense. The state legislature had decided to impose a mandatory sentencing scheme for the use of a firearm when committing a crime in order to protect human life. Dixon challenged the statute as being a violation

of his due process rights. Specifically, he argues that the law infringes on his constitutional rights because the legislation ignores the right of the judge to sentence a defendant to a shorter term in jail. In other words, the law prohibits a court from imposing a shorter sentence because of mitigating factors such as the defendant's being a first-time offender. Does the statute violate Dixon's substantive due process rights? **Commonwealth of Pennsylvania v. Carl Cooke, 492 A.2d 63 (Pa. Super. 1985).**

Section 3.8

Internet References

For more information about the topics in this Chapter, see:

A. *The Legislative Process*

- **www.loc.gov**
  The Library of Congress maintains this website which provides access to legislative information, the copyright office, and other governmental related functions.

- **http://lcweb.loc.gov/global/legislative/congress.html**
  This is the official website for the Unites States Legislative Branch. It provides detailed information about the U.S. Congress, Committees of Congress, Congressional Organizations, and the legislative process.

- **http://thomas.loc.gov**
  This site provides general legislative information. An interested party may look up summaries of the law, the status of legislation, text of bills, Committee reports, and other information concerning pending legislation.

B. *Due Process*

- **www.wld.com/conbus/weal/wdueproc.htm**
  West Legal Dictionary provides a fairly detailed discussion o Due Process at this internet address.

- **http://encarta.msn.com/find/Concise.asp?ti=(04950000)**
  Encarta Encyclopedia maintains a site that provides a history of the Due Process Clause.

- **http://supreme.findlaw.com/constitution/amendment14**
  Find Law provides an internet link which contains an in-depth look into the Fourteenth Amendment, including its text, history, and related cases.

- **http://supreme.findlaw.com/constitution/amendment05**
  This website deals with the Fifth Amendment and provides a detailed listing of the various issues that arise from this Constitutional provision.

Footnotes:

1. *Due Process of Law: Procedural and Substantive Issues,* http://faculty.ncwc.edu/mstevennns/ 410/4101ect06.htm (6/25/03).

2. *Rochin v. California* 342 U.S. 1165 (1952).

3. *See*: Willett, "How Our Laws Are Made," H.R. Doc. No. 99-158, 99 Cong., 2d Sess. (1986).

4. Harris, "Innocent-Owner Defense Succeeds Under Nassau's DWI Law," New York Law Journal, August 30, 2005.

KEY TERMS

Article One	Impartial Tribunal
Bill	Joint Resolution
Bill of Rights	Magna Carta
Congress	Ordinance
Concurrent Resolution	Procedural Due Process
Doctrine of Incorporation	Procedural Law
Drug Testing	Reconstruction Amendment
Due Process	Statute
Fifth Amendment	Substantive Due Process
Fourteenth Amendment	Substantive Law
Hopper	United States Senate
House of Representatives	Veto

CHAPTER 4

CRIMINAL LAW AND PROCEDURE

SECTION 4.1
CRIMES

"The real significance of crime is in its being a breach of faith with the community of mankind."

Joseph Conrad
Lord Jim, 1900

As a general rule, an individual can engage in any type of conduct that he or she wishes unless the law specifically prohibits those actions. The legislature, however, will intercede whenever necessary to regulate and prohibit conduct that society deems inappropriate.

A **crime** is an offense against society as determined by the legislature or it is considered a public wrong that carries the punishment of imprisonment or some other public sanction. Crimes number in the thousands, and specific definitions will vary from jurisdiction to jurisdiction. The offense is investigated by law enforcement officials who usually file the criminal charges against the accused, and a governmental agency, such as the District Attorney or United States Attorney, prosecutes the defendant. These crimes range from felonies to summary offenses.

The United States Department of Justice maintains statistics on the categories of crimes committed each year in this country. The most frequently charged offenses deal with non-violent crimes and make up about three-fourths of all arrests. Drug trafficking and other drug related crimes constitute the single largest category of all arrests and make up 36% of the total arrests made in the United States. Violent crimes account for one-fourth of all arrests and assault and robbery lead this category. The Southern states have the highest rate of violent crimes and account for 42% of all violent crimes committed in this country.

Statistically, men are the victims of killings about three-fourths of the time and commit this violent act in almost 90% of the cases. About one-third of murder victims are under 25 and about one-half of the perpetrators are in this age category. Louisiana and Maryland have the highest murder rate by 100,000 people.[1] At what age, however, is a person most likely to die by homicide? According to the Centers for Disease Control, an individual is ten times more likely to be murdered at birth than any other time during one's life. Most of these deaths occurred to children not born in a hospital and the perpetrators were the children's adolescent mothers.[2] Police investigations have determined that arguments are the leading reason for murder in the United States and handguns are by far the weapon of choice.[3]

Not all homicides are illegal nor are all killings punished equally. The law has created a number of categories to reflect these facts with crimes ranging from first degree murder to involuntary manslaughter.

The first part of this chapter will provide definitions for some of the more well-known crimes, such as murder, rape, burglary, and theft. The second part of the chapter will discuss criminal procedure with a focus on the law of search and seizure, police questioning of suspects and will provide a step by step analysis of the arrest procedure through trial.

HOMICIDE

A **homicide** is the killing of another human being but a homicide does not automatically mean that the killing is illegal. In fact, three categories of homicide have been created to designate if the killing is legal or illegal:

1. justifiable homicide;

2. excusable homicide; and

3. criminal homicide.

Justifiable homicide is the killing of another person in self-defense or the execution of an individual carried out by the state or federal governments. California, Michigan, Oklahoma and Louisiana lead the country in justifiable homicides and account for nearly half of these types of killings even though they have only 18% of the population.[4] It is anticipated that the number of justifiable homicides will increase with the growing number of states that have enacted "Make My Day" laws. At least 15 states, including Florida, Colorado, Arizona, and Kentucky, now allow a person to use deadly force against an intruder or attacker in a dwelling, residence, or vehicle and the law provides immunity from for using deadly force. In fact, these laws allow the use of deadly force whenever a person feels threatened in a public area without first having to retreat. An **excusable homicide** is a killing by accident or mistake where the wrongdoer does not have any criminal culpability. A child who is accidentally killed by a car when he darts out between parked vehicles in pursuit of a ball is an example of a homicide that is excusable. **Criminal homicide,** on the other hand, is the unlawful killing of another that includes the crimes of murder and manslaughter. **Murder** is considered the most serious crime by society and it is divided into different degrees depending on how the crime is committed. For instance, first degree murder or premeditated murder represents the conscious attempt to take the life of another.

Manslaughter is considered less serious because the killing is committed through gross negligence or under mitigating circumstances such as when a person kills his spouse in a fit of rage after finding her in bed with another man.

The definition of **first degree murder** varies by state but it is generally considered to be the unlawful killing of another human with malice aforethought, and with the specific intent to kill. This type of deliberate homicide is commonly referred to as premeditated murder and involves a killing by such means as torture, ambush, poisoning, or lying in wait. It is this element of a premeditated and deliberate killing that distinguishes first-degree murder from all other types of criminal homicide. A contract killing or an assassination are classic examples of premeditated murder. Specific intent to kill may also be inferred from the surrounding circumstances, such as the use of a deadly weapon upon a vital part of the victim's body. For example, purposely shooting a person in the head or chest would demonstrate a specific intent to kill that individual; shooting the person in the foot would not.

Malice aforethought describes conduct that exhibits a wanton disregard for the safety of others. This legal term has been defined to include not only ill will towards a person, but a wickedness of disposition, hardness of heart, and recklessness of consequences. In other words, malice aforethought includes such things as discharging a gun into a crowd, throwing a rock off the top of a building, cutting a person with a knife or other sharp object, or punching another in the face. These acts show a disregard for the rights of others and demonstrate a wickedness of disposition.

How much time must elapse between forming the intent to kill and the actual act in order to establish premeditation or specific intent to kill? There is no exact time requirement; instead, premeditation may be proven by a person's words or conduct. For instance, premeditation may be inferred by the intentional use of a deadly weapon upon a vital part of the body, regardless of the passage of time between when the shooter formed the intent to pull the trigger and the actual act.

STATE OF NORTH CAROLINA v. EDWARD HORNSBY
567 S. E. 2D 449 (CT. APP. N. C. 2000)

On the morning of March 21, 2000, Adam Barefoot, the "adopted" son of defendant and Moore, overheard defendant and Moore arguing, and Moore saying something like, "Don't be pointing no gun at me." Soon after, Barefoot went to school. When Barefoot returned home that afternoon, he began working on his homework, a report on John F. Kennedy, and talked to defendant and Moore about the report. According to Barefoot, defendant stated, "Ain't the person who killed him Lee Harvey Oswald?" Barefoot responded that Oswald had shot Kennedy in the head with a rifle. Defendant then went into the bedroom, retrieved a rifle, and aimed it at Moore. Defendant told Moore that she better leave before he killed her. Moore got up, took Barefoot's hand, and stated, "Well, if I go, he is going with me." Defendant then responded, "Everything's cool," placed the gun back in its case, and stated, "All right. Let's just watch some TV."

Later the same evening, defendant became angry and went into the bedroom and retrieved his gun. When he returned to the living room, defendant pointed the gun barrel at Moore's head. Moore attempted to knock the barrel away with her right arm while she was holding Barefoot with her left arm. Defendant shot Moore in the head, then walked back into the bedroom and put the gun away. He returned to the living room, picked up the telephone, and called 911. During the 911 call, defendant stated that he "killed the devil" and referred to Moore's body as a dead snake.

First degree murder is the intentional and unlawful killing of a human being with malice and with premeditation and deliberation. Premeditation means that the act was thought out beforehand for some length of time, however short. Deliberation means that the fatal act was "executed with a fixed design to kill notwithstanding defendant was angry or in an emotional state at the time."

The evidence in the present case showed: defendant pointed a gun at Moore in the morning; he again threatened Moore that evening at supper by stating, "That will be your last supper, Renee;" he pointed his rifle at Moore shortly before shooting her; and he fired the fatal shot at point blank range. The State's evidence established each and every element of first degree murder, including premeditation and deliberation, and there was no evidence to negate these elements. Accordingly defendant's assignment of error is overruled.

QUESTIONS FOR DISCUSSION:

1. Dudley, Stephens and another sailor were cast adrift in a small boat following a storm with no food or water. Dudley and Stephens discussed sacrificing one of the three so that the remaining two could survive. The two sailors then killed the decedent and fed upon his body for nourishment. The survivors were tried for first degree murder even though all three would have died of starva-

tion. The decedent was chosen because he would have expired first due to his frail and deteriorating health. Are Dudley and Stephens guilty of first degree murder? **Regina v. Dudley and Stephens, 14 Q. B. D. 273 (1884).**

2. Mr. Carrol was selected to attend an electronic's school for nine days. His wife greeted the news with a violent argument. Prior to his departure, and at the request of his wife, Mr. Carrol put a loaded 22 caliber pistol on the window sill, at the head of the common bed. Later than evening, the parties engaged in another protracted argument. Carrol's wife proceeded to follow her husband into the bedroom as they continued to argue. Mr. Carrol remembered the gun on the window sill, so he grabbed the pistol, and spontaneously shot his wife twice in the back of the head. Is this a case of premeditated murder? **Commonwealth v. Carrol, 194 A.2d 911 (Pa. 1963).**

3. In the book and movie *Alive*, a plane carrying 15 members of the Uruguay national rugby team crashed in the Andes Mountains. The survivors ate the flesh of their dead friends in order to stay alive until they were rescued. How does this case differ from **Regina v. Dudley and Stephens?**

Second-degree murder or **felony murder,** is the unintentional killing of another committed during the commission of a felony. An example of felony murder is demonstrated by a person who sets fire to a building unaware that the owner is inside. Since the owner died during the commission of an arson, Jones is guilty of felony murder even though he did not know the owner was inside the building. If, however, a criminal specifically kills another during the commission of a felony, such as a robbery, the crime would constitute first-degree murder and not felony murder.

If the crime is committed by more than one person, all participants in the criminal enterprise can be equally found guilty regardless of their involvement. This is called the **co-felons rule**. For instance, the driver of the get-away car in a grocery store robbery is just as liable for the killing of a store clerk as the person who pulls the trigger.

Some states do not make a distinction between first degree and felony murder and treat both crimes the same.

Is it a defense to felony murder that the killing was an accident or unintentional?

STATE OF NEW JERSEY V. HERBERT SMITH
509 A. 2D 206 (N. J. SUPER. 1986)

Defendant was convicted of felony murder as a result of the death of a man who suffered a heart attack when his car was involved in an accident with the one driven by the defendant fleeing from the scene of an armed robbery. We hold that the proofs could justify a conviction for felony murder.

Julia McCarthy was working at the courtesy desk at the Mayfair Foodtown when she was confronted by defendant pointing a handgun at her. Defendant instructed her to fill a bag with money and said, "Give me five minutes" as he left the store. A customer of the store, observed defendant get into the car and Tresch chasing the car. He testified that the car was going fast as it exited the parking lot.

A few minutes later, Edwin L. Mackie was by the window of his store, when he heard a "loud thunderous" noise outside. He ran outside in time to see a brown car driving away, which did not stop at the stop sign at the end of the street. Mackie also saw a man, later identified as Kelton Barnes, emerging from a damaged vehicle. Barnes told Mackie that the other car had come "barreling out of the side street," hit him, and continued on. Mackie took Barnes into his office to call the police. However, Mackie had to place the call because Barnes' hands were shaking so badly that he was unable to dial.

Officer Powell found Barnes walking back and forth outside his car in the heavy rain. Barnes seemed very nervous and upset, but the only observable injury was a laceration on his hand. At first, Barnes said that he was all right, but as he sat with Powell in the patrol car for a credentials check, he began shaking and said that he didn't feel well. Barnes then slumped over in the seat. Powell performed CPR until a medical unit arrived, but Barnes was declared dead on arrival at the hospital.

Smith was charged with felony murder which imposes liability where the actor is engaged in the commission of, or an attempt to commit, or flight after committing or attempting to commit (a felony), and in the course of such crime or of immediate flight, causes the death of a person other than one of the participants.

Felony murder is a crime of transferred intent, based on a showing of intent to commit the underlying felony even though there is no intent to kill. Thus, in this case, the jury would have to find that the heart attack was a probable consequence of defendant's conduct incident to the felony.

Defendant claims that the State failed to produce sufficient evidence to show a causal link between defendant's conduct and Barnes' heart attack. The State offered the testimony of Dr. Schoss who stated that Barnes had very severe heart disease, but, in his opinion, Barnes died as a result of the stress he was subject to prior to the time he died. In contrast, defendant's medical expert, testified that Barnes could have died at any time, just in the course of his normal activities without any stress, because his heart was that bad. It then became a question for the jury to weigh that testimony and to reach a conclusion.

The question of causation with respect to felony murder was addressed in **People v. Martin, 112 Ill. App.3d 48 (1983).** In that case, the stress of an assault inflicted upon the victim who had severe heart disease caused such a strain on the victim's heart that he died. The court concluded that, "The fact that a person without the deceased's history of heart disease probably would have survived the attack is immaterial. The determination of whether there was a causal relationship between the defendant's conduct and the decedent's death is a matter properly left to the trier of fact."

We are satisfied that the jury had sufficient medical evidence from which it could conclude that the accident was the precipitating factor of Barnes' heart attack and, therefore, his death.

Generally, **third-degree murder** is the killing of another with malice aforethought but with no specific intent to kill and not occurring during the commission of a felony. As an illustration, Minnesota law defines third degree murder as "Whomever, without intent to effect the death of any person, causes the death of another by perpetrating an act eminently dangerous to others and evidencing a depraved mind, without regard for human life, is guilty of murder in the third degree."

For example, if an individual is intentionally shot in the foot and dies as a result of medical complications, that action will give rise to third-degree murder. The shooting itself is evidence of malice but no specific intent to kill existed.

COMMONWEALTH OF PENNSYLVANIA V. JOHN KLING
731 A.2D 145 (PA. SUPER. 1999)

John Kling was driving his red Chrysler Conquest near McConnellsburg when he noticed a black Camaro in his rear-view mirror. The Camaro took off, and both automobiles began racing up a curvy mountain road known as Scrub Ridge. At speeds in excess of 80 mpm, both vehicles reached the crest of Scrub Ridge, and with Kling in the lead, the improvident competitors began descending the mountain road.

The first downside mile from the top of Scrub Ridge is riddled with eight substantial curves and five cautionary speed signs. Nevertheless, Kling maintained his excessive speeds, pulling away from the Camaro and disappearing into the blind curves.

Approaching the eighth major curve on the downslope, Kling swung into the no-passing zone and blew past two pickup trucks traveling in front of him. He then headed into the sharp double curve at nearly 70 mpm, crossed the centerline again, and struck a vehicle driven by Helen Mellott. The collision killed Ms. Mellott instantly.

Third degree murder occurs when a person commits a killing, which is neither intentional nor committed during the perpetration of a felony, but contains the requisite malice. Malice exists where there is a wickedness of disposition, hardness of heart, cruelty, recklessness of consequences, and a mind regardless of social duty, although a particular person may not be intended to be injured. Where malice is based on a reckless disregard of consequences, it is not sufficient to show mere recklessness; rather, it must be shown the defendant consciously disregarded an unjustified and extremely high risk that his actions might cause death or serious bodily injury.

Kling was deliberately racing his high-powered car at speeds of 75-80 mpm on a two and one-half mile stretch of a curvy mountain road. He passed five cautionary signs warning him to slow down around the treacherous curves. In spite of these warnings, Kling proceeded at high rates of speed and, cutting the curves in order to negotiate the road. Without a doubt, the aggregate of these circumstances plainly warned Kling his conduct was nearly certain to result in disaster.

Kling chose to play Russian roulette with the other drivers on Scrub Ridge. By speeding through the curves, he pulled the trigger four or five times with one near miss; on the last pull, however, he killed a person. This conduct exhibited the sustained recklessness, in the face of warnings, necessary to prove a knowing and conscious disregard that death or serious bodily injury was reasonably certain to occur. We therefore uphold Kling's convictions for third degree murder.

The last category of criminal homicide is **manslaughter** which is divided into voluntary and involuntary manslaughter.

The reader might remember the bizarre case in Germany that gained worldwide attention. Armin Meiwes admitted to slaying and consuming a man's body who had volunteered to be killed after reading an internet message from Meiwes' about his perverted fantasy. The communication by Meiwes read: "Seeking well-built man, 18-30 years old for slaughter." The victim responded: "I offer myself to you and will let you dine on my live body. Not butchery, dining!!" Because the victim had willingly volunteered to be killed, the crime did not fit the German definition of murder, and the act was classified as manslaughter. What then is manslaughter?

Voluntary manslaughter is the intentional killing of another committed in the heat of passion and as a result of provocation that would arouse the passions of an ordinary person beyond the power of his or her control. Courts recognize that these elements will eliminate malice aforethought in what would normally be a first-degree murder case.

Certain types of conduct can provoke a reasonable person to act without consideration for his or her actions. Provocation has been recognized in cases where one spouse finds the partner in bed with another person, or if an assailant learns that a spouse or child has been the victim of a sexual attack.

Words alone, however, are not considered sufficient provocation to cause a person to use deadly force regardless of how insulting or inciteful they might be. This principle will apply in most cases even if the words are spoken just to inform the defendant that a provocative event has occurred. In evaluating the facts of the killing, the courts will use an objective person standard in determining whether sufficient provocation existed to bring about the fit of rage.

To provide an example of a definition for this crime, Ohio provides: "No person, while under the influence of sudden passion or in a sudden fit of rage, either of which is brought on by serious provocation occasioned by the victim that is reasonably sufficient to incite the person into using deadly force, shall knowingly cause the death of another."

Is a person guilty of voluntary manslaughter if she finds her boyfriend in a sexual liaison with another woman? The courts have traditionally ruled that if an accused catches his or her spouse in the act of adultery, the circumstances establishes heat of passion for the crime of voluntary manslaughter. Will the same rule apply if the parties are not married but are boyfriend and girlfriend?

GAIL TURNER V. STATE
708 SO. 2D 232 (CT. APP. ALA. 1997)

Gail Turner, was found guilty of murder. Evidence at trial tended to show that the appellant had lived with James Stephens for two and one-half years. On June 22, 1995, Stephens and Cockerham, went out for the evening. Cockerham picked up Stephens and the two went to New Country, a nightclub in Decatur. While at New Country, Stephens met a female whom he knew, Cindy Adams. Later that night, Stephens and Adams both went with Cockerham to his apartment. Cockerham went to bed, instructing the other two to lock the door when they left. Stephens and Adams turned off the lights, placed pillows on the floor and started kissing. Stephens had removed Adam's blouse.

After noticing that Cockerham's truck was parked in the parking lot, Ms. Turner walked to Cockerham's apartment. The appellant began banging on the door, and when no one came to answer, she screamed, "I know you are in there" and "open the door." When Stephens finally answered the door, she yelled, "I can't believe you're with a bitch like this." Turner left the apartment and Stephens followed her outside. According to the appellant, Stephens said something to her, she turned around, and they "struggled." She said the next thing she knew, he was on the ground. She said she remembers that she did not have a gun when she left Cockerham's apartment, but does not recall where the gun that killed Stephens came from.

The sole issue in this appeal is whether there is a reasonable theory to support the theory that the appellant killed Stephens out of heat of passion caused by provocation recognized by law.

A person commits the crime of manslaughter if: He causes the death of another person under circumstances that would constitute murder; except that he causes the death due to a sudden heat of passion caused by provocation recognized by law, and before a reasonable time for the passion to cool and for reason to reassert itself."

In order to reduce murder to (voluntary) manslaughter, the heat of passion must have been caused by a provocation recognized by law. Alabama courts have acknowledged such legal provocation in two circumstances: (1) when the accused catches his/her spouse in the act of adultery; and (2) when the accused has been assaulted or was faced with what appeared to be an imminent assault. The appellant contends that both circumstances were present in this case and that, therefore, the heat of passion was the result of a provocation legally sufficient to reduce her murder conviction to manslaughter. However, although there was evidence that the killing resulted from heat of passion, the evidence does not support the contention that either circumstance of a legally sufficient provocation was present in this case.

The evidence showed that the appellant immediately became enraged when she discovered Stephens "kissing and fondling" Ms. Adams. While this situation appears comparable to the circumstance of catching a spouse in the act of adultery, courts have required that, for heat-of-passion manslaughter to be available, the party caught by the accused having a sexual or romantic relationship with another must actually be the spouse of the accused. Thus, the accused must be married to one of the parties caught in the compromising situation before the killing of either party can be reduced to manslaughter.

Involuntary manslaughter lacks an essential element to make the crime murder and it is considered a lesser included offense. This crime is defined as the unintentional killing of another resulting from outrageous conduct or criminal negligence that demonstrates a reckless disregard for the safety of another. For example, an intoxicated driver who causes an accident and kills another person is guilty of this crime which is also called vehicular manslaughter.

The Missouri Criminal Code provides an example of a definition for this crime. That law states: "A person commits the crime of involuntary manslaughter if he: (1) recklessly causes the death of another person; or (2) while in an intoxicated condition operates a motor vehicle with criminal negligence to cause the death of any person.

One of the more publicized cases of involuntary manslaughter, dubbed the "Nanny Murder Trial," involved Louise Woodward. She was the au pair from England who came to the United States to work as a baby sitter. Woodward was in charge of an eight month old infant that died in her care. The case was tried in Massachusetts and the evidence demonstrated that the baby died from being shaken to death. Woodward was initially convicted of murder but the judge reduced the finding to involuntary manslaughter. Following the trial, Woodward returned to Europe, attended law school and is now an attorney in England.

COMMONWEALTH OF PENNSYLVANIA V. HICKS
201 A.2D 294 (PA. 1964)

The offense of involuntary manslaughter consists of the killing of another person without malice and unintentionally, but in doing some unlawful act not amounting to a felony, or in negligently doing some lawful act. Where the act in itself is not unlawful, to make it criminal, the negligence must be such a departure from prudent conduct as to evidence a disregard of human life or an indifference to consequences. Reckless driving upon the highway is such a departure from prudent conduct.

A review of the evidence in a light most favorable to the verdict establishes the following:

Arthur Gilmore, an eyewitness, testified that at 7:15 p.m. on March 4, 1963, Harry Yeager, a pedestrian was struck by a 1955 or 1956 Chrystler or Plymouth car which was being driven south on 17th Street. The accident occurred at the intersection of 17th Street and Columbia Avenue, in Philadelphia. Mr. Gilmore described the car as being black with a red top. He estimated the speed of the car at fifty miles-per-hour as the light turned amber. The light was red as the car passed through the intersection. The front of the car struck Yeager, who was crossing the street, throwing his body eleven feet into the air and a distance of thirty feet. He further testified that the driver stopped for a few seconds but made no move to leave the car or render assistance to Yeager. When Gilmore called to the driver to halt, the driver turned off his lights and "took off," throwing a lot of smoke.

It is our conclusion that the evidence is sufficient to support the verdict of involuntary manslaughter.

RAPE

Sexual violence affects millions of people a year and is a dramatically unreported crime with only about 39% of the cases being reported to the police. Females are the usual victims but anyone can be a target. Some victims cannot refuse the sexual advances because of threats or intimidation while others are unable to consent because of mental illness, physical disability, age, or because they have been drugged.[5]

The National Institute for Justice reports that one in every six women have been the victim of an attempted or completed rape in their lifetime and about three percent of men have also been the victim of a sex crime. Statistically, 44% of rape victims are under the age of eighteen and 15% have not reached their twelfth birthdays.

The common law definition of **rape** is the unlawful carnal knowledge of a woman by a man through force or the threat of force and without consent. The crime does not require the assailant to complete the act of sexual intercourse. Rape merely requires penetration, no matter how slight.

Is it a defense to rape that the defendant is impotent and unable to perform the act of sexual intercourse? This is the issue in **Arizona v. Kidwell.**

STATE OF ARIZONA V. RAYMOND KIDWELL
556 P. 2D 20 (ARIZ. APP. 1976)

KIDWELL, Raymond appeals his conviction of rape.

Kidwell argues that the trial court erred in refusing to direct a verdict on the rape charge. Appellant maintains that the evidence only supports a conviction for attempted rape on the grounds that the proof showed he had no erection at the time of the act and one who is impotent cannot be convicted of rape.

This issue appears to be one of first impression in Arizona. Although we have discovered no case law holding to the contrary, we hold that under Arizona law proof of impotency does not constitute a defense to a charge of rape.

A.R.S. §13—612 provides: The essential guilt of rape consists in the outrage to the person and feelings of the female, and any sexual penetration, however, slight is sufficient to complete the crime.

The critical element of rape is sexual penetration. The slightest penetration of the vulva is sufficient to complete the offense. Whether this penetration is accomplished by an erect or nonerect penis is not, in our opinion, relevant if penetration is established.

In the instant case, it was not disputed that Kidwell was impotent, in that he did not have an erection at the time of the offense. The victim, however, testified that a slight penetration of approximately one inch was accomplished. Kidwell's expert medical witness stressed the difficulty of achieving penetration in light of the victim's position and appellant's lack of an erection, but admitted that penetration as defined by our law could have taken place. This evidence is sufficient to uphold Kidwell's conviction.

The judgment and sentence are affirmed.

The elements of rape are not always easy to ascertain. Courts have struggled with two major questions over the years: (1) what constitutes force?; and (2) did the victim consent to the sexual act? These are especially difficult questions in instances of date rape and where the woman has been psychologically coerced into having sex.

What kind of behavior amounts to a threat, and how vehement must the woman be in resisting the sexual advance? In **Commonwealth v. Rhodes, 510 A.2d 1217 (Pa. 1986),** the Pennsylvania Supreme Court held that force implies more than just physical force; it may also include psychological coercion. Before that ruling, rape convictions were not upheld when the assailant threatened his victim with sending her back to a juvenile detention center if she did not comply with his sexual advances, **(Commonwealth v. Mlinarich, 498 A.2d 395 (Pa. Super. 1985)),** and when a father told his daughter that the Bible commanded her to have sex with him. **Commonwealth v. Biggs, 467 A.2d 31 (Pa. Super. 1983).**

Sex-offense laws have been recently modified to reflect the changing attitudes of society in making it easier to sustain a conviction. Some jurisdictions have made date rape a specific crime and have eliminated the requirement of force as an element of the offense. Pennsylvania is an example of a state that has revamped its law to reflect this change. In **Commonwealth v. Berkowitz, 641 A.2d 1161 (Pa. 1991),** a female college student, who had been drinking, claimed that another student raped her after she entered his dormitory room looking for a mutual friend. The victim testified that although he did not shove her or apply force, she continued to say "no" throughout the encounter. The Pennsylvania Supreme Court found that although the victim established her lack of consent, she did not establish a threat of force or psychological coercion, which is a necessary requirement for rape. The court remanded the case for trial on the charge of indecent assault, which is a misdemeanor, as opposed to rape, which is a felony.

Criticism of this decision prompted the sex offense laws in Pennsylvania to be amended and the crime of **sexual assault** was added. It is now a felony to engage in sexual intercourse with a person who does not consent to the act. What is obviously missing from this definition is the element of force. The result of this legislation is that "no" now means "no."

The legislature further amended the rape statute to afford greater protection to victims by prohibiting sexual conduct where the complainant is unconscious or the person knows that complainant is unaware that sexual intercourse is occurring. Rape also exists where the person has substantially impaired the complainant's power to control his or her conduct by employing, without the knowledge of the complainant, drugs or intoxicants. This change was made in response to those cases in which women have been raped after a drug has been placed in a victim's drink without her knowledge, rendering the victim unconscious.

The following is the current rape statute in Pennsylvania:

A person commits a felony of the first degree when he or she engages in sexual intercourse with a complainant:

1. By forcible compulsion.

2. By threat of forcible compulsion that would prevent resistance by a person of reasonable resolution.

3. Who is unconscious or where the person knows that the complainant is unaware that the sexual intercourse is occurring.

4. Where the person has substantially impaired the complainant's power to appraise or control his or her conduct by administering or employing, without the knowledge of the complainant, drugs, intoxicants or other means for the purpose of preventing resistance.

5. Who suffers from a mental disability which renders the complainant incapable of consent.

6. Who is less than 13 years of age.

The Pennsylvania legislature has addressed the issue of rape between spouses by providing that forcible sex between spouses is rape.

Is it rape when the victim is tricked into having sexual intercourse? The courts make a distinction between cases where the woman does not know that a sexual act is about to occur (fraud-in-factum) and where the victim consents to the sexual act but the permission is obtained through fraud (fraud-in-the-inducement). Fraud-in-factum is rape, but fraud-in-the-inducement is not. For instance, a person who consents to intercourse under the fraudulent promise that the parties will marry knows that a sexual act is to occur so rape has not been committed. A woman, however, who consents to a gynecological examination believing that a metal instrument is being inserting when the doctor is really performing sexual intercourse has been raped.

Statutory Rape

Children are protected by the law in a variety of ways. The reader has already learned that children have a degree of immunity for their torts and they may disaffirm a contract unless it is for a necessity such as food or shelter. These protections are also extended to the voluntary sexual acts of children where adults may be prosecuted for having sexual relations with a child under a certain age. This is the crime of **statutory rape**.

Traditionally, **statutory rape** occurs when a man over the age of 16 has sexual relations with the consent of a female under 16 who is not his spouse. Because of the tender years of the female, she is presumed incapable of giving a meaningful consent, and the man is responsible for statutory rape regardless of his knowledge of her age.

In some states, the required age of the parties will differ. In Pennsylvania, for example, a person is guilty of statutory sexual assault when "that person engages in sexual intercourse with a complainant under the age of 16 years and that person is four or more years older than the complainant and the complainant and that person are not married to each other."

In Re J.M.
2003 WL 79330 (Ga. 2003)

The juvenile court found that sixteen-year-old J.M. violated Georgia's fornication statute, by having sexual intercourse with his sixteen-year-old girlfriend G.D. in her bedroom and adjudicated him delinquent. On appeal, J.M. contends that his constitutional right of privacy prohibits the State from criminalizing his conduct.

G.D. lived with her parents. Between 2 a.m. and 5 a.m. on September 16, 2001, she brought J.M. into her bedroom. She placed a stool next to the closed bedroom door, and she and J.M. engaged in sexual intercourse on the floor. When G.D.'s mother walked in and discovered them having sexual intercourse, J.M. jumped out of the bedroom window and ran.

We begin our analysis by considering whether J.M.'s right to privacy encompassed his sexual liaison with G.D. Both were sixteen years old at the time of the act, and the General Assembly has established sixteen as the age at which a person can legally consent to sexual intercourse. They willingly engaged in sexual intercourse, and there was no force involved.

Finally, J.M. and G.D.'s acts were private. The bedroom was G.D.'s personal bedroom, and she invited J.M. to enter the house and her bedroom. Although G.D.'s mother did not condone her daughter's behavior, she acknowledged that G.D. could reasonably expect privacy in various parts of the family home, including in

G.D.'s bedroom. Before beginning her intimacies with J.M., G.D. ensured the bedroom door was closed and placed a stool against the door, further evidencing her and J.M.'s efforts to keep their acts private. Under these facts, we find that they intended to keep their sexual activity private and took reasonable steps to ensure their privacy. Accordingly, Georgia's right to privacy encompassed J.M.'s actions.

We next examine whether the State had a compelling interest that it vindicated through means that were narrowly tailored to accomplish only that compelling interest. Here, the State's interest in "shielding the public from inadvertent exposure to the intimacies of others" is not at issue because the intercourse occurred in a private residence. The State's interests in protecting people from engaging in sexual acts against their will, whether through force or inability to consent, are not implicated because J.M. and G.D. were legally capable of consenting, and they willingly engaged in sexual intercourse. Likewise, the State's interest in restricting commercial sexual activity is not involved.

The State offers its interest in regulating the behavior of "minors" as grounds for prohibiting J.M. and G.D.'s conduct. Whether labeled "minor" or "adult," however, the General Assembly has already determined that persons who are at least sixteen years old are sufficiently old to decide whether to engage in sexual intercourse. Because the State cannot use Georgia's criminal laws to proscribe J.M.'s conduct in this case, we reverse his adjudication as a delinquent.

OPEN LEWDNESS

Society has become much more tolerant in sexual matters between consenting adults. The law, however, remains critical of obscene conduct that is committed in public. For example, streaking and publicly exposing a private body part is not tolerated and fall within the definition of **open lewdness.**

A person is guilty of the crime of open lewdness when he or she commits any lewd act that the individual knows is likely to be observed by others who would be affronted or alarmed.

STATE OF HAWAII V. DON WHITNEY
912 P. 2D 596 (CT. APP. HAWAII 1996)

On June 14, 1993, Don Whitney was convicted of open lewdness. **HRS § 712-1217** states: "Open lewdness: A person commits the offense of open lewdness if in a public place the person does any lewd act, which is likely to be observed by others who would be affronted or alarmed."

Officer Kobayashi was assigned to monitor complaints of "open lewdness" and other sexual activity at the Ala Moana Beach Park in Honolulu. The officer was dressed in "plain clothes" and was acting in an undercover capacity. The officer entered the men's public rest room and shower area. There he observed defendant standing on a bench in the men's shower area. Defendant was dressed in a shirt and blue jeans. Defendant then pulled his pants and underwear down to his knees and stroked his penis. The officer testified he was "affronted and alarmed" by defendant's behavior.

In construing **HRS § 712-1217**, Hawaii's Supreme Court indicated that the "public place" element of **HRS § 712-1217** is determined by an objective standard. What constitutes a "public place" depends upon the circumstances of each particular case. Thus, the fact that defendant was in a male shower area does not render the shower area non-public. Whether a place is owned by the State or whether the accused believes he or she is in a remote area is not dispositive of whether a particular place is deemed "public" or "private."

The pertinent question is not whether defendant's act was actually seen by a number of casual observers but whether it was likely to be seen by a number of casual observers. Here, the offense took place in a public rest room and shower area. Members of the public would frequent a public rest room and shower area. The room was freely accessible to the public, and the area was open to public use by males. Defendant's act occurred where anyone entering the rest room and shower area would have seen him. Defendant could reasonably be deemed to have intended, or known, that his conduct was likely to be seen by members of the public. Under these circumstances, defendant's act occurred in a "public place" because it

was likely to be seen by any number of casual observers.

Defendant further contends that the evidence was insufficient because Officer Kobayashi stated he was "surprised" rather than affronted and alarmed. On the contrary, Officer Kobayashi did also testify that he was affronted and alarmed. We reiterate, however, that whether Officer Kobayashi was personally affronted or alarmed is not dispositive because **HRS § 712-1217** requires only that the act be one which is likely to be observed by others who would be affronted and alarmed, and not that there be proof that a particular person was in fact affronted and alarmed. For that reason, the fact that no one may testify to being shocked or offended by a defendant's act does not necessarily mean the exposure was not indecent, because the common sense of the community, as well as the sense of decency and morality, which most people entertain, must be the guide.

By his act, defendant knew the nature of his conduct. Defendant's act was "lewd." The rest room and shower area was open and accessible to others. From the surrounding circumstances, there can be no doubt that defendant was conscious of his act and that he committed the act without any regard to the risk that his act was likely to cause others who might enter the area to be affronted or alarmed. That being so, we hold that there was sufficient evidence to support the conclusion that defendant was aware of the substantial risk that his act would result in the prohibited conduct.

Judgment is affirmed.

BURGLARY

According to the FBI, more than two million burglaries occur each year and two-thirds of these offenses are of residential structures. Burglars invade homes primarily during the day through forcible entry while business structures are usually entered at night. The average loss per illegal entry is a little more than $1,700. The Northeast has the fewest number of burglaries while the South has the highest rate for these crimes. As for what month has the highest burglary rate, that distinction goes to July. February by far has the fewest.

The definition of burglary has changed over time. At common law, **burglary** was defined as the breaking and entering of a building at night with the intent of committing a felony. Since the purpose of this law is to allow people to be secure in their homes, should it matter whether the offense occurs during the day or night? The modern definition of burglary provides that a person is guilty of the crime if he enters a building or occupied structure with the intent to commit a crime unless the premises are open to the public. The distinction of committing the crime between the day or night has been eliminated, as well as the requirement of a breaking and entering.

By way of comparison, England defines burglary as the entry into "any building, part of a building, inhabited vehicle or vessel with the intent to steal, cause grievous bodily harm, criminal damage, or to commit rape."

Burglary is a crime in and of itself and does not require the substantive offense to be committed by the criminal. For example, if a person breaks into a home to steal a rare painting, but the painting is no longer there, the individual is still guilty of burglary.

Does the definition of burglary include a person who enters a tent with the intent to commit a crime? That is the issue in **People v. Wilson.**

PEOPLE V. JOHN WILSON
15 CAL. RPTR. 2D 77 (CAL. APP. 1992)

Wilson appeals his conviction for burglary. We affirm.

The charge arose from Wilson's relationship with Sherry Parsons. Wilson and Parsons met in March of 1991, and Wilson moved into the trailer where Parsons was staying. Parsons discovered that Wilson was aggressive, profane, and dominating, and asked him to move out three or four days later.

On May 1, 1991, Wilson and Parsons were at the grocery store when Wilson grabbed her by the hair, threw her down, and broke the grocery bag. Daniel Brackett, who knew Wilson, drove up with Sean Pray and saw Wilson pulling Parsons by the hair. Brackett calmed Wilson and took Parsons and Wilson to another location. Parsons said she was afraid of Wilson and stayed with Pray and Brackett.

In the early morning of May 11, 1991, Wilson appeared at Pray's tent. He unzipped the tent, stepped inside and said, "I've come to get you. You're going with me. Get up, get your clothes on and get your stuff. You're going to go with me or I'm going to kick your ass."

While Parsons was packing her belongings, Wilson pointed his knife at Pray, who was in his sleeping bag. Wilson threatened to burn Pray and set fire to the tent. Wilson ripped a gold chain off Pray's neck and said, "You're lucky it isn't your throat." Wilson slashed the tires of Pray's car with his knife, and kicked a lantern near his head, shattering glass over the bed.

Wilson argues that a tent is not an inhabited dwelling, house or a building for purposes of burglary. He bases his argument on the common definitions of "house" and "building." We find no merit in this point.

Courts have defined "building" broadly, to include such structures as a telephone booth, a popcorn stand on wheels, and a loading dock constructed of chain link fence. A "house" has also been broadly defined as "any structure, which has walls on all sides and is covered by a roof."

We reject Wilson's claim that a tent does not fall within the dictionary definition of a "building." The term inhabited dwelling house means a structure where people ordinarily live and which is currently being used for dwelling purposes. A place is an inhabited dwelling if a person with possessory rights uses the place as sleeping quarters intending to continue doing so in the future. The place—whether dwelling house or building—must be inhabited.

We conclude that it is the element of habitation, not the nature of the structure that (establishes) the crime of burglary. An "inhabited dwelling house," must be defined as a person's actual place of abode, regardless of the material of which it is built. Applying that conclusion to the instant case, we find that the tent having four sides and a roof and being inhabited by Pray and Parsons and used for sleeping and storage of their possessions, is a dwelling house, for purposes of (burglary).

The judgment is affirmed.

How would you answer the following questions?

1. If a person breaks into a car to steal the radio, does it constitute burglary?

2. If a person enters a mobile home to assault the occupants, is this burglary?

3. If a person enters a department store while it is open in order to steal a coat, is this burglary?

Has a person committed a crime if he or she purposely comes onto the land of another but has no intent to commit a crime? For example, is it a crime if a camper comes upon a home in the woods and enters the structure to take a shower or if one climbs over a fence on someone's property to go hunting on that land? **Criminal trespass** laws have been enacted to protect the unlawful intrusion onto real estate. The crime occurs when a person enters the land of another without permission or with no legal right to be there. For instance, some states make it a crime if a person:

1. Enters, gains entry by subterfuge or surreptitiously remains in any building or occupied structure; or breaks into any building or occupied structure or separately secured or occupied portion thereof, or

2. Knowing that he is not licensed or privileged to do so, enters or remains in any place as to which notice against trespass is given by:

    i.   actual communication to the actor;

    ii. posting in a manner prescribed by law or reasonably likely to come to the attention of intruders;

    iii. fencing or other enclosure manifestly designed to exclude intruders; or

    iv. an actual communication to the actor to leave school grounds as communicated by a school, center or program official, employee or agent or a law enforcement officer.

THEFT RELATED CRIMES

Consider the following cases to ascertain if there is a common thread. In 1980, two men rigged the Pennsylvania State Lottery by placing counterfeit balls in the machine insuring that 666 would be the winning number. A bank clerk mistakenly deposited ten thousand dollars into a customer's checking account which was promptly withdrawn by the recipient. A student gave his ATM card to roommate to withdraw $20 from his checking account as a loan. Instead, the roommate withdrew $500. A person walked into a jewelry store and sold a new $9,000 Rolex watch to the merchant for $100. The common thread in these cases is that they are all examples of theft related offenses.

The Federal Bureau of Investigation determined that over seven million theft related crimes were committed in 2002 with an estimated loss of $4.9 billion dollars in property. These figures represent a very sizable portion of the total crimes committed during the year with theft related offenses ranging from larceny to receiving stolen property.

Larceny is the taking and carrying away of property that belongs to another without the owner's consent and with the intention of depriving the owner of the goods permanently.

Because of the difficulty in distinguishing larceny from embezzlement and other theft-related crimes, these offenses have been consolidated into the crime of theft. No degree of force, however, may be used in taking the property or else the theft will be transformed into robbery.

Robbery consists of all of the elements of larceny with the additional requirement that the taking be accomplished by force or the threat of force.

The Federal Bureau of Investigation reports that most robberies occur on streets and highways and firearms are used almost half of the time. The average dollar value of the items taken per robbery is $1,230.

The force needed to accomplish a pick-pocket is not the type ordinarily required for robbery. If a weapon is used, however, the crime will be considered robbery. For instance, a purse snatch in which the victim is knocked to the ground is considered robbery.

A person commits the crime of **receiving stolen property** if he intentionally obtains or disposes of property of another knowing that it has been stolen, or believing that it has probably been stolen.

As a sign of our dependence on the Internet, states have added the offense of **electronic fencing.** This crime occurs when one uses the Internet to sell property gained through unlawful means. This variation of receiving stolen property is demonstrated by Illinois Public Act No. 94-179 which provides:

> A person commits the offense of electronic fencing when he or she uses or accesses the Internet with the intent of selling property gained through unlawful means knowing that the property was stolen. A person who unknowingly purchases stolen property over the Internet does not violate this provision.

This crime is aimed at penalizing those who take possession of stolen merchandise. The court looks at the circumstances behind the transaction to decide the criminal intent of the person who obtained the goods.

Identity theft is a recent phenomenon that involves using the victim's personal information to obtain a financial advantage such as the misappropriation of a credit card or money from a bank account. Criminals have even assumed the unsuspecting person's identify to obtain a fraudulent driver's license or to apply for a job. In fact, the United States Postal Authority estimates that nearly 10 million people are the victims of identify theft at the cost of about $5 billion dollars.

In 1998, Congress enacted the **Identity Theft and Assumption Deterrence Act** by making it a crime to misuse the personal identifying information of another. A number of states have followed suit by passing similar legislation. For example, Wisconsin provides that: "Whoever intentionally uses or attempts to use any personal identifying information or personal identification documents of an individual to obtain credit, money, goods, services or anything else of value without the authorization or consent of the individual and by representing that he or she is that individual, is guilty of a felony."

It is not necessary to break into someone's home to steal a person's private information. For instance, some thieves engage in "shoulder surfing" which involves watching an unsuspecting victim punch in a password on an automated teller machine or by listening in on a conversation while the person discloses a credit card number over the telephone. Some criminals even engage in "dumpster diving" by looking through discarded trash for copies of checks, or credit card statements. A recent expansion of this crime has occurred with the Internet. People frequently receive spam e-mails requesting personal information under a false pretense and people unwittingly provide that data.[6]

Victims of identify theft need to take four protective steps as quickly as possible after learning of the problem. Contact each of the three major credit reporting agencies and place a fraud alert on your credit card report. Those agencies are as follows:

1. Equifax
    P.O. Box 749241
    Atlanta, GA 30374-0241

2. Experian
    P.O. Box 9532
    Allen, TX 75013

3. TransUnion
    Fraud Victim Assistance Division
    P.O. Box 6790
    Fullerton, CA 9283-6790

Once a fraud alert is issued, the credit agency will provide a free copy of your credit report if requested. Review that document carefully and check to see if any inquiries have been made about your credit history from companies that you have not contacted or accounts you did not open. If fraudulent information is discovered, request that it be removed.

The next step in the process of protecting and restoring your credit history is to notify credit card companies and banks in writing about the problem. If you discover an improper entry on an account, file a written dispute with the company and immediately close the account. Also, file a complaint with the police in the location where the identity theft took place and obtain a copy of the police report or report number. Finally, contact the Federal Trade Commission and file a complaint online at www.consumer.gov/idtheft.[7]

COMMONWEALTH OF PENNSYLVANIA V. MATTHEWS
632 A.2D 570 (PA. SUPER. 1993)

William Murphy discovered that his home had been burglarized. Among the items taken were the keys to his automobile. The car had also been stolen.

A few days later, Officer Bush spotted Matthews driving the stolen car. Bush asked Matthews to produce his driver's license and owner's registration. Matthews was unable to produce either. The officer then informed Matthews that the vehicle had been reported stolen.

At trial, Matthews testified that he had rented the car from Charles Lewis in exchange for two "rocks" of crack cocaine. Matthews testified that he needed the car in order to perform a plumbing job at the home of Edward Thorton, and, at the time he was stopped by Officer Bush, he was on his way to return the car to Charles Lewis.

It is undisputed that the vehicle showed no physical manifestations of theft, such as signs of forced entry, broken ignition system or obliterated vehicle identification number.

In order to obtain a conviction for receiving stolen property, the Commonwealth must prove beyond a reasonable doubt that the property was stolen, the defendant was in possession of the property and the defendant knew the property was stolen or had reason to believe the property was stolen.

A permissible inference of guilty knowledge may be drawn from the unexplained possession of recently stolen goods. The mere possession of stolen property, however, is insufficient to permit an inference of guilty knowledge. There must be additional evidence, circumstantial or direct, which would indicate that the defendant knew or had reason to know that the property was stolen.

In this case, we find that the evidence presented by the Commonwealth was insufficient to establish that Matthews knew or had reason to believe that the vehicle in question had been stolen. Matthews was cooperative with the police; the car showed no physical signs that it had been stolen; and, Matthews offered an explanation for his possession of the vehicle at trial which was consistent with his statement to police at the time of his arrest. Accordingly, we reverse the judgment of sentence for receiving stolen property.

Conspiracy

Labeled by the court more than 80 years ago as the "darling of the modern prosecutor's nursery," **conspiracy** is an all encompassing crime that allows the government to file charges against anyone who has participated in the planning or committing of a crime and to hold each liable for the actions of the other. For example, the following is Pennsylvania's definition of a conspiracy:

A person is guilty of conspiracy with another person or persons to commit a crime if with the intent of promoting or facilitating its commission he or she:

1. agrees with such other person or persons that they or one or more of them will engage in conduct which constitutes such crime or an attempt or solicitation to commit such crime; or

2 agrees to aid such other person or persons in the planning or commission of such crime or of an attempt or solicitation to commit such crime.

3. No person may be convicted of conspiracy to commit a crime unless an overt act in pursuance of such conspiracy is alleged and proved to have been done by him or by a person with whom he conspired.

4. It is a defense that the actor, after conspiring to commit a crime, thwarted the success of the conspiracy, under circumstances manifesting a complete and voluntary renunciation of his criminal intent.

Conspiracy is a separate crime from the actual substance offense that is to be committed. The agreement to commit the crime does not have to be in writing and can be informal. A mere tacit understanding is sufficient and each participant becomes the agent of the other for purposes of criminal responsibility.

Anthony Hankinson v. Wyoming
47 P.3d 623 (Wyo. 2002)

Anthony Hankinson was convicted of conspiracy to commit aggravated assault and battery. He submits this appeal contending that there is not sufficient evidence to sustain the conviction.

Hankinson and Lester Poague got drunk on July 25, 2000. They decided to go to the business owned by Daryl Coast and give him a beating, because of grievances against Coast. After drinking most of the day, Hankinson and

Poague went to Coast's place of business and broke in the door. Once inside, they looked for Coast because they wanted to "kick his ass." Because Coast was a much bigger man than Poague, Poague had armed himself with an axe handle. However, Coast was not at his business, so the two vandals scattered business papers and poured fingernail polish on a credit card machine. Hankinson subsequently was charged with burglary, attempted assault and conspiracy.

The central thrust of Hankinson's appeal is that he was too drunk to have formed the intent to conspire with Poague and, to the extent they discussed a "plan" to beat up Coast using the axe handle, it did not rise to the level of a conspiracy, as that word is viewed in the context of the criminal law.

In **Jasch v. State,** 563 P.2d 1327, 1332 (Wyo. 1977), we defined a conspiracy as an agreement between two or more persons to do an unlawful act. The crime of conspiracy is complete when an agreement has been made and overt acts are performed to further the unlawful design. A conspiracy is completed when an agreement has been made and some overt act is performed in furtherance of the conspiracy. A mere tacit understanding will suffice, and there need not be any written statement or even a speaking of words, which expressly communicates agreement.

If it is established that a conspiracy existed and that the Defendant was one of its members, then the acts and declarations of any other member of such conspiracy in or out of such Defendant's presence, done in furtherance of the objects of the conspiracy, and during its existence, may be considered as evidence against such Defendant.

Whether or not Hankinson was so drunk that he could not form the requisite intent, and whether Hankinson actually engaged in a conspiracy to commit the crime of assault and battery on Coast, were questions for the jury. There was evidence that suggested that Hankinson was relatively lucid on the night of the crime. During the crimes, Hankinson had to make decisions and take actions that required some presence of mind, even if those actions were only the basest form of stupidity. In light of this evidence, the jury could reasonably have inferred that Hankinson acted with specific intent, even though there was a great deal of evidence to indicate that Hankinson was drunk. Likewise, though the agreement that Poague and Hankinson made to assault Coast was crude and ill conceived, the jury could reasonably have inferred that a conspiracy was present. Hankinson's argument focuses on his own view of the facts, rather than that view which might have been taken by reasonable jurors. The Judgment of the district court is affirmed.

WHITE COLLAR CRIME

From Martha Stewart to Enron, the news is replete with stories about corporate wrongdoing, improper accounting practices, and stock manipulation. Illegal actions perpetuated in a business setting are generally classified as **white-collar crimes**. It has been estimated that the dollar loss from this offense is larger than all other crimes put together. In fact, the figure has been placed at a staggering $400 billion dollars a year and the crime is on the rise. While there is no one exact definition for this offense, the Federal Bureau of Investigation has defined white collar crime as "...those illegal acts which are characterized by deceit, concealment, or violation of trust and which are not dependent upon the application or threat of physical force or violence." This catch-all phrase includes computer fraud, health care fraud, securities fraud and insider trading, counterfeiting, theft of trade secrets, embezzlement, and tax evasion. The problem is so pervasive that the FBI estimates that white-collar crime accounts for 4% of all reported crime with the majority of these offenses being for fraud, counterfeiting, and forgery. The National White Collar Crime Center has determined that one in every three American households has been victimized by white-collar crimes. While individuals are the largest group of victims, businesses, financial institutions, governments, religious organizations, and other public entities have all been victimized.

Because of the difficulty and expense in uncovering white-collar crime, as well as the public's low tolerance for corporate wrongdoing, the state and federal governments have become more aggressive in prosecuting these cases. Some legislative bodies have even increased the penalty for white collar crime by imposing mandatory jail time. California is an example of a state that now imposes a minimum jail sentence for anyone convicted of economic or white collar crime. The rationale for this mandate is discussed in **People v. Alejandro.**

PEOPLE V. ALEJANDRO
28 CAL. 4TH 481 (CAL. 2002)

On April 18, 1997, a complaint was filed charging defendant with the theft of a trade secret. It was further alleged that the loss exceeded $2.5 million. Defendant pleaded no contest to the theft charge, a charge based upon evidence that he had printed out confidential design specifications for certain computer chips on the last day of his employment as an electrical engineer at Digital Equipment Corporation. Defendant objected to the potential application of **Section 1203.044** to his sentence.

Defendant stands convicted of theft, specifically a violation of **Section 499c**, which provides: "Every person is guilty of theft who, with in-

tent to deprive or withhold the control of a trade secret from its owner, or with an intent to appropriate a trade secret to his or her own use or to the use of another, does any of the following: steals, takes, carries away, or uses without authorization, a trade secret."

The trial court determined that **Section 1203.044** applies to such a theft. This statute, entitled The Economic Crime Law, requires that a defendant who is convicted of certain theft offenses and is granted probation shall be sentenced to at least 90 days in the county jail as a condition of probation.

The Legislature declared in enacting **Section 1203.044:** "Major economic or white collar crime is an increasing threat to California's economy and the well-being of its citizens. The Legislature intends to deter that crime by ensuring that every offender, without exception, serves at least some time in jail. White collar criminals granted probation too often complete their probation without having compensated their victims or society. Probation accompanied by a restitution order is often ineffective because county financial officers are often unaware of the income and assets enjoyed by white collar offenders. Thus, it is the Legislature's intent that the financial reporting requirements of this act be utilized to achieve satisfactory disclosure to permit an appropriate restitution order. White collar criminal investigation and prosecutions are unusually expensive. These high costs sometimes discourage vigorous enforcement of white collar crime laws by local agencies. Thus, it is necessary to require white collar offenders to assist in funding this enforcement activity."

We observe that the term "white collar crime" is a relatively broad one and is not limited to losses involving cash or cash equivalents. It generally is defined as "a nonviolent crime usually involving cheating or dishonesty in commercial matters. Examples include fraud, embezzlement, bribery, and insider trading." **Black's Law Dict. (7th ed.1999).** The Legislature has applied the term "white collar crime" to fraud and embezzlement in **Section 186.11,** a statute that provides for enhanced prison terms for recidivists committing these offenses when the offense involves a pattern of "taking more than one hundred thousand dollars." Like the crime of theft, fraud and embezzlement are not limited to the unlawful acquisition of cash or cash equivalents. Indeed, frequently fraud and embezzlement simply are methods by which a charged theft is accomplished.

Because the crime of theft includes a wide range of property and the term "white collar crime" has a broad meaning, we find it improbable that the Legislature intended to address only the theft of cash or cash equivalents in adopting The Economic Crime Act. It is far more reasonable to conclude that the Legislature intended the provision to apply to all thefts of property of a particular value. Any other interpretation would permit many white collar thieves to continue to receive light probationary sentences and to evade strict restitution requirements. From the usual meaning of the terms used in **Section 1202.044,** the purpose of the enactment, and the Legislature's parallel use of the same terms in other statutes, one must conclude that **Section 1203.044** is not limited to thefts of cash or cash equivalents.

We find it clear from the words employed in **Section 1203.044** and the declaration of intent accompanying its enactment, that **Section 1203.044** does not apply solely to thefts of cash or cash equivalents, but rather that it addresses thefts of property, including trade secrets, exceeding specified values.

SECTION 4.2
DEFENSES TO A CRIME

A criminal act may be considered justified or excusable under certain limited circumstances. Defenses in this category include **self-defense** and actions in defense of others. The law recognizes the right of a person unlawfully attacked to use reasonable force in self-defense. However, only a person who reasonably believes there is imminent danger of bodily harm can use a reasonable amount of force under the circumstances.

Some defenses to a crime rest on the defendant's assertion that he or she lacked criminal responsibility for the criminal act. As a general rule, **intoxication** is not a defense unless it negates a specific mental state, such as specific intent to kill, which is required to prove the crime. Some defendants invoke the defense of **insanity** as demonstrating lack of criminal responsibility. Insanity rests on the theory that people who suffer from a mental disease or defect should not be convicted if they fail to appreciate that what they are doing is wrong or if they do not know the difference between right and wrong. The insanity defense only applies if the accused was insane at the time of the crime. Insanity during or after the trial does not affect criminal liability.

In many states, there are at least four possible verdicts: guilty; not guilty; no contest; and not guilty by reason of insanity. **Not guilty by reason of insanity** results in the automatic commitment to a mental institution. Recently, states have created another verdict: **guilty but mentally ill**. This option arose from the shooting of President Reagan by John Hinkley. The assailant shot the President in order to impress actress Jodie Foster, with whom he became infatuated after watching the movie *Taxi Driver*. Pennsylvania has adopted the verdict of guilty but mentally ill, which means that a jury that returns with such a finding is saying that the defendant has criminal responsibility for his actions, but it is acknowledged that the defendant suffers from a mental problem.

The following explanation of the insanity defense was offered in **Commonwealth v. Bowers**:

> The verdict of not guilty by reason of legal insanity labels a defendant as a sick person rather than a bad person. It signifies that in the eyes of the law that person, because of mental abnormality at the time of the crime, does not deserve to be blamed and treated as a criminal for what he did.

> The verdict of guilty but mentally ill labels a defendant as both bad and sick. It means that in the law's eyes that person at the time of the crime was not so mentally abnormal as to be relieved from blame and criminal punishment for what he did, but that he was abnormal enough to make a prime candidate for special therapeutic treatment.

Defendants found guilty but mentally ill will be sent to a hospital or mental institution for treatment and will then be transferred to prison after they have recovered.

Entrapment is also a defense to an arrest. This defense is designed to deter impermissible police conduct that entices a person to commit a crime that he or she had no previous inclination to perpetrate. The defense, however, is not available to a party who has no hesitation in committing the crime and the police merely presented the opportunity to act on the impulse. The test for determining entrapment is whether the actions of the police officer are likely to induce a normal law-abiding citizen to commit the crime. As the court noted in **Department of Alcoholic Beverage Control v. Alcoholic Beverage Control Appeals Board of California,** two guiding principles determine whether the defense of entrapment exists. The first deals with the actions of the law enforcement agent and whether those actions would generate in a normal law-abiding citizen a motive to commit the crime. The second inquiry is whether the conduct of the police would make the commission of the crime unusually attractive.

DEPARTMENT OF ALCOHOLIC BEVERAGE CONTROL v. ALCOHOLIC BEVERAGE CONTROL APPEALS BOARD OF CALIFORNIA
122 CAP. RPTR. 2D 854 (CT. APP. CAL. 2002)

Dream Girls serves food and beverages and provides adult entertainment. Detective Nelson did an undercover inspection of Dream Girls' premises. He sat at a table, ordered a beer and watched dancer Mary Gast perform two dances on stage. After Gast finished on stage, Detective Nelson approached her as she sat at the bar and requested that she perform a couch dance for him. Gast escorted Detective Nelson to a couch and danced for him.

After finishing the first couch dance, Gast inquired if Detective Nelson wanted another dance. He responded by asking if there would be "more skin involved," but did not offer to pay Gast any additional money for complying with his request. Gast performed a second couch dance, during which she exposed her breasts and buttocks to Detective Nelson.

The relevant issue presented is whether Detective Nelson's question about whether there would be "more skin" amounted to entrapment as a matter of law.

The test for determining entrapment is whether the acts of the law enforcement agent are "likely to induce a normally law-abiding person to commit the offense." Although this test focuses primarily on the conduct of the law enforcement agent, it also requires consideration of the effect that the conduct would have on a normally law-abiding person under the circumstances presented. Thus, for example, "the transactions preceding the offense, the suspect's response to the inducements of the officer, the gravity of the crime, and the difficulty of detecting instances of its commission" are relevant to a determination of whether the officer's conduct constituted entrapment. However, the test is objective rather than subjective and thus the suspect's character, predisposition to commit the offense and subjective intent in committing the crime are irrelevant.

Dream Girls argues that Detective Nelson's conduct amounted to entrapment because Gast did not have a preexisting intent to violate the regulation, but engaged in the illegal dance only at his behest. The Board concluded that although the officer's request to see "more skin" was not "overbearing" the conduct constituted entrapment because it was an affirmative act the officer knew was likely to induce Gast to commit a violation.

To the extent that Dream Girls and the Board rely on the notion that Gast did not harbor a preexisting criminal intent but instead merely responded to Detective Nelson's request, this reliance is misplaced, for several reasons. First, such an analysis is based on a subjective standard that focuses on the suspect's state of mind, rather than an objective standard that focuses primarily on the conduct of the officer, to de-termine the issue of entrapment. Second, even if the officer was aware that Gast had a financial motivation to commit the violation, this does not render his request overbearing or make the request anything more than the mere opportunity for Gast to act on her financial motivation by committing the regulatory violation.

For purposes of determining the issue of entrapment, Detective Nelson's conduct is indistinguishable from the conduct of officers involved in undercover drug operation, in which an officer approaches a possible drug source on the street and offers to buy drugs. Such a request has been uniformly held to be a permissible police stratagem absent additional overbearing conduct or pressure by the officer.

Detective Nelson's conduct was not of such a nature that it was "likely to induce a normally law-abiding person to commit the offense. The Board erred in concluding that Detective Nelson's conduct amounted to entrapment. Accordingly, we remand the matter for further proceedings.

SECTION 4.3
POLICE INVESTIGATION

Most crimes require the police to conduct an investigation in order to ascertain the identity of the perpetrator. This process requires the police to examine the crime scene, and to question witnesses.

While justice demands that the culprit be apprehended, the government must not violate the constitutional rights of the suspect in their zest to solve the crime. Over the years, the police have developed a number of tools and procedures to help identify the criminal. Suspects will be questioned and search warrants will be issued. Several of these police methods are discussed in the following sections.

SECTION 4.4
POLICE SKETCH

During the initial meeting with the victim or witnesses, the identity of the assailant is a focal point of the investigation. When possible, a sketch of the assailant is made by a police artist or detective through the use of an identification kit or computer.

The following sketch is an example of a drawing made by the use of a kit. The unit consists of hundreds of plastic overlays that show different parts and shapes of the face.

The artist puts the sketch together with the assistance of the witness and is able to quickly change the shape of the nose, eyes, or mouth to create an accurate representation of the accused.

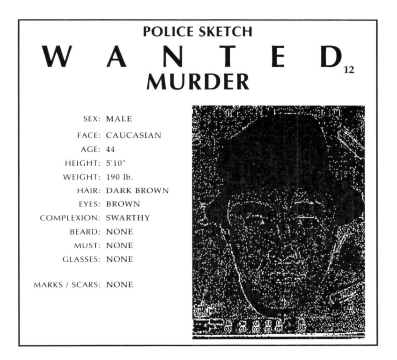

POLICE SKETCH
W A N T E D$_{12}$
MURDER

SEX: MALE
FACE: CAUCASIAN
AGE: 44
HEIGHT: 5'10"
WEIGHT: 190 lb.
HAIR: DARK BROWN
EYES: BROWN
COMPLEXION: SWARTHY
BEARD: NONE
MUST: NONE
GLASSES: NONE

MARKS / SCARS: NONE

**SECTION 4.5
THE POLYGRAPH**

The police will frequently ask suspects and complainants to submit to a **polygraph** or "lie detector" examination. No one can be forced to take the test, and the results are generally not admissible in court since the polygraph is subject to error.

POLYGRAPH EXAMINATION REPORT

The machine itself fits into a small case and consists of devices to measure skin temperature, blood pressure, and respiration. The person to be tested is told of the questions that will be asked in advance of the examination. The test is then administered with the questions being repeated and the responses recorded on graph paper.

The scientific community remains divided over the accuracy of the lie detector. The advocates of the test praise the machine's ability to detect deception with an accuracy rate of at least 85%. The critics of the polygraph place the accuracy of the test at less than 50%. For the most part, state and federal courts continue to question the validity of the polygraph, and the results of the test are not admitted into court as accurate scientific evidence.

In **United States v. Scheffer,** the Supreme Court was asked to decide whether an individual who had passed a polygraph examination concerning his use of drugs but had tested positive on his urine analysis could use the test results of the lie detector in the defense of his case. In excluding the polygraph evidence, the Court reconfirmed the inadmissibility of the test results because of the lack of uniform scientific opinion concerning the validity of the test.

UNITED STATES OF AMERICA V. EDWARD SCHEFFER
118 S. CT. 1261 (1999)

In March 1992, Edward Scheffer volunteered to work as an informant on drug investigations for the Air Force Office of Special Investigations (OSI). In early April, one of the OSI agents supervising respondent requested that he submit to a urine test. Shortly after providing the urine sample, but before the results of the test were known, respondent agreed to take a polygraph test administered by an OSI examiner. In the opinion of the examiner, the test "indicated no deception" when respondent denied using drugs since joining the Air Force.

On April 30, Scheffer was absent without leave until May 13, when an Iowa State patrolman arrested him following a routine traffic stop and held him for return to the base. OSI agents later learned that respondent's urinalysis revealed the presence of methamphetamine.

Scheffer was tried by general court-martial on charges of using methamphetamine.

Scheffer sought to introduce the polygraph evidence in support of his testimony that he did not knowingly use drugs. The military judge denied the motion, relying on **Military Rule of Evidence 707**, which provides, in relevant part:

> (a) Notwithstanding any other provision of law, the results of a polygraph examination, the opinion of a polygraph examiner, or any reference to an offer to take, failure to take, or taking of a polygraph examination, shall not be admitted into evidence.

A defendant's right to present relevant evidence is not unlimited, but rather is subject to reasonable restrictions. A defendant's interest in presenting such evidence may thus bow to accommodate other legitimate interests in the criminal trial process.

Rule 707 serves several legitimate interests in the criminal trial process. These interests include ensuring that only reliable evidence is introduced at trial, preserving the jury's role in determining credibility, and avoiding litigation that is collateral to the primary purpose of the trial.

The contentions of Scheffer notwithstanding, there is simply no consensus that polygraph evidence is reliable. To this day, the scientific community remains extremely polarized about the reliability of polygraph techniques. Some studies have concluded that polygraph tests overall are accurate and reliable. See, e.g., S. Abrams, *The Complete Polygraph Handbook* 190-191 (1968) (reporting the overall accuracy rate from laboratory studies involving the common "control question technique" polygraph to be "in the range of 87 percent"). Others have found that polygraph tests assess truthfulness significantly less accurately and that scientific field studies suggest the accuracy rate of the "control question technique" polygraph is "little better than could be obtained by the toss of a coin," that is, 50 percent. See Iacono & Lykken, *The Scientific Status of Research on Polygraph Techniques: The Case Against Polygraph Tests,* in 1 Modern Scientific Evidence, supra, § 14-5.3, p. 629.

The approach taken by the President in adopting **Rule 707**–excluding polygraph evidence in all military trials–is a rational and proportional means of advancing the legitimate interest in barring unreliable evidence. Although the degree of reliability of polygraph evidence may depend upon a variety of identifiable factors, there is simply no way to know in a particular case whether a polygraph examiner's conclusion is accurate, because certain doubts and uncertainties plague even the best polygraph exams. Individual jurisdictions therefore may reasonably reach differing conclusions as to whether polygraph evidence should be admitted. We cannot say, then, that presented with such widespread uncertainty, the President acted arbitrarily or disproportionately in promulgating a rule excluding all polygraph evidence.

For the foregoing reasons, Military Rule of Evidence 707 does not unconstitutionally abridge the right to present a defense. The judgment of the Court of Appeals is reversed.

SECTION 4.6
QUESTIONING
OF A SUSPECT

Nearly everyone has seen a movie or television show in which a police officer reads a suspect his rights as the person is being handcuffed. Is this something that has been added to the film for drama or is a law enforcement agent really mandated to tell the suspect that he has the right to remain silent? **Custodial interrogation** by the police is considered inherently coercive so the Supreme Court has mandated specific procedures to be followed in obtaining statements. More specifically, the Fifth Amendment provides that no person may be compelled to be a witness against himself. This fundamental guarantee is the basic cornerstone for the **Miranda Warnings.** If a person is the subject of custodial interrogation, the police must inform the suspect that he or she has the right to remain silent, that anything said can and will be used against the individual in court, and the accused has the right to have a lawyer present during the questioning. If the accused cannot afford counsel, the government will supply an attorney for free.

Custodial interrogation has been defined as "questioning initiated by law enforcement officers after a person has been taken into custody or otherwise deprived of his or her freedom of action in any significant way." Custody is much broader than being incarcerated for purposes of the Miranda Warnings. A suspect must be told of his right to remain silent if his freedom of movement or liberty is significantly restricted. In practical terms, the issue is whether the suspect is free to walk away from the interrogation. If not, the suspect must be read his rights. For example, a suspect is considered in custody while in the back of a police car or while in bed and surrounded by the police. Interrogation, on the other hand, involves more than merely asking the suspect questions about routine information such as the person's name and address. The questions must focus on the crime to trigger the reading of the warnings.

How broad is the Fifth Amendment right against self-incrimination? The courts have ruled that this guarantee does not protect an individual from being fingerprinted or photographed, since these procedures are not testimony.

COMMONWEALTH OF PENNSYLVANIA V. GRAHAM
703 A.2D 510 (PA. SUPER. 1997)

In this appeal we decide whether a provision of the Motor Vehicle Code is constitutional that permits the Commonwealth to introduce into evidence the fact that a defendant refused to be tested for alcohol or drugs where the defendant is charged with driving under the influence.

The fatal automobile accident occurred on August 2, 1994. On that evening, appellant was driving northbound on Interstate 95, weaving back and forth between lanes at an estimated speed of seventy miles per hour. As appellant made one of his abrupt lane changes, his vehicle collided with another vehicle. Several persons were seriously injured, and one person was killed.

After the accident, Sergeant Stieber noticed that appellant was agitated, had difficulty standing and had a strong odor of alcohol on his breath.

Lieutenant Nestel administered the "one leg stand" and the "walk and turn" tests, neither of which appellant could successfully complete.

Appellant was then transported to police headquarters where Officer Waerig told appellant that the rights provided by **Miranda v. Arizona, 384 U.S. 436, 86 S.Ct. 1602, (1966),** do not apply to chemical testing, and if the accused refuses to consent, his driver's license will be suspended for one year. Appellant agreed to submit to the breathalyzer test.

The results of the breathalyzer test revealed that the alcohol level of appellant's blood was within the legal limit. An analysis of appellant's blood revealed the presence of cocaine metabolite, marijuana and marijuana metabolite.

Appellant argues that the results of his blood test should not have been admitted at trial. He maintains that his consent to the blood test was invalid because the officer coerced him to incriminate himself in violation of his Fifth Amendment rights. He asserts that he consented to the test only because he was afraid of the inferences the fact finders would draw if they learned he refused to take the blood test. He contends that such consent deprived him of his right not to incriminate himself.

The United States Supreme Court has made it clear that a defendant does not have a constitutional right to refuse blood tests. **Schmerber v. California, 384 U.S. 757, 86 S.Ct. 1826, 16 L.Ed.2d 908 (1966).** While blood test evidence may be "an incriminating product of compulsion," such evidence in no way implicates an accused's *testimonial* capacities and therefore, its admission does not offend the privilege against self incrimination embodied in the Fifth Amendment. The Court noted that the Fifth Amendment privilege relates to testimony or communication from an accused. The privilege does not prevent the police from using the accused's body or blood as physical evidence when it is material.

Because it is clear that appellant had no constitutional right to refuse the blood test, the Motor Vehicle Code does not burden appellant's constitutional rights by allowing evidence of his refusal to consent to be admitted at trial. As such, a defendant's consent to a blood test after being informed that his refusal could be admitted at trial, is valid and not coerced.

SECTION 4.7
COMMONWEALTH
v. CHRISTOPHER

PROBLEM FOUR

PARK, BROWN & SMITH, P.C.
ATTORNEYS AT LAW
M E M O R N D U M

To: All Law Clerks

From: Peter Smith, Esquire

Re: Commonwealth v. Peter Christopher
In Court Identification

Kathy Roberts often stayed after school to workout. The wrestling team was usually there practicing but they were away at a match on the evening in question.

Kathy was so busy exercising that she didn't notice the presence of a stranger—at least not until it was too late. Kathy first realized that she wasn't alone when she looked up and saw what appeared to be a shark staring back at her. When she looked again, she realized it was a man with a tattoo of a shark on his left shoulder. The strange thing was that he was wearing a ski mask. Before she had time to realize what was happening, she was assaulted and her pocketbook was stolen.

Afterward, Kathy was extremely troubled by the incident. She could not stop thinking about the tattoo, since she knew she had seen the image before. To her shock and amazement, Kathy soon realized that she knew her assailant. It was her next door neighbor, Peter Christopher. He had a tattoo of a shark on his shoulder, and he intensely disliked the family.

Ms. Roberts reported her suspicions to the police and their investigation lead to the arrest of Peter Christopher on a variety of criminal charges. During the second day of trial, the District Attorney requested Peter Christopher to stand before the jury and remove his shirt so the panel could ascertain whether the defendant had a tattoo of a shark on his shoulder. The defense vigorously objected to this in-court identification, claiming that it would violate Christopher's Fifth Amendment rights against self-incrimination. The issue before the court concerns these identifying marks on the defendant's shoulder. The Fifth Amendment guarantees that no person shall be compelled to testify against himself. According to **Morgan v. State**, can the District Attorney compel Christopher to remove his shirt to show the jury his shoulder? Why would this type of in-court identification violate (or not violate) the Constitution?

GLENMORE MORGAN v. STATE OF MARYLAND
558 A.2D 1226 (MD. APP. 1989)

We are called upon to decide whether requiring a defendant to don an article of clothing in the courtroom in front of the jury so that the jury may see if the article of clothing fits violates his privilege against self-incrimination under the 5th Amendment.

In the case before us, Glenmore Morgan, defendant, was charged with possession of cocaine with intent to distribute, possession of cocaine and possession of controlled paraphernalia. During a jury trial, the court required the defendant to put on a jacket seized by officers of the Montgomery County Police Department pursuant to a search warrant.

At the time the search warrant was executed, defendant and two other men were present in the living room of the residence. After the two other men retrieved their coats, Morgan queried, "What about my jacket?" When asked by the police if a jacket located on the loveseat in the living room was his, Morgan hesitated be-

fore responding, "No." Police search of the jacket revealed a small quantity of cocaine, a beeper, keys to the residence and a key to a safe in the kitchen. During a search of the safe, the police discovered bottles of inositol powder, several baggies, razor blades, measuring spoons, a box containing a grinder, and twenty-three grams of cocaine. Morgan was convicted on all charges.

The Fifth Amendment of the United States Constitution provides: "No person... shall be compelled in any criminal case to be a witness against himself." Defendant contends that the court's order requiring him to put on the jacket in front of the jury violated his constitutional right against compelled self-incrimination.

The Court of Appeals in **Andrews v. State** upheld a trial court order restraining Andrews from shaving his head or facial hair until the conclusion of this trial. Purportedly, he had changed his appearance immediately after the crime in question by shaving his head and beard. The trial court order was designed to prevent the defendant from defeating "legitimate avenues of identification" by disguising his appearance.

In **Schmerber v. California, 384 U.S. 757 (1966),** the Supreme Court stated that the privilege against compelled self-incrimination "protects an accused only from being compelled to testify against himself or otherwise provide the State with evidence of a testimonial or communicative nature…" Requiring a defendant to put on an article of clothing, simply does not constitute an act compelling a testimonial or communicative response. The fact that an article of clothing fits may give rise to a inference of ownership, which under the facts of any given case could be incrimination, is not a communicative response from the defendant.

By granting the prosecutor's request to order the defendant to don the coat in the presence of the jury, the trial court compelled the defendant to disclose nothing of his personal knowledge. This is not communication within the meaning of the Fifth Amendment. Moreover, it is of no consequence that the defendant declined to take the stand to testify on his own behalf; his physical display simply does not constitute "testimony."

In this case, the trial court order requiring defendant to don a coat, which admittedly contained incriminatory evidence, to determine whether it fit him did not constitute a compulsion to elicit communicative or testimonial evidence from the defendant.

Judgment affirmed.

ANSWER SHEET
PROBLEM FOUR

Name   **Please Print Clearly**

1. According to **Morgan v. State,** can the District Attorney compel Christopher to remove his shirt to show the jury his tattoo? Explain your answer.

2. Why would this type of in court identification violate or not violate Christopher's constitutional rights? Explain your answer.

_____

_____

_____

_____

_____

_____

_____

_____

_____

_____

_____

_____

_____

_____

_____

_____

_____

_____

_____

_____

_____

SECTION 4.8
SEARCH AND SEIZURE

Roy Caballes' car was stopped by the police for a traffic violation. A drug-detecting dog was then walked around the vehicle while another officer wrote the traffic ticket. The canine soon became agitated alerting the police to the presence of drugs. A search of the car's trunk yielded several hundred pounds of marijuana. Is there anything wrong with allowing a police dog to randomly walk around a person's car? The court found that the canine sniff was an illegal search and seizure. What exactly is a search and seizure?

The **Fourth Amendment** prohibits unlawful **search and seizure** and requires that all warrants be issued upon probable cause. This protection against overzealous police conduct usually requires a police officer to appear before a judge to establish probable cause for the issuance of a search warrant. Probable cause, however, is not defined in the Constitution. Over the years, the courts have determined probable cause to exist when the information on which the warrant is based is such that a reasonable person would believe that what is being sought will be found in the location to be examined. The judge, however, may consider the opinion of an experienced law enforcement officer in making the probable cause determination for a search warrant. An affidavit based on mere suspicion, or stating a conclusion with no supporting facts, however, is insufficient. If the court is satisfied that sufficient evidence exists to issue a warrant, that document must be specific as to the location and evidence that is the subject of the search warrant.

The general test to determine whether a warrant is needed by the police to conduct a lawful search and seizure is to ascertain whether the person had a reasonable expectation of privacy. If the individual enjoyed a reasonable expectation of privacy, a warrant must be obtained before the search can be undertaken. For example, a person has an expectation of privacy while at home, but the police would not need a warrant to seize a gun that a person is brandishing while walking down the street.

The police may also seize property that has been discarded or abandoned by a person since there is no longer an expectation of privacy.

MISSOURI V. CORDELL MOSBY
94 S. W. 3D 410 (MISSOURI CT. APP. 2003)

On September 2, 2001, Officer C. Barbosa was on patrol and observed the defendant while the defendant was sitting on the steps in front of a dwelling at 500 E. Armour. Officer Barbosa testified that there was a "No Trespassing" sign posted on the dwelling. Officer Barbosa exited his vehicle and approached the defendant who then attempted to walk away. The officer observed the defendant drop a beige rock-like substance on the ground between two cars. The beige rock-like substance was recovered. It was later field tested with positive results for cocaine.

The State's claim that Mosby lacked standing to challenge the seizure of the cocaine and the handgun because he did not have any legitimate expectation of privacy with regard to those items. In order for the defendant's Fourth Amendment rights to be violated or for the defendant to have standing to assert a violation of those rights, the defendant must have a legitimate expectation of privacy in the place or thing searched. To determine whether a criminal defendant has a legitimate expectation of privacy in the place or thing searched, the defendant must have an actual subjective expectation of privacy in the place or thing searched and this expectation must be reasonable or legitimate.

The Fourth Amendment, in protecting against unreasonable searches and seizures, do not give the courts general supervision over police practices and conduct. Evidence is excludable only if it has been obtained through an unreasonable search and seizure. In order to have standing to complain, a defendant must have a reasonable expectation of privacy related to that property *at the time of the allegedly improper search and seizure.*

Mosby has never asserted that he had any legitimate expectation of privacy in the public street where the clear plastic bag was located or in the stairwell where the white plastic bag was located. Indeed, there is no reasonable expectation of privacy subject to Fourth Amendment protection where the public at large is welcome.

Law enforcement officers do not violate the Fourth Amendment by merely approaching a person on the street and asking questions. Consequently, even when law enforcement officers have no basis for suspecting a particular individual, they may ask to see the person's identification and request consent to search, so long as they do not convey that compliance with those requests is required. Nothing in the record supports a finding that the officer exceeded these bounds.

We next turn to whether the record could support a finding that Mosby had a legitimate and reasonable expectation of privacy related to the two bags and their contents at the time he was seized. Officer Barbosa saw Mosby drop that bag on the ground between two cars while Mosby was attempting to walk away from the officer.

When property is abandoned, the constitutional protections against unreasonable search and seizure no longer apply, because those protections are designed to protect one's person and dwelling. Therefore, a person has no standing to complain of the search or seizure of property that he has voluntarily discarded, left behind, or otherwise relinquished his interest so that he no longer retains a reasonable expectation of privacy with regard to it at the time of the search or seizure. Where, as here, an individual drops, throws, or otherwise discards contra-band while being followed or pursued by a police officer, the contraband is deemed to have been abandoned, and Fourth Amendment protections no longer apply.

Police generally need to obtain a **search warrant** when there is a reasonable expectation of privacy. There are, however, a number of exceptions to this rule. The police are not required to obtain a search warrant in the following situations:

1. **Plain View:** If the subject of the search is readily observable, in other words, in plain view, there is no reasonable expectation of privacy. For instance, if marijuana is growing in one's backyard and is visible from the sidewalk, the police do not need a search warrant to seize the plants. An improper search, however, will occur if the police peer into a basement window, and with the aid of a flashlight uncover contraband, since the homeowner would have a reasonable expectation of privacy against this type of intrusion.

2. **Emergency:** If the time delay in obtaining the warrant will defeat the ends of justice, the police can engage in the search without the warrant. Car searches generally fall within this exception since vehicles are mobile and can avoid the police by merely being driven away. The police, however, must still have probable cause for the search. If the vehicle is towed to the police station and impounded, a search warrant will have to be obtained in order to conduct a lawful search since the vehicle is no longer mobile. The emergency situation would no longer be present, since the car would be in the possession of the authorities.

3. **Search Incident to an Arrest:** Police officers can search a defendant and the area within that person's immediate reach for weapons and other contraband. This exception was established to protect the public from possible harm.

4. **Hot Pursuit:** If the police are pursuing a suspect who is fleeing the scene of a crime, they may make a reasonable search of the area looking for the suspect.

5. **Consent:** The police are not required to obtain a search warrant when a suspect consents to a search. The consent, however, must be freely and voluntarily given, and not be coerced by law enforcement officials. Certain third parties may also consent to a search.

For instance, parents may allow the police to search a child's room, and a school principal is authorized to allow the police to search student lockers at the educational institution. While a roommate may allow the police to search the common areas in an apartment, a landlord does not have the authority to allow the police to search the leased premises without a search warrant.

6. **Search Incident to a General Police Measure:** Border and custom searches are allowed to prevent the entry of illegal aliens and contraband. Custom agents can check everyone's luggage regardless of the existence of probable cause. Other examples include searches of passengers at the airport, and individuals can be required to pass through a metal detector before being allowed to enter a courtroom. Both of these measures are designed to protect the safety of the public. The police, however, may not selectively discriminate against a particular racial group under the auspices of conducting a search incident to a general police measure. For example, the police may not stop young African-American males on the New Jersey Turnpike merely because the individual may match a racial profile.

7. **Stop and Frisk:** Police officers may conduct "pat-down" searches when there is probable cause to believe that a crime is about to occur and the suspect may possess a weapon. If the police find contraband during the "pat-down" that is instantly recognizable by feel, it may be seized without a warrant. This seizure is called **plain feel**. This exception has the potential for abuse, so courts generally require that the officers present very specific facts that lead to a conclusion of probable cause.

STATE V. THOMAS HOSKINS
2002 WL 1453811 (OHIO APP. 2002)

Officer Martin and his partner witnessed a vehicle driving with its passenger door wide open. The officers stopped the vehicle for possible violations of ordinances pertaining to driving in traffic with an open door and reckless driving.

Because of the high incident of drug and gun activity in the vicinity in conjunction with the passenger door being open, both officers approached the vehicle. Officer Martin, trained to watch the occupant's hands for signs of danger, noticed Hoskins' right hand placed down the front of his pants. Concerned Hoskins was concealing or reaching for a gun, Officer Martin ordered Hoskins out of the car, handcuffed him, and conducted a pat down search for the presence of weapons.

During the pat down, Officer Martin felt an object he immediately identified as crack cocaine in the area of Hoskins' right thigh near the area where his hand had been. Officer Martin retrieved the object, which was determined to be a baggie of crack cocaine.

Hoskins argues the trial court erred by denying his motion to suppress the crack cocaine found on his person following the traffic stop. We disagree.

Our first query is whether the police officers justifiably stopped the vehicle in which Hoskins rode. Under **Terry v. Ohio**, a police officer may make a brief, investigatory stop of an individual without probable cause if the officer reasonably suspects the individual is, or has been, involved in criminal activity. This standard for evaluating the officer's conduct is objective: would the facts available at the moment of seizure or search warrant a man of reasonable caution in the belief that the action was appropriate?

As Hoskins argues, the police lacked a reasonable suspicion to stop him. Nevertheless, reasonable suspicion of criminal activity sufficient to stop the vehicle in which he was riding existed because of the observed violations of Cleveland ordinances.

In determining the propriety of the Terry search, the question is whether the officer had a reasonable, objective basis for frisking the defendant after ordering him out of the car.

When Officer Martin approached the vehicle he noticed Hoskins' right hand placed down the front of his pants in a posture leading him to believe Hoskins was hiding or retrieving a weapon. Further, this incident occurred in an area Officer Martin recognized as a high drug area where shootings have occurred. Also, in Officer Martin's experience, driving with an open car door is indicative of an attempt to dispose of drugs or weapons. Based upon the totality of these circumstances, we conclude Officer Martin had a reasonable, objective basis for conducting a Terry search of Hoskins.

In **Minnesota v. Dickerson**, the United States Supreme Court adopted the "plain feel" doctrine. In doing so, the Supreme Court stated: "If a police officer lawfully pats down a suspect's outer clothing and feels an object whose contour or mass makes its identity immediately apparent, there has been no invasion of the suspect's privacy beyond that already authorized by the officer's search for weapons."

Here, the record establishes that Officer Martin, during the course of a lawful Terry search, discovered what he immediately determined to be crack cocaine. Because the contraband was in "plain feel," Officer Martin did not violate Hoskins' constitutional right to be free from unreasonable searches. The crack cocaine discovered on Hoskins' person was admissible into evidence.

Section 4.9
The Progress of a
State Criminal Case[8]

1. **The Obligations of Crime Victims and Witnesses**: A victim or witness to a crime is expected to report the crime to the police, and to testify in court about what happened. The police will take a statement and file a *criminal* complaint, which is a statement of facts about the crime and later becomes the basis of the formal charges against the accused. After the complaint is drafted, a judge will issue a warrant for the offender's arrest or a summons commanding the accused to appear for a preliminary hearing.

STATE CRIMINAL PROCEDURE

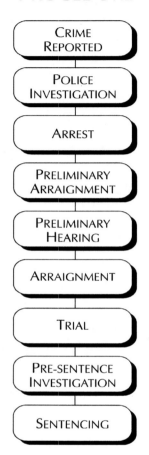

CRIME REPORTED

POLICE INVESTIGATION

ARREST

PRELIMINARY ARRAIGNMENT

PRELIMINARY HEARING

ARRAIGNMENT

TRIAL

PRE-SENTENCE INVESTIGATION

SENTENCING

2. **Preliminary Arraignment**. In cases where the offender is arrested he or she, now called the *defendant*, appears within hours for a preliminary arraignment, which is held before the district justice in the district where the offense occurred or at the Roundhouse if the crime occurred in Philadelphia. It is not necessary that a victim appear for the preliminary arraignment.

One of the purposes of this hearing is to set *bail*. Bail is a means of insuring that the defendant will continue to appear at scheduled court appearances. In setting bail, the judge considers such factors as the seriousness of the crime, the circumstances of the defendant, his age, employment status, etc., and whether the accused is likely to flee if released. Bail may take several forms, but it usually involves the use of money or property of the defendant or someone on his behalf along with the promise of the defendant to remain available. If the defendant fails to appear for a scheduled court appearance, the court may issue a bench warrant for the defendant's arrest and order revocation or forfeiture of bail.

The preliminary arraignment is also held to advise the defendant of his or her constitutionally guaranteed rights and to set a date for preliminary hearing. At the end of the preliminary arraignment, the defendant is released on bail or placed under confinement.

3. **Preliminary Hearing:** This hearing is held before the District Justice or a Municipal Court Judge in Philadelphia, and is usually the First Hearing at which the victim or witness will be called to appear. The purpose of the hearing is to determine whether there is probable cause that the defendant committed the offense or offenses charged. A police officer or prosecutor asks questions of witnesses and sometimes of the defendant. Counsel for the defendant may conduct cross-examination. It is important to remember that this hearing is not to determine guilt; only whether it is more likely than not that the defendant committed the crime charged. If the Judge determines that the defendant probably committed the offense, the case is bound over for further proceedings in the Court of Common Pleas. If no probable cause has been established, the defendant is released and the case is over.

4. **Arraignment:** When a case is bound over to Common Pleas Court, the records and transcripts from the earlier proceedings are sent from the District Justice to the appropriate county courthouse. Once the Court Clerk amasses a file, and the District Attorney draws up an *information*, which is a formal list of charges against the defendant.

The purposes of arraignment are to insure the defendant's awareness of the formal charges against him, to determine whether he has a lawyer, to establish time periods for the filing of various motions, and to set a date for a trial. An arraignment is very informal, often conducted without the defendant being present, since he or she may forego or "waive" formal notice of the charges in the information. The presence of a victim or witness is not necessary at the arraignment.

5. **Trial**: After thirty days have passed since the arraignment, the case may be scheduled for trial. Once a specific date, time, and courtroom are assigned, the defendant is notified, and witness subpoenas are dispatched in the mail. A witness should receive a subpoena to appear in court about a month before trial. Unless the case is *continued*, or postponed to a later date, the case is called before the court at the designated time.

   Many cases are resolved prior to trial. Often the defendant decides to plead guilty. When this happens, or when the case is postponed, the witness should be contacted by the District Attorney's Office and be informed that his or her presence for the date listed in the subpoena will be unnecessary.

   When a case does proceed to trial, the trial may take place before a judge and jury or just before a judge. In jury trials, the jury decides factual questions based on the evidence and on the law as provided by the judge. In other words, the jury decides what actually happened on the occasion in question and then renders a decision on the defendant's guilt or innocence. This is called the *verdict*. In non-jury or *bench* trials, the judge decides both factual and legal questions.

   A trial consists of several phases. After a jury is picked, the prosecution makes an *opening statement*. The purpose of this statement is for the prosecutor to describe what the evidence will prove. The defense makes its opening statements, either right after the Commonwealth's or at the beginning of the defense case. After opening statements, the Commonwealth presents its *case in chief*. That is, the prosecutor calls witnesses and puts on evidence aimed at establishing the defendant's guilt. This is the phase at which a witness will testify if needed. After the prosecution concludes, or *rests*, the case for the defense is presented. After all the evidence has been heard, each side is permitted to make a *closing speech* to the jury. In these speeches, the attorneys argue to the jury how and why the evidence supports their view or theory of the case, asking respectively for verdicts of guilt and innocence. Afterwards, the judge *charges* the jury, explaining what law they must consider in reaching a verdict. The jury deliberates until it reaches a verdict. Once a decision of guilt or innocence is made, the verdict is announced and the court makes it final by pronouncing a *judgment* on the verdict. The trial is now concluded.

6. **Sentencing:** In cases where the defendant pleads guilty, sentencing is usually immediately imposed by the court. In other cases, a future date for sentencing is set by the court. Sometimes the court orders the filing of a *pre-sentence investigation report*. The purpose of the report is to advise the court of the circumstances of the defendant which could affect the type of sentence to be imposed. The Commonwealth and the defense may ask for punishment of greater or lesser severity. The court considers these arguments, the contents of the pre-sentence investigation report, as well as any input made by the victim, and then pronounces sentence on the defendant. Sentencing may call for fines, imprisonment, or both. In addition, the defendant is required to pay court costs and, whenever feasible, to make restitution to victims for lost or damaged property or other financial losses. The sentence is carried out by the offices of parole or probation.

SECTION 4.10
THE PROGRESS OF A
CRIMINAL CASE IN
FEDERAL COURT

An arrest may be initiated following a grand jury presentment or by a complaint and warrant.

The Fifth Amendment of the Constitution guarantees that "no person shall be held to answer for a capital, or otherwise infamous crime unless by presentment or indictment by a grand jury…" The **grand jury indictment** is utilized to determine that probable cause exists that a crime has been committed and that the target of the investigation probably did commit the crime. A grand jury consists of twenty-three people, and a majority vote is required to indict. The proceedings are conducted in secret, and a witness does not have the right to have counsel present.

Following indictment, a bench warrant is issued for the arrest of the suspects, and they are brought before a Federal Magistrate for an Initial Appearance.

Federal prosecutions can also be initiated by a complaint and warrant. This method is used when immediate arrest is necessary because of fear of flight by the suspect. The Complaint is prepared by the United States Attorney with the assistance of a federal law enforcement agent who narrates the facts of the case. A judge then examines the document, and a federal agent must be present to attest to its veracity. By issuing the warrant, the Court determines that probable cause exists for arrest.

Federal arrestees are often detained in local detention centers where cells are reserved and paid for by the federal government. An initial hearing is held promptly after the defendant's arrest. If a defendant is arrested on a weekend, he will be brought in for the initial hearing on the next business day following his arrest. At the initial hearing, bail is set, the defendant is advised of his rights, and legal counsel is appointed if the defendant has none.

If the arrest was made pursuant to a grand jury indictment, the case proceeds to arraignment where the charges are read, pleas are entered, and a trial date is selected. If the arrest is made pursuant to the complaint and warrant procedure, a grand jury indictment will follow unless waived and replaced with an information (formal list of charges). The arraignment follows in either case within thirty days of the arrest, and the trial occurs within seventy days of the initial appearance. This is required by the Speedy Trial Act. Fewer cases go to trial in the federal system, since 95% of federal criminal cases are resolved through guilty pleas.

FEDERAL CRIMINAL PROCEDURE

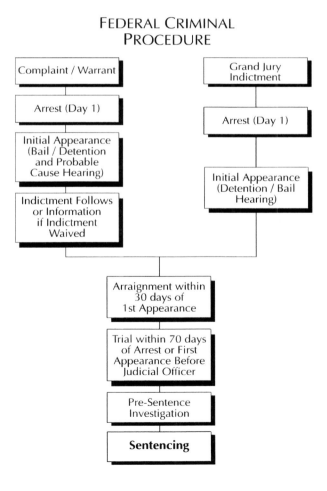

SECTION 4.11
THE GRAND JURY[9]

The grand jury is a group of people chosen from the same pool of citizens used to select trial jurors but it serves a very different function. The **grand jury** determines whether there is probable cause to believe that a crime was committed and that a specific person or persons committed it. If the grand jury finds that probable cause exists, it will then return a written statement of the charges called an **indictment**. After that, the accused will go to trial.

The grand jury normally hears only that evidence presented by an attorney for the government which tends to show the commission of a crime. The grand jury must determine from this evidence, and usually without hearing evidence for the defense, whether a person should be tried for a serious federal crime, referred to in the Bill of Rights as an **infamous crime**. An infamous crime is one which may be punished by imprisonment for more than one year. As a general rule, no one can be prosecuted for a serious crime unless the grand jury decides that the evidence it has heard so requires. In this way, the grand jury operates both as a "sword," authorizing the government's prosecution of suspected criminals, and also as a "shield," protecting citizens from unwarranted or inappropriate prosecutions. A person may, however, waive grand jury proceedings and agree to be prosecuted by a written charge of crime called an **information**.

The major portion of the grand jury's work is concerned with evidence brought to its attention by an attorney for the government. The grand jury may consider additional matters otherwise brought to its attention, but should consult with the United States Attorney or the court before undertaking a formal investigation of such matters. This is necessary because the grand jury has no investigation staff, and legal assistance will be necessary in the event that an indictment is voted.

It should be kept in mind that a federal grand jury can take action upon federal crimes that have been committed within the district in which it has been impaneled. Furthermore, a federal grand jury is not authorized to investigate situations involving the conduct of individuals, public officials, agencies or institutions that the grand jury believes is subject to mere criticism rather than a violation of federal criminal statutes. Its concern must be devoted solely to ascertaining whether there is probable cause to believe that a federal crime has been committed and to report accordingly to the court.

SECTION 4.12
VERDICTS AND
SENTENCING

At the completion of a criminal trial, the fact finder may return with a variety of verdicts, including: **(1)** Not guilty; **(2)** Guilty; **(3)** Not guilty by reason of insanity; and **(4)** Guilty but Insane.

The verdicts of **not guilty** and **guilty** are easy to understand. If the defendant is found innocent, the case is over and the accused may not be prosecuted again for the same crime.

This result is mandated by the **double jeopardy** clause contained in the Fifth Amendment which provides: "nor shall any person be subject for the same offense to be twice put in jeopardy of life or limb." This concept is such a basic tenant of civilized law whose origins can be traced back to the ancient Roman Empire where it was proclaimed that the "governor should not permit the same person to be again accused of a crime of which he has already been acquitted."

The premise of the double jeopardy is to protect people against three distinct risks: (1) a second prosecution for the same offense after acquittal, (2) a second prosecution for the same offense after conviction, and (3) multiple punishments for the same offense.

As the reader may remember from Chapter Two, it is not a violation of the double jeopardy clause if both criminal charges and a civil lawsuit are brought against a person for the same event. On rare occasions, a person may even be prosecuted in both federal and state courts for the same act based on the logic that the state and federal governments are separate sovereigns. The Rodney King trial is a classic example. A California jury found the Los Angeles police officers involved in the filmed assault not guilty. The defendants were then successfully prosecuted in federal court for violating King's constitutional rights.

The idea of a defendant being found insane in response to a crime is not a novel idea. It was first introduced in England during the late 1800's and it continues to be a viable verdict. The fact finder is the ultimate judge of a person's mental capacity, and if the jury is convinced that the defendant was mentally ill at the time of the commission of the crime, they may return with a verdict of **not guilty by reason of insanity** or **guilty but mentally ill.** A person will be found not guilty by reason of insanity if he or she does not know the difference between right and wrong because of a defective thought process caused by mental illness. If a jury concludes that a person is insane at the time of the crime, the defendant will be sent to a mental institution instead of prison. Once the individual regains his sanity, he will be released from the mental facility.

Guilty but mentally ill offers the jury an "in-between" verdict. The defendant is still responsible for his criminal conduct, but is provided treatment for the mental illness. Only a minority number of states have adopted this approach including Pennsylvania and Delaware. Juries who determine that the accused suffered from a psychiatric disorder that left him with insufficient willpower to choose whether to commit the act or refrain from doing it, may return with a verdict of guilty but mentally ill.

The distinction between "not guilty by reason of insanity" and "guilty but mentally ill" lies in the degree of mental illness. The verdict of not guilty by reason of insanity reflects a finding that the defendant is so mentally impaired that he lacks the ability to appreciate the wrongfulness of his criminal conduct. A person who is guilty but mentally ill appreciates the inappropriateness of his conduct but due to a psychiatric disorder, lacks sufficient willpower to choose whether to do a particular act or refrain from doing it.

Perhaps the reader may remember John DuPont and his killing of an Olympic wrestler who trained at the DuPont estate. The accused admitted that he shot the athlete but claimed that he was insane at the time. The defendant introduced evidence to show that his paranoia resulted in his installing razor wire in the walls to prevent people from hiding there, and he had excavators dig on his property in search of underground tunnels that he thought led to his home. On the day of the incident, DuPont walked up to the wrestler, asked the athlete if he had a problem with the defendant, and then shot the man three times with a .44 Magnum revolver. The jury found that the multimillionaire suffered from a mental disease process but it was not severe enough to prevent DuPont from understanding the difference between right and wrong. He was found guilty but mentally ill and sentenced to thirteen to thirty years in jail.

If the defendant is found not guilty, the case is concluded. The government can generally not appeal an adverse determination because of the concept of double jeopardy. If the defendant is found guilty, however, the case proceeds to the sentencing phase of the trial which phase rarely takes place immediately following conviction.

There is usually a short delay to allow counsel to file post-trial motions and for the court to conduct a background check on the defendant. Rarely, does the jury participate in the sentencing aspect of the trial except in capital murder convictions.

The idea of punishment for a crime is not novel and can be traced back to historical times. Most people are aware of the biblical reference by Matthew of "an eye for an eye and a tooth for a tooth." This quote is often used as the justification for retribution against a criminal which punishment is also thought to be a deterrent. That famous quote, however, is not the only reference in the bible for punishment. For instance, the bible also states that "he that killeth any man shall surely be put to death" or "he that killeth a beast shall make it good; beast for beast."

The Bureaus of Justice Statistics estimates that nearly 2.2 million people are confined in prisons across the United States and this figure represents a 33-year continuous rise in the prison population which makes this country number one in the world in people that are incarcerated at any given time. In fact, 1 out of every 136 people in this country is incarcerated despite a falling crime rate.[10]

Judges have a degree of discretion in the types and lengths of sentences that may be imposed in order for the penalty to fit the crime.

Punishment can range from incarceration to non-reporting probation or community service. Jail time remains the most frequent penalty with 72% of defendants being incarcerated for serious felonies while 25% receive probations.[11]

Prison sentences are usually indeterminate with a minimum and maximum term of incarceration. For instance, a defendant will be sentenced to five to ten years in a state penitentiary. This range allows the prisoner to be paroled after the minimum time period if he has been a model prisoner and has shown evidence of rehabilitation.

Mandatory sentencing is the legislature's attempt to take away the sentencing decision from the judge so that people who commit certain types of crimes will be treated the same. For example, committing a crime with a gun, selling drugs within a school zone, and the commission of three separate felonies will result in the imposition of mandatory jail time. Proponents of mandatory sentencing believe that it acts as a deterrent since it sends a clear message to criminals that they will face real prison time if they commit certain types of crimes. Not everyone, however, is sold on the idea since it removes the discretion from the judge in cases with extenuating circumstances and it does not consider the role of a particular defendant in the crime.

Judges can be creative in their sentences, and the newspapers occasionally contain stories about the more unusual punishments. For instances, novel penalties have included sex offenders being castrated, defendants having to put bumper stickers on their cars advertising their crimes, and a rap fan who was forced to listen to Wayne Newton's music for violating a sound ordinance.

Regardless of whether the penalty seems excessively harsh or whimsical, they involve the same issue. Does the punishment violate the person's constitutional rights on the basis that is it humiliating or barbaric?

The **Eighth Amendment** prohibits punishment that is cruel and unusual. This guarantee is frequently asserted by a defendant in response to a prison term that seems excessively harsh, or a penalty that seems a little too creative. The Constitution does not define what constitutes cruel and unusual punishment but is clear that the guarantee is intended to limit those entrusted with the sentencing power. Courts have interpreted the clause to mean that the penalty must be proportionate to the crime. That determination changes with evolving standards of decency but it is directed to punishments that *shock the conscious of civilized man*. The Eighth Amendment encompasses more than barbarous physical punishment. It also includes the unnecessary infliction of pain and those sentences that are grossly disproportionate to the severity of the crime.

Much litigation exists over what is and is not an appropriate sentence. Incarceration does deprive inmates of a number of life's pleasures but the courts hold that these restrictive and harsh conditions are part of the penalty that offenders must pay for their offenses against society.

Constitutional violations, however, have been found in cases of prison overcrowding, insufficient bathroom facilities, serving insect infested food, and in not supplying toothpaste, shampoo, and shaving cream.

The reader may remember the 1995 movie *Murder in the First* starring Kevin Bacon. The film chronicled the story of Henry Young and his confinement at Alcatraz Federal Penitentiary. Young was convicted of involuntary manslaughter in the stabbing death of a fellow inmate but many events in the film were fictional recreations. The movie, however, did portray a chilling account of solitary confinement. This drastic measure of total isolation is not cruel and unusual punishment when administered within proper bounds. Solitary confinement, however, for an excessive duration of time violates the Eighth Amendment. The following confinements have been found to be improper: confinement in a solid-door solitary confinement cell for more than fifteen days; confinement in a barred-door solitary confinement cell for more than thirty days; and depriving an inmate of the clothing necessary for warmth and modesty.

The death penalty has had a varied course before the United States Supreme Court. Between 1930 and 1965, almost four thousand people were executed. In the 1960's, the death penalty was considered cruel and unusual punishment. About ten years later, the Supreme Court in **Furman v. Georgia** invalidated the death penalty statutes in forty states citing to the law's arbitrary nature since the jury had too much discretion in the process. Within a few years, thirty-five states reinstituted the death penalty with legislation that provided guidelines for the jury in deciding when a sentence of death is the appropriate penalty. These guidelines allow for the examination of aggravating and mitigating factors.

The death penalty was routinely carried out through the 1990's and beginning of the twenty-first century. For instance, sixty-five people were executed in 2003 and more than three thousand prisoners are under sentences of death at the beginning of 2004. Nevertheless, controversy continues to surround the death penalty. Amnesty International has determined that more than half of the countries in the world have abolished the death penalty and eighty percent of recent executions have taken place in the United States, China, Iran, and Vietnam.

Court decisions no longer focus on the constitutionality of the death penalty but on specific aspects of this ultimate penalty. For example, the death penalty for rape has been found unconstitutional because the sentence is disproportionate to the crime. The Supreme Court has found it improper to execute a person who is insane but it did not prohibit the killing of a mentally handicapped individual found guilty of capital murder. The court also ruled it to be unconstitutional to execute a person who was under the age of 18 at the time of committing the crime. The justices felt that the death penalty is "disproportionate punishment for juveniles."

The United States ended the twentieth century with a great deal of dissatisfaction over use of the electric chair. This controversy has now abated since lethal injection has supplanted the electric chair as the method of choice for execution. It is claimed that this new procedure is painless and humane. Death row inmates, however, have started to attack lethal injection as cruel and unusual punishment. For instance, a prisoner in Tennessee challenged that state's procedure for administering the lethal dose of medicine. Apparently, Tennessee prohibits a health care professional from administering the injection and the defendant maintained that safeguards are not in place to insure that mistakes will not cause inhumane deaths. An inmate in Alabama received a stay from the Supreme Court moments before his execution in order to appeal his sentence on the basis that his execution would be unconstitutional harsh. The inmate is a former drug addict whose damaged veins make it difficult to inject him without cutting into his muscle to administer the fatal injection. Another prisoner in Indiana contended that lethal injection was cruel and unusual because his obesity resulted in the inability to locate a suitable vein. Regardless of the merits of these arguments, as long as the death penalty is legal in the United States, there will be challenges to the sentence regardless of how the punishment is carried out.

Larry Hope v. Mark Pelzer
122 S. Ct. 2508 (2002)

In 1995, Alabama followed the practice of chaining inmates to one another in work squads. It was also the only State that handcuffed prisoners to "hitching posts" if they either refused to work or otherwise disrupted work squads. Hope was handcuffed to a hitching post on two occasions. On May 11, 1995, while Hope was working in a chain gang, he got into an argument with another inmate. Both men were taken back to the prison and handcuffed to a hitching post. During his two hours on the post, Hope was offered drinking water and a bathroom break every 15 minutes, and his responses to these offers were recorded on an activity log.

On June 7, 1995, Hope was punished more severely. He took a nap during the morning bus ride to the chain gang's worksite, and when he arrived, he was less than prompt in responding to an order to get off the bus. An exchange of vulgar remarks led to a wrestling match with a guard. Four other guards intervened, subdued Hope, handcuffed him, placed him in leg irons and transported him back to the prison where he was put on the hitching post. He remained attached to the post for approximately seven hours. During this 7-hour period, he was given water only once or twice and was given no bathroom breaks.

The unnecessary and wanton infliction of pain constitutes cruel and unusual punishment forbidden by the Eighth Amendment. We have said that "among 'unnecessary and wanton' inflictions of pain are those that are 'totally without penological justification.'" **Rhodes v. Chapman, 452 U.S. 337 (1981).** In making this determination in the context of prison conditions, we must ascertain whether the officials involved acted with "deliberate indifference" to the inmates' health or safety.

As the facts are alleged by Hope, the Eighth Amendment violation is obvious. Any safety concerns had long since abated by the time the prisoner was handcuffed to the hitching post because Hope had already been subdued, handcuffed, placed in leg irons, and transported back to the prison. Despite the clear lack of an emergency situation, the guards knowingly subjected him to a substantial risk of physical harm, to unnecessary pain caused by the handcuffs and the restricted position of confinement for a 7-hour period, to unnecessary exposure to the heat of the sun, to prolonged thirst and taunting, and to a deprivation of bathroom breaks that created a risk of particular discomfort and humiliation. The use of the hitching post under these circumstances violated the "basic concept underlying the Eighth Amendment, which is nothing less than the dignity of man." This punitive treatment amounts to gratuitous infliction of "wanton and unnecessary" pain that our precedent clearly prohibits.

**SECTION 4.13
PROBLEM CASES**

1. Three packages containing more that $500,000 fell out of the back of an armored truck. Morant, an individual walking down the street, retrieved and carried away the bags. The money was not returned immediately nor were the police notified that the money had been located. A couple of days later, the armored truck company posted a $75,000 reward, and Morant came forward with the money in order to claim the reward. Has this individual committed the crime of theft by retaining the money until a reward was posted?

2. Anthony Saduk filled a muzzleloader rifle with gun powder, cigarette butts, and paper-towel wadding. As a practical joke, he shot the gun in the direction of his roommate, but three of the cigarette butts penetrated his friend's chest causing death. Since Saduk had no intention of hurting his friend, and was merely carrying out a practical joke, did he have the necessary intent to be found guilty of any type of criminal homicide?

3. The police suspected that Gindlesperger was growing marijuana in his basement. An officer aimed a thermal detection device at the home from the street in order to measure the heat emissions coming from the defendant's house. The temperature of the home was felt to be consistent with marijuana production activities. Did the warrantless search of the house, with a thermal detection device, constitute an unlawful Search and Seizure? **Commonwealth of Pennsylvania v. Gregory Gindlesperger, 706 A.2d 1316 (Pa. Super. 1997).**

4. The police set up a road block as part of a program to interdict drunk drivers. Schavello, who was driving towards the road block, made a U-turn in order to avoid police contact. He was then stopped by the police a short distance away, and alcohol was detected on his breath. Schavello failed a field sobriety test and was arrested for driving under the influence of alcohol. Is avoiding a road block sufficient probable cause to stop a motor vehicle when it makes a U-turn without any further suspicion by the police of illegal activity? **Commonwealth of Pennsylvania v. Schavello, 734 A.2d 386 (Pa. 1999).**

5. The manager of an apartment building was making yearly repairs and maintenance inspections. The date of these inspections were posted throughout the building. During his examination of one of the units, the manager observed drugs on the kitchen table and immediately contacted the police. The manager then led the officers into the apartment with a pass key. The police observed five plastic bags containing crack cocaine on the kitchen table. Based upon their observations, one officer left the apartment in order to

obtain a search warrant. The other officer remained behind and arrested Davis when he entered the apartment. The lease agreement provided: "Landlords and anyone allowed by the landlord, may enter the leased unit after first notifying tenant." Was the entry by the police into the apartment without a search warrant legal? **Commonwealth of Pennsylvania v. Curtis Davis, 743 A.2d 946 (Pa. Super. 1999).**

6. Booth disregarded a stop sign while he was driving and collided with the car of Nancy Boehm. She was 32 weeks pregnant at the time and lost the fetus as a result of the trauma. Booth's alcohol level was .12, and he was charged with involuntary manslaughter or homicide by vehicle. The Motor Vehicle Code provides that any person who unintentionally causes the death of another individual as the result of driving under the influence of alcohol or controlled substances has committed the crime of involuntary manslaughter. Is an unborn fetus, a person for the purposes of involuntarily manslaughter? **Commonwealth of Pennsylvania v. Jeffrey Booth, 2001 WL 166998 (Pa. 2001).**

SECTION 4.14
INTERNET REFERENCES

To learn more information about the topics in this chapter, see the following internet references:

A. *Criminal Law*

- **www.crimelibrary.com**
  The Crime Library has assembled various stories about famous criminal cases, classic crime stories, mass and serial murders, as well as terrorists, spies, and assassins at this location.

- **www.talkjustice.com**
  A person is able to post messages at this location about the criminal justice system and can access Cybrary, an online library which provides 12,000 links to different web sites relating to criminal justice.

- **www.law.indiana.edu/law/crimlaw.html**
  This site by Indiana University School of Law-Bloomington allows a user to downloads short speeches about different aspects of criminal law, such as double jeopardy and being called as a witness.

- **www.thebestdefense.com**
  Information about specific crimes and the process of a criminal case is offered at this criminal law firm's website.

- **www.raperecovery.terrashare.com**
  The Rape Recovery Help Line and Information Page is located at this site.

- **www.softport-co.com/safety/home.html**
  The Los Angeles County Sheriff presents an article on how to prevent a home burglary at this location.

- **www.usdoj.gov**
  The United States Department of Justice provides information on criminal justice programs and initiatives, as well as other information on the United States criminal justice system.

- **www.ncjrs.org**
  The Justice Information Center provides information on criminal and juvenile justice throughout the world at this address.

- **www.fbi.gov**
  The Federal Bureau of Investigation's site provides information and statistics on crime, including concerning FBI investigations, international crime, wiretapping, electronic surveillance, and economic espionage.

- **www.aclu.org**
  The American Civil Liberties Union offers information on the protection of a person's constitutional rights within the criminal justice system at this address.

B. *The Polygraph*

- **www.polygraph.org**
  This site by the American Polygraph Association offers a variety of information on the lie detector.

- **www.truthorlie.com**
  This site provides answers to frequently asked questions about the polygraph test.

C. *Miranda Warnings*

- **www.courttv.com/legalhelp/lawguide/criminal/91.html**
  This site provides general information about Miranda Warnings and its history.

D. *Search and Seizure*

- **www.supreme.findlaw.com/constitution/amendment04/**
  The Constitutional Law Center provides a variety of information relating to the law of Search and Seizure at this site, including the history, cases, and statutes concerning this Amendment.

E. *Grand Jury*

- **www.archive.abcnews.go.com/sections/us/DailyNews clinton_jury.html**
  ABC News has created this link to explain the inner workings of the grand jury system.

- **www.udayton.edu/~grandjury**
  This site explains how the federal and state grand jury systems work.

F. *Sentencing*

- **www.sentencing.org**
  This is the site for the Coalition for Federal Sentencing Reform, and it provides articles, history, and links to relevant sites.

Footnotes:

1. U.S. Department of Justice –Office of Justice Programs, *Homicides Trends in the United States; Long Term Trends and patterns.*

2. "CDC: Newborns Face Highest Murder Risk," http://usgovinfo.about.com/-library/weekly/aa031202a.htm.

3. "Murder Victims-Circumstances and Weapons Used or Cause of Death," U. S. Census Bureau, Statistical Abstract of the United States: 2000, page 206.

4. Hallinan, "California Leads in Justifiable Killings, http://www.trosch.org/tro/mpr-7g30.htm.

5. "Sexual Violence," National Center for Injury Prevention and Control, http://www.cdc.gov/ncipc/factsheets/svoverview.htm.

6. Identify Theft and Identify Fraud, www.usdoj/gov/criminal/fraud/idtheft.html.

7. Fighting Back Against Identify Theft: Deter, Detect, Defend, www.ftc.gov/bcp/edu/microsites/idtheft/consumers/defend.html.

8. This summary has been partially reproduced from the "Victim's Rights Handbook" written by the District Attorneys' Office of both Bucks and Montgomery Counties and has been reproduced with their permission.

9. This has been reprinted in part from a manual entitled "Handbook for Federal Grand Jurors," published by the Administrative Office of the United States Supreme Court. Washington, D.C. 20544.

KEY TERMS

Arraignment

Arrest

Arson

Bail

Burglary

Carnal Knowledge

Conspiracy

Crime

Criminal Complaint

Criminal Homicide

Criminal Trespass

Cruel and Unusual Punishment

Custodial Interrogation

Date Rape

Eighth Amendment

Electronic Fencing

Entrapment

Excusable Homicide

Expectation of Privacy

Federal Rule of Criminal
   Procedure

Felony Murder

Fifth Amendment

First Degree Murder

Fourth Amendment

General Police Measure

Grand Jury

Gross Negligence

Guilty

Guilty but Insane

Heat of Passion

Homicide

Hot Pursuit

Identity Theft

Indictment

Innocent

Insanity

Intentional Killing

Involuntary Manslaughter

Justifiable Homicide

Larceny

Malice Aforethought

Mandatory Sentencing

Miranda Warnings

Murder

Not Guilty by Reason of Insanity

Open Lewdness

Overt Act

Plain View

Plain Feel

Polygraph

Preliminary Arraignment

Preliminary Hearing

Premeditation

Pre-Sentence Investigation

Probable Cause

Rape

Receiving Stolen Property

Robbery

Search and Seizure

Search Incident to an Arrest

Search Incident to a General
   Police Measure

Search Warrant

Second Degree Murder

Self-defense

Sentencing

Speedy Trial Act

Statutory Rape

Stop and Frisk

Theft

Third Degree Murder

Trial

Voluntary Manslaughter

White Collar Crime

CHAPTER 5

CONSUMER PROTECTION[1]

SECTION 5.1
INTRODUCTION

Fans of Miss Cleo the "Jamaican" television "psychic" must be suffering withdrawal pains since the famous seer packed her tarot cards in the fall of 2002. Miss Cleo, who reportedly was more a California Valley Girl than the Jamaican shaman she claimed, evidently did not foresee the weight of the American legal system coming down on her.

Under pressure from the U.S. Federal Trade Commission, two companies associated with Cleo, Access Resource Services and Psychic Readers Network, Inc., agreed to pay a $5 million fine and cancel $500 million in billings. Smaller settlements were subsequently reached with at least five states. Before her legal problems, Miss Cleo had been a spectacular financial success:

> Her honeyed words persuaded millions to pick up the phone and call, bringing in millions of dollars. . . . But the calls also generated 2,000 complaints across the United States from people who said they had been the victims of duplicitous marketing and outright fraud. Miss Cleo herself has not been charged; as it turns out she rarely answered the phone. Instead callers were farmed out to contract workers. . . . At $4.99 a minute, the numbers quickly added up. . . . People who had asked to be placed on a "do not call" list were contacted, while others received up to 10 calls a day, usually automated messages telling them, "Miss Cleo had a dream about them and they should call back."[2]

Doubtless the government should not always protect us from our own foolishness, but costly consumer fraud and other forms of consumer abuse (invasion of privacy, dangerous products, identity theft, false advertising, and so on) are not unusual in our consumption driven lives. Historically we relied on the market to address those problems; but in recent decades legislatures, courts, and administrative agencies have developed laws and rulings to protect us where the market arguably has failed. This chapter surveys some of those legal interventions.

SECTION 5.2
COMMON LAW
CONSUMER PROTECTION

Later in this chapter we will explore government efforts to protect consumers from dangerous products, unfair lending practices, and the like. Before turning to that legislation, we need to appreciate the common law (judge-made law) that preceded and, in some respects, provided the foundation for the many federal, state, and local initiatives of recent years.

If the market is to operate efficiently, the buyer must be able to rely on the truth of the seller's affirmations regarding a product. Regrettably, willful untruths appear to be common in American commerce. A victim of fraud is entitled to rescind the contract in question and to seek damages, including, in cases of malice, a punitive recovery. Although **fraud** arises in countless situations and thus is difficult to define, the legal community has generally adopted the following elements, each of which must be proven:

1. Misrepresentation of a material fact.

2. The misrepresentation was intentional.

3. The injured party justifiably relied on the misrepresentation.

4. Injury resulted.

In identifying a **fraudulent expression**, the law distinguishes between statements of objective, verifiable facts and simple expressions of opinion. The latter ordinarily are not fraudulent even though they are erroneous. Thus, normal sales puffing ("This baby is the greatest little car you're ever gonna drive.") is fully lawful, and consumers are expected to exercise good judgment in responding to such claims. However, if a misleading expression of opinion comes from an expert, and the other party does not share that expertise (such as in the sale of a diamond engagement ring), a court probably would offer a remedy.

In limited circumstances, **silence** may constitute fraud. Typically, that problem may emerge where party A misunderstands the facts of the situation and party B both knows the true facts and knows that A does not know those facts and cannot reasonably be expected to discover them. An example would be a cracked engine block, where the cracks were filled with a sealer and covered with a compound such that the crack is unlikely to be discovered even by capable inspection.[3] In such situations, the knowledgeable party may be under a duty to speak. Nonetheless, the general rule is that silence is fully permissible.

Of course, fraud can involve false conduct as well as false expression. A familiar example is the car seller who rolls back an odometer with the result that the buyer is misled.

A variation on the general theme of fraud is **innocent misrepresentation**, which differs from fraud only in that the falsehood was unintentional. The wrongdoer believed the statement or conduct in question to be true, but he or she was mistaken. In such cases, the wronged party may secure rescission of the contract, but ordinarily damages are not awarded. The following case involves a fraud claim against Harley-Davidson.

Tietsworth v. Harley-Davidson
677 N.W. 2d 233 (Wis. S. Ct. 2004)

Plaintiff Steven C. Tietsworth and the members of the proposed class own or lease 1999 or early-2000 model year Harley motorcycles equipped with Twin Cam 88 or Twin Cam 88B engines. Harley's marketing and advertising literature contained the following statement about the TC-88 engines:

> Developing [the TC-88s] was a six-year process. . . . The result is a masterpiece. We studied everything from the way oil moves through the inside, to the way a rocker cover does its job of staying oil-tight. Only 21 functional parts carry over into the new design. What does carry over is the power of a Harley-Davidson™ engine, only more so.

Harley also stated that the motorcycles were "premium" quality, and described the TC-88 engine as "eighty-eight cubic inches filled to the brim with torque and ready to take you thundering down the road."

On January 22, 2001, Harley sent a letter to owners of Harley motorcycles informing them that "the rear cam bearing in a small number of Harley-Davidson's Twin Cam 88 engines has failed. While it is unlikely that you will ever have to worry about this situation, you have our assurance that Harley-Davidson is committed to your satisfaction." The letter went on to explain that the company was extending the warranty on the cam bearing from the standard one-year/unlimited mileage warranty to a five-year/50,000 mile warranty. Separately, Harley developed a $495 "cam bearing repair kit" and made the kit available to its dealers and service departments "to expedite rear cam bearing repair."

The complaint alleges that the cam bearing mechanism in the 1999 and early-2000 model year TC-88 engines is inherently defective, causing an unreasonably dangerous propensity for premature engine failure. The complaint alleged that Harley's failure to disclose the cam-bearing defect induced the plaintiffs to purchase their motorcycles by causing them to reasonably rely upon Harley's representations regarding the "premium" quality of the motorcycles.

The complaint further alleges that if the plaintiffs had known of the engine defect, they either would not have purchased the product or would have paid less for it. The amended complaint does not allege that the plaintiffs' motorcycles have actually suffered engine failure, have malfunctioned in any way, or are reasonably certain to fail or malfunction. Nor does the complaint allege any property damage or personal injury arising out of the engine defect. Rather, the complaint alleges that the plaintiffs' motorcycles have diminished value, including diminished resale value, because Harley motorcycles equipped with TC-88 engines have demonstrated a "propensity" for premature engine failure and/or fail prematurely.

The plaintiffs' common-law fraud claim is premised on the allegation that Harley failed to disclose or concealed the existence of the cam bearing defect prior to the plaintiffs' purchases of their motorcycles. It is well established that a nondisclosure is not actionable as a misrepresentation tort unless there is a duty to disclose. **Ollerman v. O'Rourke Co., Inc., 94 Wis. 2d 17, 26, 288 N.W. 2d 95 (1980).** Our decision in Ollerman outlined the three categories of misrepresentation in Wisconsin law—intentional misrepresentation, negligent misrepresentation, and strict responsibility misrepresentation—

and described the common and distinct elements of the three torts.

All misrepresentation claims share the following required elements: (1) the defendant must have made a representation of fact to the plaintiff; (2) the representation of fact must be false; and (3) the plaintiff must have believed and relied on the misrepresentation to his detriment or damage. The plaintiffs here allege intentional misrepresentation, which carries the following additional elements: (4) the defendant must have made the misrepresentation with knowledge that it was false or recklessly without caring whether it was true or false; and (5) the defendant must have made the misrepresentation with intent to deceive and to induce the plaintiff to act on it to his detriment or damage.

Ollerman reiterated the general rule that in a sales or business transaction, "silence, a failure to disclose a fact is not an intentional misrepresentation unless the seller has a duty to disclose." Ollerman held that "a subdivider–vendor of a residential lot has a duty to a 'noncommercial' purchaser to disclose facts which are known to the vendor, which are material to the transaction, and which are not readily discernible to the purchaser." We specified that this was a "narrow holding," premised on certain policy considerations present in noncommercial real estate transactions.

The transactions at issue here, however, are motorcycle purchases, not residential real estate purchases, and it is an open question whether the duty to disclose recognized in Ollerman extends more broadly to sales of consumer goods...

[W]e have generally held that a tort claim is not capable of present enforcement (and therefore does not accrue) unless the plaintiff has suffered actual damage... Actual damage is harm that has already occurred or is "reasonably certain" to occur in the future.

The injury complained of here is diminution in value only—the plaintiffs allege that their motorcycles are worth less than they paid for them. However, the amended complaint does not allege that the plaintiffs' motorcycles have diminished value because their engines have failed, will fail, or are reasonably certain to fail as a result of the TC-88 cam-bearing defect. The complaint does not allege that the plaintiffs have sold their motorcycles at a loss because of the alleged engine defect. The complaint alleges only that the motorcycles have diminished value—primarily diminished potential resale value—because Harley motorcycles equipped with TC-88 engines have demonstrated a "propensity" for premature engine failure and/or will fail as a result of the cam bearing defect. This is insufficient to state a legally cognizable injury for purposes of a fraud claim.

Diminished value premised upon a mere possibility of future product failure is too speculative and uncertain to support a fraud claim. The plaintiffs do not specifically allege that their particular motorcycles will fail prematurely, only that the Harley product line that consists of motorcycles with TC-88 engines has demonstrated a propensity for premature engine failure. An allegation that a particular product line fails prematurely does not constitute an allegation that the plaintiffs' particular motorcycles will do so, only that there is a possibility that they will do so.

We certainly agree with the court of appeals that the damage allegations in a fraud complaint are not evaluated against a standard of "absolute certainty" for purposes of a motion to dismiss for failure to state a claim. But an allegation that a product is diminished in value because of an event or circumstance that might—or might not—occur in the future is inherently conjectural and does not allege actual benefit-of-the-bargain damages with the "reasonable certainty" required to state a fraud claim.

Reversed.

The **doctrine of unconscionability** emerged from court decisions where jurists concluded that some contracts are so unfair or oppressive as to demand intervention. The legal system intrudes on contracts only with the greatest reluctance. Mere foolishness or want of knowledge does not constitute grounds for unconscionability, nor is a contract unconscionable and hence unenforceable merely because one party is spectacularly clever and the other is not. Unconscionability takes two forms:

1. *Procedural unconscionability* is a situation where the bargaining power of the parties was so unequal that the agreement, as a practical matter, was not freely entered. Procedural unconscionability usually arises from lack of knowledge or lack of choice. A consumer may not be reasonably knowledgeable about a contract because of the use of fine print, inconspicuously displayed contract terms, or complex legalese. A consumer may not have voluntarily entered a contract because of lack of time, pressing circumstances, or market conditions.

2. *Substantive unconscionability* is a situation where the clause or contract in question was so manifestly one-sided, oppressive, or unfair as to "shock the conscience of the court." A contract price dramatically exceeding the market price, a contract that does not provide a remedy for a breach, or contract terms completely out of line with the relative risks assumed by the parties are among the conditions that might lead to a finding of substantive unconscionability.

SECTION 5.3
STATE CONSUMER LAWS

Having looked at the common law foundation of consumer protection, we turn to some of the many governmental measures that provide shelter in the marketplace. Many states have enacted comprehensive consumer protection statutes, such as Pennsylvania's **Unfair Practices and Consumer Protection Law.** States also have specific statutes addressing such problems as door-to-door sales, debtor protection, and telemarketing fraud. We will look at only one of those, the so-called **lemon laws**, which address the particularly frustrating problem of a hopelessly defective vehicle.

New car purchases are covered by warranty laws; in addition, all 50 states have some form of law designed to provide recourse for consumers whose new vehicles turn out to be defective such that they cannot be repaired after a reasonable effort. The quarrel, of course, is about when a car is truly a lemon. Lemon laws differ significantly from state to state, but they often cover new cars for one to two years or 12,000 to 18,000 miles after purchase. Typically, state laws provide that the vehicle must have been returned to the manufacturer or dealer three or four times to repair the same defect and that defect must substantially impair the value or safety of the vehicle, *or* the vehicle must have been unavailable to the consumer for a total of at least 30 days in a 12-month period. Such a vehicle is a lemon, and the purchaser is entitled to a replacement vehicle or full refund of the purchase price. In some states, used cars may also be treated as lemons. In almost all states, the determination about whether a car is a lemon is handled by an arbitration panel. If dissatisfied with the ruling, the consumer may then file suit.

General Motors Corporation v. Dohmann
722 A.2d 1205 (Conn. S. Ct. 1998)

The sole issue in this appeal is whether the Connecticut "lemon law" requires the plaintiff, General Motors Corporation, to provide the defendant, Eugene Dohmann, with a replacement vehicle.

On October 26, 1996, the defendant purchased a new Chevrolet S-10 pickup truck (truck) from Maritime Motors (Maritime), a General Motors dealership located in South Norwalk. The following day, the defendant noticed defects in the paint on the truck's hood, roof, and bumpers. The defendant promptly notified Maritime of the defects and requested that the dealership provide him with a replacement vehicle. Maritime agreed to inspect the truck for defects, but refused the defendant's request for a replacement vehicle.

After inspecting the truck, Maritime agreed that the truck's paint was defective, but again refused to provide a different vehicle. Instead, the dealership offered to replace the truck's hood, the part of the truck on which the paint defects were most visible, with a hood taken from another vehicle of the same color. The defendant allowed Maritime to undertake that repair attempt. The replacement hood, however, did not fit properly and the paint was not an exact match. Dissatisfied with the repair attempt, the defendant told Maritime to reinstall the original hood, and Maritime complied.

Maritime subsequently suggested two other possible methods of curing the defects in the paint: (1) wet sanding and (2) repainting the affected areas of the truck. The defendant, however, rejected these suggestions because he believed that both wet sanding and repainting would remove the truck's original factory finish. In the defendant's view, the factory process produces a paint finish superior to that of a bodyshop. . . .

Thereafter, the defendant initiated an arbitration proceeding against the plaintiff. After a hearing, a three-member arbitration panel determined that (1) the truck had been subject to a reasonable number of unsuccessful repair attempts, and (2) the defective paint substantially impaired the truck's value to the defendant. Consequently, the panel concluded that the defendant was entitled to a new, comparably equipped replacement vehicle.

On appeal, the plaintiff claims that the trial court improperly affirmed the decision of the arbitration panel. Specifically, the plaintiff maintains that the record does not contain substantial evidence to support the arbitrators' findings that (1) the truck had been subject to a reasonable number of repair attempts, and (2) the defects in the paint substantially impaired the value of the truck to the defendant.

Our analysis begins with a brief overview of Connecticut's lemon law legislation. For consumer buyers of new motor vehicles, the act provides supplemental remedies of repair, replacement, and refund to facilitate the enforcement of express warranties made by the manufacturers of such vehicles. These supplemental remedies come into play whenever a manufacturer or authorized dealer, after a reasonable number of repair attempts, is unable substantially to conform a new vehicle to the terms of the express warranty...

The plaintiff first claims... that, because the additional repairs suggested by the dealership were capable of producing a paint finish that met factory standards, the single attempt to cure the defect by replacing the truck's hood was insufficient to constitute the requisite reasonable number of repair attempts. We disagree.

Section 42–179 provides in relevant part: "(d) If the manufacturer, or its agents or authorized dealers, are unable to conform the motor vehicle to any applicable express warranty by repairing or correcting any defect or condition which substantially impairs the use, safety, or value of the motor vehicle to the consumer *after a reasonable number of [repair] attempts*, the manufacturer shall replace the motor vehicle with a new motor vehicle acceptable to the consumer... (e) It shall be presumed that a reasonable number of [repair] attempts have been undertaken... if... the same nonconformity has been subject to repair four or more times... No claim shall be made under this section unless at least one attempt to repair a nonconformity has been made."

Generally a reasonable number of repair attempts is defined as four attempts during the first 18,000 miles or two years and the problem continues to exist. In some instances, less than four repair attempts is allowed if the problem is one for which evidence exists that no repair will bring the vehicle back into conformance." The report further states, "In cases involving problems with the paint on a vehicle, a determination may be made that it is impossible for any dealer to repaint the vehicle in a manner that would match the type of finish originally achieved at the manufacturer's plant when the car was built." Consequently, if the record contains substantial evidence to support a finding that proposed additional repair attempts would not have produced a paint finish that satisfied factory paint specifications, arbitrators reasonably may find that a single repair attempt is sufficient.

The record before us reveals the following regarding the utility of additional repair attempts. The plaintiff presented affidavits of two automobile body experts who stated that body shop paint processes are capable of producing results equal to, and in some cases superior to, those produced by the original factory paint process. The state's technical expert, Gregory Carver, however, testified that the conditions under which the factory originally paints a vehicle are superior to those that exist in a body shop. Specifically Carver stated that paint bonds to the surface of a vehicle most successfully the first time it is applied, and that, therefore, it is impossible for a body shop to duplicate the bond achieved at the factory. Carver further stated that the finish of a repainted vehicle is less durable than the finish applied at the factory.

We conclude, therefore, that the record contains substantial evidence to support the conclusion that, under the circumstances, Maritime's attempt to replace the truck's hood constituted a reasonable number of repair attempts.

The plaintiff claims that the arbitrators improperly concluded that the paint defects substantially impaired the value of the truck to the defendant. Section 42–179 (d) provides; "If the manufacturer, or its authorized dealers, are unable to conform the motor vehicle to any applicable express warranty by repairing or correcting any defect or condition which *substantially impairs the . . . value of the motor vehicle to the consume. .* the manufacturer shall replace the motor vehicle."

We conclude that under the lemon law the standard for determining whether a defect substantially impairs the use, safety, or value of a motor vehicle to the consumer is both subjective and objective. The standard is subjective in that the fact finder first must examine the subjective desires, needs, and circumstances of the particular consumer. In light of those desires, needs, and circumstances, the fact finder then must make an objective determination as to whether the value of the motor vehicle to the consumer has, in fact, been substantially impaired. In making this determination, the fact finder must determine that the consumer's subjective desires, needs, and circumstances are reasonable.

Having articulated the standard for substantial impairment under the lemon law, we address the plaintiff's claim that the record does not contain substantial evidence to support a finding that the evident defects in the paint substantially impaired the truck's value to the defendant.

During the arbitration hearing, the defendant testified that he takes great pride in the appearance of the vehicles that he owns and maintains the finish of those vehicles in factory condition. Moreover, he stated that appearance was a major factor in his decision to purchase a new truck rather than a used one. On the basis of that testimony, the arbitrators reasonably could have concluded that, had the defendant known of the defects in the paint before accepting delivery, he would not have purchased the truck, and that the statutory requirement of subjective substantial impairment had been satisfied.

Carver, the state's technical expert, testified that, on a scale of 1 to 10, with 10 representing the worst amount of damage, the damage to the truck constituted a 3. Carver further stated that the paint defects could not be removed easily. Moreover, Carver corroborated the defendant's contention that wet sanding and repainting the truck would remove its finish. Finally, Carver stated that the paint defects possibly could affect the resale value of the vehicle and that if the vehicle was not maintained meticulously, the affected areas could deteriorate further. Thus, on the basis of Carver's testimony, the arbitrators reasonably could have concluded that the statutory requirement of objective substantial impairment had been satisfied.

We conclude, therefore, that the record contains substantial evidence to support a finding that the defects in the truck's paint substantially impaired its value to the defendant.

Affirmed.

SECTION 5.4
FEDERAL CONSUMER LAWS

The **Federal Trade Commission** was created in 1914 to prevent "unfair methods of competition and unfair or deceptive acts or practices in and affecting commerce." In conducting its business, the FTC performs as a miniature government with extensive and powerful quasi-legislative and quasi-judicial roles.

The FTC's primary legislative direction is in issuing trade regulation rules to enforce the intent of broadly drawn congressional legislation. That is, the rules specify particular acts or practices that the commission deems deceptive.

The FTC's quasi-legislative or rule-making power is extensive, as evidenced by the following examples:

- The Federal Trade Commission's "Do Not Call" Registry forbids telemarketers, with certain exceptions, from placing calls to the 85 million Americans who have added their phone numbers to the Federal Trade Commission's list. In February 2005 the FTC announced its first settlements in Do Not Call disputes. In this instance, two time-share sellers and a telemarketer agreed, without admitting any wrong, to pay civil penalties for the hundreds of thousands of calls placed to consumers on the Do Not Call list.

- The FTC announced in 2000 that the largest cigar companies had agreed to include health warning labels on packaging and in advertising. Cigar consumption grew by 70 percent from 1993 to 1998, and premium cigar sales grew by 250 percent. One 45-year-old smoker was not happy about the new rules: "It feels like King George is here," said Pat Godine, a Treasury Department employee. "It's a natural leaf. What if a few people die? I don't want to live 120 lives. It's a solution to overpopulation."[4]

On its own initiative or as a result of a citizen complaint, the FTC may investigate suspect trade practices. At that point the FTC may drop the proceeding, settle the matter, or issue a formal complaint.

Where an agreement cannot be reached, the FTC may proceed with a **formal complaint,** in which case the matter proceeds essentially as a trial conducted before an administrative law judge. The FTC has no authority to impose criminal sanctions.

Unfair and deceptive trade practices, including those in advertising, are forbidden under Section 5 of the Federal Trade Commission Act. An unfair trade practice (1) must be likely to cause substantial injury to consumers, (2) must not be reasonably avoidable by consumers themselves, and (3) must not be outweighed by countervailing benefits to consumers or to competition. The FTC test for deception requires that the claim is (1) false or likely to mislead the reasonable consumer and (2) material to the consumer's decision making. Deception can take many forms, including, for example, testimonials by celebrities who do not use the endorsed product or do not have sufficient expertise to evaluate its quality. The primary areas of dispute involve quality and price.

"Fewer calories," "faster acting," and "more effective" are the kinds of claims that may lead to allegations of deception unless they are factually supportable. Under the FTC's ad substantiation program, advertisers are engaging in unfair and deceptive practices if they make product claims without some reasonable foundation for those claims. For example, credible survey evidence must be in hand if an advertiser says, "Consumers prefer our brand two to one." Indeed, in recent years the FTC has settled many such claims, including a 2002 agreement with the makers of Wonder Bread regarding their claims that the bread included added calcium that could improve children's brain function and memory. The FTC said Wonder Bread had no proof that calcium helps children's brain performance. Wonder Bread has agreed not to make such claims without reliable scientific substantiation.

Deception in price advertising sometimes takes the form of the so-called *bait and switch* practice, where a product is advertised at a very low price to attract customers although the seller actually has no intention of selling at that price. Once the customer is in the door (having taken the bait), the strategy is to switch the customer's attention to another, higher-priced product.

Sale pricing also sometimes leads to claims of deception. Do some retailers offer phony markdowns based on inflated "original" or "regular" prices? The FTC has long maintained guidelines for proving that a former price was genuine, but the problem is one that has been left largely to the states.

All-terrain vehicle accidents caused 357 deaths in 2002, up 67 percent from 1997. That total exceeded the 2002 deaths on snowmobiles or personal watercraft, but the federal government has asserted little regulatory oversight. In 2005, the **Consumer Product Safety Commission** has been urged to ban the sale of adult-sized ATVs for use by children under 16; but the commission, skeptical about the wisdom of a ban, has instructed its staff to carefully review the ATV safety record to determine whether new rules are needed. The commission claims the power to ban the vehicles or order redesign if a substantial risk is established, but considerable evidence suggests that riding practices rather than design flaws are at issue.[5] The Consumer Product Safety Commission is the federal agency charged with protecting us from defects in consumer products; but with only a $62 million annual budget, the CPSC does not have the resources to routinely challenge corporations and to undertake careful investigations of thousands of products. Indeed, a 2004 *Consumer Reports* study concludes that the agency's inflation-adjusted budget has declined about 50 percent over 30 years, the staff has likewise shrunk by about 50 percent during that time, and enforcement actions were down 35 percent in 2003 from 2001.[6]

In many instances, however, product recalls are undertaken voluntarily by the manufacturer. When the CPSC does decide to act, enforcement can be painfully slow. The child-safety standard for lighters, for example, required 10 years for commission approval.

On the other hand, the CPSC can be quite aggressive in encouraging industry cooperation. Graco Children's Products agreed in 2005 to pay $4 million to settle Consumer Product Safety Commission charges that Graco failed to notify the CPSC in a timely manner that some 12 million of its products could be hazardous to children. The company allegedly received reports of hundreds of injuries from its high chairs, swings, beds, and the like but failed to report the problems as the law requires.[7]

The CPSC, created in 1972, is responsible for reducing the risks in using consumer products such as toys, lawn mowers, washing machines, bicycles, fireworks, pools, portable heaters, and household chemicals. The CPSC pursues product safety, initially, by *collecting data* and *issuing rules*. The commission conducts research and collects information as a foundation for regulating product safety. Via its rule-making authority, the CPSC promulgates mandatory consumer product safety, performance, and labeling standards. Public comments and suggestions are encouraged, but industry trade associations appear to have the bigger voice with the commission.

To enforce its policies and decisions, the CPSC holds both *compliance* and *enforcement* powers. In seeking compliance with safety expectations, the commission can exert a number of expectations. Manufacturers must certify before distribution that products meet federal safety standards. Manufacturing sites may be inspected and specific product safety testing procedures can be mandated. Businesses other than retailers are required to keep product safety records. In cases of severe and imminent hazards, the CPSC may enforce its decisions by seeking a court order to remove a product from the market. In less urgent circumstances, the commission may proceed with its own administrative remedy. Preferring voluntary compliance, the commission may negotiate with the company to issue notice of its defective product or to repair or replace the product.

Where voluntary negotiations fail, the commission may proceed with an adjudicative hearing before an administrative law judge or members of the commission. That decision may be appealed to the full commission and thereafter to the federal court of appeals. Civil or criminal penalties may result. Only a few products have actually been banned from the market.

The following case deals with an alleged "bait and switch" violation that had its origins in a newspaper advertisement that offered a $500 coupon off the purchase price of a car.

ROBERT CONLEY, JR. V. HAYDOCY PONTIAC-GMC TRUCK, INC.
WL 655267 OHIO APP. 10 DIST., 1998

Plaintiff-appellant, Robert Conley, Jr., appeals from a judgment of the Franklin County Court of Common Pleas dismissing his complaint.

In 1996, defendant, Haydocy Pontiac-GMC Truck, Inc. ("Haydocy"), a car dealership, ran a print advertisement in a local newspaper which contained language offering $500 off the purchase of any vehicle. The relevant language of the coupon, as attached to plaintiff's complaint, states "NOW THAT THE SHOW IS OVER ⋯ $500 COUPON expires on 3/31/96 * * * On All Pontiacs."

Plaintiff gathered $69,000 worth of coupons, went to Haydocy on March 22, 1996, and test drove a 1996 Bonneville SSEI. When the sales person asked plaintiff how he intended to pay for the vehicle, plaintiff responded that he would pay the entire purchase price with coupons. In response, the sales person took an auto show bonus cash rebate from Pontiac out of his desk and tried to exchange with plaintiff "from the coupons I had brought in." Haydocy refused to allow plaintiff to pay for the automobile with coupons. Plaintiff filed a two-count complaint on June 28, 1996, alleging that (1) Haydocy had breached its implied contract with plaintiff, and (2) Haydocy had committed a breach of the Consumer Sales Practices Act in refusing to honor all the coupons, as the coupons lacked any language limiting plaintiff to one coupon per purchase.

Plaintiff filed a motion for summary judgment on his Consumer Sales Practices Act claim, contending that because the coupons lacked any material exclusions, reservations, limitations, modifications, or conditions, the coupons could not rightfully be limited to one coupon per customer per purchase. Defendant filed a motion for partial dismissal, seeking that the court dismiss plaintiff's breach of contract claim. Defendant later filed a motion for summary judgment regarding damages on plaintiff's claim under the Consumer Sales Practices Act.

While the motions were pending, plaintiff filed a motion for leave to file a second amended complaint, seeking to raise a bait and switch claim arising out of the attempt by defendant's sales person to replace defendant's print advertisements in plaintiff's possession with an auto show rebate coupon issued by the manufacturer. Despite defendant's opposition, the trial court granted the motion on May 20, 1997. On the same day, the trial court denied plaintiff's summary judgment motion, denied defendant's summary judgment motion, and granted defendant's motion to dismiss plaintiff's breach of contract claim.

The case ultimately was scheduled for trial in October 1997. At that time, defendant apparently argued that plaintiff's case should be dismissed based on this court's decision in **Conley v. Lindsey Acura, Case No. 97APE04-**

557. By entry of dismissal filed October 28, 1997, the trial court dismissed plaintiff's action for the reasons set forth in *Lindsay Acura*. Plaintiff appeals, assigning the following error:

Plaintiff's single assignment of error no longer contends he could use an unlimited number of coupons toward the purchase price of a car at Haydocy. Rather, plaintiff contends that when he "went to the dealership to use his coupon(s), he was met with a classic bait and switch attempt although the bait and switch did not involve a vehicle; instead, it involved the coupons themselves." Similarly, plaintiff's affidavit, filed with the trial court on January 13, 1997, states that defendant's agent "tried to switch my coupons with another, but I saw what they were doing and would not accept the other one." Accordingly, plaintiff asserts on appeal that the trial court improperly dismissed his "bait and switch" allegations on the authority of *Lindsay Acura*.

Given this court's opinion in *Lindsay Acura*, plaintiff properly has abandoned his contention that he could use an unlimited number of coupons to purchase an automobile at Haydocy. *Lindsay Acura* explicitly rejected that contention on virtually identical facts. *Lindsay Acura*, however, did not directly address the "bait and switch" argument raised in plaintiff's second amended complaint and argued on appeal.

Nonetheless, *Lindsay Acura* is relevant. Plaintiff's "bait and switch" claim reduces the contention that defendant's sales person attempted to substitute the print advertisement bearing no limits on the number of coupons to be used per purchase, with a manufacturer's rebate coupon containing such restrictions. Because *Lindsay Acura* rejected the argument that plaintiff could use an unlimited number of print advertisements per purchase, defendant's attempt to substitute the manufacturer's rebate coupon for the print advertisement caused plaintiff no injury: either way he received a $500 discount. Plaintiff nonetheless attempts to support his "bait and switch" contentions with further allegations that Haydocy procured his presence at the dealership through deception via the print advertisements. *Lindsay Acura*, however, found no deception under the Consumer Sales Practices Act, even though the coupon there lacked language limiting a customer to one coupon per purchase. Similarly, the lack of restrictive language in the print advertisement at issue here does not constitute the deception plaintiff asserts.

Given the foregoing, the trial court did not err in dismissing plaintiff's complaint on the authority of *Lindsay Acura*. We overrule plaintiff's single assignment of error and affirm the judgment of the trial court.

Judgment affirmed.

The Food and Drug Administration is responsible for protecting the public from dangerous processed food (except meat and poultry), seafood, drugs, medical devices, radiation-emitting products, and cosmetics and for ensuring the effectiveness of drugs.

The FDA plays a broad, important role in the health and welfare of America. In recent years, the agency has, for example, banned the words *sunblock* and *waterproof* from sunscreen labels, declared nicotine-laced lollipops and lip balm illegal, and generally ensured that ad language is supported by scientific evidence. For example, Tropicana, a PepsiCo unit, settled an FTC complaint in 2005 that some of its ads saying that "heart healthy" orange juice could lower blood pressure were misleading. The settlement forbids Tropicana from making claims that "any food will have an effect on the risk of heart disease, stroke, or cancer" unless sound scientific evidence supports those claims. At this writing in 2005, the FDA is in the midst of one of its most highly publicized and interesting investigations. At FDA insistence, anti-inflammatory prescription painkillers Vioxx and Bextra have been removed from the market, and a competitor, Celebrex, is being sold only with a "black box" warning, the FDA's firmest. Scientific evidence satisfied the FDA that the enormously successful drugs dangerously raise the risk of heart attacks and strokes and may have caused, in the case of Vioxx alone, as many as 139,000 heart attacks, strokes, and deaths.[8]

Historically, the FDA was criticized for being too cautious and slow in allowing potentially helpful, new drugs on the market. The drug industry and free market advocates argued for greater faith in the market, and in 1992 the agency accelerated its drug approval process so that approval time fell from 27 to 14 months. However, at the same time the proportion of new drugs removed from the market for safety reasons jumped from 1.5 percent to 5 percent.[9] FDA officials have long complained that they do not have the financial resources to fully monitor drugs following their market entry, and some FDA scientists have said that they have felt pressure from their bosses to mute their findings and concerns about some drugs. Of course, differences of scientific opinion among experts are inevitable.

A 2004 survey found about two-thirds of FDA scientists are less than fully confident about the FDA's safety monitoring of prescription drugs now on the market, and one-third have some doubts about the process of approving new drugs.[10] One reason for those concerns is that drug companies may not be playing one of their crucial roles in the free market process by revealing what they know about the dangers of their own products. One Stanford University medical professor told Congress that Merck for several years had suppressed internal studies showing increased heart risks associated with Vioxx; and internal Merck e-mail suggests that Merck may have known about the increased risks as early as 1996.[11] But Merck argues that it acted responsibly in studying Vioxx carefully and removing it from the market when the evidence warranted that decision. One of the results of this regulatory battle is that thousands of lawsuits have been filed against Merck and others. The FDA, of course, is left with the very difficult job of balancing the benefits of a drug against its risks.

SECTION 5.5
CONSUMER PRIVACY

Adelaide Andrews and Andrea Andrews aren't related. But for a while, a lot of people thought they were the same person. Andrea may have wanted it that way. The two met in 1993 when Adelaide visited a doctor. Andrea, the physician's receptionist, copied Adelaide's personal data, including her Social Security number and address—and then assumed her identity. Masquerading as Adelaide, Andrea racked up thousands of dollars in debt and ruined Adelaide's credit rating, which took years to put right. Such identity theft... has ensnared a number of prominent victims, including Tiger Woods, Ted Turner, and Oprah Winfrey.[12]

Identity theft has exploded in recent years. In February 2005, for example, more than 145,000 personal records may have been breached at information broker Choice Point.[13] Choice Point, which collects and sells information, holds some 19 billion Social Security numbers, credit histories, job applications, vehicle registrations, lawsuits, and so on.[14] About 9.3 million U.S. adults suffered identity theft between October 2003 and September 2004.[15] Dumpster diving, stolen mail, computer hacking, a corrupt co-worker, or a credit card application improperly disposed of can lead to big financial losses and a nightmare of months or more. In most cases, consumers learn about such theft only after their Social Security numbers, credit card numbers, and other vital information have been used to make purchases, drain bank accounts, and so on. The odds of catching the bad guys in identity theft are estimated at about 1 in 700.[16]

The Choice Point scandal has critics calling for government intervention in the lightly regulated information industry. Only one state, California, requires data companies to notify consumers when their records have been compromised. California and a few other states have laws allowing consumers to completely "freeze" their credit records so that they cannot be accessed by anyone. Of course, to the credit industry, laws allowing a freeze amount to inefficient overkill. Marc Rotenberg, a privacy advocate, says the current problems "end the discussion on whether self-regulation works."[17] Nonetheless, proposed federal legislation has yet to gain traction.

Smoothly flowing information, on the other hand, is vital to efficiency in a free market economy. In some sense, we must pay for our privacy. A recent study concludes that "credit card interest rates as low as 6.9 percent are the direct result of competition in the financial services industry."[18] The authors, two university professors, argue that tighter privacy requirements could increase costs to consumers. The study examined the effects of proposed "opt-in" rules that would require express permission from consumers before their personal information could be shared. Those rules, according to the study, would "have the effect of choking off competition, raising costs, and possibly increasing the number of mailings required to achieve the same level of return."[19] So increased personal privacy may be paid for, at least in part, by reduced financial efficiency. But the potential for privacy abuse is chilling even if it might mean cheaper groceries:

> You swipe your savings card against a screen mounted on a supermarket shopping cart. As you move about the store, the screen flashes ads for products you usually buy, notes you haven't bought toothpaste in six months, and provides recipes and health information. All the while your every move—including which aisles you go down and how long you spend in each department—is tracked for marketing purposes via the savings cards, also known as loyalty cards. Such technology is in the works, and privacy advocates are outraged.[20]

QUESTION FOR DISCUSSION:

Mark Johnson of the *Tampa Tribune:*

> Comfort Inn has your number—*your credit card number,* that is.

> It only takes spending one night at a hotel or motel to put a customer and his or her credit card information into that company's database file. That dossier, however, can grow to include details such as what movies guests ordered, if they used the health club, and whether they golf.

> More sophisticated computer systems also can cull information from outside sources such as mailing lists, online public records, and census data to assemble a customer profile. The hotel may know the value of your house or whether you own a dog.[21]

What benefits come to customers and marketers from these intrusions on consumer privacy?

SECTION 5.6
DEBTOR/CREDITOR LAWS

Perhaps you are operating a business selling furniture, appliances, cars, or other consumer goods, and your customers ordinarily do not pay in cash. You may have strong faith in the free market; however, Congress, the state legislatures, and most American people have decided that credit arrangements are so important, so confusing, and so potentially hurtful that they have supplemented the market's powerful messages with specific government rules. We will take an abbreviated look at several particularly important pieces of federal consumer credit legislation.

As we increasingly turned to credit financing, consumers often did not understand the full cost of buying on credit. The **Truth in Lending Act (TILA)** is part of the Consumer Credit Protection Act of 1968. Having been designed for consumer protection, it does not cover all loans. The following standards determine the TILA's applicability:

1. The debtor must be a "natural person" rather than an organization.

2. The creditor must be regularly engaged in extending credit and must be the person to whom the debt is initially payable.

3. The purpose of the credit must be "primarily for personal, family, or household purposes" not in excess of $25,000. However, "consumer real property transactions" are covered by the act. Hence home purchases fall within TILA provisions.

4. The credit must be subject to a finance charge or payable in more than four installments.

The TILA and **Regulation Z** interpreting the act were designed both to protect consumers from credit abuse and to assist them in becoming more informed regarding credit terms and costs so they could engage in comparison shopping. Congress presumed the increased information would stimulate competition in the finance industry. The heart of the act is the required conspicuous disclosure of the amount financed, the finance charge (the actual dollar sum to be paid for credit), the annual percentage rate (APR—the total cost of the credit expressed at an annual rate), and the number of payments. The finance charge includes not just interest but service charges, points, loan fees, carrying charges, and other costs. The TILA covers consumer loans generally, including credit cards and auto purchases, but its impact is somewhat limited by its $1,000 cap on penalties for personal property loans, as affirmed by the Supreme Court's 2004 decision in **Koons v. Nigh (543 U.S. 50).**

As an aggressive marketer, you may want to hand out credit cards in your student union, but the TILA provides that credit cards cannot be issued to a consumer unless requested. Cardholder liability for unauthorized use (lost or stolen card) cannot exceed $50, and the cardholder bears no liability after notifying the issuer of the missing card. The **Fair Credit and Charge Card Disclosure Act of 1988** creates extensive disclosure requirements for card issuers. The act requires notification of various cost factors when card issuers solicit applications. Details vary, depending on whether the card application was solicited by mail, telephone, or "take ones" (such as a magazine insert). In general, issuers must disclose key cost features, including APR, annual membership fees, minimum finance charges, late payment charges, and so on.

Having a favorable credit rating is a vital feature of consumer life, and having reliable credit information is essential to efficient business practice. Thus the three national credit information giants, Equifax, Experian, and TransUnion, as well as local credit bureaus, provide retailers, employers, insurance companies, and so on with consumers' detailed credit histories. The federal **Fair Credit Reporting Act** (FCRA) affords consumers the following credit reporting protections, among others:

- Anyone using information from a credit reporting agency (CRA), such as Equifax, to take "adverse action" against you (denying you credit, a job, insurance) must notify you and tell you where it secured the information.

- At your request, a CRA must give you the information in your file and a list of all those who have recently sought information about you.

- If you claim that your credit file contains inaccurate information; the CRA must investigate your complaint and give you a written report. If you remain unsatisfied, you can include a brief statement in your credit file. Notice of the dispute and a summary of your statement normally must accompany future reports.

- All inaccurate information must be corrected or removed from the file, usually within 30 days.

- In most cases, negative information more than seven years old must not be reported.

- You must provide written consent before a CRA can provide information to your employer or prospective employer.

- You can sue for damages if your rights under the act have been violated.[22]

To provide consumers a ready opportunity to check the accuracy of their own credit information, the federal **Fair and Accurate Credit Transactions Act of 2003** (FACT Act) guarantees consumers the right to receive free annual copies of their credit reports.

The **Fair Credit Billing Act (FCBA)** provides a mechanism to deal with the billing errors that accompany credit card and certain other "open-end" credit transactions. A cardholder who receives an erroneous bill must complain in writing to the creditor within 60 days of the time the bill was mailed. The creditor must acknowledge receipt of the complaint within 30 days. Then, within two billing cycles but not more than 90 days, the creditor must issue a response either by correcting the account or by forwarding a written statement to the consumer explaining why the bill is accurate. The creditor cannot threaten the consumer's credit rating or report the consumer as delinquent while the bill is in dispute, although the creditor can report that the bill is being challenged. Where a "reasonable investigation" determines the bill was correct but the consumer continues to contest it, the consumer may refuse to pay, and the creditor will then be free to commence collection procedures after giving the consumer 10 days to pay the disputed amount. If the bill is reported to a credit bureau as delinquent, that report must also indicate the consumer's belief that the money is not owed, and the consumer must be told who received the report. Penalties for a creditor in violation of the act are quite modest. The creditor forfeits the right to collect the amount in question and any accompanying finance charges, but the forfeiture cannot exceed $50 for each charge in dispute.

With ATMs, point-of-sale machines, electronic deposits, and the like we are deeply immersed in an era of "electronic money." The **Electronic Fund Transfer Act** provides remedies for consumers confronting electronic banking problems such as liability for lost or stolen cards and billing errors.

The **Equal Credit Opportunity Act** is designed to combat bias in lending. Credit must be extended to all creditworthy applicants regardless of sex, marital status, age, race, color, religion, national origin, good-faith exercise of rights under the **Consumer Credit Protection Act**, and receipt of public assistance (like food stamps). ECOA was in large part a response to anger over differing treatment of women and men in the financial market place. Creditors often would not lend money to married women in the women's own names, and single, divorced, and widowed women were similarly disadvantaged in securing credit.

Lucas Rosa v. Park West Bank & Trust Co.
214 F.3d 213 (1st Cir. 2000)

On July 21, 1998, Lucas Rosa came to the Park West Bank to apply for a loan. A biological male, he was dressed in traditionally feminine attire. He requested a loan application from Norma Brunelle, a bank employee. Brunelle asked Rosa for identification. Rosa produced three forms of photo identification: (1) a Massachusetts Department of Public Welfare Card; (2) a Massachusetts Identification Card; and (3) a Money Stop Check Cashing ID Card. Brunelle looked at the identification cards and told Rosa that she would not provide him with a loan application until he "went home and changed." She said that he had to be dressed like one of the identification cards in which he appeared in more traditionally male attire before she would provide him with a loan application and process his loan request.

Rosa sued the Bank. Rosa charged that "by requiring him to conform to sex stereotypes before proceeding with the credit transaction, the Bank unlawfully discriminated against him with respect to an aspect of a credit transaction on the basis of sex." He claims to have suffered emotional distress.

Without filing an answer to the complaint, the Bank moved to dismiss… The district court granted the Bank's motion. The court stated, The issue in this case is not Rosa's sex, but rather how he chose to dress when applying for a loan. Because the Act does not prohibit discrimination based on the manner in which someone dresses, Park West's requirement that Rosa change his clothes does not give rise to claims of illegal discrimination. Further, even if Park West's statement or action were based upon Rosa's sexual orientation or perceived sexual orientation, the Act does not prohibit such discrimination.

Price Waterhouse v. Hopkins, which Rosa relied on, was not to the contrary, according to the district court, because that case "neither holds, nor even suggests, that discrimination based merely on a person's attire is impermissible."

On appeal, Rosa says that the district court "fundamentally misconceived the law as applicable to the Plaintiff's claim by concluding that there may be no relationship, as a matter of law, between telling a bank customer what to wear and sex discrimination."

The Bank says that Rosa loses for two reasons. First, citing cases pertaining to gays and transsexuals, it says that the ECOA does not apply to cross-dressers. Second, the Bank says that its employee genuinely could not identify Rosa, which is why she asked him to go home and change.

The ECOA prohibits discrimination, "with respect to any aspect of a credit transaction, on the basis of race, color, religion, national origin, sex or marital status, or age." Thus to prevail, the alleged discrimination against Rosa must have been "on the basis of… sex."

While the district court was correct in saying that the prohibited basis of discrimination under the ECOA do not include style of dress or sexual orientation that is not the discrimination alleged. It is alleged that the Bank's actions were taken, in whole or in part, "on the basis of… [the appellant's] sex."… Whatever facts emerge, and they may turn out to have nothing to do with sex-based discrimination, we cannot say at this point that the plaintiff has no viable theory of sex discrimination consistent with the facts alleged.

The evidence is not yet developed, and thus it is not yet clear why Brunelle told Rosa to go home and change. It may be that this case involves an instance of disparate treatment based on sex in the denial of credit… It is reasonable to infer that Brunelle told Rosa to go home and change because she thought that Rosa's attire did not accord with his male gender: in other words, that Rosa did not receive the loan application because he was a man, whereas a similarly situated woman would have received the loan application. That is, the Bank may treat, for credit purposes, a woman who dresses like a man differently than a man who dresses like a woman. If so, the Bank concedes, Rosa may have a claim. Indeed, under Price Waterhouse, "stereotyped remarks [including statements about dressing more 'femininely'] can certainly be evidence that gender played a part." It is also reasonable to infer, though, that Brunelle refused to give Rosa the loan application because she thought he was gay, confusing sexual orientation with cross-dressing. If so, Rosa concedes, our precedents dictate that he would have no recourse under the federal Act. It is reasonable to infer, as well, that Brunelle simply could not ascertain whether the person shown in the identification card photographs was the same person that appeared before her that day. If this were the case, Rosa again would be out of luck. It is reasonable to infer, finally, that Brunelle may have had mixed motives, some of which fall into the prohibited category.

It is too early to say what the facts will show; it is apparent, however, that, under some set of facts within the bounds of the allegations and nonconclusory facts in the complaint, Rosa may be able to prove a claim under the ECOA. We reverse and remand.

Personal debt is at an all-time high in America. Perhaps we live beyond our means, but Congress and the states have recognized that financial reversals are inevitable for many. Laws have been developed to protect consumers from unfair debt collection methods and to provide a way out via bankruptcy.

The **Fair Debt Collection Practices Act** (FDCPA) is designed to shield debtors from unfair debt collection tactics by debt collection agencies and attorneys who routinely operate as debt collectors. The act does not extend to creditors who are themselves trying to recover money owed to them. Several thousand debt collection agencies nationwide pursue those who are delinquent in their debts. The agencies are normally paid on a commission basis and are often exceedingly aggressive and imaginative in their efforts. The FDCPA requires the collector to include a warning in the first communication with the debtor that the communication is an attempt to collect a debt, and any information obtained will be used for that purpose. In any subsequent communication except a court pleading, the collector must always disclose his or her role as a collector.

The FDCPA forbids, among others, the following practices:

- Use of obscene language.
- Contact with third parties other than for the purpose of locating the debtor.
- Use of or threats to use physical force.
- Contact with the debtor during "inconvenient" hours. For debtors who are employed during "normal" working hours, the period from 9 PM to 8 AM would probably be considered inconvenient.
- Repeated phone calls with the intent to harass.
- Contacting the debtor in an unfair, abusive, or deceptive manner.

The Federal Trade Commission is responsible for administering the FDCPA. A wronged debtor may also file a civil action to recover all actual damages (for example, payment for job loss occasioned by wrongful debt collection practices as well as damages for associated embarrassment and suffering).

The following case discusses whether a collection letter from a lawyer constitutes a violation of the Fair Debt Collection Practices Act.

TERRY BRUESEWITZ V. LAW OFFICES OF GERALD MOORE ASSOCIATES
2006 WL 3337361 W.D. WIS. 2006

Plaintiff Terry Bruesewitz commenced this action against defendants Law offices of Gerald E. Moore & Associates, P.C. ("GEMA") alleging that GEMA and Hill violated certain provisions of the Fair Debt Collection Practices Act, 15 U.S.C. § 1692, *et. seq.,* (FDCPA).

Plaintiff failed to make timely payments on his credit card account with MBNA America Bank, N.A. In September 2004 MBNA assigned plaintiff's account to Worldwide Asset Purchasing, LLC, which retained GEMA, a collection law firm, to pursue collection on the account.

On November 28, 2005 GEMA sent a letter, signed by Hill, to plaintiff. The letter provided in part:

Name of Creditor:	Worldwide Asset Purchasing, LLC, successor in interest to MBNA America Bank, N.A.
Account Number:	5329033800000477
Amount of Claim:	$5,631.43
GEMA No.	01106541

NOTICE OF INTENT TO ARBITRATE & SETTLEMENT OFFER

Dear TERRY BRUESEWITZ:

It is this firm's understanding that you have sufficient resources with which to make a settlement of this account, but you have failed to do so. Your refusal to make suitable arrangements for settlement has left my client no alternative but the exercise of its remedy under your card member agreement: the submission of this claim to binding arbitration before the National Arbitration Forum.

At this time, my client would like to offer you the opportunity to settle your account for 80% of your current balance as listed above. Receipt of these monies within ten (10) days from receipt of this letter will prevent the filing of a claim. If you are unable to take advantage of this one-payment settlement offer, we wish to give you the opportunity to honor your outstanding obligation by making monthly payments. In order to set up acceptable payment arrangements please contact us directly.

On February 8, 2005 plaintiff's counsel sent GEMA a letter advising that it represented the plaintiff and requesting verification of the debt and original creditor. Thereafter GEMA suspended all direct contact with plaintiff.

GEMA routinely initiates arbitration on behalf of its clients and has filed 29,946 arbitration claims since 2004.

Plaintiff maintains that defendants' letter violates four sections of the FDCPA. Section 1692e of the FDCPA makes it unlawful for a debt collector to use "any false, deceptive, or misleading representation or means in connection with the collection of any debt." Section 1692f prohibits the use of "unfair or unconscionable means" to collect a debt. Section 1692e(5) makes it unlawful to threaten to take action that is not intended to be taken. Section 1692e(3) makes it unlawful to falsely imply that a communication is from an attorney.

When assessing whether any of these violations occurred the Court views the letter from the standpoint of "the unsophisticated debtor." The unsophisticated debtor standard is an objective one. The unsophisticated debtor is "uninformed, naive, or trusting," but is also considered to have a "rudimentary knowledge of the financial world and is capable of making basis logical deductions and inferences." Accordingly, the issue before the Court is whether it can be determined as a matter of law that under the unsophisticated debtor standard, the challenged provisions of the letter violate the statutory prohibitions.

The Court finds that the amount of the debt is clearly stated in the letter and is not misleading. Under a reasonable reading of the letter the balance owed on plaintiff's account was $5,631.43 as prominently listed at the top of the letter as "Amount of Claim." Defendants are offering to settle plaintiff's claim for 80% of that amount. Plaintiff advances a strained interpretation that would permit a finding that the amount of claim listed at the top is 80% of the total account balance. Plaintiff offers no objective evidence of confusion.

Where it is apparent that a collection letter would not confuse a significant fraction of the population, summary judgment should be granted in favor of the defendant unless the plaintiff has presented "objective evidence of confusion."

Plaintiff contends that defendants' threat to commence arbitration proceedings violates § 1692(e)(5) because defendants did not intend to initiate arbitration on the claim. In support of this argument plaintiff offers only the fact that defendant did not actually initiate arbitration notwithstanding plaintiff's failure to respond or pay. Although the defendant did not commence an arbitration proceeding the undisputed evidence is overwhelming that it intended to do so when the letter was sent. First, it is undisputed that defendants routinely initiate arbitration proceedings for their collection clients and have done so in 29,946 cases since 2004. GEMA presently has 2,858 arbitration cases pending. There is nothing to suggest that defendants were not following their ordinary procedure in this case, which includes the initiation of arbitration if other collection efforts are unsuccessful. Defendants deviated from their ordinary procedure only as a result of the intervention in the case by plaintiff's attorney.

Plaintiff offers the additional argument that the letter threatens immediate arbitration at the end of the ten-day opportunity for settlement. The language of the letter does not support a time restriction. The letter provides that an 80% payment within ten days "will prevent the filing of a claim." The plain meaning of that sentence is that the 80% settlement offer is closed after ten days. It says nothing about when arbitration might be initiated in the event the offer is not accepted. Accordingly, the threat to commence an arbitration proceeding was clearly intended to be carried out in the ordinary course but the ordinary process was interrupted by the intervention of plaintiff's counsel. Summary judgment in defendants' favor is appropriate.

IT IS ORDERED that defendants' motion for summary judgment is GRANTED.

SECTION 5.7
BANKRUPTCY

Fresh Start? Should we lend a hand to those who are down on their luck? Bankruptcy law was specifically designed to provide a fresh start for those whose financial problems were insurmountable. We believed that both the debtor and society benefited from the new beginning. Now, as bankruptcy filings have skyrocketed, we are downsizing the fresh start.

In 2004, new bankruptcy filings totaled some 1.59 million, up from 780,000 ten years earlier.[23] Approximately 1 in 73 American households filed for bankruptcy during a 12-month period ending in March 2004.[24] Interestingly, bankruptcy patterns vary dramatically by region, with the highest rates in the southeast (such as Tennessee, with one household in every 38.7 filing for bankruptcy in that 12-month period) and the lowest rates in parts of the West and Midwest along with the Northeast (one in 156.2 households in Vermont filed for bankruptcy).[25] The credit industry sees the bankruptcy wave as more evidence of declining personal responsibility, while consumer advocates say the bankruptcies are the product of tragedies spurred by medical emergencies, job losses, and an explosion of credit cards:

> How is it that the person who wants to do right ends up so worse off?" asked Cleveland municipal judge Robert Triozzi… when he ruled against Discover in the company's breach-of-contract suit against another struggling credit cardholder, Ruth Owens. Owens tried for six years to pay off a $1,900 balance on her Discover card, sending the credit company a total of $3,492 in monthly payments between 1997 and 2003. Yet her balance grew to $5,564.28, even though… she never used the card to buy anything more. Of that total, over-limit penalty fees alone were $1,158. Triozzi denied Discover's claim, calling its attempt to collect more money from Owens "unconscionable."[26]

In 2005, with President Bush in the White House and strong Republican majorities in both houses of Congress, a new bankruptcy reform law is in place after many years of political struggle. The thrust of the new legislation is to force more bankrupt parties to repay their creditors. In brief, the new legislation forces some bankruptcy filers to enter their claim under Chapter 13 of the bankruptcy code rather than the more forgiving Chapter 7. Those with income above their state's median who can pay $6,000 over five years—$100 per month—probably would be forced into Chapter 13, where the court would order a repayment plan. Those not meeting that test could file under Chapter 7, thereby achieving a fresh start by escaping most repayment responsibilities while their nonessential property would be sold to pay debtors. The new law also requires those filing for bankruptcy to pay for credit counseling. Supporters of the new law argue that it will reduce the cost of credit for all Americans, whereas opponents see the bill as a punitive assault on those already down on their luck

Bankruptcy in the United States is governed exclusively by federal law; the states do not have the constitutional authority to enact bankruptcy legislation, but they do set their own rules within the limits provided by Congress. Our attention will be limited to the principal federal statute, the **Bankruptcy Reform Act of 1978**, as amended.

Bankruptcy is an adjudication relieving a debtor of all or part of his or her liabilities. Any person, partnership, or corporation may seek debtor relief. Three forms of bankruptcy action are important to us:

1. **Liquidation** (**Chapter 7** of the Bankruptcy Act), in which most debts are forgiven and all assets except exemptions are distributed to creditors.

2. **Reorganization** (**Chapter 11**), in which creditors are kept from the debtor's assets while the debtor, under the supervision of the court, works out a plan to continue in business while paying creditors.

3. **Adjustment of debts** of an individual with regular income **(Chapter 13)**, in which individuals with limited debts are protected from creditors while paying their debts in installments.

A Chapter 7 liquidation petition can be *voluntarily* filed in federal court by the debtor (individual, partnership, or corporation), or creditors can seek an *involuntary* bankruptcy judgment. A Chapter 7 liquidation is commonly called a "straight" bankruptcy.

In a voluntary action, the debtor files a petition with the appropriate federal court. The court then has jurisdiction to proceed with the liquidation, and the petition becomes the *order for relief*. The debtor need not be insolvent to seek bankruptcy. Creditors often can compel an involuntary bankruptcy.

The debtor may challenge that bankruptcy action. The court will enter an order for relief if it finds the debtor has not been paying his or her debts when due or if most of the debtor's property is under the control of a custodian for the purpose of enforcing a lien against that property.

After the order for relief is granted, voluntary and involuntary actions proceed in a similar manner. Creditors are restrained from reaching the debtor's assets. An interim bankruptcy trustee is appointed by the court. The creditors then hold a meeting, and a permanent trustee is elected. The trustee collects the debtor's property and converts it to money, protects the interests of the debtor and creditors, may manage the debtor's business, and ultimately distributes the estate proceeds to the creditors. Debtors are allowed to keep exempt property, which varies from state to state but typically includes a car, a homestead, some household or personal items, life insurance, and other "necessities." Normally a dollar maximum is attached to each.

The debtor's nonexempt property is then divided among the creditors according to the priorities prescribed by statute. Secured creditors are paid first. If funds remain, "priority" claims, such as employees' wages and alimony/child support, are paid. Then, funds permitting, general creditors are paid. Each class must be paid in full before a class of lower priority will be compensated. Any remaining funds will return to the debtor.

When distribution is complete, the bankruptcy judge may issue an order *discharging* (relieving) the debtor of any remaining debts except for certain statutorily specified claims. Those include, for example, taxes and educational loans. The debtor might fail to receive a discharge if he or she had received one in the previous six years, if property was concealed from the court, or if good faith in the bankruptcy process was lacking in other respects.

Chapter 11 is available to individuals and most businesses. The basic thrust of this type of bankruptcy is to allow financially troubled enterprises to continue in operation while debtor adjustments are arranged. Thus both debtor and creditor may ultimately benefit more than from a straight liquidation. The debtor may voluntarily seek reorganization, or the creditors may petition for an involuntary action. When a reorganization petition is filed with the court and relief is ordered, one or more committees of creditors are appointed to participate in bankruptcy procedures. Typically the debtor continues to operate the business, although the court may appoint a trustee to replace the debtor if required because of dishonesty, fraud, or extreme mismanagement. The company, its bankers, and its suppliers will meet to work out a method for continuing operations. A plan must be developed that will satisfy the creditors that their interests are being served by the reorganization. Perhaps new capital is secured, or perhaps creditors receive some shares in the company. The plan must be approved by the creditors and confirmed by the court. The company is then required to carry out the plan.

Under Chapter 13, individuals (not partnerships or corporations) can seek the protection of the court to arrange a debt adjustment plan. Chapter 13 permits only voluntary bankruptcies and is restricted to those with steady incomes and somewhat limited debts. The process can begin only with a voluntary petition from the debtor. Creditors are restrained from reaching the debtor's assets. The debtor develops a repayment plan. If creditors' interests are sufficiently satisfied by the plan, the court may confirm it and appoint a trustee to oversee the plan. The debtor may then have three to five years to make the necessary payments.

Aggressive consumer protection measures of the kind we have studied in this chapter are unknown to much of the world, but change is coming. European nations certainly are not new to consumer protection initiatives; but the European Union has recently recognized that a more organized, consistent, and responsive effort is necessary for economic progress and for fairness. The European Union has adopted a consumer policy strategy for the period 2002–2006. A key ingredient in this plan is to build consumer confidence in cross-border shopping, thus strengthening the European Union as a unified economic entity. That goal would be achieved with more uniform rules across EU nations, consistent enforcement, increased consumer education, and the like.

The growth of formal consumer protection efforts is an acknowledgment of the market's imperfections and the need for some government intervention. As the following article suggests, China is quickly learning that lesson. Remember that China remains formally a communist state with central control. But in a burst of entrepreneurial zeal, the Chinese have adapted free market principles to fit their needs. With that growing acceptance and understanding of the market, the government and the people now see a role for legal measures to curb unscrupulous behavior.

SECTION 5.8 PROBLEM CASES

1. An online "Ask a Lawyer" service received the following question: "Can I sue a creditor who is harassing me?" Answer that question and explain how the wronged consumer would go about that lawsuit.

2. What do I do if someone "steals my identity?"

3. Snow wrote a $23.12 check to a convenience store, Circle K. The check bounced, and Circle K sent the check to its attorney, Riddle, for collection. Riddle sent Snow a letter demanding payment along with a $15 service fee. Snow paid the $23.12, but refused to pay the $15. Then Snow sued Riddle for violating the Fair Debt Collection Practices Act because the collection letter did not include the required "validation notice" telling him about his legal rights under the FDCPA. Riddle responded by saying that the FDCPA does not apply to dishonored checks. Does a dishonored check constitute a debt such that the FDCPA would apply? Explain. See **Snow v. Riddle, 143 F.3d 1350 (10th Cir. 1998).**

4. Jenny Craig, Inc., reached a 1997 agreement with the Federal Trade Commission providing that the company must include the following statement in most ads: "For many dieters, weight loss is temporary." In your view, is that requirement a wise use of FTC authority? Explain.

5. Roseman resigned from the John Hancock Insurance Company following allegations of misuse of his expense account. He reimbursed the account. Subsequently he was denied employment by another insurance firm after that firm read a Retail Credit Company credit report on him. The credit report included accurate information regarding Roseman's resignation. Was Retail Credit in violation of the Fair Credit Reporting Act in circulating information regarding the resignation? Explain. See **Roseman v. Retail Credit Co., Inc., 428 F. Supp. 643 (Pa. 1977).**

6. Consumers sometimes abuse sellers. One familiar technique is shoplifting. Of course, shoplifting is a crime. However, the criminal process is cumbersome and often does not result in monetary recoveries for sellers. As a result, at least 43 states now have laws permitting store owners to impose civil fines, the collection of which is usually turned over to a lawyer or collection agency with a threat to sue in civil court, file criminal charges, or both if payment is not forthcoming. Fines may range from $50 to $5,000 or more, depending on the value of the item stolen. Defense lawyers say this civil fine system is unfair. Why? On balance, is the civil fine approach to shoplifting a good idea? Explain.

7. Goswami failed to pay her $900 credit card bill. A collection agency, ACEI, mailed her a collection letter with a blue bar across the envelope saying "Priority Letter." The letter did not, in fact, constitute priority mail. The purpose of the bar was to encourage Goswami to open the envelope. Was the bar a deceptive practice in violation of the Fair Debt Collection Practices Act? Explain. See **Goswami v. American Collections Enterprise, Inc., 377 F.3d 488 (5th Cir. 2004); cert. den. 2005 U.S. LEXIS 5511.**

Footnotes: 1. Reprinted with permission from "Consumer Protection**," Law, Business, and Society**, by McAdams, Neslund and Neslund. Copyright 2005 by the McGraw-Hill Companies.

2. Araminta Wordsworth, "Miss Cleo Didn't See $5M Fine in Her Future," *National   Post*, November 16, 2002, p. A21.

3. **Lindberg Cadillac Co. v. Aron**, 371 S.W.3d 651 (Mo. App. 1963).

4. Knight Ridder Newspapers, "Fuming—Government Intervention Has Cigar Smokers Red Hot," *Waterloo/Cedar Falls Courier*, July 14, 2000, p. A5.

5. John J. Fialka, "As ATVs Take Off in Sales, Deaths and Injuries Mount," *The Wall Street Journal*, February 10, 2004, p. A1.

6. *Washington Post*, "Study: Dangerous Products Widely Available," *Waterloo/Cedar Falls Courier*, October 5, 2004, p. B6.

7. Christopher Conkey, "Safety Agency Takes Action on Baby Gear," *The Wall Street Journal*, March 22, 2005, p. D1.

8.   Knight Ridder Newspapers, "Merck Accused of Concealing Side Effects of Vioxx during Senate Hearings," *Waterloo/Cedar Falls Courier*, November 19, 2004, p. A1.

9. Marie McCullough, "Journal Speaks Out against FDA," *Des Moines Register*, November 23, 2004, p. 3A.

10. Paul Recer, "Most FDA Scientists Critical of Drug Monitoring," *Des Moines Register*, December 17, 2004, p. 3A.

11. Knight Ridder Newspapers, "Merck Accused of Concealing."

12. Robert S. Greenberger and Glenn R. Simpson, "Identity Theft Dogs Credit Firms in the Supreme Court, Congress," *The Wall Street Journal*, April 12, 2001, p. A18.

13. Jennifer Saranow and Ron Lieber, "Freezing Out Identity Theft," *The Wall Street Journal*, March 15, 2005, p. D1.

14. Rachel Konrad, "Identity Theft Scandal Widens," *Des Moines Register*, February 19, 2005, p. 8C.

15. Saranow and Lieber, "Freezing Out Identity Theft."

16. Knight Ridder Newspapers, "Identity Thieves Get More Sophisticated," *Waterloo/Cedar Falls Courier*, October 7, 2004, p. A1.

17. Evan Perez, "Identity Theft Puts Pressure on Data Sellers," *The Wall Street Journal*, February 18, 2005, p. B1.

18. "Study Finds Privacy 'Protections' Could Increase Cost to Consumers," *Business Wire*, May 22, 2002.

19. "Study Finds Privacy 'Protections' Could Increase Costs."

20. Associated Press, "Consumers Decide: Privacy or Savings?" *Waterloo/Cedar Falls Courier,* January 18, 2002, p. C5.

21. Mark Johnson, "Credit Card Use Helps Businesses Sell Personal Data," *Tampa Tribune,* August 5, 1999, Business and Finance Section, p. 7.

22. This summary of FCRA requirements was drawn largely from the FTC document, "A Summary of Your Rights under the Fair Credit Reporting Act"

23. Michael Schroeder and Suein Hwang, "Sweeping New Bankruptcy Law to Make Life Harder for Debtors," *The Wall Street Journal,* April 6, 2005, p. A1.

24. Constance Mitchell Ford, "Creditor-Friendly South Offers Preview of Bankruptcy Changes," *The Wall Street Journal,* March 10, 2005, p. A1.

25. Ford, "Creditor-Friendly South."

26. *The Washington Post,* "Punitive Charges Dog Credit Card Users," *Waterloo/Cedar Falls Courier,* March 7, 2005, p. A1.

KEY TERMS

Adjustment of debts
Bankruptcy
Bait and switch practice
Chapter 7 of the Bankruptcy Act
Chapter 11 of the Bankruptcy Act
Chapter 13 of the Bankruptcy Act
Consumer Product Safety
  Commission
Doctrine of unconscionability
Electronic Fund Transfer Act
Equal Credit Opportunity Act
Fair Credit and Charge Card
Disclosure Act
Fair Credit Reporting Act
Fair Debt Collection Practices Act

Federal Trade Commission
Food and Drug Administration
Fraud
Identity theft
Innocent Misrepresentation
Lemon Law
Liquidation
Puffing
Reorganization
Regulation Z
Truth in Lending Act
Unfair Practices and Consumer
Protection Law
Unfair and deceptive trade
  practices

CHAPTER 6

RACE, LAW & REALITY

BY: VANESSA J. LAWRENCE, ESQ.

SECTION 6.1
INTRODUCTION

"We hold these truths to be self-evident, that all men are created equal, that they are endowed by their Creator with certain unalienable rights, that among these are life, liberty and the pursuit of happiness."

Declaration of Independence 1776

Our country was founded upon the principle that all men are created equal. However, these noble words were not all inclusive: they did not include a large segment of the population. This chapter will explore how the color of one's skin or ancestry has played a role in what constitutional rights a person enjoys. With more than two and one half centuries of history as a guide, the civil rights movement in the United States will be explored in a chronological fashion.

Great strides have been made to insure that people are treated equally and are given the same opportunities for advancement. The public's understanding of past mistakes in the area of race relations is also well known and is continually reinforced through educational programs and court pronouncements.

So, is **racial discrimination** still an issue? Are insensitive comments and discriminatory conduct still part of American life? Is it still necessary to seek court intervention because of unequal treatment due to one's race?

Consider the following comments. Radio announcer and television host, Don Imus, referred to the women's college basketball team from Rutgers University, composed mainly of African American players, as "...some nappy-headed hos." During a nationally televised basketball game, sportscaster Billy Packer described then Georgetown basketball player Allen Iverson as a "tough monkey." Democratic Presidential aspirant, Joe Biden, referred to another Presidential candidate, Barack Obama, as "the first mainstream African American who is articulate, bright, clean and a nice-looking guy." Former U. S. Education Secretary, William Bennett, commented during a radio talk show that "I do know that it's true that if you wanted to reduce crime, you could, if that were your sole purpose, you could abort every black baby in this country, and your crime rate would go down." Richmond, Virginia General District Judge Ralph Robertson during an internet chat room discussion stated "African Americans are prone to crime and violence because it is in their genes" and he agreed with another chat-room writer who said that some minorities are "people who have no regard for sanitation, courtesy, private property, etc."[1]

Various situations have also taken place in retail sales that raise issues of race relations. For example, The Children's Place, a nationwide children's clothing chain, agreed to a 22-step settlement after an employee reported that during her training process she was instructed to shadow African American customers in hopes of preventing theft. She was also instructed not to give large shopping bags to this client base, nor to tell them about sales or invite them to apply for store credit cards. The employee contacted the state after her complaints to the chain's district manager brought no response. The settlement was reached after an investigation revealed enough evidence to prepare a lawsuit against the store.[2]

In 2004, the U. S. Department of Justice filed a lawsuit alleging racial discrimination against African American customers by Cracker Barrel Restaurant and Old Country Store, Inc., a nationwide family restaurant chain. The complaint alleged that Cracker Barrel allowed Caucasian servers to refuse to wait on African American customers, to segregate patron seating by race, to seat white customers before African American patrons who had arrived earlier, to provide inferior service to African American customers after they were seated, and to treat African Americans, who complained about the quality of food or service, less favorably than white customers who lodged similar complaints. The Justice Department's investigation revealed evidence of such conduct in approximately 50 different Cracker Barrel restaurants in seven states. Eventually, the litigation was settled and Cracker Barrel agreed to implement an effective nondiscrimination policy, to implement an improved system for investigating, tracking, and resolving discrimination complaints, and to retain an outside contractor to test the compliance.[3]

The U. S. Equal Employment Opportunity Commission (EEOC) filed a lawsuit on behalf of approximately 10,000 African Americans against Walgreens, the Illinois-based national drug store chain. The suit alleged that Walgreens discriminated against African American retail management and pharmacy employees in promotion, compensation and assignment. In July 2007, the EEOC announced a $20 million proposed consent decree resolving the systematic race discrimination dispute, pending court acceptance.[4]

How do you explain these actions or court settlements in a context other than race?

SECTION 6.2
RACE IS AN ISSUE

Race remains an issue despite this country's many attempts to remedy the injustices committed over the years but why was race ever a question? Why does race continue to be a problem? How did the government deal with questions of race over the years and how do our laws address issues of race in today's society? The phrase **affirmative action** is part of our vocabulary but what does it mean? Why does any group have preferential treatment and does preferential behavior apply only to race?

The Fourteenth Amendment of the United States Constitution states: "…nor shall any State…deny to any person within its jurisdiction the **equal protection** of the laws."

Despite this mandate, the Constitution has not always afforded equal protection to all people. When this historic document was ratified in 1787, slavery not only existed but also was protected by the Constitution. The migration and importation of Africans was left up to the individual states and Congress was prohibited from amending this clause until 1808. The original Constitution also counted African Americans as only 3/5 of a person for purposes of determining taxation and representation. On the other hand, Native Americans were not counted at all on the premise they were not taxed. Census figures from 1790 determined that African Americans composed 19.3% of this country's population and 92.15% of these individuals were slaves. Race was, therefore, an issue.

Advancing the clock seventy years, race continued to be an issue. This is demonstrated by the plight of Dred Scott who sued for his freedom after he returned with his master from residing in a free state. The United States Supreme Court denied his request declaring that African Americans were not citizens of the United States.

This decision dramatically set back race relations in this country. The **Dred Scott** decision follows.

DRED SCOTT V. SANDFORD
19 HOW. 393 (1857)

The question is this: Can a Negro become a member of the community formed and brought into existence by the Constitution of the United States, and become entitled to all the rights, and privileges guaranteed by that instrument to the citizens?

This plea applies to that class of persons only whose ancestors were Negroes of the African race, imported into this country, and sold and held as slaves. The only issue is, whether the descendants of such slaves, when they shall be emancipated, or who are born of parents who had become free before their birth, are citizens of a State, in the sense the word citizen is used in the Constitution.

The question then arises, whether the provisions of the Constitution embraced the African race, at that time in this country, or who might afterwards be imported, who had then or should afterwards be made free in any State?

The court thinks the affirmative of these propositions cannot be maintained. And if it cannot, the plaintiff could not be a citizen, within the meaning of the Constitution.

It becomes necessary to determine who were citizens of the States when the Constitution was adopted. In order to do this, we must refer to the Governments and institutions of the thirteen colonies, when they separated from Great Britain. We must inquire who, at that time, were recognized as citizens of a State, whose rights and liberties had been outraged by the English Government; who declared their independence, and assumed the powers of Government to defend their rights by force of arms.

In the opinion of the court and the language used in the Declaration of Independence, neither the class of persons who had been imported as slaves, nor their descendants, were intended to be included in the general words used in that memorable instrument.

It is difficult to realize the state of public opinion in relation to that unfortunate race, which prevailed in the civilized and enlightened portions of the world at the time of the Declaration of Independence. But the public history of every European nation displays it in a manner too plain to be mistaken.

They had for more than a century before been regarded as beings of an inferior order, and unfit to associate with the white race, either in social or political relations; and so far inferior, that they had no rights which the white man was bound to respect; and that the Negro might justly and lawfully be reduced to slavery for his benefit. He was bought and sold, and treated as an ordinary article of merchandise. This opinion was at that time fixed and universal in the civilized portion of the white race.

And in no nation was this opinion more firmly fixed or more uniformly acted upon than by the English Government and English people. They not only seized them off the coast of Africa, and sold them in slavery for their own use; but they took them as ordinary articles of merchandise to every country where they could make a profit on them, and were far more extensively engaged in this commerce than any other nation in the world.

(Colonial laws and the state of feeling toward blacks) show that a perpetual and impassable barrier was intended to be erected between the white race and the one which they had reduced to slavery, and governed as subjects with absolute and despotic power, and which they then looked upon as so far below them in the scale of created beings, that intermarriages between white persons and Negroes or mulattoes were regarded as unnatural and immoral, and punished as crimes, not only in the parties, but in the person who joined them in marriage. And no distinction in this respect was made between the free Negro or mulatto and the slave, but this stigma, of the deepest degradation, was fixed upon the whole race.

The Declaration of Independence proceeds to say: "We hold these truths to be self-evident: that all men are created equal; that they are endowed by their Creator with certain unalienable rights; that among them is life, liberty, and the pursuit of happiness; that to secure these rights, Governments are instituted, deriving their just powers from the consent of the governed."

The general words above quoted would seem to embrace the whole human family. But it is too clear for dispute that the enslaved African race were not intended to be included, and formed no part of the people who framed and adopted this declaration; for if the language would embrace them, the conduct of the distinguished men who framed the Declaration of Independence would have been utterly inconsistent with the principles they asserted.

Yet the men who framed this declaration were great men, and incapable of asserting principles inconsistent with those on which they were acting. They perfectly understood the meaning of the language they used, and how it would be understood by others; and they knew that it would not in any part of the civilized world be supposed to embrace the Negro race, which had been excluded from civilized Governments and the family of nations and doomed to slavery.

The unhappy black race was separated from the white by indelible marks, and laws long before established, and were never thought of or spoken of except as property.

The court is of opinion, that Dred Scott was not a citizen within the meaning of the Constitution of the United States.

Mr. Justice McLean dissenting.

In the argument, it was said that a colored citizen would not be an agreeable member of society. This is more a matter of taste than of law. Several of the States have admitted persons of color to the right of suffrage, and in this view have recognized them as citizens; and this has been done in the slave as well as the free States.

QUESTION FOR DISCUSSION:

1. Relying upon at least two passages from the Supreme Court's majority opinion, discuss how each provides insight into how African Americans were viewed in 1857.

The Chief Justice of the Supreme Court stated in the majority opinion in **Dred Scott v. Sandford** that "[a black man] had no rights which the white man was bound to respect." This was how African Americans were viewed by society at the time. The court also stated, "…that the Negro might justly and lawfully be reduced to slavery for his benefit." These statements and others in the Dred Scott decision demonstrate that an individual's race was an issue.

SECTION 6.3
THE FIRST STEPS
TOWARDS CHANGE

Steps to eradicate these perceptions were taken following the Civil War. Three Constitutional Amendments were added that are collectively known as the **Civil War Amendments**: **Amendment Thirteen** abolished slavery,

Amendment Fourteen made all persons born or naturalized in the United States citizens of the United States, determined that each person would be counted as a whole person (but excluded Native Americans), and it established the equal protection and due process clauses. **Amendment Fifteen** gave the right to vote to all citizens.

During this same period, Congress passed the first two Civil Rights Acts. The **Civil Rights Act of 1866** was enacted over the veto of President Andrew Jackson and provided that all persons born in the United States must be considered citizens, without regard to race, color, or previous condition of slavery. The Native American, however, was not protected by this legislation. It also gave citizens of every race the right to make contracts, sue, purchase, sell, and convey real and personal property and to have full and equal benefits of the laws as enjoyed by white citizens. A violation of this law was a crime and carried a fine not to exceed $1,000, or imprisonment of up to one year.

The **Civil Rights Act of 1875** mandated that all public accommodations and facilities be made available to people regardless of race and there must be equality in the use of transportation, theaters, and other places of public amusement.

QUESTIONS FOR DISCUSSION:

1. The Fifteenth Amendment states: "(t)he right of citizens of the United States to vote shall not be denied or abridged by the United States or by any State on account of race, color, or previous condition of servitude." Does this Amendment guarantee the right to vote?

2. Does the Civil Rights Act of 1866 apply to individual or private discrimination against another based on race?

3. What do you think is the current status of the Civil Rights Act 1875? Support your response.

4. Congress passed the Civil War Amendments and Civil Rights Acts in an attempt to bring about racial equality following the abolition of slavery. Do you think the U. S. Supreme Court's decisions that were rendered after the passage of those laws continued the march towards equality?

SECTION 6.4
THE SUPREME COURT

In reality, the Civil Rights Act of 1875 was largely ignored. The Supreme Court was also asked to pass upon the constitutionality of this legislation. Not only did the Justices find the Civil Rights Act of 1875 unconstitutional but it also ruled that the Fifteenth Amendment did not guarantee all people the right to vote, only a right not to be discriminated against in voting.

Many of the southern states seized upon these court pronouncements to support the enactment of various ways to dilute the African American's right to vote. Methods such as poll taxes, literacy tests, and **Grandfather Clauses** were enacted that were either administered in a discriminatory fashion or had a disparate impact upon African

Americans. Out of all of the impediments enacted, Grandfather Clauses had the greatest impact. Eleven states had such statutes or clauses in their constitution. For example, Louisiana's Grandfather Clause stated, "you could vote, if your father and grandfather could vote as of January 1, 1867." On its face, this type of clause appears to be fair, and to apply to all people regardless of race. However, it had a desperate impact on the African American race. In 1896, there were 130,344 African Americans registered to vote in Louisiana, thereby constituting a majority in 26 parishes in that state. By 1900, or just two years after the adoption of that state's new constitution, only 5,320 African Americans were on the voter registration books. Of 181,471 African American males of voting age in Alabama in 1900, only 3,000 registered after the new constitutional provision went into effect.[5] Race was an issue.

SECTION 6.5
SEPARATE BUT EQUAL

Once the federal troops left the south following the end of the Civil War, barriers were erected to maintain the discriminatory practices against African Americans. Known as **Jim Crow Laws**, states passed legislation that required businesses to maintain separate facilities for people based upon race. This practice came to a head in 1892 when Homer **Plessy** refused to sit in a railroad car designated for African Americans. This act of defiance found its way to the Supreme Court where the court sanctioned the concept of **separate but equal.** Arguably, that principle is still having lingering effects on race relations today.

PLESSY V. FERGUSON
163 U.S. 537 (1896)

This case turns upon the constitutionality of an act of the General Assembly of Louisiana, providing for separate railway carriages for the white and colored races.

The statute enacts "that all railway companies carrying passengers in their coaches, shall provide equal but separate accommodations for the white, and colored races. No person shall be admitted to occupy seats in coaches other than the ones assigned to them on account of the race they belong to."

The information filed in the criminal District Court charged that **Plessy** was assigned to the coach used for the race to which he belonged, but he insisted upon going into a coach used by the race to which he did not belong.

Plessy was seven-eighths Caucasian and one-eighth African blood; that the mixture of colored blood was not discernible, and that he was entitled to every right, privilege and immunity secured to citizens of the United States of the white race; and he took possession of a vacant seat in a coach where passengers of the white race were accommodated, and was ordered by the conductor to vacate said coach and take a seat in another assigned to persons of the colored race, and having refused to comply with such demand he was forcibly ejected with the aid of a police officer, and imprisoned to answer a charge of having violated the above act.

The constitutionality of this Act is attacked upon the ground that it conflicts both with the Thirteenth Amendment abolishing slavery, and the Fourteenth Amendment that prohibits certain restrictive legislation on the part of the States.

A statute which implies merely a legal distinction between the white and colored races and which must always exist so long as white men are distinguished from the other race by color has no tendency to destroy the legal equality of the two races, or reestablish a state of involuntary servitude. Indeed, we do not understand that the Thirteenth Amendment is strenuously relied upon by the plaintiff in error in this connection.

By the Fourteenth Amendment, the object of the Amendment was undoubtedly to enforce the absolute equality of the two races before the law, but in the nature of things it could not have been intended to abolish distinctions based upon color, or to enforce social equality, or a commingling of the two races upon terms unsatisfactory to either. Laws permitting, and even requiring, their separation in places where they are liable to be brought into contact do not necessarily imply the inferiority of either race to the other, and have been generally, if not universally, recognized as within the competency of the state legislatures in the exercise of their police power.

So far, then, as a conflict with the Fourteenth Amendment is concerned, the case reduces itself to the question whether the statute of Louisiana is a reasonable regulation. In determining the question of reasonableness the legislature is at liberty to act with reference to the established usages, customs and traditions of the people, and the preservation of the public peace and good order. Gauged by this standard, we cannot say that a law that authorizes or even requires the separation of the two races in public conveyances is unreasonable.

We consider the underlying fallacy of the plaintiff's argument to consist in the assumption that the enforced separation of the two races stamps the colored race with a badge of inferiority. If this were so, it is not by reason of anything found in the act, but solely because the colored race chooses to put that construction upon it. If the two races are to meet upon terms of social equality, it must be the result of natural affinities, a mutual appreciation of each other's merits and a voluntary consent of individuals. If one race were inferior to the other socially, the Constitution of the United States cannot put them upon the same plane.

The judgment of the court below is, therefore, *affirmed.*

This decision by the Supreme Court provided the legal authorization for maintaining two separate societies within the United States. While slavery was abolished in 1865, the segregation of the races was now authorized by the highest court in this country.

QUESTIONS FOR DISCUSSION:

1. What do you think may have been the relationship between the races if the Supreme Court had reached the opposite decision from the one rendered in **Plessy?**

2. What are some reasons why the separate but equal standard announced in **Plessy** should not be maintained?

3. Does separation of a race stamp a race with a badge of inferiority?

SECTION 6.6
THE JAPANESE
AMERICAN EXPERIENCE

From a historical perspective, most of the legal issues involving race focused on whites, Native Americans and African Americans. This changed during World War II when the court examined certain discriminatory practices directed to those of Japanese decent residing in this country.

As a result of the attack on Pearl Harbor, President Roosevelt authorized directives that placed a curfew and another that excluded Japanese people from certain military zones in the United States irrespective of whether they were American citizens.

Hirabayashi was a student at the University of Washington, and he refused to obey a curfew imposed against the Japanese. His disobedience resulted in a criminal conviction. The Supreme Court considered the constitutionality of that conviction in **Hirabayashi v. United States**, 320 U.S. 81 (1943). The order in question required all persons of Japanese ancestry to be confined to their home between the hours of 8 p.m. and 6 a.m. The Court concluded that this curfew was a constitutional exercise of power by the government to take steps necessary to prevent espionage and sabotage in an area threatened by Japanese attack.

A short time later, the Supreme Court was again called upon to determine the constitutionality of an even more restrictive executive order.

KOREMATSU V. UNITED STATES
323 U.S. 214 (1944)

The petitioner, an American citizen of Japanese descent, was convicted for remaining in San Leandro, California, a "Military Area," contrary to Civilian Exclusion Order No. 34, which directed that all persons of Japanese ancestry be excluded from that area. No question was raised as to petitioner's loyalty to the United States.

Exclusion Order No. 34, which the petitioner knowingly and admittedly violated, was one of a number of military orders issued after we were at war with Japan, declaring that the successful prosecution of the war requires every possible protection against espionage and sabotage to national-defense material, national-defense premises, and national-defense utilities.

One of the series of proclamations, a curfew order, which like the exclusion order here was promulgated pursuant to Executive Order 9066, subjected all persons of Japanese ancestry in prescribed West Coast military areas to remain in their residences from 8 p.m. to 6 a.m. As is the case with the exclusion order here, that prior curfew order was designed as a "protection against espionage and against sabotage."

Exclusion from the area in which one's home is located is a far greater deprivation than constant confinement to the home from 8 p.m. to 6 a.m. Nothing short of apprehension by the proper military authorities of the gravest imminent danger to the public safety can constitutionally justify either. The military authorities, charged with the primary responsibility of defending our shores, concluded that curfew provided inadequate protection and ordered exclusion. They did so in accordance with Congressional authority to the military to say who should, and who should not, remain in the threatened areas.

We uphold the exclusion order and in doing so, we are not unmindful of the hardships imposed by it upon a large group of American citizens. But hardships are part of war, and war is an aggregation of hardships. All citizens alike feel the impact of war in greater or lesser measure. Citizenship has its responsibilities as well as its privileges, and in time of war the burden is always heavier. Compulsory exclusion of large groups of citizens from their homes, except under circumstances of direst emergency and peril, is inconsistent with our basic governmental institutions. But when under conditions of modern warfare our shores are threatened by hostile forces, the power to protect must be commensurate with the threatened danger.

It is said that we are dealing here with the case of imprisonment of a citizen in a concentration camp solely because of his ancestry, without evidence or inquiry concerning his loyalty and good disposition towards the United States. Our task would be simple were this a case involving the imprisonment of a loyal citizen in a concentration camp because of racial prejudice. Regardless of the true nature of the assembly and relocation centers — and we deem it unjustifiable to call them concentration camps with all the ugly connotations that term implies — we are dealing with nothing but an exclusion order. To cast this case into outlines of racial prejudice, without reference to the real military dangers that were presented, merely confuses the issue. Korematsu was not excluded from the Military Area because of hostility to him or his race. He was excluded because we are at war with the Japanese Empire, because the properly constituted military authorities feared an invasion of our West Coast and felt constrained to take proper security measures, because they decided that the military urgency of the situation demanded that all citizens of Japanese ancestry be segregated from the West Coast temporarily. There was evidence of disloyalty on the part of some, the military authorities considered that the need for action was great, and time was short. We cannot — by availing ourselves of the calm perspective of hindsight — now say that at that time these actions were unjustified. *Affirmed.*

Mr. Justice Roberts, dissenting.

I dissent, because I think the indisputable facts exhibit a clear violation of Constitutional rights.

This is not a case of temporary exclusion of a citizen from an area for his own safety or that of the community, nor a case of offering him an opportunity to go temporarily out of an area where his presence might cause danger to himself or to his fellows. On the contrary, it is the case of convicting a citizen as a punishment for not submitting to imprisonment in a concentration camp, based on his ancestry, and solely because of his ancestry, without evidence or inquiry concerning his loyalty and good disposition towards the United States. If this is a correct statement of the facts disclosed by this record, and facts of which we take judicial notice, I need hardly labor the conclusion that Constitutional rights have been violated.

Mr. Justice Murphy, dissenting.

This exclusion of "all persons of Japanese ancestry from the Pacific Coast on a plea of military necessity in the absence of martial law ought not to be approved. Such exclusion goes over "the very brink of constitutional power" and falls into the ugly abyss of racism.

Being an obvious racial discrimination, the order deprives all those within its scope of the equal protection of the laws. It further deprives these individuals of their constitutional rights to live and work where they will, to establish a home where they choose and to move about freely.

That this forced exclusion was the result in good measure of this erroneous assumption of racial guilt rather than bona fide military necessity is evidenced by the Commanding General's Final Report on the evacuation from the Pacific Coast area. In it he refers to all individuals of Japanese descent as "subversive," as belonging to "an enemy race" whose "racial strains are undiluted," and as constituting "over 112,000 potential enemies." In support of this blanket condemnation of all persons of Japanese descent, however, no reliable evidence is cited to show that such individuals were generally disloyal, or had generally so conducted themselves in this area as to constitute a special menace to defense installations or war industries, or had

otherwise by their behavior furnished reasonable ground for their exclusion as a group.

Similar disloyal activities have been engaged in by many persons of German, Italian and even more pioneer stock in our country. But to infer that examples of individual disloyalty prove group disloyalty and justify discriminatory action against the entire group is to deny that under our system of law individual guilt is the sole basis for deprivation of rights.

I dissent from this legalization of racism. Racial discrimination in any form and in any degree has no justifiable part whatever in our democratic way of life.

Mr. Justice Jackson, dissenting.

Korematsu was born on our soil, of parents born in Japan. The Constitution makes him a citizen of the United States and a citizen of California by residence. No claim is made that he is not loyal to this country. There is no suggestion that apart from the matter involved here he is not law-abiding and well disposed. Korematsu, however, has been convicted of an act not commonly a crime. It consists merely of being present in the state whereof he is a citizen, near the place where he was born, and where all his life he has lived.

Even more unusual is the series of military orders that made this conduct a crime. They forbid such a one to remain, and they also forbid him to leave. They were so drawn that the only way Korematsu could avoid violation was to give himself up to the military authority. This meant submission to custody, examination, and transportation out of the territory, to be followed by indeterminate confinement in detention camps.

A citizen's presence in the locality, however, was made a crime only if his parents were of Japanese birth. Had Korematsu been one of four — the others being, say, a German alien enemy, an Italian alien enemy, and a citizen of American-born ancestors, convicted of treason but out on parole — only Korematsu's presence would have violated the order. The difference between their innocence and his crime would result, not from anything he did, said, or thought, different than they, but only in that he was born of different racial stock.

In 1988, Congress enacted the **Civil Liberties Act** formally recognizing the injustice done to those of Japanese ancestry in the United States by the evacuation, relocation, and internment of civilians during World War II.

Congress found that the internments by the government were carried out without adequate security reasons and were motivated primarily by racial prejudice, wartime hysteria, and failure of political leadership.

Because the excluded individuals suffered incalculable losses in education and job training, surviving internees were declared eligible to receive restitution of $20,000 each from the federal government.

QUESTIONS FOR DISCUSSION:

1. Which opinion of the court in **Korematsu v. United States** do you agree with and why?

2. Do you believe the American government in 1988 should have compensated the survivors of the internment camps for the actions that took place during World War II? What is your opinion on the amount of money that was awarded?

3. How did the actions taken by the U. S. Government during WWII deprive its Japanese citizens of their "due process rights" guaranteed by the 14th Amendment?

4. Is there any way that the U. S. Government could have protected itself from espionage and sabotage and at the same time afforded its Japanese citizens their Constitutional guaranteed rights.

SECTION 6.7
EQUALITY IN EDUCATION

In 1954, the Supreme Court was again called upon to decide an issue involving the segregation of the races. This time the question was whether segregation in public schools is constitutional? Now that the composition and philosophy of the Supreme Court had changed since the 1896 decision in **Plessy v. Ferguson** and the separate but equal doctrine had come under increasing criticism, the time for change was in the wind. This occurred in **Brown v. Board of Education, (Brown I)** when the court ruled that segregation in public education was inherently unconstitutional.

This case has been declared one of the most important rulings during the twentieth century since it reversed many years of legally authorized segregation and disparate treatment of African Americans.

BROWN V. BOARD OF EDUCATION
347 U.S. 483 (1954)

These cases come to us from the States of Kansas, South Carolina, Virginia, and Delaware.

In each, minors of the Negro race seek the aid of the courts in obtaining admission to the public schools of their community on a non-segregated basis. In each instance, they had been denied admission to schools attended by white children under laws requiring or permitting segregation according to race. This segregation was alleged to deprive the plaintiffs of the equal protection of the laws under the Fourteenth Amendment.

The doctrine of "separate but equal" did not make its appearance in this Court until 1896 in **Plessy v. Ferguson** involving not education but transportation. American courts have since labored with the doctrine.

In the instant cases, there are findings that the Negro and white schools involved have been equalized with respect to buildings, curricula, qualifications and salaries of teachers, and other "tangible" factors. Our decision, therefore, cannot turn on merely a comparison of these tangible. We must look instead to the effect of segregation on public education.

Education is perhaps the most important function of state and local governments. Compulsory school attendance laws and the great expenditures for education both demonstrate our recognition of the importance of education to our democratic society. In these days, it is doubtful that any child may reasonably be expected to succeed if he is denied the opportunity of an education.

We come to the question presented: Does segregation of children in public schools solely on the basis of race, even though the physical facilities and other "tangible" factors may be equal, deprive the children of the minority group of equal educational opportunities? We believe that it does.

Segregation of white and colored children in public schools has a detrimental effect upon the colored children. The impact is greater when it has the sanction of the law, for the policy of separating the races is usually interpreted as denoting the inferiority of the Negro group. A sense of inferiority affects the motivation of a child to learn. Segregation with the sanction of law, therefore, has a tendency to [retard] the educational and mental development of Negro children and to deprive them of some of the benefits they would receive in a racially integrated school system.

We conclude that in the field of public education, the doctrine of "separate but equal" has no place. Separate educational facilities are inherently unequal. Therefore, we hold that the plaintiffs and others similarly situated are, by reason of the segregation complained of, deprived of the equal protection of the laws guaranteed by the Fourteenth Amendment.

The Supreme Court in **Brown v. Board of Education (Brown 1)** did not fashion a remedy so the court revisited the case in 1955, **(Brown II)** and noted that the school districts needed to desegregate with "all deliberate speed." Did the public school systems, particularly some of the ones in the southern states, desegregate with all deliberate speed?

Needless to say, there was massive resistance to the Court's ruling. Many saw this as an issue involving states' rights v. federal law. Local school districts in states such as Virginia closed school districts to avoid desegregation. They did not want white and African American children to go to school together. In Little Rock, Arkansas, Governor Faubus used the National Guard to prevent nine African American students, who had been selected by the school board, from desegregating Central High School. Upon the intervention of President Dwight Eisenhower, the Governor withdrew the National Guard leaving the local police to handle the volatile situation. The President had to summon the elite 101st Airborne Division of the United States Army to Little Rock, thus removing the issue of desegregation from the Governor's control. Race was still an issue in this country.

**SECTION 6.8
CIVIL RIGHTS
LEGISLATION**

Congress continued in its struggle to pass remedial legislation that would bring about racial equality. After an 82-year gap in legislation, the Civil Rights Acts of 1957, 1960, and 1964 were enacted. Each built upon the other and provided additional legal tools to fight unequal treatment solely because of the color of one's skin.

The **Civil Rights Act of 1957** established the Commission on Civil Rights and gave this organization the power to investigate allegations of discrimination and deprivation of the right to vote. The Act also established the Civil Rights Division within the Justice Department with an Assistant Attorney General to head that special division and to impose fines if convicted of unlawful conduct.

The **Civil Rights Act of 1960** strengthened existing laws on obstruction of court orders and imposed criminal penalties for violence and destruction. It also provided for court appointed referees to monitor voting rights.

In 1963, President Kennedy was instrumental in the introduction of a bill to ban discrimination in the work place regardless of one's racial makeup. Because of his assassination, however he never saw his ideas come to fruition. Instead, the **Civil Rights Act of 1964** became the law under the guidance of President Lyndon Johnson. The purpose of this progressive legislation was multifaceted including the enforcement of the constitutional right to vote, to confer jurisdiction upon the federal courts, to provide injunctive relief against discrimination in public accommodations, to authorize the Attorney General to institute suits to protect the constitutional rights in public facilities and public education, to prevent discrimination in federally assisted programs, to establish the **Equal Employment Opportunity Commission (EEOC)**, and for other purposes.

There are three sections of the Civil Rights Act of 1964 that are of particular relevance. **Title IV** addresses public education and calls for desegregation within public education at all levels, elementary, secondary and college. **Title VI** focuses on federally assisted programs and provides for nondiscrimination within those federal programs. In fact, federal funds will be terminated if the party receiving the money refuses to voluntarily comply with the statute. Of the three titles, however, **Title VII** is the most commonly recognized section. Its purpose is to eliminate job discrimination in employment by making it illegal to discriminate in employment based on race, color, religion, sex or national origin. It also created the Equal Employment Opportunity Commission to enforce the law.

Relying upon the Civil Rights Acts as its foundation, Congress passed the **Elementary and Secondary Education School Act of 1965**, which provided for federal school aid for the first time to insure that the poor received a proper education. In order to receive federal funds, the local school districts had to abide by the requirements of the Civil Rights Acts. Local districts had to choose between whether to maintain segregation or receive the massive federal funding that had been made available. Needless to say, they opted for the money, thereby bringing segregation in public education to an end. In some districts, however, segregation continues due to factors such as housing patterns, neighborhood school systems, and economics.

SECTION 6.9
RACE AND INTER-
PERSONAL RELATIONSHIPS

In 1967, the Supreme Court reviewed one of the most sensitive areas in race relations, inter-racial marriage. The court was called upon in **Loving v. Virginia, 388 U.S. 1**, to determine the constitutionality of **miscegenation statutes**; laws that prohibit interracial marriage. The law in question provided: "If any white person intermarries with a colored person, or any colored person intermarries with a white person, he shall be guilty of a felony and shall be punished by confinement in the penitentiary for not less than one nor more than five years." At the time, Virginia and fifteen other states had statutes that prevented marriages between persons solely on the basis of race.[6] In declaring these laws unconstitutional on the basis of the Equal Protection Clause, the court stated, "there can be no question but that Virginia's miscegenation statutes rest solely upon distinctions drawn according to race."

Further, "there is patently no legitimate overriding purpose independent of invidious racial discrimination which justifies this classification."

QUESTIONS FOR DISCUSSION:

1. Why do you think this area of inter-racial relationships was one of the last to be addressed by the Supreme Court?

2. Is there any justifiable area in our daily existence when racial segregation does not violate the Constitution?

3. Is it ever "o.k." to discriminate based upon race?

SECTION 6.10
AFFIRMATIVE ACTION

An outgrowth of the Civil Rights Acts is the concept of **affirmative action**. This phrase was not mentioned in any previous legislation. Affirmative action as it applies to race has become controversial. This concept attempts to achieve racial equality by recognizing that certain employers and educational facilities need to create affirmative goals so that disadvantaged groups are placed upon a level playing field with other candidates when employment and admission decisions are made. The term was first coined by President Kennedy in Executive Order 10925. Among other things, that Order required projects financed with federal funds to "take affirmative action" to ensure that hiring and employment practices are free of racism.

President Johnson outlined the premise for "affirmative action" in a speech at Howard University, when he stressed that civil rights laws are not enough to fix years of discrimination. He stated:

> You do not wipe away the scars of centuries by saying: now, you are free to go where you want, do as you desire, and choose the leaders you please. You do not take a man who for years has been hobbled by chains, liberate him, bring him to the starting line of a race, saying, you are free to compete with all the others, and still justly believe you have been completely fair. This is the next and more profound stage of the battle for civil rights. We seek not just freedom but opportunity—not just legal equity but human ability—not just equality as a right and a theory, but equality as a fact and as a result.

Subsequently, he issued an Executive Order mandating affirmative action for the first time. It required government contractors to "take affirmative action" toward minorities in all aspects of hiring and employment. Also, contractors must take and document all measures to ensure equality in hiring. A few weeks later, the Order was amended to cover discrimination on the basis of gender as well.

In 1969, President Nixon implemented the **Philadelphia Order**, which is the most forceful program to guarantee fair hiring practices in construction jobs. Philadelphia was selected as the test case because, as Assistant Secretary of Labor Arthur Fletcher proclaimed, "The craft unions and the construction industry are among the most egregious offenders against equal opportunity laws . . . openly hostile toward letting blacks into their closed circle." This order also included specific goals and timetables, which had to be followed.

President Nixon said, "We would not impose quotas, but would require federal contractors to show affirmative action to meet the goals of increasing minority employment."

Affirmative action is a polarizing subject in many circles. Opponents maintain that affirmative action is nothing more than reverse discrimination and allows for the admission or employment of less qualified persons. Advocates argue that it is merely an attempt to level the playing field. What is often missed in these arguments it that affirmative action, or preferential treatment, is not limited to African Americans, but applies equally to other minorities, women, and in many instances to other subgroups such as military veterans and the handicapped.

It must be acknowledged that the idea of affirmative action existed long before the 1960's and continues to this day. It just was not labeled affirmative action nor was it applied to minorities. For example, legacy preferences in college admissions, in-state tuition reduction, free college tuition to employees, spouses, and children, and the "old boy network" are just some examples of preferential treatment afforded to certain classes of people.

The **legacy preference**, as it is known, is nearly as widespread as those affirmative action programs based on race and ethnicity. Colleges like these preferences because it keeps alumni happy and more inclined to donate. But overwhelmingly, the legacy preference benefits Caucasians.

For example, 91% of the legacy applicants at the University of Virginia accepted on an early-decision basis for the fall of 2003 were white; 1.6% were black, 0.5% were Hispanic, and 1.6% were Asian. Among applicants whose parents were not alumni of the University, the pool of those accepted was more diverse: 73% were Caucasians, 5.6% African American, 9.3% Asian and 3.5% Hispanic. About half of the legacy applicants accepted at Virginia were children of out-of-state alumni. Virginia gives these applicants a break by grouping them with its in-state applicants. The SAT scores of accepted state residents averaged about 30 to 35 points lower than those of accepted out-of-state applicants.[7]

It must not be overlooked, however, that elimination of this form of preferential treatment would have serious financial implications for colleges and universities. Alumni provide approximately 28% of the private donations to higher education.

At most Ivy League schools, it is estimated that sons and daughters of graduates make up 10% to 15% of the student body and enjoy a sharply higher rate of acceptance. For instance, Harvard accepts 40% of legacy applicants, compared with an 11% overall acceptance rate of its applicants. Princeton accepts 35% of the children of alumni who apply, but only 11% of the overall applicant pool. The University of Pennsylvania accepts 41% of legacy applicants, compared with an admission rate of 21% overall.

Acceptance based upon legacy is not always as clear-cut as awarding additional points or placement in a different applicant pool. It may include favoritism based on social class or a specific high school. President George W. Bush attended Yale. While the University did not have an explicit point system in 1964, Bush received preferential treatment. After all, he was the product of an exclusive prep school, the son and grandson of alumni, and a member of a politically influential family. His admission to this prestigious University was not based solely upon his SAT scores: 566 verbal and 640 math.[8] These forms of affirmative action programs continue; they just have a different label or no label.

Affirmative action programs stemming from the civil rights movement focus primarily on education and employment. These policies require that active measures or affirmative steps, be taken to ensure that women, African Americans, and other minorities and subgroups enjoy the same opportunities for employment, promotions, salary increases, career advancements, school admissions, scholarships, and financial aid that had been the nearly exclusive province of Caucasians in this country.

These initiatives have met with resistance on many levels. For instance, the Supreme Court considered the issue of reverse discrimination in **Regents of the University of California v. Bakke,** 438 U.S. 265 (1978). **Bakke** is a white male, who had been rejected two times by a medical school in California. The institution had two separate admissions pools, one for standard applicants, and another for minority students. The school maintained a quota in which it reserved 16 of its 100 places for minority students. **Bakke** was refused admission while minority applicants with lower scores were granted admission. The Supreme Court ruled that a fixed quota system was unlawful. However, it upheld affirmative action by ruling that it was lawful to consider race as a factor in school admissions.

In 1995, the Supreme Court refined its affirmative action position in **Adarand Constructors, Inc. v. Pena** by imposing a "strict scrutiny" test in determining whether discrimination exists before a federal affirmative action program may be implemented. This meant that an affirmative action program must fulfill a "compelling governmental interest," and it has to be "narrowly tailored" to fit the particular situation. The Court's majority held that "the unhappy persistence of both the practice and the lingering effects of racial discrimination against minority groups" justified the use of race-based correctional measures only under particular circumstances.

The following month, President Clinton acknowledged this new standard for affirmative action programs and stated, "...it actually reaffirmed the need for affirmative action and reaffirmed the continuing existence of systematic discrimination in the United States." On the same day, he issued a White House memorandum that called for the elimination of any program that creates a quota, establishes preferences for unqualified individuals, mandates reverse discrimination, or continues after its equal opportunity purposes have been achieved.

The up and down history of affirmative action continued when in 1996, a United States Court of Appeals in **Hopwood v. University of Texas Law School**, suspended the University of Texas' affirmative action admissions program and opined that the **Bakke** decision was invalid. The appellate court rejected diversity as a goal, asserting that "educational diversity is not a compelling state interest." The U. S. Supreme Court did not hear the appeal so the decision was allowed to stand.

In 1997, the Texas Attorney General announced that all "Texas public universities (should) employ race-neutral criteria." In that same year, California enacted "**Proposition 209**" which banned all forms of affirmative action. That mandate provided: "The state shall not discriminate against, or grant preferential treatment to, any individual or group on the basis of race, sex, color, ethnicity, or national origin in the operation of public employment, public education, or public contracting."

The pendulum continued to swing away from affirmative action at a state level in several other jurisdictions. For instance, in 1998, the State of Washington enacted Initiative 200 making it the second state to completely abolish state affirmative action measures. In 2000, the Florida legislature approved the education component of Gov. Jeb Bush's "One Florida" initiative. This ended admission programs based on affirmative action in all of Florida's colleges and universities.

The United States Supreme Court, however, spoke again in 2003 on affirmative action. The University of Michigan's undergraduate and law school affirmative action policies were called into question in **Gratz**

v. Bollinger and **Grutter v. Bollinger** respectively. The highest court determined that modification was needed to the undergraduate policy of awarding additional points to minorities during the admission process. The law school's admission policy of merely taking race into account as one of many factors considered in the process was upheld because it furthers "a compelling interest in obtaining the educational benefits that flow from a diverse student body." Unlike the undergraduate program that utilized a formula, the law school's affirmative action program provided "individualized consideration" which the Supreme Court allowed. This decision effectively over ruled the **Hopwood** case from Texas.

In June of 2007, the Supreme Court re-examined the issue of race in a case involving integration in the public school systems of Seattle and Louisville. The Court rejected the integration plans that had been implemented but left the door open for using race to assign students in limited circumstances. As the court stated, "A district may consider [race] a compelling interest to achieve a diverse student population…Race may be one component of that diversity."[9] At the present time, affirmative action continues to be viable because race is still an issue.

SECTION 6.11
CURRENT ISSUES

Race intersects with many issues including immigration. The United States is composed of people from numerous countries, some of whom are here illegally. It has been estimated that there are approximately 12 to 20 million illegal aliens currently residing in the U. S. This issue intersects with race because many of the illegal aliens are of Hispanic background. In an attempt to address the illegal alien issue, Congress debated the **Comprehensive Immigration Reform Act of 2007**. This bill offered citizenship to the millions of illegal aliens currently residing in the U. S. The proposed legislation created a new class of visa (Z visa) that would be given to anyone who was living illegally in this country as of January 1, 2007. This visa would provide its holder with the right to remain in this country for the rest of his or her life, and access to a Social Security number. After eight years, those individuals would be eligible for a "green card" if they paid a $2,000 fine and back taxes for some of the period in which they worked. Based upon the existing immigration rules concerning green cards, five years later these illegal immigrants could begin the process of becoming U. S. citizens. The bill created another new category of visa (Y visa) that would let temporary guest workers stay in the U. S. for two years, after which they would have to return home. The proposed legislation also contained **The Dream Act**, which would provide a fast-track to citizenship for illegal-immigrant minors who either go to college or serve in the U. S. military. It would also guarantee minors lower, in-state tuition rates if they attended a public university in their home state. Finally, the bill had provisions for added enforcement of the United States-Mexico border by increasing the number of border patrol agents to 20,000 and by adding another 370 miles of fencing. On June 28, 2007, the Immigration Reform Act of 2007 effectively died due to the inability of Congress to garner the necessary votes to end the debate on the bill.

In February 2007, the Equal Employment Opportunity Commission (EEOC) "launched a national initiative to bring a fresh, 21st century approach to combating racism, which remains the most frequent claim filed with the agency." In an effort to identify and implement new strategies that will strengthen its enforcement of Title VII of Civil Rights Act of 1964 and advance the statutory right to a workplace free of race and color discrimination, the EEOC instituted the **E-RACE Initiative** (Eradicating Racism and Color in Employment).

Allegations of race discrimination, racial harassment, or retaliation arising from opposition to race discrimination are the most frequently filed claims with the EEOC. In 2006, 36% of the charges filed with EEOC alleged race-based discrimination.[10]

New forms of discrimination are emerging based on race and color. Recent studies have shown that employees with lighter colored skin are paid more or favored over a darker skinned employee even though the darker skinned employee had higher educational credentials.[11] Facially neutral employment criteria are significantly disadvantaging applicants and employees on the basis of race and color. Practices such as employers using names as a basis for making selection decisions, employment and personality tests, use of credit scores or video resumes can all have a disparate impact. With a growing number of interracial marriages and families and increased immigration, racial demographics of the workforce have changed and the issue of race discrimination in America is multi-dimensional.[12]

E-Race is a multi-faceted approach. It involves outreach, education, and an enforcement campaign. EEOC chairperson stated, "New times demand new strategies to stay ahead of the curve. These old evils are still around in new forms and we intend to act vigorously to eradicate them."[13]

> *The enduring hope is that race should not matter; the reality is that too often it does.*
>
> *Justice Anthony Kennedy 2007*

SECTION 6.12
INTERNET REFERENCES

- **http://www.infoplease.com/spot/affirmative1.html**
  This site provides a history of affirmative action.

- **www.civilrights.org/issues/affirmative**
  The Civil Rights Coalition can be accessed at this site.

- **www.law.cornell.edu/wex/index.php/Equal_protection**
  The Equal Protection Clause is explained in detail by this site maintained by Cornell Law School.

- **www.pbs.org/wgbh/aia/part4/4p2932.html**
  This site maintained by PBS discusses Dred Scott and his case.

- **http://teachingamericanhistory.org/library/index.asp?document=52**
  This site contains a speech by Abraham Lincoln on the Dred Scott Decision.

- **http://afroamhistory.about.com/od/jimcrowlaw1/Jim_Crow_Laws.htm**
  A number of articles about Jim Crow laws can be found at this site.

- **http://www.asianamericanmedia.org/jainternment**
  This site offers more information about the Japanese interment during World War II.

- **http://www.eeoc.gov/initiatives/e-race/index.html**
  This site provides information on EEOC E-Race Initiative.

Footnotes:

1. The Richmond Free Press

2. Entrepreneur Magazine, May 2001, *Colorblind Collaring*, by Steven Bahls and Jane Easter Bahls.

3. See http://usdoj.gov/crt/housing/caselist.htm for the terms of the consent degree.

4. http://www.eeoc.gov/press/7-12-07.html, U.S. Equal employment Opportunity Commission, Press Release, July 12, 2007.

5. See *From Slavery to Freedom: A History of Negro America*, 5th edition, by John Hope Franklin, Alfred A. Knoph, Inc, 1980 at page 265.

6. In 1954, the year **Brown I** was decided, 30 states had statutes outlawing interracial marriages.

7. See The Wall Street Journal, *Admissions Preferences for Alums' Kids Draw Fire*, by Daniel Golden, January 2003.

8.   See CNN.com/inside politics, *How Affirmative Action Helped George W.*, by Michael Kinsley, January 20, 2003.

9.   See Parents Involved in **Community School v. Seattle School District #1** and **Meredith v. Jefferson County Kentucky Board of Education**.

10. www.eeoc.gov/initiatives/e-race/why_e-race.html, the United States Equal Employment Opportunity Commission, *The E-Race Initiative*, February 28, 2007.

11. Ibid.

12. Ibid.

13. Ibid.

KEY TERMS

Affirmative Action
Amendment Thirteen
Amendment Fourteen
Amendment Fifteen
Civil Liberties Act
Civil Rights Act of 1866
Civil Rights Act of 1875
Civil Rights Act of 1957
Civil Rights Act of 1960
Civil Rights Act of 1964
Civil War Amendments
Comprehensive Immigration Reform Act of 2007
The Dream Act
E-RACE Initiative

Elementary and Secondary Education School Act of 1965
Equal Employment Opportunities Commission
Equal Protection
Grandfather Clauses
Jim Crow Laws
Legacy Preference
Miscegenation Statutes
Philadelphia Order
Proposition 209
Racial Discrimination
Title IV
Title VI
Title VII

Part Two

The Procedural Law

CHAPTER 7

THE JUDICIAL SYSTEM

SECTION 7.1
THE FEDERAL
COURT SYSTEM

"A Court is only as sound as its jury, and a jury is only as sound as the men who make it up."

Harper Lee
"To Kill a Mockingbird," 1960

Article III of the Constitution provides that "the judicial power of the United States shall be vested in one Supreme Court, and in such other inferior courts as Congress may from time to time establish."

The court is the last branch of the government to be addressed by the Constitution and very little direction is provided by the framers in that historic document. Article III merely creates the **Supreme Court** of the United States and it glaringly fails to set forth that Court's powers, composition or jurisdiction. In what one may call a lack of respect, the framers also gave Congress the power to create the remaining courts thereby making the court system seem subservient to the legislature.

The First Congress of the United States accepted this grant of power when it enacted the Judiciary Act of 1787. Through the efforts of Senator Oliver Ellsworth of Connecticut, the legislature created thirteen judicial districts and three circuit courts throughout the country. Initially, the Supreme Court consisted of one chief justice and five other jurists who met twice a year in the Nation's Capital, the initial session commencing on the first Monday of February, and the other on the first Monday in August.

The Supreme Court was given exclusive jurisdiction over all controversies of a civil nature in which a state is a party and it has exclusive jurisdiction over proceedings against ambassadors or other public ministers consistent with the law of nation. The Supreme Court is also given appellate jurisdiction or the ability to hear cases on appeal from the federal circuit courts and courts of the states.

During its first few years, the Supreme Court heard very few cases and was viewed as the weakest branch of the government. This perception changed dramatically in 1801 when John Marshall became the Chief Justice and issued the landmark ruling in **Marbury v. Madison**. This case established the fundamental principle that the Supreme Court uniquely has the power to declare a law of Congress unconstitutional. It is also the final arbiter of the meaning of the Constitution. With these powers, the Supreme Court became an equal partner in the government, and it has enjoyed that status ever since.[1]

Presently, the court of **original jurisdiction** or trial court in the federal system is the District Court, and appeals are entertained by the Circuit Court of Appeals. On rare occasion, the Supreme Court of the United States will review a lower court's decision if it presents a compelling national question that needs to be answered.

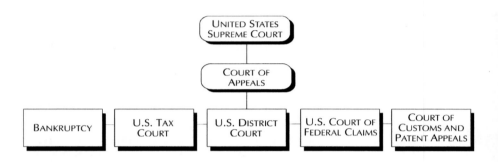

The **United States District Court**, or trial court, is in direct contact with the parties, hears the evidence, and applies the appropriate law to the facts of a case. There are ninety-four district courts in the United States and its territories. A state may have one or more district courts within its boundaries depending on its population. For example, the state of New York has four district courts within its boundaries, whereas Maine only has one.

The type of cases the federal court may hear are limited to questions involving federal law, the United States Constitution, and disputes between citizens of different states where the amount in controversy exceeds $75,000. Congress has also created several specialized courts that hear cases involving very narrow issues, such as tax matters and customs or patent appeals.

The **Court of Appeals** is the intermediate appellate court within the federal court system. There are thirteen circuit courts throughout the United States. Eleven of the circuit courts hear cases on appeal from the district courts. The twelfth circuit is devoted to hearing cases from the District of Columbia. Congress has also created one specialized court called the United States Court of Appeals for the Federal Circuit. This Federal Circuit hears appeals involving tort claims against the United States government, patent cases, and appeals from the United States Court of Federal Claims and the Court of International Trade. Parties may appeal to the Circuit Courts of Appeal as a matter of right.

Because the Supreme Court's decision to hear a case is discretionary, the Courts of Appeal are usually the last place that a party will appeal a federal case. When a Court of Appeals decides a case, that decision is binding over all of the district courts within that circuit.

The **Supreme Court of the United States** is the final arbiter of all legal disputes. As a result, it often decides very controversial issues that affect our daily lives. Supreme Court decisions establish precedent and bind all other courts. Commentators and constitutional scholars analyze each word of an opinion and predict how a particular holding will impact society.

The Court has undergone significant changes over the past forty years and established legal doctrines have changed drastically. For example, the death penalty was unconstitutional but is now considered appropriate punishment under certain circumstances.

What has caused this change in judicial philosophy? Shifting attitudes of the public certainly has an influence in court interpretation. The modification of the law, however, is more a reflection of the personalities of the members of the Supreme Court. There has been a dramatic turnover of Supreme Court justices during the past four decades, which has altered the judicial philosophy of the Court. Today a conservative majority rules the court. What has lead up to this shift is worthy of examination.

The Warren Court, named after Chief Justice Earl Warren during the 1960s, was viewed as a liberal body that went to great lengths to ensure that all individuals be treated equally regardless of their social status. Suspects in criminal proceedings were guaranteed the right to have an attorney present when questioned, and the issue of busing became viewed as the only way that children of all races could receive an equal education. The death penalty was treated as cruel and unusual punishment, and affirmative action programs took hold as the only way to overcome centuries of racial discrimination.

However, when Warren Burger was elevated to Chief Justice in 1969, the court began a subtle transformation. As liberal members of the court resigned, middle-of-the road or conservative jurists took their place. The liberal tendency of the Court became more tempered and reflective of the opinions of the conservative jurists. Decisions were frequently decided by a single vote. Nevertheless, it was during this period that **Roe v. Wade** decided the constitutionality of a woman's right to an abortion and the justices prohibited discrimination against women. The court also lifted the moratorium on the death penalty.

The composition of the Supreme Court at the start of the twenty-first century was divided into three groups. Justices Sandra Day O'Connor and Anthony Kennedy, President Reagan appointees, joined Justice Souter and Stephen Breyer to form a moderate voting block. Rehnquist, Thomas, and Antonin Scalia collectively practiced judicial restraint. John Paul Stevens, a Ford appointee, usually maintained the liberal or Activist position.

Justices Ruth Bader Ginsberg and Stephen Breyer were appointed by President Clinton and their votes helped shift the Court's voting record to a more middle-of-the road position. This "do not rock the boat" philosophy continued until the death of Chief Justice Rehnquist in 2005 and the retirement of Sandra Day O'Connor in 2006. These vacancies provided President George W. Bush with the opportunity to appoint their replacements. John Roberts, Jr. was selected as the new Chief Justice and Samuel Alito, Jr. became the newest Associate Justice. Both individuals were judges on the Circuit Court of Appeals and were conservative in their judicial thinking. During their early tenure, these individuals have maintained their conservative judicial philosophies, and have joined Clarence Thomas, and Antonin Scalia to form a solid conservative voting block.

It is not technically accurate to use the labels liberal and conservative when speaking about members of the Court. The proper terms for current judicial philosophies is activist v. judicial restraint oriented. An **activist** is one who views his or her role as bringing about social change. If there is something wrong with the system, a justice will take an active stance in imposing remedial measures to correct a problem. A justice that is **judicial restraint-oriented** tends to believe that his or her role is merely to make sure that a rule is constitutional. If there is something wrong with the system, it is up to the legislature to bring about the necessary change.

The operational aspects of the Supreme Court reveal that its term starts on the first Monday in October and ends when the list of scheduled cases is reached during the summer. Before World War II, the Supreme Court had 1,300 docketed cases. Today, about 8,000 cases are appealed each year and an additional 1,200 applications are filed that can be acted upon by a single Justice.[2] The Supreme Court is also a court of both original and appellate jurisdiction. Cases involving Ambassadors, Consuls, litigation between the federal government and a state as well as suits between states may be heard directly by the Supreme Court. There are no appeals of these decisions. Most cases, however, reach the Supreme Court on appeal of a lower court's decision. These appeals are originated by the filing of a **writ of certiorari** which is Latin for "we wish to be informed."[3]

History demonstrates that few appeals are actually heard by the court. In 2000, the Justices decided only 74 cases even though it takes a mere four of nine jurists to agree to hear the appeal. This has become known as the "Rule of Four." The Justices meet on Wednesdays and Fridays to review recent appeals and the junior most Justice acts as the "doorkeeper" when it is necessary to retrieve materials. Their deliberations are secret and what is said among the justices is not available for public consumption.[4]

Supreme Court Rule 10 governs these petitions and provides that the acceptance of a case on a Writ of Certiorari is not a matter of right but within the sound discretion of the court and the appeal will only be entertained for compelling reasons. Some of the factors the court considers in determining whether to grant an appeal include:

A. A conflict in United States Court of Appeal decisions on the same issue;

B. A state's highest court has issued a ruling on an issue that conflicts with a decision of another state's highest court or with a United States Court of Appeal; or

C. A state court or a United States Court of Appeal has decided an important question of federal law that has not been, but should be, settled by the Supreme Court.

A Petition for a Writ of Certiorari is rarely granted when the alleged error merely consists of factual mistakes or the misapplication of a properly stated rule of law.

For additional reading about the workings of the United States Supreme Court, see *Gideon's Trumpet* by Anthony Lewis and *The Brethren* by Bob Woodward and Scott Armstrong.

The official web address for the United States Supreme Court is:

- **www.supremecourtus.gov**
  This site provides information about the high court, including biographies of the current Court members, an overview of how the court works, Supreme Court Rules, and Supreme Court decisions.

SECTION 7.2
THE STATE
COURT SYSTEM

We are a nation of states with each maintaining its own independent court system. While the configuration of the court system will vary from state to state, each will have a trial court and at least one appellate court. The National Center for States Courts is an organization created to improve the administration of justice through leadership and service to state courts and courts around the world. They maintain a website that provides links to each state court in the country. That site may be accessed at http://www.ncsconline.org/D_KIS/info_court_web_sites.html. The state court system in Pennsylvania is provided as an illustration.

The court of original jurisdiction in Pennsylvania is known as the **Court of Common Pleas** and they were established as part of the Pennsylvania Constitution in 1776 and it is subdivided into the following three divisions: (1) The Trial Court; (2) the Family Court; and (3) Orphan's Court.

The Trial Division will hear both civil and criminal cases. Orphan's Court is concerned with matters involving estates, such as will contests, trusts, and incompetence hearings. Family Court decides juvenile cases and matters involving the family unit such as divorce, custody, support, paternity, and domestic violence.

To reduce the backlog of cases, a specialized court has been created to handle small disputes. In Philadelphia, this court is called the Municipal Court and is divided into civil and criminal divisions. It handles all landlord/tenant problems, civil disputes of $10,000 or less, criminal cases where the penalty involves five years or less imprisonment, and code violations. In the surrounding counties, magesterial district justices who have offices in the various townships throughout the Commonwealth handle these matters. Parties appearing in Municipal Court do not enjoy the right to a jury trial, so most cases can be appealed directly to the Court of Common Pleas at which time the person will receive a new trial equipped with a jury if so desired.

Pennsylvania State Judicial System

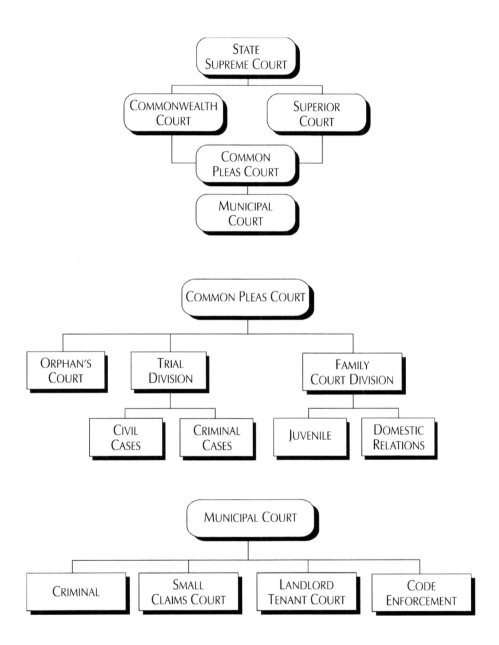

SECTION 7.3
THE JURY SYSTEM

The right to a trial by one's peers is a basic building block of American democracy guaranteed by the United States Constitution. In fact, it has been estimated that this country accounts for 95% of all jury trials in the world.[5] As the Supreme Court noted, "The guarantees of a jury trial reflect a profound judgment about the way in which the law should be enforced and justice administered. Providing an accused with the right to be tried by a jury of his peers gives him an inestimable safeguard against the corrupt or overzealous prosecutor and against the compliant, biased, or eccentric judge."[6]

While the right to a jury trial is firmly engrained in our system of jurisprudence, it was not conceived by the founders of this country. Jury trials have been in existence in England for centuries and some scholars contend that the concept originated in thirteenth-century England as an outgrowth of the *Magna Carta*.

During the founding days of this country, the right to a jury trial was brought to America by the English colonists. In fact, it was adopted by the First Congress of the American Colonists in 1765 with the declaration that "trial by jury is the inherent and invaluable right of every British subject in these colonies."

The founding fathers considered the concept to be so fundamental that it is contained in two different Amendments to the United States Constitution. The Sixth Amendment guarantees the defendant in a criminal case the right to a speedy and public trial by an impartial jury. The Seventh Amendment entitles citizens to a jury trial in civil cases involving a dispute of more than twenty dollars.

In application, a judge presides over the trial and decides questions-of-law. The jury, on the other hand, is the ultimate arbiter of the facts. They decide which party should win a controversy based upon the evidence presented at trial.

To better understand the distinction between a question of law and a question of fact, consider the following hypothetical situation:

> Joe Roberts is driving his car south on Broad Street and enters the intersection on what he maintains is a green light. Bill Smith is proceeding east on Montgomery Avenue and enters the same intersection on what he too alleges is a green light. The vehicles collide on Broad Street, and Roberts maintains that he is injured. Joe institutes suit against Smith for personal injuries.

The judge will inform the jury that a party who enters an intersection against a red light is negligent and responsible for the injuries caused by that negligence. This is a statement of law. On the other hand, it is up to the jury to decide which party entered the intersection after the light turned red. This is a determination of fact.

A jury in a criminal trial generally consists of twelve people whose decisions must be unanimous. The origin of this number is not clear. Some say it represents the number of apostles from the bible, Solomon's officers which numbered twelve, or twelve was a favorite number in mid-evil times. The Supreme Court, however, has noted that the number is an historical accident that became fixed in the fourteenth century. The essential feature of a jury lays in the collective judgment of a group of people, and in the community participation that results from that group's determination of innocence or guilt. The performance of this role is not dependent on a specific number of citizens that make up the jury.[7] Jury requirements, therefore, vary by state and type of proceeding. For instance, Pennsylvania requires that a defendant in a criminal trial be provided with twelve jurors and all must agree on the verdict. In a civil case, however, the verdict need not be unanimous, and the jury will consist of eight members unless a litigant specifically demands a trial by twelve.

More than 120,000 jury trials a year are conducted in the United States. In contrast, only about one-percent of trials in England are conducted with the help of a jury. France utilizes juries for only the most serious crimes, and Italy uses panels of three judges. Germany, Finland and Sweden have mixed tribunals of a professional judge and several laymen.[8] Russia has only recently reinstituted the use of jury trials in serious criminal matters, and Japan will utilize six-person juries starting in 2009.

Mark Twain stated in a 1873 speech that: "We have a criminal jury system which is superior to any in the world; and its efficiency is only marred by the difficulty of finding twelve men every day who don't know anything and can't read."

Is the jury system the best way of having a matter decided in a court of law? The verdict in the O.J. Simpson case left many people questioning the validity of the jury system, and who can forget the two-million dollar award against McDonald's for the coffee that spilled on a woman's leg as she rode in a car. Fortunately, these examples are not representative of jury verdicts. Most legal experts agree that it is the best system available despite certain recognized short comings and occasional erroneous verdicts. After all, it is better to be tried by the collective judgment of one's peers than by the wisdom of a single individual. This is the backbone of a democracy.

The jury system does have inherent weaknesses. The law is very complicated, and a trial is an intimidating proceeding. Jurors are thrust into the role of deciding complex cases without the proper legal training or experience. As a generalization, they tend to be plaintiff oriented and are more apt to award money than to find for the defense. Verdicts also tend to be higher in metropolitan cities than those in rural counties.

An analysis of civil jury verdicts by the United States Department of Justice determined that in 53% of the cases, the jury found in favor of plaintiffs and awarded a total of $3.9 billion dollars in compensatory and punitive damages during the one-year period under review. The average finding was $37,000 and juries awarded punitive damages in 6% of the cases with a median punitive damage award of $50,000.[9]

On the other hand, some scholars have found the very weaknesses of the jury system to be its strength. In a speech given by Oliver Wendell Holmes on January 17, 1899, he stated:

> *"I confess that in my experience I have not found juries especially inspired for the discovery of truth…they will introduce into their verdict a…large amount…of popular prejudice, and thus keep the administration of the law in a court with the wishes and feelings of the community."*[10]

**SECTION 7.4
VOIR DIRE**

Voir Dire is French for *"to speak the truth"* and refers to the jury selection process. Many lawyers consider jury selection one of the most important parts of the trial. It is through this procedure that prospective members of the jury are questioned by the judge or attorneys to ascertain whether they are suitable to serve at the trial. Issues of prejudice, conflicts of interest, and philosophies on life will be explored.

In theory, the attorneys are trying to find objective and unbiased citizens who can render a fair decision. In reality, the individual attorneys are trying to find prospective jurors who are most sympathetic to his or her cause.

Percy Foreman, a famed criminal attorney, once noted:

> The classic adversary system in the United States not only encourages, it demands that each lawyer attempt to empanel the jury most likely to understand his argument or least likely to understand that of his opponent. You don't approach the case with the philosophy of applying abstract justice. You go in to win.[11]

The O.J. Simpson trial, dubbed as the trial of the twentieth century, generated a great deal of controversy regarding the actual fairness of jury trials and whether the process of voir dire is a successful means of obtaining a fair and impartial jury. Indeed, a Gallup Poll showed that public interest in serving on juries dropped more than 50 percent during the duration of the Simpson trial.[12]

A prominent concern is that juries do not reflect the racial make-up of the community. Voter rolls don't always reflect minority participation, and some minority communities feel alienated from the process. Minnesota has taken direct action by posting billboards in predominately minority communities encouraging jury participation. New York has added unemployment and welfare participants to its jury lists. Some jurisdictions obtain their jury pools from both the voter registration lists and the drivers license records in order to have a better cross-section of the population.

There are also concerns that jurors feel underappreciated. While most states have laws that prohibit employers from firing people who are called for jury duty, only six states (Alabama, Colorado, Connecticut, Massachusetts, Nebraska and Tennessee) require employers to keep paying the person while on jury duty. According to surveys, however, jurors are more concerned about inconvenience than a lack of adequate compensation.[13] Jurors are often left sitting around for days waiting to be called. To help solve this problem, many states have switched to a one-day, one-trial jury process where a person is summoned to appear only on one day. If not chosen for service that day, the individual's jury duty is over.

As for the jury selection process, judges in England summon the first twelve potential jurors and ask a very basic question: "Can you give a fair hearing to both the Crown and the defense?" If the potential jurors respond in the affirmative, they are impaneled as part of the jury. The jury selection process in the United States, however, is much more complicated.[14]

In this country, a prospective juror may be challenged on two grounds. Counsel may challenge a juror for cause or exercise a peremptory challenge. A **challenge for cause** is utilized when an individual is biased or unable to render a fair verdict. For instance, the court will exclude a relative of the victim or a person that has a preconceived opinion on the defendant's innocence or guilt. The number of challenges for cause is unlimited, and the judge is the final arbiter as to whether the juror can be fair and impartial. **Peremptory challenges** are discretionary with the attorney and are used to exclude those who are perceived to be least sympathetic to a litigant's position. These individuals are dismissed without reason or justification. The number of peremptory challenges will vary. In a civil suit, an attorney generally receives a modest number of peremptory challenges such as three. In a criminal case, the number will be significantly higher and will increase with the severity of the crime.

For instance, North Carolina provides both the government and the defense with fourteen peremptory challenges in murder cases, and eight in other criminal trials. In a civil case, such as a malpractice lawsuit or car accident, each side is given eight discretionary challenges. Georgia allows twelve peremptory challenges in criminal cases and twenty in matters where the prosecution seeks the death penalty.

Attorneys are afforded great latitude in choosing the individuals they can remove from a jury panel as long as the peremptory challenges are not used on a discriminatory or improper basis. For instance, the Supreme Court has found that using peremptory challenges to systematically exclude African Americans, Latinos, Hispanics, or women is "an unconstitutional proxy for juror competence and impartiality." Would the exclusion of the gay community from a jury panel also constitute an unconstitutional application of a peremptory challenge? That is the issue in **People of California v. Garcia.**

PEOPLE V. CANO GARCIA
77 CAL. APP. 4TH 1269 (CAL. 2000)

Garcia was charged with burglary. During his trial, it became known that two members of the jury panel were lesbians and the prosecution excused both women.

In 1986, the Supreme Court decided the Constitution prohibits jury selection based upon racial stereotyping. Eight years later, it extended the rationale to gender discrimination. To date, those are the only two classifications the Supreme Court has recognized as prohibited bases for exclusion of jurors.

Our only issue is whether lesbians-and gay males-constitute a cognizable class whose exclusion resulted in a jury that failed to represent a cross-section of the community and thereby violated Garcia's constitutional rights. We are convinced they do.

Sexual orientation is not something likely to be volunteered, and it is even less likely to be the subject of inquiry by court or counsel. We re-gret that our record in this case does not clearly reveal how it came up here. But it has come up, and it is our obligation to determine its import in this case of first impression.

Two requirements must be met in order to qualify an asserted group as cognizable for purposes of the representative cross-section rule. First, its members must share a common perspective arising from their life experience in the group, i.e., a perspective gained precisely *because* they are members of that group. The characteristic must also impart to its possessors a common social or psychological outlook on human events.

Lesbians and gay men qualify under this standard. It cannot seriously be argued that homosexuals do not have a common perspective – "*a common social or psychological outlook on human events*"– based upon their membership in that community. They share a history of persecution comparable to that of Blacks and women.

When any large and identifiable segment of the community is excluded from jury service, the effect is to remove from the jury room qualities of human nature and varieties of human experience, the range of which is unknown and perhaps unknowable. The Attorney General contends, however, that the group does not qualify because it is heterogeneous in all other respects: its membership cuts across racial, religious, sexual, economic, social, and occupational lines.

The question, then, is whether another group- or groups-in the community could adequately represent the views of homosexuals. We cannot think of anyone who shares the perspective of the homosexual community. Outside of racial and religious minorities, we can think of no group which has suffered such "pernicious and sustained hostility" Both the defendant and the community are entitled to have that perspective represented in the jury panel.

The length of jury duty will vary depending upon the jurisdiction. Jury duty in federal court ranges between two and three weeks unless an individual is selected to serve on a case that extends beyond this time period. While the length of jury duty in state courts vary by jurisdiction, a number of courts utilize the "One Day or One Trial" program. Under this system, a person who is not selected to serve on a jury during the first day of jury duty is discharged. If a person is selected to sit on a panel, that individual's civic obligation is fulfilled upon completion of the one case.

SECTION 7.5
COMMONWEALTH
v. CHRISTOPHER

SELECTION
OF THE JURY

PROBLEM SEVEN—A

PARK, BROWN & SMITH, P.C.
ATTORNEYS AT LAW
MEMORANDUM

TO: All Law Clerks

FROM: Peter Smith, Esquire

RE: Jury Selection

The selection of a jury is not an exact science and requires an attorney to make quick decisions about the suitability of a potential juror based upon a short conversation with that individual. The ultimate goal of counsel is not to find a jury that will be fair and unbiased but to select jurors that will favor the client.

To gain an appreciation for this important trial task, the following case is presented so that the reader may experience firsthand the jury selection process. You will learn the background of the case by reviewing the following news broadcast.

TRANSCRIPTION OF NEWS BROADCAST

In local news, a 16-year-old girl was assaulted at her high school gym last night and her handbag was stolen. The student, whose name is not being released because of her age, was confronted around 8:00 p.m. while working out in the nautilus room. The victim is unable to identify the thief, since he was wearing a green and white ski mask. She did, however, notice a tattoo of a shark on his bare left shoulder. According to police, the suspect is 5' 10" and weighs approximately 160 pounds. He was last seen wearing a red and white striped shirt, denim pants, and sneakers.

The police eventually arrested an individual who lived near the school who matched the thief's description. The suspect even had a tattoo of a shark on his shoulder. The suspect was charged with theft and other related offenses. The criminal case is about to commence and twenty-one potential jurors are sitting in the courtroom. Biographical sketches are provided of the individual members of the jury pool to assist you in selecting a jury of twelve people.

You should review the biographical data for each prospective juror to see which individuals should be challenged for cause and which people should be considered for use of a peremptory challenge. When reviewing the sketches, first analyze the problem as though you represent the defendant and make your selections. You should then examine the biographical sketches and assume that you represent the prosecution.

For the purposes of this exercise, each side is given three peremptory challenges. The goal is to select twelve jurors suitable to both the prosecution and defense. A worksheet is provided for your selections following the biographical sketches.

Sample questions have also been provided and will be used by the defense and prosecution at the time of the jury selection process. They will give you an idea of the types of issues that are of concern to each side.

QUESTIONS FOR DEFENSE COUNSEL TO ASK THE PANEL:

1. Is anyone familiar with any of the parties, counsel, or the judge in this case?

2. Does anyone know anything about this case?

3. Has anyone ever been the victim of a crime?

4. Is anyone a member of the police force, or does anyone have a close family member on the police force?

5. Has anyone heard or read anything about this case?

6. Does anyone believe that the testimony of a police officer should be given more credence than any other witness?

7. The government has the burden of proving the defendant guilty. Would anyone draw an adverse inference if the defendant didn't testify?

QUESTIONS FOR THE DISTRICT ATTORNEY TO ASK THE PANEL:

1. Has anybody ever been accused of committing a crime?

2. Does anyone believe that they cannot be fair and impartial in the hearing of this matter?

3. Does anyone believe that he or she will have a difficult time in finding the defendant guilty if he could go to jail as a result of the conviction?

4. Will serving on this jury be a hardship or an inconvenience?

BIOGRAPHICAL SKETCHES OF PROSPECTIVE JURORS:

Our consultant service has provided us with 21 biographical sketches of the jurors that we may encounter at trial. Please review the sketches and make your decision on jury selection for both the prosecution and defense.

JUROR 1   *Marilyn Trainer*—Female, 40-year-old mother with three daughters, ages 18, 15 and 12. She claims that she can be fair in the case, even though she has three daughters. She is an unemployed housewife.

JUROR 2   *John McNamara*—Male, 35 years old, married, no children. He is a police sergeant.

JUROR 3   *Hans Forrestor*—Male, single, 30-year-old philosophy professor at Penn who has been mugged on the subway. The police never found his attacker. He claims that he can be fair in the rape case.

JUROR 4   *Star Jackson*—Female, 26-year-old rock singer, single, and a member of Women Organized Against Rape.

JUROR 5   *Chip Wright*—Male, 22 years old, single, college student who resides in fraternity house.

JUROR 6   *Jeanette Williams*—Female, 29-year-old civil litigation paralegal, married, no children. Her husband is a doctor (gynecologist).

JUROR 7   *Duke Septa*—Male, 50-year-old, divorced bus driver with four sons. His marriage represented the "worst years of his life." He believes women should not work and should only take care of the household.

JUROR 8   *Vincent Serino*—Male, 60-year-old gym teacher, not married. Teaches at a girls' Catholic school.

JUROR 9   *Lola Thomas*—Female, 21-year-old exotic dancer. Single, lives with her boyfriend.

JUROR 10   *Alice B. Davis*—Female, 58-year-old housewife with two sons, ages 28 and 30. She has never worked because her household duties keep her busy enough. Her husband is a traveling salesman for an encyclopedia company.

JUROR 11   *Andrew Hoffman*—Male, 23 years old and single. He has heard about the case from the neighborhood, and believes that the defendant has a bad reputation. He does not think he can be impartial.

JUROR 12   *Joseph Hammer*—Male, 23-year-old, unemployed construction worker who lives at home with family. He has two sisters and a brother.

JUROR 13   *Louis Waterman*—Male, 40-year-old, retired sailor who was in the Navy for 20 years. He is single.

JUROR 14   *Anna Klein*—Female, 43-year-old, widowed fashion designer with no children.

JUROR 15   *Desmond Lovejoy*—Male, 28-year-old florist. He is not married.

JUROR 16   *Aileen Wheeler*—Female, 33-year-old, divorced cab driver. She has one 16-year-old son.

JUROR 17   *Elizabeth Addis*—Female, college student at Princeton. She is awaiting trial for a streaking incident.

JUROR 18   *Thomas Bradford*—Male, 50-year-old, disabled veteran on Social Security. He is married with eight children and ten grandchildren.

JUROR 19   *Rose Kelly*—Female, 45-year-old, married waitress whose husband is a roofer. She was convicted of prostitution when she was 18 years old.

JUROR 20   *Margaret Jones*—Female, 35-year-old, single, psychiatrist. Her practice involves drug therapy. She was in the Peace Corps.

JUROR 21   *Jane Sullivan*—Female, 28-year-old lawyer who works for the Office of the Public Defender. She is single.

JURY SELECTION WORKSHEET

Juror Number (For Government)		Juror Number (For Defense)	
1. Yes/No	12. Yes/No	1. Yes/No	12. Yes/No
2. Yes/No	13. Yes/No	2. Yes/No	13. Yes/No
3. Yes/No	14. Yes/No	3. Yes/No	14. Yes/No
4. Yes/No	15. Yes/No	4. Yes/No	15. Yes/No
5. Yes/No	16. Yes/No	5. Yes/No	16. Yes/No
6. Yes/No	17. Yes/No	6. Yes/No	17. Yes/No
7. Yes/No	18. Yes/No	7. Yes/No	18. Yes/No
8. Yes/No	19. Yes/No	8. Yes/No	19. Yes/No
9. Yes/No	20. Yes/No	9. Yes/No	20. Yes/No
10. Yes/No	21. Yes/No	10. Yes/No	21. Yes/No
11. Yes/No		11. Yes/No	

Record of Peremptory Challenges:		Record of Challenges For Cause:	
Government:	Defendant:	Government:	Defendant:
1.	1.	1.	1.
2.	2.	2.	2.
3.	3.	3.	3.

SECTION 7.6
DISCHARGE OF
AN EMPLOYEE FOR
JURY SERVICE

Employers are often confronted with the difficult problem of what to do when an employee announces that he or she has been selected for jury duty. The worker's absence can have a disruptive influence on production schedules and cause economic hardship. Can the employer discharge the worker and hire a replacement to minimize the impact of the juror's absence?

Federal law prohibits the discharge, intimidation, or coercion of any permanent employee because of jury service **(28 U.S.C.A. § 1875).** Penalties for a violation of the statute include reinstatement of the worker, recovery of lost wages, other loss of benefits suffered by the employee, and attorney's fees.

An individual claiming that the employer has violated this law may file an application with the Federal District Court in the locale where the employer maintains a place of business. Upon a finding of probable merit in the claim, the court will appoint counsel to represent the employee in any federal court action necessary to resolve the dispute.

Court cases that have dealt with this legislation have prohibited the recovery of mental pain and suffering for the employer's actions and have based the recovery of attorney's fees on a per-hour basis rather than on a percentage of recovery. A court has even granted a discharged employee a preliminary injunction reinstating him to his job pending the outcome of the trial for wrongful discharge.

SECTION 7.7
JURISDICTION

Jurisdiction refers to the power of a court to determine the merits of a dispute and to grant an aggrieved party relief. In order for a court to properly entertain an action, it must have jurisdiction over the subject matter in dispute and jurisdiction over the parties involved.

Subject matter jurisdiction is quite simple. The particular court where the dispute is heard must have the power to hear the kind of case that is in controversy. The courts are very specialized, and the plaintiff must institute suit before the proper court. For instance, a divorce proceeding may not be instituted in tax court. The court's power to hear these specific types of cases is usually granted by the legislature.

Jurisdiction over the person requires the court to have power to exercise its authority over the defendant. Traditionally, suit was instituted where the defendant could be found. This was either in the state where he resided or where he worked. Now, a court is considered to have jurisdiction over the parties when the defendant has "minimum contacts" with the state where the court is located (the **forum state**). **Minimum contacts** are generally deemed to exist when the defendant takes actions that are purposefully directed toward the forum state.

The rule of serving a defendant where the defendant can be found was expanded over time by the passage of long arm statutes that allow a jurisdiction to reach beyond the state boundaries to serve a defendant with the lawsuit. The most common **long arm statutes** deal with a non-resident who commits a tort within a state, a party who owns property in a state, and one doing business in a state.

In order to satisfy the requirements of due process, the Supreme Court has ruled that a state court may exercise personal jurisdiction over a non-resident defendant as long as there are *minimum contacts* between the defendant and the state in which the suit has been filed. The concept of minimum contacts protects defendants against the burdens of litigating in a distant or inconvenient court. Usually, a defendant will have some kind of presence in the forum. In the case of transacting business within a state, however, it is not necessary to have an office in that jurisdiction. Soliciting business through sales representatives or by placing an advertisement in a local newspaper have been held to constitute minimum contacts.

NIKE, INC. v. MADONNA CICCONE
1990 WL 96681 (D. OR.)

NIKE is an Oregon corporation with its principal place of business in Oregon. Boy Toy is a corporation with its principal place of business in New York. The purpose of Boy Toy is to promote the professional services of Madonna to third parties who use her name for promotional purposes. Boy Toy does not maintain an office in Oregon and has no employees or bank accounts in Oregon. Boy Toy owns no real or personal property in Oregon.

Madonna is a resident of California who travels worldwide. Madonna does not own or possess property or have a bank account in Oregon and has never paid property or income taxes to Oregon. Madonna has performed a concert in Oregon, and her music recordings are distributed in Oregon.

During the fall of 1989, Frederick DeMann, acting on behalf of Boy Toy and Madonna, telephoned Mark Thomas how, an employee of NIKE, at NIKE's corporate headquarters in Oregon. Thomas how was unavailable but returned DeMann's call the same day. At that time, DeMann suggested that NIKE, Boy Toy and Madonna begin contract negotiations relating to Madonna's promotion of NIKE products. DeMann's telephone call was unsolicited, and it was the first contact between the respective parties.

Thereafter, representatives of NIKE engaged in contract negotiations with agents of Boy Toy and Madonna through an extensive series of mail, telephone and facsimile communications. Neither Madonna nor her agents traveled to Oregon to meet with representatives of NIKE.

Boy Toy and Madonna move to dismiss this action for lack of personal jurisdiction. Boy Toy and Madonna argue that this court cannot exercise jurisdiction over them because the parties negotiated the contract outside of Oregon, and performance of the contract was commenced in California when Madonna filmed the video.

NIKE argues that this court has jurisdiction over Boy Toy and Madonna because Madonna received profits from her music recordings sold in Oregon, and because Madonna performed a concert in Oregon.

Due process requires that nonresident defendants have certain minimum contacts with the forum so that maintenance of a suit does not offend traditional notions of fair play and substantial justice. A court may exercise jurisdiction when a defendant's contacts with the forum are significant in relation to the specific cause of action. To establish jurisdiction, a plaintiff must demonstrate the following:

> (1) The nonresident defendant must do some act or consummate some transaction with the forum or perform some act by which he purposefully avails himself of the privilege of conducting activities in the forum, thereby invoking the benefits and protections of its laws. (2) The claim must be one which arises out of or results from the defendant's forum-related activities. (3) Exercise of jurisdiction must be reasonable.

Jurisdiction may exist even if a defendant has never physically entered the forum state. It is an inescapable fact of modern commercial life that a substantial amount of business is transacted solely by mail and wire communications across state lines, thus obviating the need for physical presence within a State in which business is conducted. So long as a commercial actor's efforts are "purposefully directed" toward residents of another State, we have consistently rejected the notion that an absence of physical contacts can defeat personal jurisdiction there.

Since NIKE has demonstrated that Boy Toy and Madonna have purposefully availed themselves of the forum's benefits within Oregon, the court's exercise of jurisdictions is presumptively reasonable.

It would be no more a hardship for Madonna or representatives of Boy Toy to travel to Oregon to defend this suit than it would be for NIKE to travel to New York to pursue the case. Oregon has a strong interest in providing NIKE, its resident, with a forum to settle its dispute. NIKE personnel involved in the contract negotiations are located in Oregon, and NIKE's interests clearly favor the state of Oregon as a forum.

The motion of Boy Toy and Madonna to dismiss for lack of personal jurisdiction is denied.

With the advent of websites and their ability to convey information to people around the world, additional jurisdictional issues arise. For instance, is a business that places information about itself on the internet subject to lawsuits in any place where an individual can access the site even if the business has no presence in that state and has not solicited business in that state? This is the issue in **Michael Hurley v. Cancun Playa Oasis International Hotels**. In this case, the court found that a website by itself is not sufficient contact to confer jurisdiction in a state just because a person may be able to access the site from that state. The plaintiff must still establish that the defendant has maintained continuous, systematic, and substantial business contacts within the state where the lawsuit has been filed.

MICHAEL HURLEY V. CANCUN PLAYA OASIS INTERNATIONAL HOTELS
1999 WL 718556 (E. D. PA. 1999)

Plaintiff Michael Hurley ("Hurley") has filed this action against defendants Cancun Playa Oasis International Hotels ("Cancun Playa") and Reserve Hotel ("ReservHotel"). Hurley alleges that as a result of defendant's negligence, he suffered personal injuries while staying at Cancun Playa's hotel in Mexico. Defendant ReservHotel, a Georgia corporation which

Hurley claims is liable as an agent of Cancun Playa, has filed a motion to dismiss for lack of personal jurisdiction.

For a court properly to exercise jurisdiction under the Due Process Clause, the plaintiff must satisfy a two-part test. First, the plaintiff must demonstrate that the defendant had the constitutionally sufficient "minimum contacts" with the forum. Second, the court must determine that the exercise of specific jurisdiction is consistent with traditional notions of fair play and substantial justice.

In his response to defendant's motion to dismiss, Hurley offers no evidence that his contacts with ReservHotel gave rise to his personal injury claim. For example, Hurley notes that ReservHotel maintains a website and a 1-800 telephone number. Hurley does not contend, however, that he visited the website, knew of the phone number prior to filing his complaint, or used either medium to make reservations in Cancun.

The exercise of general personal jurisdiction does not require that the subject matter of the cause of action ha[ve] any connection to the forum. Rather, a court has jurisdiction over a nonresident corporation only if the corporation's contacts with the forum are continuous, systematic, and substantial. In fact, only a showing of "significantly more than mere minimum contacts" will suffice.

It is undisputed that ReservHotel is not registered to conduct business in Pennsylvania. It has no assets, bank accounts, or property in Pennsylvania. No officers, agents, or employees of ReservHotel reside or work in Pennsylvania. ReservHotel does not have a Pennsylvania telephone listing. Finally, ReservHotel "has never met, contracted with, or been in contact with any individual traveler or travel agent" in Pennsylvania, including the plaintiff.

Hurley nevertheless asserts that ReservHotel maintained "continuous and systematic business contact" with Pennsylvania through its 1-800 telephone number and Internet website, both of which are accessible in Pennsylvania.

The first type of contact is when the defendant clearly does business over the internet.... The second type of contact occurs when "a user can exchange information with the host computer. The third type of contact involves the posting of information or advertisements on an internet website "which is accessible to users in foreign jurisdictions."

ReservHotel's website meets the requirements of the second type of internet contact. ReservHotel's website accepts and confirms reservations for various hotels. These characteristics give ReservHotel's website an interactive quality that goes beyond a passive website that simply advertises.

Personal jurisdiction, however, requires more than a recognition that a nonresident corporation has an "interactive" website. Rather, the "nature and quality of the commercial" contacts actually conducted over the internet must be continuous, systematic, and substantial.

In this case, the record lacks a single instance of deliberative contact between ReservHotel and Pennsylvania through the internet. Hurley, for example, has not demonstrated that ReservHotel has formed contracts with any Pennsylvania entity. In fact, Hurley has not shown that any resident of the Commonwealth has even visited ReservHotel's Web page. ReservHotel's website, as far as the record in this case demonstrates, has not been a place of any commercial activity here. Plaintiff has simply not established that ReservHotel has maintained continuous, systematic, and substantial business contacts with Pennsylvania.

Accordingly, the court will grant ReservHotel's motion to dismiss plaintiff's complaint for lack of personal jurisdiction.

SECTION 7.8
VENUE

Venue is the place where a case should be heard. The plaintiff decides where to institute suit. This decision will rarely be disturbed unless the defendant can demonstrate a compelling reason to remove the matter to another jurisdiction. This will occur if the defendant cannot obtain a fair trial in the location where the lawsuit was filed because of prejudice or bias. For instance, in the case of the Oklahoma City bombing, Timothy McVeigh requested a change of venue because of the potential bias of the jury pool. The 1995 bombing destroyed a large part of the Alfred P. Murrah Federal Building and left 169 people dead and 500 injured. The original judge was removed from the trial because of doubts about his impartiality since the bombing had destroyed his office. The defense also asserted that the trial should take place outside of Oklahoma to insure an unbiased jury because of the intense pre-trial publicity surrounding the heinous crime, and the effect the criminal activity had on the people in Oklahoma. The trial was eventually moved to Denver, Colorado.

The second reason for requesting a change of venue derives from the concept of **forum non-conveniens**. This Latin term means that the place of the trial is inconvenient for the parties and the witnesses involved in the litigation. A court may refuse to exercise jurisdiction over the parties if it would be more convenient for a court in another jurisdiction to hear the case. This was the issue in a lawsuit involving the 1992 film "Sister Act" and the charge that various defendants wrongfully misappropriated the idea for the movie. The lawsuit was filed in New York but the defendants requested the litigation be transferred to California where all of the defendants except one had their principal place of business in that West Coast state.

ASSOCIATED ARTISTS ENTERTAINMENT, INC. v. WALT DISNEY PICTURES
1994 WL 708142 (S.D. N.Y.)

On June 11, 1993, Associated Artists Entertainment, Inc., an Oklahoma corporation brought suit in New York alleging the wrongful misappropriation of a movie proposal. All of the defendants, except for Paul Rudnick, have their principal place of business in, or reside in, California.

Walt Disney Pictures, Buena Vista Pictures Distribution, Inc., and Scott Rudin Productions, Inc. are all California corporations with their principal places of business in California. The individual defendants, Bette Midler and Scott Rudin, are both residents of California. Only defendant Paul Rudnick is a resident of New York. Nevertheless, he conducts extensive business in California and joins with the other defendants in this motion to transfer venue.

Associated claims that the defendants developed the highly successful film "Sister Act" based on a concept submitted to them by plaintiff several years earlier. In 1987, Associated submitted a formal proposal to Disney which Disney subsequently rejected. Plaintiff then developed a screenplay, a business plan, and a joint venture proposal and submitted these again to Disney in 1990. In 1992, Disney released the film "Sister Act" which plaintiff claims strongly resembles its proposal.

The defendants seek a change of venue based primarily on convenience of the parties, given their extensive contacts with California.

28 U.S.C. § 1404(a) states: "For the convenience of parties and witnesses, in the interest of justice, a district court may transfer any civil action to any other district where it might have been brought."

Proper jurisdiction having been established in California, this Court must now balance several factors to determine the propriety of transfer. These include (1) the place where the operative facts occurred; (2) the convenience to the parties; (3) the convenience of witnesses; (4) the relative ease of access to sources of proof; (5) the availability of process to compel attendance of unwilling witnesses; (6) the plaintiff's choice of forum; (7) the forum's familiarity with the governing law; and (8) trial efficiency and the interests of justice.

In support of their motion, defendants argue that a New York forum would greatly inconvenience them. All of the defendants are located in or conduct extensive business in California and, other than Rudnick, have limited contacts with the State of New York.

Courts give a plaintiff's choice of forum varying degrees of weight. When a plaintiff sues in a district other than the one in which it resides, however, that choice is entitled to far less deference than a decision to sue in plaintiff's home forum. Associated is an Oklahoma corporation doing business primarily in that state. This, together with the fact that California is the home state of all but one of the defendants, diminishes the weight of Associated's choice of a New York forum.

Numerous witnesses involved in the making of "Sister Act" and all of the documents pertaining to the film's production are located in California.

All of the documents and most of the key witnesses are located in California. Finally, there is no reason for this Court to find that justice is better served by retaining this action, especially since all other factors favor transfer to the California.

Defendants' motion to transfer this action to the United States District Court for the Central District of California is granted.

Section 7.9
Standing

In accordance with the United States Constitution, courts are only permitted to hear actual cases or controversies. That is, courts cannot offer advisory opinions to people who are not actually involved in a dispute. The plaintiff in a lawsuit must have a direct and substantial interest in the outcome of the case that he or she intends to bring. This concept is referred to as **standing**. To meet this requirement, the plaintiff must show that he or she has actually been injured by the action that is the subject of the lawsuit. The injury can be physical, economic, environmental, or aesthetic, but must injure the plaintiff in fact. To have standing to have a case heard, it is also necessary that the relief sought by the plaintiff either correct or compensate for the harm alleged in the lawsuit.

Consider this example: Estelle was in the process of researching the environmentally fragile nature of the Nevada mountains when she discovered that someone planned to build an amusement park in that area. The park would have a detrimental effect on the environment in the mountain region. If Estelle makes no allegation of the way in which the building of the park would cause an actual injury to her personally, she will be denied standing to bring that case.

Elton John authored the composition *Can You Feel the Love Tonight* as the featured song in the Disney film, *The Lion King*. Subsequently, two publishing companies instituted suit over the composition, claiming it infringed on their copyright to a previous work, *Listen to Your Heart*. Since only one company may be the proper owner of the song, the court had to ascertain which publisher had standing to maintain the action for copyright infringement.

HALWILL MUSIC, INC. v. ELTON JOHN
2000 U.S. DIST. LEXIS 7067 (S.D. N.Y. 2000)

Two different companies seek to assert the same copyright against the same purported infringers; but only one has the right to do so, and the other must be dismissed.

The first suit was brought by plaintiff Gold-Rhyme Music Company ("GoldRhyme") against The Walt Disney Company and other defendants, alleging that the Elton John composition *Can You Feel the Love Tonight,* featured in connection with the film *The Lion King,* infringed the copyright on a previous work, *Listen To Your Heart,* composed by Glenn Medeiros. Subsequently, however, Halwill Music, Inc. ("Halwill") filed suit, making essentially the same claim against essentially the same defen-

dants and further alleging that Medeiros had conveyed to Halwill the sole and exclusive right to sue for copyright infringement with respect to *Listen To Your Heart.*

The Court hereby grants Halwill's motion and dismisses the action brought by GoldRhyme for lack of standing.

Under the **Copyright Act of 1976,** "the legal or beneficial owner of an exclusive right under a copyright is entitled…to institute an action for any infringement of that particular right committed while he or she is the owner of it."

It is undisputed that in 1988, as part of an agreement conveying to Halwill an undisputed half-interest in certain of Medeiros' musical compositions (including *Listen to Your Heart)*, Medeiros agreed that Halwill shall have the sole and exclusive right to administer and protect the Musical Compositions on behalf of both parties throughout the world. Pursuant to that 1988 agreement, Halwill registered a claim for copyright in *Listen To Your Heart* in 1993.

In 1996, Medeiros entered into a separate agreement with GoldRhyme that gave GoldRhyme the exclusive right to initiate all actions for infringements of any Medeiros compositions covered by that agreement. This 1996 agreement, however, was limited to compositions "that have not been assigned in writing to any third party as of the date hereof." Therefore, the 1996 agreement does not in any way pertain to *Listen To Your Heart* which was covered by the 1988 agreement.

Although GoldRhyme attempts to attack the validity of the 1988 agreement between Halwill and Medeiros, its arguments in this regard are without merit. For example, GoldRhyme contends that the 1988 agreement is not signed and is therefore invalid. In fact, however, the signed amended agreement between Halwill and Medeiros specifically refers to and incorporates prior agreements,

Accordingly, the Court hereby grants plaintiff Halwill's motion and dismisses with prejudice GoldRhyme's action against defendants for lack of standing.

SECTION 7.10
FULL FAITH AND CREDIT

Full Faith and Credit is a constitutional mandate that requires each state to uphold the laws and decrees of every other state. As the Supreme Court noted in **Sherrer v. Sherrer**, 334 U.S. 343, the Full, Faith and Credit Clause "is one of the provisions incorporated into the Constitution by its framers for the purpose of transforming an aggregation of independent sovereign states into a nation." This guarantee is contained in **Article Four** of the United States Constitution which provides that full, faith and credit shall be given in each state to the public acts, records, and judicial proceedings of every other state. Essentially, this means that a judgment in one state will be enforced in another state as long as the first state has jurisdiction. Without this provision, the legal system would become uncertain and chaotic. People would never know if a different state would enforce a validly obtained judgment in another jurisdiction. How does this concept work in reality?

Assume that John Smith, a New Jersey resident and college student, goes to Florida for spring break. Upon his arrival in Florida, he rents a car, but unfortunately Smith runs over the clerk as he is pulling away from the rental agency. He is so distraught by the incident that he takes the next plane back to Newark International Airport in New Jersey. The clerk files suit in Florida for her injuries. John ignores the lawsuit since he has no plans of ever returning to Florida, and a judgment is rendered against him in the amount of $100,000. Is Smith correct in assuming that nothing can be done to him as long as he stays out of Florida? Pursuant to the "Full Faith and Credit Clause" of the Constitution, the Florida judgment can be transferred to New Jersey and be enforced in that jurisdiction. Florida had jurisdiction over the New Jersey resident since he committed a tort in that state.

Are traffic tickets that are received in another jurisdiction enforceable in the state of domicile of the driver under the doctrine of Full, Faith and Credit? The answer depends upon the jurisdiction. Forty-five states and the District of Columbia have entered into the **Driver's License Compact,** which governs the enforcement of motor vehicle violations committed by a driver in another jurisdiction. Based upon this agreement, a traffic ticket received in a sister state will be enforced in the state where the driver is licensed. The only jurisdictions that do not belong to the Compact are Georgia, Massachusetts, Michigan, Tennessee, and Wisconsin. The purpose of the Compact is to maximize law enforcement efforts nationwide and to create a "one driver record" concept which requires that the complete driving record of an individual be maintained in one location–the state of licensing. The benefits enjoyed by the member states are varied and include the following: (a) law enforcement officers are not burdened with traffic ticket procedures and are able to devote more time to highway patrol, surveillance, and apprehension; (b) court revenues are increased because non-residents cannot ignore member state's citations without facing driver licenses penalties at home; and (c) there is a decrease in the number of "Failure to Appear" cases.

The Compact requires that member states report all traffic convictions which occur within its boundaries to the state where the violator was licensed. This report must describe the violation and the disposition of the charges. In return, the licensing state shall give the same effect to "serious" motor vehicle violations, as though the offense had occurred in the state of licensing in cases of vehicular manslaughter, driving under the influence, using a motor vehicle to commit a felony, or failure to stop and render aid in the event of a motor vehicle accident. Minor traffic violations, such as speeding, disregarding a stop sign, or going through a red light will be reported to the licensing state, but the conviction will not appear on the individual's driving record nor will points be assigned.

A driver will also not be detained in another jurisdiction if that state is a member of the Compact. Instead, the individual will merely receive a traffic ticket. If the operator fails to pay the fine, the licensing state will be notified of the non-compliance, and the driver's license will be suspended until the ticket is paid. Notice of non-compliance is reported to the home jurisdiction within six months from the date of the issuance of the ticket. If a traffic violation is committed in a state that is not a member of the Compact, the driver will be brought before a judge for an emergency hearing and will be required to make arrangements for the payment of the fine before being allowed to leave the jurisdiction.

There is a *public policy exception* to the Full, Faith and Credit Clause which allows a state to disregard the laws of another jurisdiction if the enforcement of those rules and acts would be inconsistent with the public policy of its own state. For example, Georgia has refused to recognize same-sex marriages even though they may be valid in another state on the basis that these unions are contrary to its public policy.

BURNS V. BURNS
560 S.E.2D 47 (GA. APP. 2002)

The sole issue in this case is whether the trial court erred in enforcing a consent decree pursuant to a divorce between the parties in which they agreed that no child visitations would occur during any time the party being visited cohabited with or had overnight stays with any adult to whom that party was not legally married or related.

Darian and Susan Burns were divorced on December 4, 1995, and Darian retained full custody of the couple's three minor children. Three years later, Susan filed a motion for contempt, alleging that Darian refused to allow her visitation with the children. As a result, the court issued an order modifying visitation rights. The modification required and the parties agreed that "[t]here shall be no visitation or residence by the children with either party during any time where such party cohabits with or has overnight stays with any adult to which such party is not legally married or to whom party is not related."

On July 1, 2000, the State of Vermont enacted a civil union law, and on July 3, 2000, Susan Burns and a female companion traveled to Vermont where they received a "License and Certificate of Civil Union." Two months later, Darian filed a motion for contempt, alleging that Susan vio-

lated the trial court's order by exercising visitation with the children "while cohabitating with her female lover." Susan opposed the motion for contempt, arguing that she was not in violation of the visitation requirements in that she had complied with the legally married requirement by virtue of her civil union with an adult female.

The trial court found that the provisions of its order applied equally to both parties and to both sexes and that a "civil union" is not a marriage. The court further found that the provisions of the order were valid and enforceable.

On appeal Susan contends that she and her female companion were married in Vermont and pursuant to "the full faith and credit doctrine they are married in Georgia as well." She argues further that she has a fundamental right to privacy which includes the right to define her own family and that the State of Georgia cannot place limitations on this right.

Susan's position, however, has a flawed premise: she and her female companion were not married in Vermont but instead entered into a "civil union." The definitional section of that statute expressly distinguishes between "marriage," which is defined as "the legally recognized union of one man and one woman," and "civil union," which is defined as a relationship established between two eligible persons pursuant to that chapter. The next section reemphasizes this distinction, requiring that eligible persons must "[b]e of the same sex and therefore excluded from the marriage laws of this state."

Moreover, even if Vermont had purported to legalize same-sex marriages, such would not be recognized in Georgia, the place where the consent decree was ordered and agreed to by both parties (both of whom are Georgia residents), and more importantly the place where the present action is brought. *OCGA § 19-3-3.1(a)* clearly states that it is the public policy of Georgia "to recognize the union only of man and woman. Marriages between persons of the same sex are prohibited in this state." Additionally, under *OCGA § 19-3-3.1(b)*:

> [n]o marriage between persons of the same sex shall be recognized as entitled to the benefits of marriage. Any marriage entered into by persons of the same sex pursuant to a marriage license issued by another state or foreign jurisdiction or otherwise shall be void in this state. Any contractual rights granted by virtue of such license shall be unenforceable in the courts of this state and the courts of this state shall have no jurisdiction whatsoever under any circumstances to grant a divorce or separate maintenance with respect to such marriage or otherwise to consider or rule on any of the parties' respective

rights arising as a result of or in connection with such marriage.

Moreover, Georgia is not required to give full faith and credit to same-sex marriages of other states.

What constitutes a marriage in the State of Georgia is a legislative function, and we are duty bound to follow the clear language of the statute. The Georgia Legislature has chosen not to recognize marriage between persons of the same sex.

It is important to note that Susan's argument that her right to privacy has been infringed upon ignores her role in creating the consent decree. Although she is correct that there is a right to privacy of intimacy between persons legally able to consent, she waived that right (to the extent that right is interfered with here) when she agreed to the consent decree. That this right may be waived is clear. Indeed, if Susan wanted to ensure that her civil union would be recognized in the same manner as a marriage, she should have included language to that effect in the consent decree itself.

Simply put, the consent order provides that visitation will not be allowed during the time that Darian or Susan cohabitates with an adult to whom he or she is not legally married, and as Susan and her companion are not legally married in the State of Vermont and clearly not legally married under Georgia law, any such activity by Susan is in violation of the court's order. Accordingly, the court did not err in its conclusion that the visitation order is valid and that such violation constitutes contempt.

Judgment affirmed.

SECTION 7.11
ROBERTS V.
COMMONWEALTH

PROBLEM SEVEN—B

PARK, BROWN & SMITH, P.C.
ATTORNEYS AT LAW
MEMORANDUM

TO: All Law Clerks

FROM: Peter Smith, Esquire

RE: Joe Roberts' Trip to Arizona

Joe Roberts recently visited Arizona for a white-water rafting adventure on the Colorado River. The weather was hot and Joe was in the sun for hours. Joe and the other rafters consumed several alcoholic beverages while shooting the rapids. At the end of the day, he drove back to Phoenix for his return flight home. Unfortunately, the excitement of the day caught up with him. About an hour outside of Phoenix, Joe fell asleep at the wheel and his vehicle became stuck in a ditch along the side of the road.

A police officer arrived and asked Joe what had happened. Mr. Roberts could not remember. Joe then exited the car but became dizzy when he stood up. The officer grabbed Joe to prevent him from falling, and smelled liquor on Joe's breath. The policeman suspected that Joe was intoxicated so he administered a breathalyzer which registered a blood-alcohol level of 0.06%. Joe was charged with violating Arizona's laws on DUI since the cop suspected that Joe was an "impaired driver" as defined by Arizona state law.

Following a contentious hearing, Mr. Roberts was convicted of the charges. The judge believed that Joe's consumption of alcohol contributed to Roberts' falling asleep behind the wheel making him an impaired driver. Joe paid the fine and returned to Pennsylvania thinking that the matter was over. Mr. Roberts received the shock of his life when he opened the mail. The Arizona Department of Transportation sent notice of his DUI conviction to the Pennsylvania authorities under the Driver's License Compact. The Pennsylvania Department of Transportation has demanded that Joe immediately surrender his license and attend a hearing next month on whether he should go to jail as a repeat DUI offender.

Joe wishes to fight the suspension by the Pennsylvania Department of Transportation. Joe insists that he did nothing wrong since his blood-alcohol level of 0.06% demonstrated that he was not intoxicated. Even using the new Pennsylvania law for intoxication of a blood-alcohol of 0.08%, Joe was not legally intoxicated.

I have located the Arizona law under which Joe was convicted. *A.R.S. §28-692(A) (1)* provides that it is unlawful for a person to drive:

1. While under the influence of intoxicating liquor, the person is *impaired to the slightest degree.*

2. If there was at the time of driving a blood-alcohol content in excess of 0.05% but less than 0.10% alcohol concentration in the defendant's blood, that fact shall not give rise to a presumption that the defendant was or was not under the influence of intoxicating liquor, but that fact may be considered with other competent evidence in determining the guilt or innocence of the defendant.

Pennsylvania's law on driving under the influence provides that:

1. An individual may not operate a vehicle after imbibing a sufficient amount of alcohol that the individual is *rendered incapable of safely driving.*

2. An individual may not operate a vehicle after imbibing a sufficient amount of alcohol such that the alcohol concentration in the individual's blood or breath is at least 0.08% but less than 0.10% within two hours after the individual has driven.

Joe maintains that it is not fair that he will lose his license because the law in Arizona is more rigid than that in Pennsylvania. Joe's conviction resulted from that part of Arizona's law that provides for a conviction if the driver is *impaired to the slightest degree.* Pennsylvania requires that the operator be rendered incapable of safely driving.

Read **Kline v. Commonwealth of Pennsylvania** and let me know whether we can successfully challenge the actions of the Department of Transportation. Keep in mind that the laws in Pennsylvania when the **Kline** case was decided required a blood-alcohol content of 0.10% for conviction. Pennsylvania has now lowered the blood-alcohol level requirement to 0.08% in order to sustain a conviction. That change in the law, however, does not affect the court's holding.

John Kline v. Commonwealth of Pennsylvania
725 A.2d 860 (Cmwlth. Court 1999)

On July 9, 1997, Kline, a Pennsylvania resident, pled guilty in Virginia, to a charge of violating Virginia's "Driving under the Influence" (DUI) statute. By pleading guilty, he admitted to driving a motor vehicle while having a blood-alcohol concentration of 0.08 percent.

The Pennsylvania Department of Motor Vehicles suspended Kline's operating privilege for one year as a result of the Virginia conviction. The Department's notice advised that the Pennsylvania Motor Vehicle Code requires the Department to treat certain out-of-state convictions as though they had occurred in Pennsylvania.

The Drivers License Compact provides that the licensing authority in the home state, shall give the same effect to the conduct reported as it would if such conduct had occurred in the home state. If the laws of the home state do not provide for the offenses described in precisely the words employed in laws of the state in which the offense occurred, such home state shall construe the law as being applicable only to violations of a *substantially similar nature.*

Kline filed an appeal with the trial court, which found that he was not convicted on the basis of conduct that would have constituted the offense of DUI in Pennsylvania. Rather, the trial court found that Kline's conviction was predicated solely upon a blood-alcohol content level below that proscribed for an adult driver in Pennsylvania which is 0.10%. The trial court concluded that Kline's Virginia conviction was not for an offense substantially similar to a violation of the Motor Vehicle Code of Pennsylvania.

Virginia's statutory provision proscribing various forms of driving while intoxicated reads as follows:

> It shall be unlawful for any person to drive or operate any motor vehicle, engine or train *(i) while such person has a blood alcohol concentration of 0.08 percent or more by weight by volume.*

Pennsylvania's DUI statute states:

> A person shall not drive, operate or be in actual physical control of the movement of a vehicle *while the amount of alcohol by weight in the blood of an adult is 0.10%.*

In determining whether a reported offense from another state may serve as a basis for suspending a Pennsylvania licensee's operating privilege, the other state's offense need only be *"substantially similar"* to the Pennsylvania Vehicle Code in order to mandate a suspension under the Compact.

Here, Kline was convicted of driving with a blood-alcohol concentration level of 0.08% or more. Looking at the offense for which he was convicted, we agree with the trial court that Kline's conduct would have no consequences under Pennsylvania law.

Similarly, in **Eck v. Department of Transportation, Bureau of Driver Licensing, 713 A.2d 744 (Pa.Cmwlth.1998),** the court confined its analysis to the language of the specific provision of the party state's DUI statute under which the licensee was convicted. The licensee in **Eck** was convicted under a subsection of Maryland's DUI statute prohibiting a person from driving under the influence of alcohol. The **Eck** court observed that the use of any amount of alcohol would support a conviction, while a conviction under Pennsylvania's law requires evidence that the licensee was under the influence of alcohol to a degree that renders him incapable of driving safely. The court concluded that the two offenses were not substantially similar. A person violates the Vehicle Code of Pennsylvania if such person has a blood-alcohol content level of 0.10% or higher, *or* if such person is under the influence of alcohol to a degree that renders the person *incapable of safe driving*. While a driver in Pennsylvania need not have a blood alcohol level of 0.10% in order to be convicted of DUI, where there is no evidence to this effect, the Department must prove that the licensee was influenced by alcohol to a degree that he could not drive safely. A person driving with a blood alcohol level of 0.08% will suffer no consequences under of the Vehicle Code of Pennsylvania if he is still capable of being a safe driver in any case.

We decline to hold that a twenty-percent difference between the two statutes' threshold blood-alcohol levels is insignificant. As it currently exists, the Vehicle Code of Pennsylvania does not prohibit the conduct for which Licensee was convicted in Virginia. Therefore, the Compact does not authorize the Department to suspend driver's operating privilege based on that conduct.

Please analyze the **Kline** decision and let me know if we will be successful in an appeal of Joe's license suspension.

Name   **Please Print Clearly**

1. What is the difference between the laws in Pennsylvania and Arizona on driving a motor vehicle after consuming acholic beverages?

_____

_____

_____

_____

_____

_____

_____

_____

2. What arguments would you make on behalf of Joe to overturn his suspension?

_____

_____

_____

_____

_____

_____

_____

_____

_____

_____

3. Will we win an appeal of Joe's suspension? Please explain.

SECTION 7.12
COMITY

Comity is derived from the Latin "comitas" which means courteous. In the arena of international law, this principle allows for the courteous recognition of the rules and laws of a foreign jurisdiction. States are simply not mandated to enforce the laws and judgments of another country. Rather, each determines on its own the extent to which it will provide courtesy and respect to a foreign sovereign taking into consideration the state's international obligations and rights of its own citizens.[15] Generally, as long as the laws of another country are not contrary to public policy or prejudicial to the interests of the forum jurisdiction, the law will be upheld.

The death penalty is not uniformly supported around the world. This issue of philosophical differences can strain relations between countries—even those sovereignties with which we otherwise maintain good relations. This fact is evident in two recent cases in which the United States has sought the return of a person from a foreign country in order to face murder charges in which the death penalty could be imposed.

A new generation has learned the name of Ira Einhorn. This 1960's activist was charged with the Philadelphia murder of Holly Maddux, whose mummified body was found in a steamer trunk in Einhorn's closet. Shortly before his criminal trial, the defendant disappeared. Nevertheless, the trial went on in his absence, and Einhorn was found guilty of first-degree murder and was sentenced to death. After twenty years on the run, Einhorn was located in France. That country, however, refused to return him to the United States because of its opposition to the death penalty. It was only after the Pennsylvania legislature agreed that Einhorn would not face the death penalty and that he would be granted a new trial that the French court ordered the fugitive's return to Philadelphia.

A similar situation occurred in Canada where two young men who were residents of that country were accused of killing three people in the state of Washington. Despite requests by the United States government to return the suspects, Canada had refused because of their opposition to the death penalty. This case went before the Canadian Supreme Court, which ruled that the suspects would not be returned until the United States guaranteed that they would not face the death penalty.

UNITED STATES OF AMERICA V. DAN BURNS
SUPREME COURT OF CANADA (2001)

Burns and Rafay are each wanted on three counts of first-degree murder in the State of Washington. If found guilty, they will face either the death penalty or life in prison without parole. The defendants are both Canadian citizens and were 18 years old when the father, mother and sister of Rafay were found bludgeoned to death in their home in Washington. Both Burns and Rafay, who had been friends at high school in British Columbia, admit that they were at the Rafay home on the night of the murders. They claim to have gone out and when they returned, they say, they found the bodies of the three murdered Rafay family members. Thereafter, the two returned to Canada. They were eventually arrested. United States authorities commenced proceedings to extradite the defendants to the State of Washington for trial. The Minister of Justice for Canada ordered their extradition without seeking assurances from the United States that the death penalty would not be imposed. The Court of Appeal set aside the Minister's decision and directed him to seek assurances as a condition of surrender.

In respect of seeking assurances, the Minister took the position that assurances were not to be sought routinely in every case in which the death penalty was applicable; such assurances should be sought only in circumstances where the particular facts of the case warranted that special exercise of discretion.

Countervailing factors favor extradition only with assurances. In Canada, the death penalty has been rejected as an acceptable element of criminal justice. Capital punishment engages the underlying values of the prohibition against cruel and unusual punishment. It is final and irreversible. The abolition of the death penalty has emerged as a major Canadian initiative and reflects a concern increasingly shared by most of the world's democracies. While the evidence does not establish an international law norm against the death penalty, it does show significant movement towards acceptance internationally of the abolition of capital punishment. It also shows that a rule requiring that assurances be obtained prior to extradition in death penalty cases not only accords with Canada's principled advocacy on the international level, but also is consistent with the practice of other countries with which Canada generally invites comparison, apart from the retentionist jurisdictions in the United States.

There is no suggestion in the evidence that asking for assurances would undermine Canada's international obligations or good relations with neighboring states. While international criminal law enforcement including the need to ensure that Canada does not become a "safe haven" for dangerous fugitives is a legitimate objective, there is no evidence that extradition to face life in prison provides a lesser deterrent to those seeking a "safe haven" than does the death penalty. Whether fugitives are returned to a foreign country to face the death penalty or to face eventual death in prison from natural causes, they are equally prevented from using Canada as a "safe haven."

A review of the factors for and against unconditional extradition leads to the conclusion that assurances are constitutionally required.

Section 7.13
Alternative
Dispute Resolution

Controversies may be resolved in ways other than by using the state and federal court systems, which may be too time-consuming or expensive. Parties may agree to submit to any of a number of alternative methods for resolving their disputes. In considering an **alternative dispute resolution** mechanism, the parties will focus on factors such as cost, who will represent them, who will arbitrate the dispute, and whether the alternative method will lead to a more helpful or fair resolution.

Arbitration is often used in a commercial setting where both parties agree to have a third party or arbitrator resolve the controversy. When the parties agree to abide by the arbitrator's decision, they are involved in binding arbitration, and the court will automatically enforce the arbitrator's award. Both parties must agree on who the impartial arbitrator will be. Arbitration proceedings are usually informal, and the parties are not bound by the rules of evidence that control court cases.

Because of the binding nature of arbitration, courts will rarely overturn an arbitrator's decision unless there is clear evidence of fraud or gross misconduct.

Mediation is used primarily in disputes between labor and management, but also is suited to disputes between neighbors and family members. Mediation is different from arbitration because it is advisory in nature. A mediator makes recommendations to the parties in order to aid them in solving their differences. Successful mediation will keep the parties out of court. Mediation is gaining popularity in divorce cases in helping the parties work out their differences.

Private judging is used when both sides are constrained by time and can afford to hire a private judge, usually a retired judge. Private judging proceeds as a normal trial would be conducted.

Non-binding or **mini-trials** are another form of private dispute resolution in which the parties may or may not be represented by a lawyer. The parties usually submit their case to a panel of experts and a neutral advisor, who aids both sides. The panel and advisor suggest the likely outcome if the case were to go to court. This method is helpful for business disputes involving long processes of fact-finding.

Neighborhood Justice Centers derive from a program initiated in the 1970s. The centers receive their cases from local police or magistrates' offices. The cases usually involve neighborhood or family disputes, in which the two sides represent themselves before a panel of local residents. The aim is to avoid having the disputes escalate to the point where the criminal court system takes over.

1. Francis Thomas received an envelope at his New Jersey home with a return address from the Philadelphia Chamber of Commerce. Upon opening the letter, he discovered two tickets to a Philadelphia 76ers game. Mr. Thomas could not believe his good fortune and took his son to the contest at the First Union Center. During the second period, the Sheriff tapped Thomas on the shoulder and served him with a lawsuit concerning a motor vehicle accident that had happened one year earlier in New Jersey. Does the Philadelphia Court have jurisdiction over this New Jersey resident because Thomas was served with the lawsuit within its boundaries? See: **M. H. Eastburn v. Saul Turnoff, 147 A.2d 353 (Pa. 1959).**

2. Robert DeLuca had a long history of being involved in violent crimes. During his criminal trial for extortion, the trial judge empaneled an anonymous jury in order to safeguard the panel members' identity and to prevent jury tampering. Spectators were also screened and had to produce identification before being allowed into the courtroom. DeLuca claimed that his Sixth Amendment right to a public trial were violated by the judge's unusual actions. Do you agree? **United States v. Robert DeLuca, 96-1173, (1ˢᵗ Cir. Ct. 1998).**

3. A franchise agreement between Charles Jones and General Nutrition Companies, Inc., required that all disputes concerning the agreement be litigated in a Pennsylvania venue. Jones operated a GNC store in California. Following a dispute, he sued GNC in his home state where his store is located, the contracts were entered into in California, and the majority of witnesses are in that state. GNC requested a change of venue so that the case could be removed to Pennsylvania based upon the forum selection clause in the contract even though California does not favor this type of clause. Where should the case be heard? **Charles Jones v. GNC Franchising, Inc., CV-98-10611-DMT (9ᵗʰ Cir. Ct. 2000).**

4. Beer Across America sold beer to a minor via the internet. The liquor was shipped from the store's location in Illinois to the child's home in Alabama. After the parents returned home from vacation, they discovered the beer in the refrigerator. This prompted the parents to file a suit in Alabama against the Illinois company for the unlawful sale of liquor to a minor. Beer Across America was not registered to do business in Alabama, and it owned no property within the state. Is a passive Internet site that can be accessed from anywhere in the world sufficient to confer jurisdiction over a nonresident defendant for doing business in Alabama? **Lynda Butler v. Beer Across America, 83 F. Supp. 2d 1261 (2000).**

SECTION 7.15
INTERNET REFERENCES

To learn more information about the court system and the jury selection process, see the following sites:

A. *The Jury Process*

- **www.fija.org**
  This is the official website for the Fully Informed Jury Association, a non-profit educational association devoted to providing information about jury duty, including a citizen's guide to jury duty, and frequently asked questions about jury duty.

- **www.edwright.com/voir_dire_intro.html**
  Tips on the voir dire process are offered on this site, which is maintained by an attorney.

- **www.geocities.com/heartland/7394/lysander.html**
  A historical justification for trial by jury is presented in this article.

B. *The Court*

- **www.law.emory.edu/caselaw**
  This site features federal court decisions from 1995 through the present.

- **http://law.about.com/newsissues/law/library/courts b1899_toc.htm**
  This site provides a general discussion on the federal court system.

- **www.uscourts.gov/faq.html**
  This Federal Judiciary homepage provides answers to frequently asked questions about the federal court system.

- **www.supremecourtus.gov**
  The Supreme Court's official site is contained at this address and contain copies of the Court's opinions, Court rules, and other general information.

- **http://vis.law.villanova.edu/locator/federalcourt.html**
  Villanova University School of Law maintains this website which provides access to federal court decisions from the district court to the United States Supreme Court. The law school's website also maintains a variety of links to legal magazines and search engines for law related subjects. You may access this site through: **http://vls.law.villanova.edu/library/express/**.

- **www.aopc.org/index/ujs/courtswork.htm**
  An overview of the Pennsylvania's court system can be found at this address.

- **http://oyez.nwu.edu**
  Northwestern University maintains this multimedia data base and virtual tour of the United States Supreme Court.

Footnotes:

1. *Marbury v. Madison* http://usinfo.state.gov/usa/infousa/facts/democrac/9.htm.
2. Supreme *Court of the United States*, Supreme Court Historical Society, http://www.supremecourthistory.org/.
3. *How the Court Works,* The Supreme Court Historical Society, www.suprmecourthistory.org.
4. Id.
5. *Williams v. Florida*, 399 U.S. 78 (1970).
6. *Duncan v. Louisiana*, 88 S. Ct. 1444 (1968).
7. *American Bar Association Points: Trial by Jury*, www.abanet.org
8. See: *Criminal Justice across Europe*, www.crimeinfo.org.uk.
9. Civil Justice Statistics, U.S. Department of Justice Bureau of Justice Statistics, http://www.ojp.usdoj.gov/bjs/civil.htm.
10. Shrager and Frost, "The Quotable Lawyer," Facts on File, at 152.
11. New York Times, February 3, 1969 as cited in the "Quotable Lawyer" at 154.
12. American Bar Association Journal, November 1995, page 72.
13. Id.
14. See: *Lesson 7-9: Voir Dire*, American Bar Association.
15. *Judgment of the Court of Foreign Countries as Entitled to Enforcement of Extraterritorial Effect in State Court*, 13 A. L R. 4th 1109.

KEY TERMS

Activist
Alternative Dispute Resolution
American Arbitration
  Association
Appellate Court
Arbitration
Article III
Article IV
Certiorari
Challenge for Cause
Circuit Court of Appeals
Comity
Commonwealth Court
Court of Common Pleas
Court of Federal Claims
District Court
Driver's License Compact
Federal Court
Federal Mediation and
  Conciliation Service
Forum Non-Conveniens
Full, Faith and Credit
Judicial Restraint Oriented
Jurisdiction
Jurisdiction over the Person
Jury

Long Arm Statute
Magna Carta
Mediation
Minimum Contacts
Municipal Court
Neighborhood Justice Centers
One-Day or One-Trial
Original Jurisdiction
Peremptory Challenge
Private Judging
Questions-of-Facts
Questions-of-Law
Rule of Hour
Service
Seventh Amendment
Sixth Amendment
Standing
State Court
State Supreme Court
Subject Matter Jurisdiction
Superior Court
Supreme Court Rule 10
United States Supreme Court
Venue
Voir Dire

CHAPTER 8

CIVIL PROCEDURE

**SECTION 8.1
THE LITIGATION PROCESS**

We live in a litigation oriented society whose members seem to institute suit over every conceivable problem. "You will be hearing from my lawyer" seems to be a frequent refrain. Cases range from class action lawsuits against the tobacco industry to suits against McDonald's for causing obesity in children.

Rules have been established to govern the conduct of these lawsuits from the filing of the claim to the verdict. These regulations are called the **Rules of Civil Procedure** and vary depending upon the type of proceeding and court. Matters before a Justice of the Peace or Municipal Court judge will be informal since they involve small amounts of money and the litigants are encouraged to represent themselves. Jury trials are more formal and the rules are complex. Failure to follow these court mandates may result in an adverse finding or dismissal of the lawsuit.

Civil litigation involves three distinctive but equally important parts:

1. Pleadings;
2. Discovery; and
3. Trial.

The **Pleadings** consist of the initial documents filed with the court that set forth the theories of liability and damages requested by the plaintiff and the defenses of the parties being sued. These documents include the Complaint, Answer, New Matter or Affirmative Defenses, and Counterclaim. The pleadings also establish the boundaries of the lawsuit, since matters not asserted are generally waived. For instance, the defense of assumption of the risk or payment of a loan must be raised at this time or it will be lost as a defense.

Discovery allows each party to find out more information about the opponent's case. It is during this stage of the lawsuit that witnesses can be questioned under oath, and counsel can obtain copies of an opponent's documents and trial exhibits. In addition, medical or psychological examinations of a party may be ordered if relevant to the case.

The **Trial** is the final stage of the litigation process. It is at this judicial proceeding that evidence will be presented, witnesses cross-examined, and factual disputes resolved by the rendering of a verdict in favor of one of the parties.

SECTION 8.2
PETER CHRISTOPHER
V. JOSEPH ROBERTS

The news is filled with stories about odd lawsuits or unusual court results. For instance, Satan was the subject of a civil rights lawsuit filed by a person who lost his home in mortgage foreclosure claiming that the devil had violated his constitutional rights. Even Bill Gates is not immune from creative lawsuits. The founder of Microsoft was sued by a person who believed that Mr. Gates and others had conspired to murder him through the Windows 95 operating system that was hooked to the claimant's mind.

Any number of lawsuits may be utilized to creatively illustrate the civil litigation process. The lawsuit against Joe Roberts by his next-door neighbor over Joe's choice of a pet rivals any for its unusual facts so it will be used to demonstrate the civil litigation process.

SECTION 8.3
FACTS

Peter Christopher v. Joseph Roberts deals with the liability attached to Joe's keeping a pet bear in his backyard. Joe purchased this unusual animal when it was a cub from a bankrupt circus. Roberts raised the animal to full maturity and the bear is named "Harry." The animal weighs a little more than 300 pounds, stands five feet tall and is able to do any number of tricks. Mr. Roberts kept Harry at his house in a residential neighborhood much to the dismay of the other homeowners.

The events leading up to the lawsuit occurred on Labor Day weekend when the bear was left unattended in Joe's backyard. It was late in the afternoon and the Roberts family went inside to eat dinner. The bear had fallen asleep by the portion of the fence that borders Mr. Christopher's property.

Peter Christopher, however, did not view the bear with quite the same admiration as that shown by the Roberts family. Christopher found the odors emanating from Joe's backyard offensive and the conditions unsanitary. Christopher's complaints to the township were being investigated, but no formal action had been taken to remove the bear from the neighborhood.

On this particular weekend, Christopher had invited 50 guests to his home for a barbecue. As Christopher was setting up his lawn area for the party, he was becoming more and more agitated by the bear's close proximity to his backyard. Brazened with the consumption of alcohol, Christopher picked up a long metal pole that was normally used to clean his pool. He then walked over to the fence and started poking the large animal with the instrument to relocate the sleeping bear to the opposite side of Joe's yard. The large animal, however, awakened from his sleep in an agitated state and mauled the next door neighbor.

Christopher was injured in the fracas and instituted suit against Joe claiming that Roberts had been negligent for keeping a non-domesticated and wild animal in his backyard.

SECTION 8.4
FEE ARRANGEMENTS

An attorney may be hired under a variety of fee arrangements including a fixed price, a per-hour billing, a retainer, and a contingent fee agreement.

In a limited number of cases, an attorney knows exactly how much time will be involved in the handling of a matter and can quote a specific price. These matters include a simple uncontested divorce, the drafting of a will, or the incorporation of a business. Most cases, however, are handled on a per-hour basis. An attorney will charge for the time spent on the file and the per-hour fee will vary depending upon the sophistication of the problem and expertise of counsel. Average rates range from $100 to $300 per hour. All case work is recorded on a time sheet, and the client is billed for that time on a periodic basis. Billable time includes telephone conferences and the writing of letters on a client's behalf. Anyone who hires an attorney on a per-hour basis should ask for an itemized bill setting forth the time spent by the attorney by date and services rendered. Bills should be sent on a periodic basis, such as each month or quarterly.

Personal injury matters are frequently handled on a contingent fee basis. This means that the attorney will take a percentage of the recovery as the legal fee. If counsel is unsuccessful in recovering money for a claimant, no legal fee is due. The contingent fee agreement varies in percentage from one-third to one-half of the recovery. The average arrangement is forty percent, but some firms will offer a staggered rate depending upon the amount of work expended to create the settlement. For instance, if a case is settled before suit, an attorney may take thirty percent of the recovery; if the settlement is achieved after the institution of suit, the percentage may increase to thirty-five percent; and if the case is tried, the fee will increase to forty percent.

SECTION 8.5
CONTINGENT FEE
AGREEMENT

In the case of **Peter Christopher v. Joseph Roberts,** Mr. Christopher signed a contingent fee agreement. The following is a sample of that document and provides for a 40 percent recovery from the gross settlement.

The undersigned hereby constitutes and appoints the law firm of London and Flanigan, P.C., as his attorney to prosecute all causes of action on account of an accident or incident which occurred on September 3, involving an assault by a non-domesticated animal.

I hereby agree that the compensation of my attorney for services shall be determined as follows:

Out of whatever sum which is secured by either my said attorney or by me from the defendant, or from anyone else, either by way of voluntary payment, settlement or verdict, my said attorney, for and in consideration of the professional services rendered in the investigation and general conduct of the said case or claim, including the institution of suit, if necessary, shall retain or be entitled to forty percent (40%) of the gross amount of any recovery.

I understand and agree that my attorney is under no obligation to represent or continue to represent me on any appeal from an adverse verdict or decision. I reserve the right to decide on the acceptability of any settlement offer that may be made and to decide whether an appeal from an adverse verdict or decision will be taken. Should no money be recovered by verdict or settlement by either my attorney, or by me, my said attorney is to have no claim against me of any kind for services rendered by him.

Peter Christopher
_____ (SEAL)
Peter H. Christopher

SECTION 8.6 HOURLY BILL

Joseph Roberts is being defended on a per-hour basis. The time expended on his case is recorded on a timelog broken down into six-minute intervals. For instance, one-tenth of an hour or ".1" is the equivalent of six minutes.

PARK, BROWN & SMITH, P.C.
1515 MARKET STREET, 6TH FL.
PHILADELPHIA, PA 19100

Joseph A. Roberts
39 Royal Court
Rydal, Pennsylvania 19000

Invoice: 1010101
Page: 1

RE: **Christopher v. Roberts**

For Professional Services Rendered:

Date	Description of Service	Hours	Rate Per Hour
1/5	Conference with client	0.5	$125
1/5	Letter to opposing counsel	0.3	$125
1/7	Legal research	3.0	$125

Total Hours: 3.8

Total Amount of Bill: *$475.00*

What happens when a client hires a lawyer on a contingent fee basis and then fires that lawyer before the case is completed? Is the attorney entitled to the full fee even though he is no longer working on the file? The courts generally award the discharged attorney a fee based on the value of services rendered to the date of discharge, or in legal terms, on a **"quantum meruit"** basis. Quantum meruit is an equitable remedy that provides for a form of restitution when one person has been unjustly enriched at the expense of another.

Some states, such as New Jersey and New York, regulate the percentage that an attorney may charge in handling a contingency fee case. Pennsylvania does not have such a restriction unless the claim involves the representation of a child.

An example of how the court will monitor a contingency fee agreement is provided in a lawsuit involving Hulk Hogan. The plaintiff's New York attorney tried to change the fee arrangement from one-third to one-half on the eve of trial. The court was very critical of this move and refused to allow the increased percentage.

Belzer v. Terry Bollea, a/k/a Hulk Hogan
571 N.Y.S. 2d 365 (N.Y. 1990)

This case having been settled on the eve of trial, plaintiff's attorney has made application to this court to approve additional compensation of 50% of the recovery, instead of the normal one-third contingency fee, for the "angst, aggravation and life's blood which this case caused."

The contingent fee rules which govern attorneys in actions involving personal injury, no matter what the agreement between the attorney and client may be, are now embodied in **22 NYCRR 603.7 (e). Subdivision (e) (1)** provides that fees in excess of those contained in the schedule of fees "shall constitute the exaction of unreasonable and unconscionable compensation," unless they have been authorized by a written order of the court. **Subdivision (e) (2)** then sets forth the schedule of presumptively reasonable fees.

Two alternatives are presented. Under schedule A, a sliding scale of permissible recovery is set running from 50 percent of the first $1,000 to 25 percent of sums over $25,000. Alternatively, the compensation may be fixed pursuant to schedule B, which calls for a flat percentage not exceeding $33\frac{1}{3}$ percent of the sum recovered.

In this action, the original retainer agreement did provide for charges in excess of the permitted contingency fees because it called for a contingent fee of $33\frac{1}{3}$ percent of the gross proceeds "or whatever the Firm's straight time billing charges would have been, whichever is greater."

The attorney here claims that on the basis of straight time charges, including over 50 hours for the preparation of an assault complaint, the value of the firm's services was well above what a one-third contingent fee would permit. But an attorney cannot have it both ways. If he fixes a one-third contingent retainer, his ultimate fee is tied in with the client's recovery, for better or for worse. He takes the risk of a loss if the ultimate recovery is too low, but he may have a windfall if the recovery is much greater. The essence of a contingent fee is risk — shared risk. Sometimes the attorney wins, sometimes he loses, sometimes he breaks even.

Pursuant to these rules, the court will treat any provision of the agreement which calls for compensation greater than 33 $^1/_3$ percent a nullity, and whether the client in fact agreed or disagreed to additional fees, and no matter how sterling the representation may have been to the time of trial, the court concludes that there is no authority for the award of additional compensation. The application of the attorneys is therefore denied.

SECTION 8.7
SERVICE OF PROCESS

Procedural due process requires that a defendant be notified of any legal proceeding that has been filed against him. This is called **service of process**. In a criminal case, this occurs when the defendant is arrested or indicted. In a civil matter, however, the defendant must be served with a copy of the lawsuit. This task is usually accomplished by having a representative of the court, such as the Sheriff, personally hand a copy of the lawsuit to the defendant. Frequently, the defendant is not at home when the Sheriff attempts to serve the legal papers. When this occurs, is the Sheriff mandated to continue the search for the defendant or may the judicial officer serve another person, such as the defendant's spouse or business partner?

Court rules allow service of a legal document upon someone other than the defendant as long as the service is reasonably calculated to notify the defendant that he or she is the subject of a claim. For example, *Pennsylvania Rule of Civil Procedure 402* provides that the defendant must be handed a copy of the legal document personally, or the Sheriff may serve an adult member of the household of the defendant at the residence.

Based upon **Rule 402**, which of the following situations constitute proper service over Joseph Roberts in the case of **Peter Christopher v. Joseph Roberts?**

1. The Sheriff serves Estelle, Joe's wife, at their home;

2. The Sheriff serves Kathy, Joe's 16-year-old daughter at the household;

3. The Sheriff hands the Complaint to a painter who is painting the Roberts' home;

4. The Sheriff proceeds to the supermarket a block away from the Roberts household and serves Estelle in the store as she is buying a watermelon;

5. The Sheriff hands the Complaint to the mailman who gives it to Joe with the other mail while making the daily mail delivery to Joe's home.

What happens if the defendant is lured or tricked into entering a state solely for purposes of serving that individual with the lawsuit? Will this type of conduct be allowed? That is the issue in **Hotlen v. Middour**.

ARTHUR HOTLEN V. CHARLES MIDDOUR
404 PA. 351 (PA. 1961)

Defendant, G. Charles Middour, is a manufacturer of aluminum storm windows and doors. His factory and principal place of business is in Waynesboro, Franklin County, Pennsylvania. Defendant does no business in Philadelphia and except for passing through on a train has been in Philadelphia only twice in the past five years. Plaintiff, Arthur M. Hotlen, (trading under the name of Easy Aluminum Products Company), has, since 1959 sold Middour's products. Hotlen's place of business is in Philadelphia.

The present controversy arose over a transaction between plaintiff (Hotlen) and one Sidney Smith, who was doing business under the name Apex Window Company. Smith had ordered a number of window frames from Hotlen. Hotlen had then ordered the frames from Middour.

While Middour was in the process of constructing the frames, and after some of them had been made, Hotlen notified him not to make shipment since Smith had not paid him (Hotlen). A number of telephone calls between Hotlen and Middour ensued. Plaintiff (Hotlen) told defendant that Smith would make payment only to defendant and that defendant would have to come to Philadelphia to discuss the deal and receive payment. It was finally agreed that defendant would come to Philadelphia on Sep-

tember 7, 1960, to meet plaintiff and Smith, and that a telephone call confirming this meeting would be made on September 6. On September 6, the prothonotary of the Court of Common Pleas of Philadelphia County issued a writ of summons against defendant. At 7:28 that evening defendant, as previously agreed, called plaintiff and at that time plaintiff told him that they would meet Smith on the sidewalk in front of Bookbinders Restaurant in Philadelphia at noon the next day, September 7.

Defendant arrived at the appointed place at noon and was met by plaintiff. Plaintiff greeted him and thereupon excused himself. A deputy sheriff then approached defendant, identified himself and handed defendant the summons, which came as a surprise and a shock to defendant. Defendant had no other business in Philadelphia nor did he do business here; and Smith never appeared or testified for plaintiff.

The general rule is as follows:

"Personal service of process, if procured by fraud, trickery, or artifice is not sufficient to give a court jurisdiction over the person thus served, and service will be set aside upon proper application."

Relief is accorded in such cases not because, by reason of the fraud, the court did not get jurisdiction of the person of the defendant by the service, but on the ground that the court will not exercise its jurisdiction in favor of one who has obtained service of his summons by unlawful means. Thus, if a person resident outside the jurisdiction of the court and the reach of its process is inveigled, enticed, or induced, by any false representation, deceitful contrivance, or wrongful device for which the plaintiff is responsible, to come within the jurisdiction of the court for the purpose of obtaining service of process on him in an action brought against him in such court, process served upon him through such improper means is invalid, and upon proof of such fact the court will, on motion, set it aside: The American Jurisprudence text is supported by **Eastburn v. Turnoff, 394 Pa. 316, 319-320, 147 A.2d 353.**

It is clear to us from the record that plaintiff tricked, lured and inveigled defendant into Philadelphia County for the purpose of serving him with process and that the pretended meeting with Smith was a sham to conceal plaintiff's real purpose.

Order reversed with directions to enter an order sustaining defendant's preliminary objections and dismissing the complaint.

SECTION 8.8
CHRISTOPHER V. ROBERTS

PROBLEM EIGHT—A

PARK, BROWN & SMITH, P.C.
ATTORNEYS AT LAW
MEMORANDUM

TO: The Law Clerks

FROM: Peter Smith, Esquire

RE: Christopher v. Roberts

Mr. Roberts has been served with the lawsuit over the attack of the next-door neighbor by Joe's pet bear. We need to file a response to the legal document and prepare a defense on his behalf. As strange as it may seem, our client really did keep a bear in his backyard and he may have supplied the animal with liquor. I fully appreciate the fact that most people would be outraged if their neighbor maintained this type of animal in the backyard so I anticipate an uphill battle in defending this litigation.

I have interviewed Joe and he swears that the bear is very gentle. His family has raised the animal since it was a cub and the animal follows the family members around like a puppy dog. In fact, Joe claims that the bear will hide if you raise your voice or yell at him.

I need to ascertain the liability of a person who keeps a non-domesticated animal in a residential setting. Does the law treat the owner of such an animal the same as it would a dog or cat who harms someone? I cannot imagine that to be the case. What I really need to ascertain is if we have any defenses to the claim by Mr. Christopher? Joe has a five-foot high fence around his backyard, and the neighbor was found about ten feet inside the client's boundary line. Since Harry is about five feet tall, I have difficulty believing Christopher's story that the bear somehow pulled him over the fence. I think it is more plausible that Christopher climbed over the fence and confronted the bear on Joe's property. If that is the case, can we argue that the neighbor assumed the risk of the attack? Also, does it matter that the bear was tame and had never hurt anyone previously?

A partner provided me with the enclosed case. Please let me know if it helps our defense.

SCOTT IRVINE V. RARE FELINE BREEDING CENTER, INC.
685 N.E. 2D 120 (CT. APP. IND. 1997)

For the past thirty years, Mosella Schaffer has lived on a fifty-acre farm where she has raised and maintained exotic animals.

In 1993, Scott Bullington was renting a room in the garage area of Schaffer's house. Aware of his friend Irvine's interest in wild animals, Bullington informed Irvine of Schaffer's farm and the animals she kept there. Over the next two years, Irvine visited Schaffer's farm several dozen times. During these visits, people would occasionally pet the tigers through a fence.

On the afternoon of December 2, 1995, Irvine arrived at Schaffer's home to see Bullington. The two men drank alcohol and watched television. Because Irvine had consumed a substantial amount of alcohol, Bullington told Irvine he could stay overnight on the couch.

Around 8:00 p.m., Irvine decided to visit the tigers before going to sleep. Irvine approached the wire caging, as he and others had done in the past, placed a couple fingers inside the enclosure, and attempted to pet a male tiger. As he was scratching the male tiger, a female tiger made some commotion, which caused Irvine to look away. At that moment, the male tiger pulled Irvine's arm through the two inch by six inch opening of the wire fence.

Upon hearing Irvine's shouts, Schaffer came out of her house, banged an object against the fence, and freed Irvine. Schaffer immediately drove Irvine to the hospital and he underwent six surgeries during a thirteen-day hospital stay.

We first address whether strict liability is the common law rule for wild animal cases. The parties have not cited and we have not found a case specifically applying strict liability to a true wild animal case. However, we have little difficulty concluding that Indiana's common law recognizes the strict liability rule for wild animal cases.

We have previously set out the rationale for imposing strict liability against owners for injuries caused by an attack by a naturally ferocious or dangerous animal. Strict liability is appropriately placed upon those who, even with proper care, expose the community to the risk of a very dangerous thing. The kind of "dangerous animal" that will subject the keeper to strict liability must pose some kind of an abnormal risk to the particular community where the animal is kept; hence, the keeper is engaged in an activity that subjects those in the vicinity, including those who come onto his property, to an abnormal risk. The possessor of a wild animal is strictly liable for physical harm done to the person of another if that harm results from a dangerous propensity that is characteristic of wild animals of that class. Thus, strict liability has been imposed on keepers of lions, tigers, elephants, wolves, and other similar animals. No member of such a species, however domesticated, can ever be regarded as safe, and liability does not rest upon any experience with the particular animal.

With the rationale for the rule in mind, we analyze whether any exceptions or defenses to the strict liability wild animal rule are appropriate. The *Restatement (Second) of Torts* provides: (1) A possessor of a wild animal is subject to liability to another for harm done by the animal to the other, his person, land or chattels, although the possessor has exercised the utmost care to confine the animal, or otherwise prevent it from doing harm. (2) This liability is limited to harm that results from a dangerous propensity that is characteristic of wild animals of the particular class, or of which the possessor knows or has reason to know.

However, a possessor of land is not subject to strict liability to one whom intentionally or negligently trespasses upon the land, for harm done to him by a wild animal that the possessor keeps on the land, even though the trespasser has no reason to know that the animal is kept there. Yet, if the invitee or licensee "knows that the dangerous animal is permitted to run at large or has escaped from control, they may be barred from recovery if they choose to act upon the possessor's consent or to exercise any other privilege and thus expose themselves to the risk of being harmed by the animal.

The plaintiff's contributory negligence in knowingly and unreasonably subjecting himself to the risk that a wild animal will do harm to his person is a defense to the strict liability. Although one harmed by a wild animal that has escaped from control of its possessor is not barred from recovery because he has not exercised ordinary care to observe the presence of the animal or to escape from its attack, he is barred if he intentionally and unreasonably subjects himself to the risk of harm by the animal. Thus one who without any necessity for so doing that is commensurate with the risk involved knowingly puts himself in reach of an animal that is effectively chained or otherwise confined cannot recover against the possessor of the animal.

The plaintiff's assumption of the risk of harm from the animal is a defense to the strict liability. In the same manner, one who voluntarily teases and provokes a chained animal, or goes within reach of a vicious dog, is barred from recovery if he does so with knowledge of the danger. Thus, a plaintiff who voluntarily and unreasonably comes within reach of an animal, which he knows to be dangerous, has no cause of action when it attacks him.

Name _____ **Please Print Clearly**

1. Is a bear a domesticated or non-domesticated animal? Please explain.

_____

_____

_____

_____

_____

_____

_____

_____

2. From a liability point of view, does the law treat the owner of a bear as the same it would a dog or cat?

_____

_____

_____

_____

_____

_____

_____

_____

_____

3. What defense can Joe Roberts assert to the lawsuit by Peter Christopher?

_____

_____

_____

_____

_____

_____

_____

_____

_____

4. Does it matter that the bear had never hurt anyone before this incident?

_____

_____

_____

_____

_____

_____

_____

_____

_____

_____

SECTION 8.9

THE PLEADINGS

The purpose of the **pleadings** is to place the parties on notice of the claim, to set forth the theories of liability and defenses, and to establish the boundaries of the litigation. In other words, if the plaintiff asserts that the defendant was negligent in the operation of a car, he cannot allege that the defendant intentionally ran him off the road at trial. Likewise, if the defendant has a defense to the lawsuit, such as assumption of the risk or comparative negligence, it must be asserted at this time or it will be waived.

The plaintiff initiates a lawsuit by filing a **Complaint** with the Clerk of the Court or **Prothonotary**. This pleading is like a short story and sets forth the plaintiff's theory of liability against the defendant, as well the damages the claimant maintains that he or she is entitled to receive.

The Complaint will generally follow the following outline:

1. It will identify the parties to the lawsuit and set forth their addresses;

2. It will set forth the facts in a light most favorable to the plaintiff;

3. It will identify the theory of liability such as negligence, invasion of privacy or breach of contract;

4. It will list the plaintiff's damages and/or injuries; and

5. It will conclude by asking for a dollar amount.

Regardless of the merits of the Complaint, the defendant must file a response to the lawsuit within a specified number of days. Generally, the response is called the **Answer** and the defendant must admit or deny each paragraph of the Complaint. The defendant is also required to assert his or her defenses at this time, such as the statute of limitations or assumption of the risk. This is done in a pleading called **New Matter or Affirmative Defenses**.

If the defendant has a cause of action against the plaintiff, it may be raised as a **Counterclaim**. In the alternative, the defendant can simply file a separate lawsuit against the plaintiff.

If a pleading is defective, a party may file **Preliminary Objections**, and the matter will be referred to a judge for a ruling.

THE LITIGATION PROCESS

1. PLEADINGS

   a. Complaint

   b. Answer

   c. Affirmative Defenses

   d. Counterclaim

   e. Preliminary Objections

2. DISCOVERY

   a. Interrogatories

   b. Depositions

   c. Request to Produce Documents

   d. Medical Examination

   e. Request for Admissions

3. TRIAL

   a. Settlement Conference

   b. Jury Selection

   c. Opening Statements

   d. Presentation of Evidence

   e. Closing Statements

   f. Court Instructions

   g. Verdict

   h. Post-trial Motions and Appeals

   i. Execution

The following documents are the pleadings in the lawsuit of **Christopher v. Roberts**.

PETER CHRISTOPHER	: Court of Common Pleas
v.	:
JOSEPH ROBERTS	: No. 2008-00653

Complaint in Civil Action

1. The plaintiff, Peter Christopher, resides at 38 Royal Court in Rydal, PA

2. The defendant, Joseph Roberts, resides at 37 Royal Court in Rydal, PA

3. On or about September 3 of Labor Day weekend, the defendant owned and kept a large and wild bear on his property which was left unchained.

4. A bear is a non-domesticated and wild animal that is dangerous to people.

5. As a result of the defendant's keeping this non-domesticated animal in his backyard, the bear attacked, mauled, and bit the plaintiff causing severe injuries to his body.

6. The defendant is both strictly liable and negligent for keeping such a wild animal on his property.

7. The carelessness and negligence of the defendant includes, but is not limited to:

    a. keeping a non-domesticated animal that possessed a dangerous propensity at a residential property;

    b. failing to keep the animal properly chained and secured; and

    c. in otherwise being negligent.

8. Solely by reason of the aforesaid occurrence, the plaintiff was made to sustain great pain and suffering, lacerations and abrasions about the body, along with lost wages, and medical expenses.

WHEREFORE, Peter Christopher demands damages from the defendant in excess of $50,000.

PETER CHRISTOPHER	: Court of Common Pleas
v.	:
JOSEPH ROBERTS	: No. 2008-00653

Answer with New Matter and a Counterclaim

1-2.   Admitted.

3.   Admitted. However, the backyard was enclosed by a five-foot high fence which the plaintiff climbed over.

4-8.   Denied. Said paragraphs call for conclusions of law to which no responsive pleading is needed. Furthermore, after reasonable investigation, the defendant lacks knowledge or information to form a belief as to the truth of these averments.

New Matter

9.   Plaintiff's claim is barred by the Comparative Negligence Act.

10.   Plaintiff's claim is barred by the doctrine of assumption of the risk.

Counterclaim

11.   Joseph Roberts is the owner of a North American brown bear that he kept secured on his fenced-in property.

12.   On the date in question, Peter Christopher trespassed on the property of Mr. Roberts and willfully attacked the bear with a metal pole thereby causing the bear to sustain injuries requiring veterinarian expenses to cure.

13.   Joseph Roberts received $8,750 in expenses to treat the bear as the result of the plaintiff's conduct.

WHEREFORE, the defendant demands that judgment be entered in his favor to the amount of $8,750.

SECTION 8.10
ANTHONY ROBERTS
v. JIM JOHNSON

PROBLEM EIGHT—B

PARK, BROWN & SMITH, P.C.
ATTORNEYS AT LAW
M E M O R A N D U M

To: All Law Clerks

FROM: Peter Smith, Esquire

RE: Roberts v. Johnson

Tony Roberts decided to visit some of his college friends in the Philadelphia area. While stopped in a southbound direction on Broad Street near its intersection with Walnut Street, his car was hit in the rear by another motor vehicle being driven by Jim Johnson.

Apparently, Johnson was so intent on changing the radio station on his stereo that he did not see Tony's car stopped in front of him. While Tony was not hurt, his Corvette sustained $10,000 in property damage. It took two weeks to fix the Corvette and Tony had to rent a substitute vehicle during this time at a cost of $420.

The firm has been hired to file a lawsuit against Mr. Johnson for the damage to Tony's car and the cost of the rental vehicle. Please prepare the pleading so that we can file it with the court. As you know, Tony lives at 37 Royal Court, Rydal, Pennsylvania. Mr. Johnson resides at 805 Broadway in Philadelphia. You are to follow the form of the Complaint involving Peter Christopher, which is described in *Section 8.9*. The cause of action should be based on allegations of negligence. Your document should set forth in detail what Mr. Johnson did wrong in causing the accident. As for the date of the accident, please assume that the collision occurred one year ago on this date.

PROBLEM EIGHT—B

Name		Please Print Clearly

Anthony Roberts   :   COURT OF COMMON PLEAS
37 Royal Court   :
Rydal, PA   :
                                   :

         v.   :

Jim Johnson   :
805 Broadway   :
Philadelphia, PA   :   No. 2008-4399

COMPLAINT

_____

_____

_____

_____

_____

_____

_____

_____

_____

_____

_____

_____

_____

_____

_____

_____

_____

Section 8.11
Discovery

Lawyers do not like surprises, so between the time that a lawsuit is filed and the case proceeds to trial, the litigants engage in **discovery**. This process allows an attorney to learn more about an opponent's case by the orderly exchange of information between counsel.

The tools of discovery may be classified as follows:

1. Interrogatories

2. Request for Production of Documents

3. Depositions

4. Submission to a Medical Examination

5. Request for Admissions

Interrogatories are written questions submitted to an opponent that must be answered in writing under oath. This discovery tool is used so frequently by attorneys that standard questions have been created for specific kinds of cases. For example, pre-set Interrogatories exist for personal injury cases involving medical malpractice, car accidents, trips and falls, and products liability. Since the issues are generally the same, standard questions may be utilized in various cases. When the circumstances warrant, additional questions can be crafted to cover any situation.

A **Deposition** is the oral questioning of a person under oath in which everything that is said is recorded by a stenographer. Depositions are informal in nature and can take place in a courthouse or an attorney's office. Anyone with knowledge about a case can be deposed.

A **Request for Production of Documents** requires an attorney to turn over to opposing counsel a copy of the file. While an attorney's work product and mental impressions are exempt, statements of witnesses, photographs, employment records, and medical reports must be exchanged.

A party may be required to submit to a **physical or mental examination** if relevant. For example, if a plaintiff institutes suit for personal injury, a defendant has the right to have the claimant examined by a doctor of the defendant's own choice.

Request for Admissions are used to narrow the issues for trial. A litigant can ask an opponent to admit certain facts about the case. If the information is admitted, then it does not have to be proven at the time of trial. For example, a defendant may ask a plaintiff to admit that the claimant had a previous back injury. If the fact is admitted, the defendant will not have to produce the medical records about the previous back injury at trial.

SECTION 8.12

SUBPOENA

A **subpoena** is a court order directing a person to appear in court or at another designated location to provide testimony in a court proceeding. Failure to obey the subpoena can result in a recalcitrant witness being held in **contempt of court**. It is through this process that parties are able to compel witnesses to testify in judicial proceedings so that the facts may best be presented to the finder of fact. Subpoenas are used both at the time of trial and through the pre-trial process of discovery.

There is nothing magical about the subpoena. The forms are generally purchased from the Clerk of the Court and kept in the attorney's office until needed. Subpoenas are pre-signed by the court, and the attorney merely fills in the appropriate biographical information on the document to identify the witness. A representative of the attorney's office, such as a private investigator, must serve the subpoena upon the witness. A witness is entitled to a modest fee for his or her appearance and compensation should be tendered at the time that the subpoena is served. That individual should never ignore a subpoena, since it carries with it the contempt powers of the court. If a problem exists with the date for the witness' testimony, the witness should contact the attorney whose name is listed on the document to see if the date can be changed.

While the court has great discretion in being able to hold a party in **contempt**, the imposition of sanctions must be fair. A finding of criminal contempt will be sustained when the Court finds: **(1)** misconduct in the presence of the court **(2)** committed with the intent to obstruct the proceeding, and **(3)** obstructs the administration of justice. An example of inappropriate behavior includes a case where the defendant removed his clothing down to his underwear, persisted in arguing with the judge, told the judge to go to hell, and failed to return to the courtroom in the afternoon. **Commonwealth v. Odom, 764 A.2d 53 (Pa. Super. 2000).**

Consider the following case in which a doctor failed to appear in court with a patient's medical records. He was held in criminal contempt by the judge.

JACK ARON V. JUDGE ARTHUR HUTOE
258 SO.2D 272 (D. CT. APP. FLA. 1972)

It appears that when Dr. Aron failed to respond to witness subpoenas served on him for his appearance with certain records at trial, the trial judge recessed the trial and issued a bench warrant for his arrest. Dr. Aron was then contacted by the Sheriff's office and thereafter appeared in court during the trial. A contempt order was rendered.

This cause was heard upon the Court's Order to have Dr. Jack D. Aron taken into custody and brought before this Court to show cause why he should not be held in contempt for failure to appear as a witness. The Court finds that Dr. Jack D. Aron had been subpoenaed to testify and to bring with him records pertaining to the treatment of the Plaintiff. The attorneys for the Defendants and Plaintiff stated that they both had subpoenaed Dr. Aron. Because the doctor failed to appear, the Court was compelled to recess the case; whereupon the doctor appeared and failed to give satisfactory reason for his failure to obey the subpoenas served upon him.

It was the finding of the court that Dr. Jack Aron is in contempt of this Court and he was sentenced to pay a fine of Three Hundred Dollars ($300.00) or serve thirty-days (30) in the Dade County Jail.

Rule 1.410 (e) R.C.P. provides that the failure by any person without adequate excuse to obey a subpoena served upon him may be deemed a contempt of the court from which the subpoena issued.

We think the rule is specifically designed to encompass such actions as those committed in this case. Much time, effort and money are spent in bringing a case to trial and the trial judge should have, and does have, authority to proceed swiftly in dealing with those who arbitrarily and capriciously disregard his proper orders. Assuming arguendo, that this contempt must be characterized as civil or criminal and as direct or indirect, we believe that it was instituted by the court to punish for disobedience of a court order and was a criminal contempt. Criminal contempt proceedings are those brought to preserve the power and vindicate the dignity of the court and to punish for disobedience of its orders.

Rule 1.830 states that a criminal contempt may be punished summarily if the court saw or heard the conduct constituting the contempt committed in the actual presence of the court.

Here, the trial judge obviously saw that Dr. Aron was not present in court and heard from counsel that the witness subpoenas had been served upon him and that he had not complied with them by attending the trial and bringing his records. The contemptuous acts were committed in the actual presence of the court when the court saw that the doctor was not present at the trial with his records and saw and heard that he had been subpoenaed by each party. In response to the bench warrant the doctor came into court during the trial and offered an inadequate explanation for his absence on the morning of the trial. He admitted he had been to the court on another case earlier the same morning but stated he 'got mixed up about this one' and went back to his office.

We believe the record establishes the trial court saw and heard a contempt committed in its actual presence and that this was a direct criminal contempt. Affirmed.

Section 8.13
Rules of Evidence[1]

Cases are tried by the presentation of evidence. Witnesses are called during trial and questioned by the attorneys. The finder of fact will listen to this testimony and decide who is telling the truth.

Rules of Evidence have been established to govern the way an attorney may examine a witness or ask a question. These Rules cover a wide range of possible situations arising in all types of trials.

The following is an overview of some of the Rules of Evidence. It has been prepared by the staff of the Law Education and Participation (LEAP) Program at Temple University School of Law for use in high school mock trial competitions. LEAP organizes the program in conjunction with the National Institute for Citizen Education in the Law of Washington, D.C.

Examination of Witnesses

A witness is questioned on **direct examination** when he or she is called by an attorney to prove the client's side of the case. The attorney who calls that witness may not ask leading questions on direct examination. A **leading question** is one that suggests to the witness the answer desired. For example, the question "Isn't it true that you last saw Mrs. Jones on January 1?" is leading. The correct way to phrase the inquiry is: "When did you last see Mrs. Jones?" In other words, a question on direct examination should be designed to obtain a short narrative answer.

An exception to the leading question rule exists if an attorney calls the opponent as a witness, or a witness is shown to be "hostile." The Court may allow the attorney to ask leading questions under these circumstances. The purpose of this exception is to prevent a hostile witness from avoiding direct, non-leading questions.

Hearsay testimony is generally prohibited in court. Hearsay is an out-of-court statement made by someone other than the witness to prove the truth of the facts contained in the statement. An example of hearsay is when Mr. Smith testifies: "Joe told me that Harry was wearing a light blue coat." The opposing attorney can object when Smith says: "Joe told me…," indicating that the witness is relying upon what someone else said. To be objectionable, the answer would also have to be relevant to the case that Harry was wearing a blue coat. The Court, however, may allow the hearsay statement if Joe is the opposing party and the out-of-court statement made by Joe was against his interest.

There are a number of exceptions to the hearsay rule. One of the more unusual exceptions deals with a **dying declaration.** If the decedent has been the victim of a crime, is critically wounded, and identifies the culprit on his deathbed, the identification will be allowed in the criminal trial even though the statement is hearsay. The idea behind the rule is that a person is not going to lie just before death. A dying declaration will be admissible even though the statement is hearsay, if **(1)** the victim identifies his attacker; **(2)** the victim believes he is going to die; **(3)** death is imminent; and **(4)** death actually occurs.

Opinion testimony is an expression of non-factual conclusions. Generally, a "lay witness" can only testify as to observed facts and those areas of "opinion" that the Court would consider to be within the general knowledge of the witness. For example, a person may testify as to the speed of a car if the witness has had some experience in driving or observing cars travelling at the speed in question. Opinion testimony, however, may be given by an expert witness. An expert is a person who can be "qualified" as having specialized knowledge in a given field because of professional credentials and/or experience acceptable to the Court. In the alternative, the attorneys for each side can agree, or **stipulate**, that a witness is an expert.

While experts must possess specialized knowledge, their testimony is entitled to no more weight than any other witness. The jury may also disregard the expert testimony if it is not found to be credible.

Relevant evidence is testimony or an exhibit that helps establish a fact which is controverted or necessary to prove one's side of the case. The Court usually allows an attorney to obtain background information from an important witness. For example, an attorney may ask the witness about his age, family, or work experience, even though it is not relevant to the central issue of the case. The opposing attorney is granted leeway in questioning the witness to explore the truthfulness of the person's direct testimony, including omitted facts, bias, or prejudice.

Not all evidence that may shed light on an issue, however, will be allowed into evidence. In federal court, the trial judge is also required to examine the prejudicial effect of the proffered evidence. If the probability of the evidence in establishing a fact is substantially outweighed by negative factors—such as confusion of the issue, unfair prejudice, or misleading the jury—the admissibility of the evidence will be denied.

Is the issuance or non-issuance of a traffic ticket by a police officer investigating a motor vehicle accident relevant in a civil lawsuit for money damages? That is the issue in the following case.

Tim Freer v. Robert Singler
1998 WL 1986997 (Mich. App. 1998)

Plaintiff argues that defense counsel committed prejudicial error by eliciting during trial, and then repeating during his closing argument, the fact that defendant did not receive a traffic ticket for the accident that caused plaintiff's injuries. Citing **Dudek v. Popp,** 129 N.W. 2d 393 (1964), defendant argues that because the expert testimony of plaintiff's accident-reconstruction expert implied that defendant had violated two provisions of the Motor Vehicle Code, he was allowed to introduce for impeachment purposes evidence that he did not receive a traffic ticket.

In **Brownell v. Brown,** 319 N.W. 2d 664 (1982), this Court observed that evidence of the issuance or non-issuance of a traffic ticket is inadmissible as substantive evidence in a civil trial because neither is relevant to the issues to be tried. According to **Dudek,** evidence of the non-issuance of a traffic ticket is admissible only to impeach an *investigating* officer who did not issue a traffic ticket at the time of the accident, and then offers at trial opinion evidence which clearly imports a violation of the motor vehicle code. The **Dudek** Court reasoned that it would be an anomaly indeed if an officer were to be permitted by the effect of his opinion evidence to imply that one participant in an accident violated a causally related motor vehicle operation regulation, but at the same time be foreclosed from any inquiry as to whether he issued a violation ticket.

In the case at hand, plaintiff's accident-reconstruction expert was not an investigating officer at the accident scene. Indeed, the witness is self-employed as a private investigator. **Dudek** is inapplicable under these circumstances. Accordingly, the admission of evidence regarding the non-issuance of a traffic ticket was error.

We conclude that the error was not harmless. The record shows that defense counsel's references to the non-issuance of a traffic ticket were not inadvertent. Twice, defense counsel brought up the matter during the presentation of evidence. And even after the trial court had ruled that the officer's motivation in not issuing a ticket was unknown and inadmissible, defense counsel stated in his closing argument, "Most telling is the fact that the defendant didn't get a ticket. The officer in charge of investigating this accident apparently satisfied himself there wasn't any fault to divide between the parties because he found that defendant didn't do anything wrong." These circumstances show that defendant was deliberately attempting to influence the jury by placing before the jury the supposed opinion of a non-testifying witness charged with the responsibility of assessing responsibility for the accident. Therefore, because plaintiff's substantial rights were improperly affected by the error, reversal is warranted.

Cross examination is the questioning of the other side's witnesses. An attorney on cross-examination may ask leading questions. For example, an attorney may ask: "Isn't it true, Mr. Jones, that you were wearing a light blue jacket on the night of January 1?" Questions that permit a witness on cross examination to explain the answer are usually avoided.

The Court should restrict the subject areas on cross examination to those matters raised by direct testimony. However, the Court does allow some leeway. Attacking the truthfulness of a witness may be attempted on cross examination if the witness has been convicted of crimes of dishonesty.

Questioning by the Court may occur at any point. These questions, however, should only clarify points that are unclear. The judge should not attempt to prove any part of either side's case.

INTRODUCING EXHIBITS

Physical evidence, if relevant, can be introduced by either attorney when presenting one's case, or during cross examination.

An attorney must follow a specified procedure when introducing exhibits into court. The attorney will ask the judge: "Your Honor, I request that this document be marked as P-1 (if it is a Plaintiff's exhibit) or "D-1" (if it is a Defendant's exhibit). The Exhibit will then be marked by the clerk of the court and will be shown to opposing counsel so that he or she knows what is being discussed. The document is then **authenticated.** This is done by showing the exhibit to the witness and asking, "Mr. Jones can you identify this exhibit for the Court?" The witness will then briefly explain the exhibit and attest to its accuracy.

After the document is shown to the judge and the witness is questioned about the exhibit, the attorney formally offers the exhibit into the record. This is done by the attorney saying: "Your Honor, I offer this exhibit into evidence."

One should note that if an exhibit is authenticated, questions can be asked about its contents even if the document is never offered into the record. Also, the exhibit can be offered into evidence at the conclusion of the attorney's case but before the attorney "rests."

Opposing counsel can always object to the exhibit being offered into evidence if it is not relevant or if it has not been properly authenticated.

OBJECTIONS

Objections are made by counsel when it is felt that the opposing attorney is violating the Rules of Evidence. Objections may be made for a number of reasons. The manner in which these objections are made are outlined below.

Leading Questions: "Your Honor, I object to counsel's leading the witness." A leading question is only objectionable if asked by the counsel on direct examination, not on cross.

Irrelevant Evidence: "I object your Honor—the question is not relevant to the facts in this case." This objection is used sparingly because opposing counsel usually does not care if the opponent is not getting to the important facts.

Non-responsive: "Your Honor, the witness is not answering the question asked." This objection may be used when the witness is not answering the questions presented.

Hearsay: "Objection, Your Honor. Counsel is asking for hearsay testimony." If the witness provides an answer that is based on hearsay, the attorney can ask the court to strike the answer from the record.

Beyond the scope of direct: "Your Honor, I object. Counsel is asking about matters that were not raised on direct examination." This objection is used to limit overly broad cross examination.

An attorney may object to testimony that violates a **confidential communication.** In striving to protect the confidentiality of certain communications, the court allows for privileged communication in four situations:

1. attorney-client privilege,
2. doctor-patient privilege,
3. priest-penitent privilege, and
4. husband-wife privilege.

In these situations, a party to the conversation cannot be forced to testify in court against the other party to the communication.

Immunity from having to testify in a legal proceeding when a privilege exists is demonstrated in a suit by Billy Joel against his former business manager. The defendant wanted the singer's former wife, Christine Brinkley, to testify but the court found that she could not be called as a witness because of the immunity that she enjoyed by being married to the plaintiff.

BILLY JOEL V. FRANK MANAGEMENT, INC.
581 N.Y.S. 2D 579 (N. Y. 1992)

The novel issue raised on this motion is whether one has absolute immunity against a claim of tortiously interfering with a contract between the person's spouse and a third party.

In his complaint, Billy Joel seeks a judgment declaring valid the termination of an agreement under which FMI served as manager of Joel's business and personal affairs. Joel asserts such right based on his discovery that FMI committed fraud in the handling of his finances and breached its fiduciary duty to him. Weber, the President of FMI, is the brother of Joel's former wife.

In the subsequent action instituted by FMI against Christine Brinkley, which has been consolidated with the Joel action, FMI alleges that Brinkley "did maliciously and without reasonable justification persuade and entice... Joel to repudiate, and break" the Agreement, resulting in damage to FMI of $11,000,000. No facts are alleged to support this contention other than an assertion that Brinkley "harbored ill feelings and malice toward FMI as a result of the involvement of Weber in the negotiation and execution" of an ante nuptial contract between Brinkley and Joel. Apparently Weber had acted as a negotiator for Joel in connection with such contract, pursuant to which FMI was to administer the household account of the parties.

In support of her motion, Brinkley asserts that as Joel's wife, she has absolute immunity against this type of claim. The allegations of the FMI complaint fail to set forth necessary facts to show conduct that could be deemed "improper." The conclusory allegations that Brinkley acted "wrongfully, knowingly, intentionally, maliciously and without reasonable justification or excuse" are insufficient to satisfy the pleading requirement. Therefore, the complaint fails to state a cause of action and is dismissed.

Moreover, it would appear that crucial testimony to support FMI's claims would be inadmissible. **CPLR 4502(b)** provides that a "husband or wife shall not be required, or without the consent of the other if living, allowed to disclose a confidential communication made by one to the other during marriage." Although this privilege does not apply to ordinary conversations relating to matters of business, here the Agreement related to more than business, as it included the handling of the household account created pursuant to the ante nuptial contract. Further, since FMI was managing the income and assets of the "marital partnership," communications between Joel and Brinkley with respect thereto would not appear to be admissible as an ordinary business conversation, but rather would constitute the type of confidential discussions between spouses relating to their personal finances which would be subject to the statutory privilege.

In light of the foregoing, Brinkley's motion to dismiss the complaint against her is granted.

Throughout a trial, both sides have the opportunity of calling witnesses and presenting evidence. Since the plaintiff has the burden of proof, that party will go first in the presentation of the evidence. In a civil case, the burden of proof is by the **preponderance of the evidence**. In other words, the plaintiff must tip the scale in his or her favor in order to win.

In **Se-Ling Hosiery, Inc. v. Margulies, 70 A.2d 854 (Pa. 1950)**, the court explained the meaning of a preponderance of the evidence with the following illustration:

> If we visualize evidence as something weighed in an ordinary balance scale, and if the evidence plaintiff offers in support of his claim is so much more weighed in probative value then the evidence offered in opposition to it that it tips the scales on the side of the plaintiff, the latter has proved his claim by a fair weight of the evidence.

Gale v. Stallone provides an application of this standard of proof in a civil case. Sylvester Stallone was sued over his alleged failure to repurchase three paintings that he drew before he became a famous actor. The court had to weigh the conflicting evidence in order to resolve the case and ended up dismissing the breach of contract claim because the plaintiff did not prove her case by a preponderance of the evidence.

SONNY GALE V. SYLVESTER STALLONE
1996 WL 197776 (S. D. N. Y. 1996)

The plaintiff in this breach of contract action seeks to recover three Sylvester Stallone paintings which plaintiff claims she sold to defendant for $25,000 each and $2,000,000 in damages. For the reasons which follow, I find that plaintiff failed to prove her claim by a preponderance of the credible evidence.

This case involves three Sylvester Stallone paintings from the late 1960's sold to a Sam Ketover, to enable Stallone to travel from Florida to New York. Eventually, the paintings came into Sonny Gale's possession.

Plaintiff claims that in 1991, she learned that Stallone paintings were being sold in Beverly Hills. Plaintiff contacted Jackie Stallone, Sylvester Stallone's mother, who put her in touch with the artist himself. Plaintiff further testified that she spoke with Stallone about the paintings and that she asked him how much the paintings were worth. According to plaintiff, Stallone informed her that the paintings were worth $25,000 each. Plaintiff testified that Stallone expressed interest in purchasing the paintings, stated that he did not need to see any pictures of the paintings and told plaintiff that his business manager, Mr. Filiti, would contact her about the paintings.

Plaintiff testified that Filiti contacted her, the two of them met several times and she told Filiti that she needed to get rid of the paintings because they were taking up too much space. Plaintiff further testified that Filiti contacted Stallone and in a three-way call including the plaintiff, Stallone directed Filiti to send the paintings to Scott Hanson.

Plaintiff also testified that she spoke with Filiti regularly and that she contacted Hanson who told her that the paintings sold for more than $200,000 each.

Filiti's version of the events differs markedly from that of plaintiff. Filiti testified that plaintiff contacted him in 1990 to inquire as to whether he or Stallone was interested in purchasing the three paintings. Filiti testified that he offered plaintiff $5,000 for each painting. Filiti considered purchasing the paintings as a surprise gift for Stallone. According to Filiti, plaintiff informed him that she was going to ship the paintings to California because a Gallery there had offered her $75,000 a piece for the paintings.

Hanson was the third witness to testify. According to Hanson, an employee of his gallery requested that plaintiff send transparencies of the three paintings to California. When plaintiff informed Hanson's employee that she did not have transparencies available, several New York area photographers were suggested who could put the transparencies together. Hanson further testified that Stallone's paintings typically sold for $5,000 and $10,000.

The burden of proof is on the plaintiff to prove each essential element of her claim by a preponderance of the credible evidence. The test is that the proof shows that something is more likely to have occurred than not. The party who has to shoulder the burden of proof must prove more than simple equality of evidence, she must prove her claim by a preponderance of the evidence.

Based on the record, I find the plaintiff failed to prove her claim by a preponderance of the credible evidence. To prove a breach of contract action, plaintiff must first prove the existence of a contract. Plaintiff failed to prove that a contract for the sale of the three paintings ever existed and even assuming that one did, plaintiff did not prove any of the terms and specificities of the contract. Plaintiff testified that Stallone used the words "how much are they going to set me back?" to convey his interest in the paintings. Yet, plaintiff did not work out any payment terms with Stallone nor did she outline any arrangement for how she would ship the paintings. In fact, on cross-examination plaintiff was unsure as to whether she worked out terms of payment and shipping or whether she simply assumed that Filiti would pick up and pay for the paintings.

In direct contrast to this story, Stallone affirmatively stated that he had never spoken with plaintiff and had no knowledge of who she was. Furthermore, there is no evidence that he ever evidenced any interest in the paintings. Stallone's story is corroborated by the testimony of both Filiti and Hanson. Filiti testified that plaintiff contacted him to see if either he or Stallone would be interested in the paintings. Hanson testified that plaintiff called Hanson Galleries, Inc. in an effort to find a place that would buy her three paintings. Thus, not only is it unclear that plaintiff ever formed a contract, it is unclear that even if there was a contract, what terms were to be imposed. In short, even accepting the plaintiff's story as true, there was no meeting of the minds and no offer and acceptance, a rudimentary concept of contract law.

Thus, the Court finds the only credible story to go something like this; plaintiff first offered to sell the three Stallone paintings to Filiti; when Filiti only offered plaintiff $5,000 per painting, plaintiff contacted the Hanson Galleries, Inc. which she knew had shown and sold pieces of Stallone's work previously; plaintiff then offered to sell the paintings to the Gallery on consignment; however, rather than follow the Gallery's policy of first supplying transparen-

cies, plaintiff crated and shipped the paintings to California where they have remained for the last five years. Based on the proceedings before this Court, plaintiff failed to prove that she reached an agreement with the requisite terms for a valid contract. For that reason, plaintiff is not entitled to monetary relief and her complaint is dismissed.

To put this burden of proof in perspective, it should be compared to the burden of proof in a criminal case, which requires the government to prove each element of the crime **beyond a reasonable doubt**. This higher burden of proof has been defined as follows:

> The defendant is presumed to be innocent and the burden is upon the Commonwealth to prove his guilt beyond a reasonable doubt. A reasonable doubt cannot be a doubt fancied or conjured up in the minds of the jury to escape an unpleasant verdict; it must be an honest doubt arising out of the evidence itself, the kind of a doubt that would restrain a reasonable person from acting in a matter of importance to himself. **Commonwealth v. Donough, 103 A.2d 694 (Pa. 1954).**

The purpose of discovery is to assist the litigants by making them aware of the various witnesses who will testify and the evidence that each side will present at trial. These pre-trial disclosures allow the attorneys to plan their strategies and to prevent surprise. What happens, however, if an attorney learns the identity of a new witness during trial? The court will not automatically allow the presentation of this new evidence because of the prejudice that may be imposed on the other side. The trial judge has several ways of handling this surprise situation: the witness may be prevented from testifying; a mistrial may be declared; or the judge may allow a brief intermission so that the other side may conduct an investigation of the new information, including taking the person's deposition.

Carney v. K-Mart Corporation provides an example of a case where the court prohibited the testimony of an expert witness because his name was not disclosed in a timely fashion.

KEN CARNEY V. K-MART CORPORATION
176 F.R.D. 227 (S. D. W. VA. 1997)

Pending is Defendant Can-Am Care Corporation's ("Can-Am") Motion for Sanctions against Plaintiffs Carney.

Carney was injured while using an allegedly faulty blood glucose test strip marketed under the name "Relief Plus." In January 1997, the parties suggested a joint discovery schedule that set June 3, 1997 as the deadline for Plaintiffs to disclose their expert witnesses. On February 19, the Court incorporated this deadline into a Scheduling Order.

On June 10, 1997 the Carneys filed a Motion seeking to extend the deadline for disclosing their experts. Judge Hogg denied the Carneys' Motion and mandated July 25 as the deadline for the Carneys' disclosure.

On July 23 the Carneys filed a disclosure of experts listing Kenneth Carney's treating physicians. On the same day, they also filed a motion to enlarge the time for disclosure of their experts. On August 12, Judge Hogg again denied the Motion.

Can-Am alleges that the Court should dismiss the case for the Carneys' failure to comply with the parties' discovery plan, or the Court's Scheduling Order.

Rule 37(b)(2) states: If a party fails to obey an order to provide or permit discovery, the court may make such orders in regard to the failure as are just. The Rule lists several possible sanctions including prohibiting the offending party from introducing evidence, striking out designated claims from the pleadings; and dismissing the action or parts thereof. The imposition of sanctions is wholly within the trial court's discretion.

A party that without substantial justification fails to disclose information required shall not, unless such failure is harmless, be permitted to use as evidence at a trial, any witness or information not so disclosed. In addition to this sanction, the court may impose other appropriate sanctions.

The Carneys cannot show "substantial justification" for their failure to disclose experts. Therefore, the Court holds the Carneys will not be permitted to introduce any expert witnesses not already disclosed to the Court and to Defendants.

SECTION 8.14
EXECUTION

Following the verdict and the court's disposition of post-trial motions, the plaintiff will move to have the verdict reduced to a **judgment**. If no appeal is taken, the aggrieved party is entitled to enforce the judgment in an attempt to collect the money owed. If the defendant will not voluntarily satisfy the award, the plaintiff may seek the help of the Sheriff in seizing the assets of the defendant and selling them at **Sheriff's sale**. For instance, a home owned by the defendant may be sold at Sheriff's sale and money in a bank account can be attached in order to satisfy the judgment. Even property that is transferred to a third person in order to make the defendant judgment-proof may be seized as a transfer to defraud a creditor.

The mere fact that a plaintiff secures a judgment, however, does not mean that the aggrieved will recover the amount owed. If the defendant is judgment-proof, or has no assets, the victorious litigant will collect no money. Certain types of property may also be exempt from execution depending upon the jurisdiction. For instance, some states will not disturb property that is owned by a husband and wife if the judgment is against only one of the marital partners. A debtor's interest in a pension fund or life insurance policy are also safe from seizure. In Pennsylvania, for example, the Judicial Code provides that wages, and commissions shall be exempt while in the hands of the employer from an attachment except for support, divorce matters, board for four weeks or less and for repayment of loans under the Pennsylvania Higher Education Assistance Agency Act. A judgment, however, is valid for a number of years so a plaintiff may be able to seize assets that a debtor accumulates several years after the entry of the judgment.

SECTION 8.15
TRIAL MEMO

PROBLEM EIGHT—C

PARK, BROWN & SMITH, P.C.
ATTORNEYS AT LAW
MEMORANDUM

To: All Law Clerks

From: Peter Smith, Esquire

Re: Christopher v. Roberts

I have returned from the trial involving Joe Roberts and the attack of his next-door neighbor by the family's pet bear. The jury is in its third day of deliberation and the judge has declared a recess for the weekend. I have received an expedited copy of the trial transcript since I plan on appealing if we lose.

To prepare you for this assignment, I have dictated the following summary of the key points from the trial transcript. Please read the material so we can talk about the case. I need your honest assessment of what happened. Please be prepared to discuss the following issues:

1. Who should win the case?

2. Were the court's evidentiary rulings correct?

3. Was the court correct in refusing to allow me to produce the bear to show the jury the animal's docile and friendly nature?

OPENING STATEMENT BY MR. LONDON

Members of the jury, my name is David London, and I represent the plaintiff, Peter Christopher. What comes to mind when I hear the words "man's best friend," are images of a dog walking side by side with his owner. In this case, a bear named "Harry" was kept by Joseph Roberts in his backyard as the family pet. You will learn that over the Labor Day weekend, two years ago, my client was viciously attacked by this wild animal. Now members of the jury, this attack did not occur in the woods but in a residential neighborhood. If keeping a bear in the backyard is not bad enough, we will also prove that Mr. Roberts gave this animal alcohol. The bear eventually fell asleep against the fence abutting my client's yard.

Mr. Christopher was cleaning his yard at the time in preparation for a barbecue. Because the bear was nestled up against the fence, Peter gently nudged the animal with a pole so the bear would move to the other side of the yard. The bear, however, awakened in a fury and pulled my helpless client over the fence mauling his leg in the process. Mr. Christopher sustained a number of large lacerations to his left leg and his femur was broken in two places. These injuries have altered my client's life. His leg hurts every day and affects his ability to work. At the conclusion of this case, we will ask you to return with a very large verdict in favor of Mr. Christopher to compensate him for this tragic incident. Thank you.

OPENING STATEMENT BY MR. SMITH

My name is Peter Smith and I represent Joseph Roberts. Members of the jury, there are two sides to every story. I admit that what happened to Mr. Christopher is a tragedy. However, the accident was not caused by Joe Roberts' conduct. Rather, Peter Christopher's injuries were the result of his own actions. While intoxicated, he climbed over a five-foot high fence into the Roberts' backyard and attacked a sleeping bear with a metal pole. I admit that the defendant's choice of a pet is eccentric and not a choice that I would make, but Mr. Christopher took his life into his own hands by confronting the animal. In other words, he assumed the risk of his injuries which the judge will tell you is a complete defense to this claim.

During the course of the trial, you will hear from Mr. Roberts, who will describe his unique pet which he saved from a bankrupt circus and raised from a small cub. The evidence will also show that Harry never hurt anyone before this incident and was a very gentle animal.

At the close of the evidence, I believe you will find for the defendant, and it is in your fair judgment that Joe Roberts places his confidence. Thank you.

THE COURT: *Mr. London, present your first witness.*

MR. LONDON: Your Honor, I call Peter Christopher.

**DIRECT TESTIMONY OF
PETER CHRISTOPHER**

Q. **Please state your name for the record.**

A. *My name is Peter Christopher.*

Q. **And what did you do for a living?**

A. *I was a private investigator and undercover surveillance specialist. Presently, I am out of work because of my injuries.*

Q. **Turning your attention to September 3, two years ago, can you tell the jury what happened?**

A. *Sure. It was Sunday of the Labor Day weekend and Joe Roberts let his bear out to roam in the backyard. The animal eventually fell asleep against the fence that abutted my property. Because I was about to have a party, I tried getting the bear to move to the other side of the yard. I even tried bribing him with a piece of meat but the bear kept sleeping. So, I gently tapped him with a pole and he was wild from the moment he opened his eyes. The animal pulled me over the fence and before I could get away, the bear had my leg in his mouth. I don't remember anything after that. It was a nightmare.*

Q. **What do you remember next?**

A. *I woke up in the hospital, and the lower part of my left leg was in a cast and the pain was unbearable.*

Q. **Are you receiving any medical treatment at the present time?**

A. *Yes. I go for physical therapy twice a week.*

Q. **Mr. Christopher, are there any activities that you can no longer perform?**

A. *I can't run or squat. This prevents me from doing surveillance.*

Q. **No further questions.**

**CROSS-EXAMINATION OF
PETER CHRISTOPHER
BY MR. SMITH**

Q. **Where were you when you "tapped" Harry?**

A. *I was in my backyard.*

Q. **Mr. Christopher, you did more than just tap the bear, didn't you?**

MR. LONDON: Objection – leading.

THE COURT: *Overruled.*

A. *I told you, I just wanted to move the animal away from my property.*

Q. You repeatedly hit the bear with a pole, didn't you, Mr. Christopher?

A. *I just tapped the animal to wake him.*

Q. Mr. Christopher, you were intoxicated at the time?

A. *I had a few beers.*

Q. You had more than just a few beers, isn't that right?

MR. LONDON: Objection. The witness has answered the question.

THE COURT: *Sustained.*

Q. How did you end up in your neighbor's backyard?

A. *The bear pulled me over the fence.*

Q. How high is the fence?

A. *I guess about five-feet high.*

Q. How big is the bear?

A. *I don't know. He is much bigger than a person and has huge teeth.*

Q. Is the bear taller than the fence?

A. *No.*

Q. You climbed over the fence, didn't you?

A. *No. The bear pulled me over.*

Q. The bear just happened to pull you over the fence even though Harry is not taller than the fence?

A. *Yeah. That is right.*

Q. How was that possible?

A. *I don't know. The bear is powerful I guess.*

Q. No further questions of this witness.

REDIRECT EXAMINATION OF PETER CHRISTOPHER BY MR. ROBERTS

Q. Mr. Christopher, tell the jury what you did with the pole.

A. *I merely nudged the bear so he would move to the other side of the property.*

Q. How did you get into Mr. Roberts' backyard?

A. *The bear pulled me over the fence with its claws.*

MR. LONDON: Thank you.

THE COURT: *Mr. London, please call your next witness.*

DIRECT EXAMINATION
OF DR. JONES
BY MR. LONDON

Q. Please state your name.

A. *My name is Dr. Donald Jones.*

Q. Where do you practice?

A. *I am a surgeon at Temple University Hospital in Philadelphia.*

MR. SMITH: We will stipulate that the doctor is qualified to perform surgery.

THE COURT: *Very well. Mr. London, proceed.*

Q. Turning your attention to September 3, did you treat Peter Christopher?

A. *Yes, I had to perform emergency surgery on the wounds to his leg.*

Q. Can you tell us the nature of that surgery?

A. *Mr. Christopher had rather large and deep lacerations on his left side and his leg had to be reset because of fractures to the distal femur. The size of the wound reminded me of a shark bite.*

MR. SMITH: Objection. The doctor is speculating.

THE COURT: *Sustained.*

Q. Doctor, were these injuries the result of a bear attack?

MR. SMITH: Objection. Leading and asking for an opinion.

THE COURT: *Sustained. You'll have to rephrase that, counselor.*

Q. Dr. Jones, were you able to discover the cause of these injuries?

A. *Yes. They appeared to have been caused by the teeth of a very large and powerful animal.*

Q. Have you treated the patient since the surgery?

A. *Yes. I continue to monitor the wounds.*

Q. Dr. Jones, did the ambulance driver say anything to you when they brought the plaintiff to the hospital?

MR. SMITH: Objection – hearsay.

THE COURT: *Sustained.*

MR. LONDON: Thank you, doctor. That is all I have.

CROSS EXAMINATION
OF DR. JONES
BY MR. SMITH

Q. **Dr. Jones, isn't it true that the plaintiff's wounds healed nicely?**

A. *Yes.*

Q. **Is the plaintiff able to ambulate successfully following your excellent medical care?**

A. *Yes. I believe so.*

Q. **Was Mr. Christopher's surgery complicated by the fact that he had been drinking?**

MR. LONDON: Objection. There is no proper foundation for the question.

THE COURT: *You'll have to rephrase that, counselor.*

Q. **Did you test Mr. Christopher's blood before the operation?**

A. *Standard procedure.*

Q. **What did you learn from the blood analysis?**

A. *There was a clear indication of alcohol in his system so we had to alter the anesthesia.*

Q. **Wasn't the plaintiff's blood/alcohol level content .25?**

A. *Yes.*

Q. **Legally intoxicated?**

A. *Yes, this is more than three times the legal standard.*

Q. **Did you find any types of drugs in his system?**

MR. LONDON: Objection. And, I move to strike the question as prejudicial.

THE COURT: *Sustained*

THE COURT: *Members of the jury, please disregard these last questions.*

Q. **Doctor, do you live near the plaintiff?**

A. *I live on the same street.*

Q. **Have you heard anything about Mr. Christopher's reputation in the community?**

MR. LONDON: Objection. This is irrelevant and hearsay.

THE COURT: *Overruled. Doctor, you may answer.*

A. *I know of his reputation first-hand. Mr. Christopher is always getting into trouble with the law and he has been in jail several times for intoxication and trespassing.*

Q. **Isn't it true that you treated the plaintiff three months before this incident for a torn cartilage in the left knee?**

MR. LONDON: Objection. The question is irrelevant to this case.

MR. SMITH: It is relevant. This man had a pre-existing left knee injury.

THE COURT: *Overruled.*

    A. *He had hurt his knee about a month before the attack and needed surgery which had not yet taken place.*

Q. **Dr. Jones, are you currently being sued by Mr. Roberts for malpractice?**

MR. LONDON: Objection. That is irrelevant.

MR. SMITH: It is relevant. It shows that the doctor could be biased against my client.

THE COURT: *Overruled.*

    A. *I don't see what relevance that claim has to this case.*

Q. **I don't care what you think, doctor, I ask the questions.**

MR. LONDON: Objection. Counsel is badgering the witness.

THE COURT: *Overruled.*

Q. **Doctor, are you being sued for medical malpractice by Joe Roberts?**

    A. *Yes.*

Q. **No further questions.**

MR. LONDON: That is the plaintiff's case and we rest.

DIRECT EXAMINATION
OF JOSEPH ROBERTS
BY MR. SMITH

Q. **Please state your name for the record.**

    A. *Joseph Roberts.*

Q. **Joe, what do you do for a living?**

    A. *Well, times were tough for the Roberts family for a long while, and…*

THE COURT: *Mr. Roberts, just answer the questions asked.*

Q. **Joe, you may answer.**

    A. *I own my own construction company. It is called Joro Construction.*

Q. **Did you own a bear?**

    A. *I had a wonderful pet bear named Harry.*

Q. **Mr. Roberts, will you please tell the court why you bought such an exotic pet?**

A. *My children saw Harry at a bankrupt circus and fell in love with him. He seemed so sad so I bought him. We raised him from a cub.*

Q. **Has Harry ever been violent before the incident on September 3?**

A. *No. He wouldn't hurt a fly.*

Q. **Turning your attention to September 3, did anything unusual happen that day?**

A. *It was the Labor Day weekend and we went inside for lunch. Harry was restless because of the heat, but he finally fell asleep by the fence that surrounds my property.*

Q. **Then what happened?**

A. *I heard shouts coming from our yard. I ran outside, and saw Christopher in my backyard, passed out. I told my wife to call an ambulance.*

Q. **Was Harry injured, Mr. Roberts?**

A. *Yes. He had several wounds which had to be treated at the Large Animal Clinic at the University of Pennsylvania.*

Q. **Do you know how Mr. Christopher got in your backyard?**

A. *He must have climbed over the fence.*

MR. LONDON: Objection. This is pure speculation.

THE COURT: *Sustained.*

Q. **How high is the fence?**

A. *It is a five-foot high fence.*

Q. **How tall is Harry?**

A. *He is a little shorter than the fence is high.*

Q. **Could the bear pull someone over the fence?**

A. *No. Harry could not reach over the top of the fence with his paws.*

MR. LONDON: Objection. This is pure speculation and I move to strike.

THE COURT: *Overruled.*

Q. **How long have you had Harry?**

A. *Two years.*

Q. Has Harry ever hurt anyone before?

A. *No. He really is very gentle.*

Q. How long have you and Mr. Christopher been neighbors?

A. *A little more than six months.*

Q. Had Mr. Christopher ever complained to you about Harry before the day in question?

A. *Never. In fact, I occasionally heard him talking to the bear.*

Q. Was Harry treated for his injuries?

A. *Yes. I had to pay $5,000 for his care.*

CROSS EXAMINATION OF JOSEPH ROBERTS BY MR. LONDON

Q. Did you have a license to keep the bear at your home?

A. *No. I didn't know that I needed one.*

Q. Isn't it true, Mr. Roberts, you enjoyed getting Harry drunk?

A. *No. I did not enjoy getting the bear drunk.*

Q. Did you give that bear liquor on the day in question?

A. *He was restless so I gave him some beer. He likes it and it relaxes him.*

Q. Didn't Harry maul your son previously or have physical contact with him?

MR. SMITH: Objection. What does counsel mean by physical contact?

THE COURT: *Rephrase your question.*

Q. Didn't the bear hurt your son previously?

A. *Yes and no., Tony was wrestling with Harry and my son was scratched by the bear's claws. It was an accident. Tony yelled at Harry and the poor animal hid the rest of the day, even though he did nothing wrong.*

Q. Isn't it true that my client was bleeding profusely when you found him in the backyard?

A. *Well, he was bleeding but so was Harry. I am not sure whose blood I was looking at.*

Q. Mr. Roberts, didn't the bear have Mr. Christopher's leg in his mouth when you saw him?

MR. SMITH: Objection, your Honor.

THE COURT: *Overruled. Answer the question.*

A. *Yes. Harry had Christopher's leg in his mouth but Christopher had that metal pole in his hand.*

Q. **No further questions.**

REDIRECT OF JOSEPH ROBERTS BY MR. SMITH

Q. **What did you do when you went outside?**

A. *I immediately wrapped Peter Christopher's leg in a towel to stop the bleeding.*

Q. **Have you ever let Harry out of the confines of your backyard?**

A. *Never. Harry was afraid of strangers and I know better than to let a bear roam the neighborhood.*

Q. **Had Harry ever hurt anyone before the day in question?**

A. *No.*

Q. **No further questions.**

MR. SMITH:	Your Honor, we have one more witness.
MR. LONDON:	Your Honor, the plaintiff is unaware of any other witness and demands an offer of proof.
MR. SMITH:	The witness played a very important part in the incident. Actually, he was there.
THE COURT:	*Really. In the interest of justice, I will allow the testimony.*
MR. LONDON:	Oh my God! Your Honor, Mr. Roberts is leading a bear into the courtroom.
THE COURT:	*Mr. Roberts, remove that animal from this courtroom immediately. Mr. Smith, what is the meaning of this stunt?*
MR. SMITH:	Your Honor, we merely wish to show that Harry is a very gentle animal.
THE COURT:	*Counselors, approach the bench immediately, and I mean now!*
MR. SMITH:	The jury is entitled to meet Harry and judge for themselves whether he is a vicious animal. If the jury could merely see Harry, they would have a better understanding of this case.
MR. LONDON:	This request is outrageous.
MR. SMITH:	Your Honor, I believe there is precedent for what I am trying to do. Dogs are routinely used by the police to establish probable cause that drugs are present and

their findings are allowed into evidence as long as the dog has a history of providing reputable information.

THE COURT: *Enough! A bear has no place in the courtroom, and the prejudicial affect of this stunt far outweighs the probative value of the evidence. You will both return to your seats and make closing arguments. Mr. Smith, you are lucky I don't hold you in contempt of court and declare a mistrial. Counsel, I suggest you make your closing arguments.*

CLOSING ARGUMENT BY MR. LONDON

Ladies and gentlemen of the jury, this case is quite simple. Is it reasonable to keep a bear in one's backyard? To make matters worse, the owner of that animal then decides to provide the thing with liquor in order to quiet it down. Are these actions normal and rational? The law is clear. One who keeps a non-domesticated animal, like a bear, on his property is liable to anyone injured by that animal. The only defense is if the injured party assumed the risk of injury. Do you really believe that Mr. Christopher thought he would be harmed by gently nudging the bear with a pole to move the animal away from the fence? I think not! The only real issue in this case is how much money my client should be awarded for his injuries and loss of business. In making this calculation, please remember the massive teeth of a bear as they crushed my client's leg. Consider also that Peter must go through the rest of his life with a permanent injury to his leg. He can't run, or do the things with his leg that we each take for granted.

Peter carries both physical and emotional scars with him everyday. Everyone can see the massive scars on his left leg. No one will hire him at the moment since he can no longer perform his job. Members of the jury, I ask that you please award my client a sum of money that will reimburse him for his past and future losses and that which will send a clear signal that we will no longer tolerate the selfish conduct of people who display a disregard for their neighbors. Thank you.

CLOSING ARGUMENT BY MR. SMITH

Members of the jury, we are truly sorry that Peter Christopher injured his leg. However, this is a legal proceeding and your duty is to assess liability based upon the law and not pity. I must admit that keeping a bear as a pet is a bit eccentric. But, do you really believe that Joe would do anything to jeopardize his family's safety? Harry is a tame pet who was kept enclosed in the backyard. The plaintiff got hurt through his own fault.

The plaintiff incited the incident by attacking the sleeping bear with a metal pole. Wouldn't it have been easier if Christopher had telephoned Joe and asked his neighbor to move Harry? The plaintiff has taken great care during the trial to tell you how he was in his own yard when the bear attacked him. How then did Peter end up in Joe's backyard? Did the bear jump the fence, attack the plaintiff and throw the plaintiff into Joe's yard? I suggest that Mr. Christopher, with pole in hand, climbed over the fence to teach Harry a lesson. After all, the bear is shorter than the fence is tall. There is only one logical answer as to how Mr. Christopher ended up in the backyard. He climbed the fence to attack the bear. By engaging in such reckless conduct, the plaintiff assumed the risk of the attack and he alone must take full responsibility for the consequences.

In fact, not only should you find against Mr. Christopher, but you should award Joe money for the injuries sustained by Harry. The animal was asleep minding his own business when he was violently struck with a metal pole. It is about time that we recognize that animals have rights too and a money judgment in favor of Harry will make more people aware of this fact. Thank you.

CHARGE BY THE COURT   *This is the most unusual case I have heard during my tenure as a judge. Issues of credibility have arisen during the trial especially as to how Mr. Christopher ended up in Mr. Roberts' backyard. You are to be guided in deciding whom to believe by your own common sense and life experiences.*

As for the law, one who keeps a non-domesticated animal on his property is liable to another who is injured by that animal. A bear is a non-domesticated animal no matter how cute or playful that animal appears to be, and the owner is liable for any harm inflicted by that creature. On the other hand, one who knows of a danger, but yet still exposes himself to that risk is barred from recovery.

You must decide where Peter Christopher was located when the incident happened. Was he in his own backyard and stuck the pole through the fence, or did he assume the risk of the attack by climbing over the fence into his neighbor's backyard in order to confront the bear? In the latter event, the plaintiff is barred from recovery.

If, and only if, you find in favor of the plaintiff, then you must award a sum of money to fully compensate Mr. Christopher for his injuries and losses. In other words, you must award a sum of money that will return the plaintiff to the condition he was in before the incident occurred. Your award will include compensation for medical expenses, past and future lost wages, and pain and suffering.

The plaintiff has the burden of proving his case by the preponderance of the evidence. This means that for the plaintiff to win, you must place all of the credible evidence on a scale, and the scale must tip no matter how slight, in favor of the plaintiff. If the scales are even or tip in favor of the defendant, then you must find in favor of Mr. Roberts. In addition, it is only after the scales tip in favor of the plaintiff that you can consider the issue of damages.

If you find that Joe Roberts is not responsible for the injuries suffered by Peter Christopher, then you will return with a verdict for the defense. In that event, you may consider an award of damages to Joe Roberts for the injuries to the bear.

Please return to the jury room and decide upon a verdict.

Name   **Please Print Clearly**

1. Who should win the case? Please explain your answer.

_____

_____

_____

_____

_____

_____

_____

_____

_____

_____

_____

_____

_____

_____

_____

_____

_____

_____

_____

_____

_____

2. Were the court's evidentiary rulings correct? Please explain.

_____

_____

_____

_____

_____

_____

_____

_____

_____

_____

3. Was the judge correct in refusing to allow Harry to be brought into court?

_____

_____

_____

_____

_____

_____

_____

_____

_____

_____

SECTION 8.16
REVIEW CASES

1. Miller was found lying face down in the street and bleeding profusely. A police officer asked Miller who shot him, and Miller identified Griffin as his assailant. At the time of trial, the District Attorney calls the police officer to introduce into evidence the statement made by Miller before he died in order to prove that Griffin committed the crime. Is this hearsay statement admissible? **Commonwealth of Pennsylvania v. Aaron Griffin, 453 Pa. Super. 657 (1996).**

2. Mathis was arrested in a stolen van. He testified that while hitchhiking from Georgia to Tennessee to attend a Rod Stewart concert, he was given a ride by an unknown person who fled when the van was stopped by the police. In rebuttal to this testimony, a state witness testified that his firm represented Rod Stewart in obtaining theatrical bookings; he had checked the company's records and they revealed that Rod Stewart was in New Mexico on the day in question. The testimony was objected to as an alleged violation of the best evidence rule. Should this testimony have been excluded on that basis? **Mathis v. The State of Georgia, 228 S.E. 2d 228 (Ga. App. 1976).**

3. During a trial concerning an automobile accident, a witness for the plaintiff was asked to estimate how fast the defendant's car was going before the accident. The defense objected on the basis that the answer would constitute opinion evidence which can only be expressed by an expert witness. Can a witness, who has no specialized technical or scientific knowledge, testify as to the speed of a motor vehicle? **Dugan v. Arthurs, 79 A.2d 626 (Pa. 1911).**

4. Haight was accused of committing burglary by moving electrical equipment from a property. At the time of trial, the prosecution was allowed to introduce into evidence the fact that Haight was unemployed and on welfare at the time of the crime. The Commonwealth argued that this evidence was relevant to show a motive for the burglary, namely a desire for money. Was this line of questioning relevant to establishing a motive for burglary? **Commonwealth of Pennsylvania v. Haight, 31 A.2d 357 (Pa. Super. 1984).**

5. Following the imposition of the sentence on robbery charges, Williams decided to express his dissatisfaction with the court's punishment. He did so by (1) raising his middle finger, and (2) stating: "F - - k you." The judge ordered Williams to return to the court room, at which time the judge found Williams guilty of two counts of contempt and imposed two consecutive sentences of six months for each of the offensive acts. Was it proper to find Williams in contempt of court because he voiced displeasure over the

sentence? Was it proper for the court to find him responsible for two separate acts of contempt over the one incident? **Commonwealth of Pennsylvania v. Walter Williams, 753 A.2d 856 (Pa. Super. 2000).**

SECTION 8.17
INTERNET REFERENCES

For more information on the topics in this Chapter, see the following internet sites:

- **www.findlaw.com/oltopics/29litigation/index.html**
  This site contains government documents, journals, newsletters and articles on litigation.

- **www.law.cornell.edu/rules/fre/overview.html**
  Cornell School of Law provides a listing of the Rules of Evidence for both criminal and civil proceedings in Federal Court.

- **www.pa-bar.org**
  This is the site for the Pennsylvania Bar Association, which includes news and information about litigation in that state.

- **www.abanet.org**
  The American Bar Association sponsors this website that provides answers to frequently asked litigation questions and offers general public resources.

- **www.brobeck.com/docs/deposition.htm**
  General information about depositions and tips on how to handle a deposition can be found at this address.

- **www.law.umich.edu/thayer**
  The University of Michigan Law School maintains this site which is dedicated to evidentiary issues and offers news and articles related to evidence.

- **www.litigationlaw.com**
  Recent news concerning litigation matters may be accessed at this address.

- **www.courttv.com**
  Court Television Network maintains a library of various courtroom materials involving well known cases.

Footnote: 1. Reprinted with permission from **Simplified Rules of Evidence,** by Temple University School of Law and the Law Education and Participation (LEAP) program.

KEY TERMS

Affirmative Defense
Answer
Authenticated
Beyond a Reasonable Doubt
Civil Procedure
Closing Statements
Complaint
Confidential Communication
Contempt of Court
Contingent Fee
Counterclaim
Court Instructions
Cross Examination
Deposition
Direct Examination
Discovery
Dying Declaration
Examination
Execution
Fee Arrangement
Fixed Price
Hearsay
Interrogatory
Irrelevant Evidence
Judgment
Leading Question
Medical Examination

New Matter
Non-Responsive
Objection
Opening Statement
Opinion Testimony
Overruled
Physical Evidence
Pleading
Post-Trial Motions
Preliminary Objections
Preponderance of the Evidence
Production of Documents
Prothonotary
Quantum Meruit
Redirect Examination
Relevant Evidence
Request for Admission
Retainer
Rules of Evidence
Service of Process
Sheriff's Sale
Submission to a Medical
Subpoena
Sustained
Trial
Verdict

CHAPTER 9

ALTERNATIVE DISPUTE RESOLUTION

By: Kathleen Daerr-Bannon, Esq.

SECTION 9.1
AN OVERVIEW

"Make the Forum Fit the Fuss"
(Source unknown)

ADR is described by its advocates as "appropriate dispute resolution." Its proper name, however, is **alternative dispute resolution** and it provides the parties with a substitute forum to resolves disputes. This is true even though some of the procedures, such as arbitration and mediation, are really modifications of the litigation process. Activities such as avoidance of a problem, physical confrontation, or walking away from a dispute could be considered alternative ways of resolving conflicts, but they are not part of ADR. This chapter will provide a brief explanation of the more commonly recognized ADR processes. Because the underlying philosophy of ADR is to make the *"forum fit the fuss,"* this alternative to court imposed litigation is a fluid system that adapts to the changing needs and interests of the parties.

Generally speaking, the voluntary nature of ADR is a key element in defining the concept. The parties to a dispute must agree to remove the matter from court in order to submit it to ADR. In certain areas, such as employment and consumer disputes, a party may not realize that the pre-printed forms require the dispute to be submitted to an alternative forum. For instance, when downloading a computer program, a user is required to go through a series of screens before completing the installation process. One of those screens may contain a requirement to submit any dispute concerning the software to binding arbitration. The customer is not able to finish the installation process unless he or she clicks the "I agree" button.

ADR and the litigation process are not always mutually exclusive. ADR does not eliminate lawsuits but offers additional options. There will always be disputes for which litigation is necessary. With the increasing use of ADR, however, the filing of a lawsuit may be seen as the last resort rather than the first. ADR can be used to bring about the resolution of a dispute in its entirety, to narrow the issues, or simply to facilitate procedures leading to ultimate litigation. ADR may involve all or only some of the parties or it may lead to a resolution in which only a dollar figure needs to be established for the dispute. This alternative forum has gained popularity as is evidenced by its accepted use in disputes ranging from complex construction or commercial disputes to community or peer mediation involving everyday disagreements between students or neighbors.

Conceptually, ADR may be classified into three groups: facilitative, evaluative, and adjudicatory. For example, **mediation** is often facilitative but it also can provide an early evaluation by a third party who makes non-binding recommendations. Facilitative and evaluative processes are different but both are non-binding. On the other hand, binding **arbitration** is adjudicative or similar to a judge's decision. The various processes may also overlap or contain elements of one or more of these classifications. For instance, the parties may submit a dispute to mediation. If a voluntary resolution is not achieved, the case will ultimately have to proceed to arbitration, litigation, or some other form of adjudication.

It is useful for people considering alternative dispute resolution to understand what is desired from the process. Have communications between the parties ceased so intervention by a third party is needed to achieve settlement? Will the case never resolve unless a third party renders a binding decision? The specific procedure that fits the needs of the parties must be carefully selected and understood.

SECTION 9.2
ADR AND LITIGATION

Litigation is the traditional method for resolving disputes and an accepted fact of life in America. In order to better understand alternative dispute resolution, however, one must compare ADR to the more established litigation process.

Litigation is the initiation of a civil action or lawsuit in a public forum, a state or federal court. With few exceptions, all parties have the right to demand a jury trial with remedies ranging from money damages to an injunction. The participants have little input in the scheduling of the trial which is usually dictated by court rules or a judge. Additionally, the selection of the judge is taken out of the hands of the litigants. By comparison, ADR allows the parties to establish their own time frame for moving forward and the contestants can choose the arbitrator to preside over the dispute.

Understanding ADR also requires one to know the difference between **adjudicative and non-adjudicative proceedings**. Like a jury or bench trial, arbitration results in the imposition of a binding resolution determined by someone other than the parties. This is what is meant by an adjudicative process: the solution to the dispute is imposed by a third party. **Mediation,** which is generally not binding upon the parties, is non-adjudicative. An impartial third party acts as a facilitator to bring about the resolution of a dispute. Clients and their counsel need to be clear about the nature and consequences of the process being utilized and, if the forum is adjudicative, to be specific regarding the scope of an appeal.

Negotiation is an informal and voluntary procedure in which the parties or their representatives try to work out a resolution of their differences without the help of a neutral third party or judge. Any issue can be negotiated if the parties are willing to participate in a fruitful manner. When engaging in negotiations, a party must be flexible and realize that he or she cannot force the other side to settle on a specific set of terms or even mandate that a party settle on any terms. Once an agreement is reached, however, it may be enforced in court like any other contract. Negotiations between an attorney and an insurance adjuster over a personal injury claim is an example.

There are several precepts for which a person should be aware. While a party engaged in negotiations is under no legal duty to provide information to an opponent; evidence of fraud, deception, or the making of a misleading statement is improper. In this regard, consider the following case dealing with a change in the law.

DOROTHEA DERCOLI V. PA. NATIONAL MUTUAL INSURANCE COMPANY
554 A. 2D 906 (PA. 1989)

Dercoli appeals from an order dismissing her lawsuit against Pennsylvania National Mutual Insurance Company (Penn National) and Grange Mutual Casualty Company (Grange) for breach of fair dealing and good faith. In her appeal, Dercoli frames two issues: (1) whether our decision in **Hack v. Hack** abolishing the defense of inter-spousal immunity is to be given retroactive application; and (2) whether the duty of fair dealing and good faith requires an automobile insurer to properly advise its insured of the entitlement to present a claim where the insurer advises its insured that legal representation is unnecessary, and induces the insured to rely upon the insurer to pay appropriate benefits.

On July 21, 1980, Mrs. Dercoli was riding in an automobile operated by her husband, Mr. Dercoli, when he fell asleep. The automobile crossed the center line of the highway and crashed into the rear wheels of an on-coming tractor-trailer. Mr. Dercoli was killed instantly. Mrs. Dercoli was severely injured. At the time of the accident, Mr. Dercoli was insured under two automobile insurance policies. One of the policies was with Penn National and the other was with Grange. In the claim process that followed, Mrs. Dercoli relied upon the advice of the insurance company's agents to receive the benefits due her under the applicable policies.

On July 14, 1981, approximately one year after the accident and while Mrs. Dercoli was relying upon the carriers' agents for advice, this Court abolished inter-spousal immunity as a bar to an action for personal injuries caused by the negligence of the injured victim's spouse. The plaintiff did not learn of the removal of this bar to suit until sometime after March of 1985. In January, 1986, Mrs. Dercoli filed a complaint against the carriers averring, a breach of the defendants' duty of fair dealing and good faith. Mrs. Dercoli avers that upon the advice and assurances of the carriers' agents, she was induced to refrain from hiring an attorney to represent her in her dealings with the defendants. She alleges that she placed her entire trust and confidence in the carriers' agents and relied upon their advice as to the extent of the benefits available to her under the applicable insurance policies.

In spite of the fact that the plaintiff was assured by the carriers' agents that they would see that the plaintiff received all benefits to which she was entitled, the carriers' agents failed to advise her of her right to seek liability damages because of the waiver of spousal immunity. On the one hand, these agents were aware of Mrs. Dercoli's injuries and of her reliance on them for advice and guidance in her claim. On the other hand, they knew that if they would ad-vise her of the **Hack** decision, and of her right to proceed against her husband's estate for damages, such proceedings would substantially increase the financial exposure of the insurers.

We have long recognized that the utmost fair dealing should characterize the transactions between an insurance company and the insured. The duty of an insurance company to deal with the insured fairly and in good faith includes the duty of full and complete disclosure as to all of the benefits provided by the applicable policy along with all requirements for making a claim. Consistent with the obligation of fair dealing and good faith, the carriers had a duty to inform the plaintiff of her right to damages against her husband's estate which ultimately would be payable under the liability provisions of the policies that insured the decedent. The carriers' failure to so inform the plaintiff was a breach of the duty of fair dealing. Assuring the plaintiff at the outset that she need not hire an attorney and that she would receive all that she was entitled to receive, and then failing to inform her of her apparent right to damages following the **Hack** decision is hardly dealing with the plaintiff fairly and in good faith.

Order of Superior Court is reversed and case remanded to the trial court for proceedings consistent with this opinion.

It is usually easier to obtain cooperation between parties when there have been prior dealings which build trust and confidence. Thus, parties with ongoing business relationships may find it more feasible to mediate or resolve a dispute instead of litigating a problem. Similarly, when parties negotiate all the details of the mediation or the shape of the table as it is called, they start to build a momentum toward cooperation leading to settlement.

What happens when the parties have no such relationship and do not trust one another? The problem that arises is illustrated by the classic prisoner's dilemma shown in the following problem.

SECTION 9.4
KATHY ROBERTS'
CRIMINAL CHARGES

PROBLEM NINE—A

PARK, BROWN & SMITH, P.C.
ATTORNEYS AT LAW
MEMORANDUM

To: All Law Clerks

FROM: Peter Smith, Esquire

RE: Kathy Roberts and Her Negotiated Guilty Plea

Kathy Roberts has requested our assistance regarding criminal charges that have been filed against her and a possible negotiated guilty plea. Please determine the best outcome for her based upon the following scenarios.

As you may remember, Kathy and her next-door neighbor, Peter Christopher, have disliked each other since Kathy purchased Christopher's car and was able to disaffirm the contract after she destroyed the vehicle.

Through a strange twist of circumstances, they have both been arrested for burglarizing a neighbor's house. Don't even ask. It is too bizarre of a story to explain for purposes of this project. Suffice it to say, neither neighbor trusts the other and the following represents their mutual dilemma.

The prosecution wants one of the suspects to confess to the burglary to ensure the conviction of both. If only one party confesses to the crime, that person will be treated leniently by the government, while the other defendant will be more severely punished. If both confess to the crime, they will each receive relatively short prison terms. If neither confesses, a more substantial prison term will be sought for both suspects.

This problem is represented by the following diagram:

If Kathy

	Does Not Confess	Does Confess
And Peter Does Not Confess	Each of them gets 5 years* in jail if convicted	Peter receives 10 years in prison if convicted and Kathy gets 6 months
And Peter Does Confess	Peter gets 6 months and Kathy gets 10 years in jail if convicted	Each of them gets 2 years** in jail

*   Cooperative Solution—Best overall for both

** Minimax Solution—Solution that offers *each* greatest promise of success in view of opponent's alternative capabilities.

Since we don't know what Peter Christopher will do, what should we recommend to Kathy, as her counsel, as the best course of action?

**ANSWER SHEET
PROBLEM NINE—A**

Name **Please Print Clearly**

1. Please provide your recommendations on what Kathy should do concerning her negotiated plea and explain your answer.

_____

_____

_____

_____

_____

_____

_____

_____

_____

_____

_____

_____

_____

_____

_____

_____

_____

_____

_____

_____

_____

_____

SECTION 9.5
MEDIATION

In **mediation**, a neutral third person is selected by the parties to assist in a voluntary effort to reach settlement of some or all of the disputed issues. Mediation is informal but more structured than unassisted negotiations where the parties discuss the dilemma between themselves in an effort to resolve the dispute. The mediator does not take sides but attempts to bring the parties together by forging a solution. In mediation, an "interest analysis" approach may be taken rather than strictly relying on what is legally correct. In this fashion, the parties can determine if a resolution of the dispute is in everyone's best interest instead of rigidly applying the law to determine the outcome. A good example of this concept is the mediation problem involving the "ugly orange."

Two people claim that they had contracted for the same order of oranges, which was the last box of fruit available from the shipper. How can they ever resolve their dispute? By focusing on the underlying interests of the parties, however, a mediator soon determines that one is a purveyor of orange juice and needs the juice; the other is a baker who requires the rinds for muffins. Obviously, the non-legal solution of cooperation involves giving the juice to one and the rinds to the other. This outcome successfully solves the dilemma. This is the type of "win-win" situation that mediation is seeking to achieve through an interest analysis approach.

The mediation process begins with the parties working out certain important details of the proceeding. How will the mediator be selected? When and where will the mediation take place? How will the parties apportion the mediator's fees?

Following a discussion of these preliminary matters, mediation usually follows a basic structure. The parties talk with the mediator to establish the boundaries of the mediation, and decide whether to file briefs explaining their positions. The parties then draft a written agreement setting forth, at a minimum, the confidentiality of the process, the identities of the participants, the name of mediator, and how the fees of the third party will be paid.

Once a meeting with the mediator is arranged, the attorneys prepare their clients and bring them to the proceeding. The process begins by the mediator offering an explanation of what is to happen and then each side orally discusses the issues in an uninterrupted fashion. The mediation may center on the underlying interests of the parties or it may focus on their respective legal positions. In all cases, however, it is useful for parties to bargain in their best interests without being legalistic or confrontational. Good practice suggests that the parties approach the process in a low-key, problem-solving mode.

Following a group session, the mediator may meet privately with each side. On occasion, the mediator may even meet with counsel alone or request permission to consult with the parties to the dispute without counsel being present. These meetings are called **caucuses,** and they are even more confidential than the joint session with the parties because the mediator is not permitted to reveal confidences to the other side without permission from the party revealing the information. A caucus, however, helps the mediator flush out the parties' positions by asking tough questions, and affords the individuals with a safe and confidential place to talk about the strengths and weaknesses of the dispute. The mediator can also help the parties move towards a settlement by suggesting alternative proposals although a settlement cannot be guaranteed. This dialogue with the mediator may continue as long as it is productive.

When the process concludes, the mediator will bring everyone back together in a closing session. Sometimes the parties are able to resolve key issues which simplify and expedite the litigation process or they may reach a global settlement. In the later event, counsel will often draft a Release or Settlement Agreement which constitutes an enforceable contract.

Many states have enacted mediation privilege or immunity statutes. For instance, Pennsylvania provides that statements or writings made for purpose of the mediation are inadmissible in a court proceeding. In federal court, mediation statements are considered compromise settlement negotiations which may not be disclosed.

Some states, such as Florida and California, provide for credentialing of mediators, and about half of the states have a mediation office or center sponsored by the government.

SECTION 9.6
ARBITRATION

A few years ago, the Supreme Court noted in **Circuit City v. Adams,** 532 U.S. 105 (2001), that the freedom of the parties to contract for arbitration is very broad. Given this stamp of approval, there is an ever-increasing use of **arbitration** clauses in employment, insurance, credit card and other business contracts. What protections does a party have, however, when he or she does sign a contract containing an arbitration clause that *privatizes public justice* by requiring the use of a resolution system outside of the court?

Generally, the courts frown upon arbitration clauses that limit remedies and damages and forbid assessment of unreasonable arbitration fees since courts are accessible without charge. The following case focuses on several of the one-sided arbitration provisions that the court will scrutinize very closely.

ANNETTE PHILLIPS V. HOOTERS OF MYRTLE BEACH, INC.
173 F. 3D 933 (4TH CIR. 1999)

Annette Phillips alleges that she was sexually harassed while working at a Hooters restaurant. After quitting her job, Phillips threatened to sue Hooters. Alleging that Phillips agreed to arbitrate employment-related disputes, Hooters preemptively filed suit to compel arbitration under the Federal Arbitration Act. Because Hooters set up a dispute resolution process utterly lacking in the rudiments of evenhandedness, we hold that Hooters breached its agreement to arbitrate. Thus, we affirm the lower court's refusal to compel arbitration.

Phillips worked as a bartender at a Hooters in Myrtle Beach, South Carolina. She was employed since 1989 by Hooters of Myrtle Beach (HOMB), a franchisee of Hooters of America (collectively "Hooters").

Phillips alleges that in June 1996, a Hooters official sexually harassed her by grabbing and slapping her buttocks. After appealing to her manager for help and being told to "let it go," she quit her job. Phillips then contacted Hooters claiming that the attack and the restaurant's failure to address it violated her Title VII rights. Hooters responded that she was required to submit her claim to arbitration according to a binding agreement to arbitrate between the parties. This agreement arose in 1994 during the implementation of Hooters' alternative dispute resolution program. As part of that program, the company conditioned eligibility for raises, transfers, and promotions upon an employee signing an "Agreement to Arbitrate Employment-Related Disputes."

The benefits of arbitration are widely recognized. Parties agree to arbitrate to secure streamlined proceedings and expeditious results that will best serve their needs. In support of arbitration, Congress passed the Federal Arbitration Act. Its purpose was to place arbitration agreements upon the same footing as other contracts.

The question remains whether a binding arbitration agreement between Phillips and Hooters exists and compels Phillips to submit her Title VII claims to arbitration.

Courts can investigate the existence of such grounds as exist at law or in equity for the revocation of a contract. In this case, the challenge goes to the validity of the arbitration agreement itself. Hooters materially breached the arbitration agreement by promulgating rules so egregiously unfair as to constitute a complete default of its contractual obligation to draft arbitration rules and to do so in good faith.

The Hooters rules are so one-sided that their only possible purpose is to undermine the neutrality of the proceeding. The rules require the employee to provide the company notice of her claim at the outset, including the nature of the claim and the specific actor omissions which are the basis of the claim. Hooters, on the other hand, is not required to file any responsive pleadings or to notice its defenses. Additionally, at the time of filing this notice, the employee must provide the company with a list of all fact witnesses, along with a brief summary of the facts known to each. The company, however, is not required to reciprocate.

Hooters is free to devise lists of partial arbitrators who have existing relationships, financial or familial, with Hooters and its management. In fact, the rules do not even prohibit Hooters from placing its managers themselves on the list.

George Friedman, of the American Arbitration Association (AAA), testified that the system established by the Hooters rules so deviated from minimum due process standards that the Association would refuse to arbitrate under those rules.

We hold that the promulgation of so many biased rules – especially the scheme whereby one party to the proceeding so controls the arbitral panel — breaches the contract entered into by the parties. By creating a sham system unworthy even of the name of arbitration, Hooters completely failed in performing its contractual duty. To uphold the promulgation of this aberrational scheme under the heading of arbitration would undermine, not advance, the federal policy favoring alternative dispute resolution. This we refuse to do.

We therefore permit Phillips to cancel the agreement and thus Hooters' suit to compel arbitration must fail.

SECTION 9.7
ARBITRATION –
SCOPE OF REVIEW

Because of the binding nature of arbitration, courts will rarely overturn an arbitrator's decision unless there is clear evidence of fraud or gross misconduct. This point is demonstrated in the court's review of an arbitrator's decision in a dispute between talk show host Kelly Ripa and a talent management agency.

KELLY RIPA v. CATHY PARKER MANAGEMENT, INC.
1998 W.L. 241621 (S.D. N.Y. 1998)

Kelly Ripa, an aspiring actress, and CPM, a talent management agency for entertainers, entered into a personal management contract whereby CPM agreed to advise Ripa on how to become a professional actress. Pursuant to this agreement, CPM allegedly arranged for Ripa to attend an audition for the soap opera "All My Children." Ripa subsequently obtained a role on the soap opera and signed with a talent agent.

On July 1, 1992, Ripa signed a one-page agreement to pay CPM 15 percent of her gross earnings from "All My Children" for a four-year period.

On July 12, 1992, Ripa and CPM signed a second contract whereby CPM agreed to serve as Ripa's Personal Manager for three years in exchange for 15 percent of her gross earnings in the entertainment industry over that period. The July 12 Agreement—unlike the July 1 Agreement—contained an arbitration clause which provided that any dispute concerning the terms of the agreement would be submitted to the American Arbitration Association.

On the last page of the July 12 Agreement was a rider providing that CPM could extend the agreement for an additional three years if CPM helped Ripa "book a commercial or opportunities to audition for commercials, pilot series and films." Thus, under the terms of the July 12 Agreement, Ripa was to pay a 15 percent commission from July 12, 1992 through July 11, 1995, and, if certain conditions were satisfied, the agreement could be extended until July 11, 1998.

Between July 12, 1992 and October 28, 1996, Ripa paid commissions to CPM totaling $161,000. This amount represented fifteen percent of Ripa's income from "All My Children." However, after October 28, 1996, Ripa made no further payments to CPM.

In December 1996, CPM served an arbitration demand on Ripa, alleging that she had breached the terms of the July 12 Agreement. Specifically, CPM contended that pursuant to the Option Rider, Ripa was obligated to pay a 15 percent commission on all her earnings from July 11, 1995 until July 11, 1998. Ripa argued that she had been fraudulently induced to sign the July 12 Agreement.

The dispute between CPM and Ripa was arbitrated and on January 21, 1998, the AAA issued an award which denied CPM's claims and awarded Ripa $96,500.86. The parties agree that this $53,528.31 damage award is equal to the total commissions that Ripa had paid to CPM after July 11, 1995 (the date on which the initial term of the July 12 Agreement expired).

Judicial review of arbitration awards is narrowly limited, for undue judicial intervention would inevitably judicialize the arbitration process, thus defeating the objective of providing an alternative to judicial dispute resolution.

A court may vacate an award if the arbitrators were guilty of misconduct in refusing to hear evidence pertinent and material to the controversy, or of any other misbehavior by which the rights of any party have been prejudiced. A court's review of arbitration procedures is limited to determining whether the procedure followed was "fundamentally unfair."

In addition, an award will be vacated if it is in "manifest disregard of the law." This standard requires more than error or misunderstanding with respect to the law. The error must have been obvious and capable of being readily and instantly perceived by the average person qualified to serve as an arbitrator.

CPM's argument for vacating the arbitration award is that the arbitrator exceeded her authority by awarding Ripa damages in the amount that she paid to CPM between July 12, 1995 (the date that the Option Rider purportedly became effective) and October 28, 1996. CPM contends that Ripa was obligated to pay commissions under the July 1 Agreement, despite having signed the July 12 Agreement, and that the arbitrator erred in relieving her of this obligation.

This argument overlooks the plain language of the July 12 Agreement, which provides that "[t]his agreement is the only agreement of the parties and there is no other or collateral agreement (oral or written) between the parties in any manner relating to the subject matter hereof." The arbitrator could reasonably have interpreted this provision as rescinding all prior commission agreements between the parties. Under this interpretation, the July 12 Agreement would have relieved Ripa of any obligation to make commission payments pursuant to the July 1 Agreement. Accordingly, the arbitrator's decision to "refund" the commissions paid by Ripa does not qualify as an error that was so clear and obvious that an average person qualified to serve as an arbitrator should have instantaneously perceived and corrected.

Consistent with the arbitration award, judgment is hereby entered against CPM.

The rights of consumers and employees who enjoy little bargaining power where arbitration clauses are unilaterally inserted in contracts for employment, mortgages, credit card loans and other everyday transactions, raise significant legal issues. These agreements are usually classified as contracts of adhesion. These types of contracts will not automatically be ruled invalid by the court unless there is a finding that the contract, as drafted, is unconscionable or violates public policy.

GREEN TREE FINANCIAL CORP. v. LARKETTA RANDOLPH
531 U. S. 79 (2000)

We turn to the question whether Randolph's agreement to arbitrate is unenforceable because it says nothing about the costs of arbitration, and thus fails to provide protection from potentially substantial costs of pursuing her claims in the arbitral forum. The Federal Arbitration Act provides that a written provision in a contract to settle by arbitration a controversy arising out of such contract shall be valid save upon such grounds as exist for the revocation of any contract.

In this case, it is undisputed that the parties agreed to arbitrate all claims relating to their contract. Randolph contends that the arbitration agreement's silence with respect to costs and fees creates a "risk" that she will be required to bear prohibitive arbitration costs if she pursues her claims in an arbitral forum. Therefore, she argues, she is unable to vindicate her statutory rights in arbitration. It may well be that the existence of large arbitration costs could preclude a litigant such as Randolph from effectively vindicating her rights in the arbitral forum. But the record does not show that Randolph will bear such costs if she goes to arbitration. Indeed, it contains hardly any information on the matter. The record reveals only the arbitration agreement's silence on the subject, and that fact alone is plainly insufficient to render it unenforceable. The "risk" that Randolph will be saddled with prohibitive costs is too speculative to justify the invalidation of an arbitration agreement.

We have held that the party seeking to avoid arbitration bears the burden of establishing that Congress intended to preclude arbitration of the statutory claims at issue. Similarly, we believe that where a party seeks to invalidate an arbitration agreement on the ground that arbitration would be prohibitively expensive, that party bears the burden of showing the likelihood of incurring such costs. Randolph did not meet that burden. The Court of Appeals therefore erred in deciding that the arbitration agreement's silence with respect to costs and fees rendered it unenforceable.

Judgment vacated and remanded.

SECTION 9.8
SETTLEMENT
CONFERENCES

Judicially sponsored **settlement conferences** are an increasingly mandated process by which a judge, magistrate, or other judicially appointed individual explores settlement possibilities in an effort to eliminate pending litigation. Because these conferences are sponsored by the court, the proceeding is viewed as persuasive and important. The conference will usually take place in the judge's chambers but it may be conducted in court or in a special room. The meeting is not open to the public and there is no cost imposed by the court for the proceeding.

The process is also one in which much may ride on its outcome so the attorneys must be prepared to respond to the judge concerning any issue in the case. There are no uniform rules on the conduct of these conferences and the process varies by judge. Nevertheless, settlement conferences allow the litigants to present their case to a court official who will place a value on the dispute and provide informal rulings on the admissibility of evidence and theories of liability. If there is no resolution of the dispute, the court has the power to impose sanctions against the losing party after trial if the judge believes that one of the sides did not make a good faith effort to settle the dispute.

SECTION 9.9
MASTERS

Masters are individuals appointed by the court to decide specific issues such as the supervision of discovery in a complicated litigation matter. These masters provide rulings and submit their findings to the appointing judge thereby freeing up the court's time to devote to the actual litigation. Masters have assisted the court in such matters as civil lawsuits for money damages, criminal cases, divorce, childcare, custody, and mental health issues.

SECTION 9.10
MINI-TRIAL

A **mini-trial** is not a trial at all, but derives its name from reliance on court-like procedures. It is a voluntary process used in complex or technical matters in which the attorneys present an abbreviated version of their case to a panel of decision makers such as a mock jury panel of people selected from the community. The summaries of the attorneys are based upon the facts and existing law. The rules of evidence are usually relaxed and the parties agree upon time limitations for their presentation. Most of the time, the mini-trial is run by a neutral third party. The agreement to submit the dispute to this type of proceeding usually is entered into after the controversy has arisen. At the conclusion of the case, the decision-makers share their view of the litigation with counsel. The process is confidential and no records are kept of the proceeding. The advantage of the mini-trial is that it can forge a settlement by providing the litigants with a realistic prediction of what may happen at trial.

SECTION 9.11
OMBUDSMAN

The **ombudsman** is a facilitator available to assist the public, employees or those served by an institution with problems, or complaints. Although hired by the organization in question, the ombudsman is considered independent and not subject to the control of the organization. For instance, many Universities retain an ombudsman to advise students of their rights and to help solve problems involving faculty or the University. Car manufacturers also employ facilitators to assist consumers with car complaints. The individuals who fulfill this role must be easily accessible to those seeking assistance and must have access to all parts of the organization in an attempt to help bring closure to the dispute. For example, the Federal Student Aid Ombudsman is part of the Department of Education and helps resolve disputes involving federal student loans. This individual conducts informal fact-finding about a complaint and will recommend solutions. The service is free and the ombudsman will contact the U.S. Department of Education, the private lender, or collection agency in an attempt to have everyone treated fairly. This officer, however, is not an advocate and will examine the problem in an impartial and objective manner.

SECTION 9.12
PRIVATE JUDGES

Often called "rent-a-judge," this process permits a retired judge or experienced attorney to hear the dispute as a temporary judge. Their decisions are not generally subject to appellate review and all parties must consent to its use. The parties to the dispute must pay for the judge's services but it does provide an alternative way of resolving a dispute in an expeditious fashion.

SECTION 9.13
SUMMARY JURY TRIAL

Summary Jury Trial is a court-sponsored settlement process in which a jury renders an advisory verdict after an abbreviated trial with all its formalities. After voir dire and jury selection, the judge presides over presentations by both sides that include arguments and a shortened version of the evidence by use of summaries and exhibits. The court gives formal instructions to the jury who then deliberates and renders a verdict. According to Judge Sharon Townsend, Texas, Florida, and Virginia have incorporated the summary judge trial into their civil practice acts and federal courts make use of this time and money saving tool. In a pilot program in New York, the system produced a 100% disposition rate without a traditional trial.

The process may satisfy the litigants' need for a trial without all of the time and expenses. The Court may recommend the process when negotiations have stalled and this modified trial has proven successful in accomplishing settlement.

SECTION 9.14
THE FUTURE OF ADR

The rapidly growing use of ADR makes it appropriate to conclude this chapter with a view towards the future. The *Alternative Paths to Justice Task Force of the Pennsylvania Futures Commission on Justice in the Twenty-First Century* provides a glimpse into the future of the courts and ADR. As is stated in its Executive Summary:

By the year 2020, the right to a trial will be preserved as essential to the very fabric of American society. At the same time, the courts will not be overburdened with disputes that are better solved with methodologies other than the traditional trial. This goal will be achieved by the creation of a multi-door justice system where the mechanism to solve a dispute is appropriate to that controversy. To do this, in the year 2020:

1. The legal system will preserve traditional trials and appellate processes, including jury trials, while providing a variety of dispute resolution processes.

2. People will take responsibility for resolving disputes themselves amicably outside of the adversarial process.

3. Disputes will be resolved quickly. Dispute resolution will be accessible and affordable to all, and will treat all fairly, regardless of culture, age, or economic status.

4. There will be coordination and mutual support between the public and private dispute resolution organizations.

5. Dispute resolution will be an integral part of the educational system with the support of families and the media.

6. There will be an adequate body of qualified and trained facilitators, in all key places in government who will have sufficient knowledge to advise citizens on appropriate dispute resolutions.

7. Technology will be used to facilitate access and provide recommendations based on precedent, but will not control the dispute resolution process.

8. The justice system will have a mechanism to anticipate new types of disputes and to provide suitable means to resolve them.

Clearly, the individual who is equipped for the use of ADR today will be ready to competently resolve legal and other disputes in the future.

SECTION 9.15
INTERPRETATION
OF AN NFL
PLAYER'S CONTRACT

PROBLEM NINE—B

PARK, BROWN & SMITH, P.C.
ATTORNEYS AT LAW
M E M O R A N D U M

To: All Law Clerks

FROM: Peter Smith, Esquire

RE: Roberts v. The Stallions

Tony Roberts is the place kicker for the Stallions football team. Tony has several problems involving the interpretation of his football contract and a serious dispute has arisen between the football player and his team.

The Stallions allege three violations of the contract. The first one relates to paragraph three of the contract. The team learned that Tony spends a considerable amount of time racing cars at various speedways around the United States. The club requested that Tony voluntarily stop his racing activities, but he refused. He asserts: "They pay me to play the game. They don't have the right to run my life off the field." The Stallions have threatened to enjoin this activity if Roberts refuses to voluntarily stop drag-racing because of safety concerns.

The other two disputes relate directly to a shooting incident involving Christopher and Tony. Because Tony is a professional athlete, the shooting generated considerable publicity for which the club is less than pleased. The Stallions claim his conduct was not in keeping with the good character and image required of professional football players. The team wants to suspend Tony without pay for one month. They maintain that the contract allows for this penalty. Tony feels this charge is ridiculous and cannot understand why he was even arrested.

Unfortunately, there is more to Tony's problem. The story doesn't stop with the young Roberts arrest for shooting Christopher who was stealing his car. Upon the football player's arrival at the police station following the incident, he submitted to a urinalysis, which test revealed traces of marijuana. According to Roberts the results reflect his exposure to his sister and her "druggie" friends. The night before his arrest, Tony had been in his basement watching a video when her group invaded the house. Normally, he went to his room when his sister's friends were around. Tony hated the drug scene, and was even more bothered by smoke-filled rooms. This night, however, he was too engrossed in his film to leave. Somehow the Commissioner learned of the drug test that was positive for marijuana. The League, however, is not interested in Tony's explanation of events. As far as they are concerned, drug use is cause for immediate suspension and possible termination of the contract.

At this point in time, neither the Stallions nor the League have taken any affirmative action. Attached is a copy of Tony's player contract. Please read the contract and provide a memorandum analyzing the following questions. According to the terms of the contract:

1. Does the Club or League have the authority to stop Tony from racing? What language in the document would support an injunction? Why would the Club or League be able to regulate Tony's conduct when he's not playing football?

2. May the NFL suspend Tony and can the league terminate his contract? May the Club sanction or punish Tony for his actions and what recourse is available to the football player to dispute any sanctions imposed by the Club? In other words, where should Tony go to challenge the Club's assertions of his wrongdoing under the contract?

3. May the Club terminate Tony Roberts' contract if he lies to the team's physician about a physical ailment? Can the Club terminate the contract if Tony believes he is in excellent physical condition but the Club thinks he is too out of shape to play football? Quote the relevant language in the contract that supports your answer.

NFL Player Contract

THIS CONTRACT is between **Anthony Roberts**, hereinafter "Player," and the **Playwell Football Association**, a Maryland corporation, hereinafter "Club," operating under the name of the "Stallions" as a member of the National Football League, hereinafter, "League."

In consideration of the promises made by each to the other, Player and Club agree as follows:

1. **TERM.** This contract covers three football seasons and will begin on the date of execution or August 1, whichever is later, and end on July 31, unless extended, terminated, or renewed as specified elsewhere in this contract.

2. **EMPLOYMENT AND SERVICES.** Club employs Player as a skilled football player. Player accepts such employment. He agrees to give his best efforts and loyalty to the Club, and to conduct himself on and off the field with appropriate recognition of the fact that the success of professional football depends largely on public respect for and approval of those associated with the game. Player will report promptly for and participate fully in Club's official pre-season training camp, all Club meetings and practice sessions, and all pre-season, regular season, and post-season football games scheduled for or by club. If invited, Player will practice for and play in any all-star football game sponsored by the League. Player

will not participate in any football game not sponsored by the League unless the game is first approved by the League.

3. **OTHER ACTIVITIES.** Without prior written consent of the Club, Player will not play football or engage in activities related to football otherwise than for Club or engage in any activity other than football which may involve a significant risk or personal injury. Player represents that he has special, exceptional and unique knowledge, skill, ability, and experience as a football player, the loss of which cannot be estimated with any certainty and cannot be fairly or adequately compensated by damages. Player therefore agrees that Club will have the right, in addition to any other right which Club may possess, to enjoin Player by appropriate proceedings from playing football or engaging in football-related activities other than for Club, or from engaging in any activity other than football which may involve a significant risk of personal injury.

4. **PUBLICITY.** Player grants to Club and League, separately and together, the authority to use his name and picture for publicity and promotional purposes in newspapers, magazines, motion pictures, game programs and roster manuals, broadcasts and telecasts, and all other publicity and advertising media, provided such publicity and promotion does not in itself constitute an endorsement by Player of a commercial product. Player will cooperate with the news media, and will participate upon request in reasonable promotional activities of Club and the League.

5. **COMPENSATION.** For performance of Player's services and all other promises of Player, Club will pay Player a yearly salary of $450,000 payable as provided in Paragraph 6; such earned performance bonuses as may be called for in Paragraph 24 of or any attachment to this contract; Player's necessary traveling expenses from his residence to training camp; Player's reasonable board and lodging expenses during pre-season training and in connection with playing pre-season, regular-season, and post-season football games outside Club's home city; Player's necessary traveling expenses to and from pre-season, regular season, and post-season football games outside Club's home city; Player's necessary traveling expenses to his residence if this contract is terminated by Club; and such additional compensation, benefits, and reimbursement of expenses as may be called for in any collective bargaining agreement in existence during the term of this contract. (For purposes of this contract, a collective bargaining agreement will be deemed to be "in existence" during its stated term or during any period for which the parties to that agreement agree to extend it.)

6. **PAYMENT.** Unless this contract or any collective bargaining agreement in existence during the term of this contract specifically provides otherwise, Player will be paid as follows: If Player has not previously reported to any NFL club's official pre-season training camp in any year, he will be paid 100% of his yearly salary under this contract in equal weekly or bi-weekly installments over the course of the regular season period, commencing with the first regular season game played by club. If Player has previously reported to any NFL club's official pre-season training camp in any year, he will be paid 10% of his yearly salary under this contract in equal weekly installments over the course of the pre-season period, commencing with the end of the first week of Club's official pre-season training camp as designated for Player and ending one week prior to the first regular season game played by Club, and 90% of his yearly salary in equal weekly or bi-weekly installments over the course of the regular season period, commencing with the first regular season gamed played by Club. If this contract is executed or Player is activated after the start of Club's official pre-season training camp, the yearly salary payable to Player will be reduced proportionately and Player will be paid the weekly or bi-weekly portions of his yearly salary becoming due and payable after he his activated. If this contract is terminated after the start of Club's official pre-season training camp, the yearly salary payable to Player will be reduced proportionately, and Player will be paid the weekly or bi-weekly portions of his yearly salary having become due and payable up to the time of termination (prorated daily if termination occurs before one week prior to the first regular season game played by Club).

   a. Club agrees to give Player a signing bonus of $50,000 at the time of the execution of this contract.

   b. Player shall receive an additional bonus of $50,000 each time Player is selected to play in an All-Star football game.

   c. Player shall receive an additional compensation of $100 for each point he scores during a regular season and playoff game.

7. **DEDUCTIONS.** Any advance made to Player will be repaid to Club, and any properly levied Club fine or Commissioner fine against Player will be paid, in cash on demand or by means of deductions from payments coming due to the Player under this contract, the amount of such deductions to be determined by Club unless this contract specially provides otherwise.

8. **PHYSICAL CONDITION.** Player represents to Club that he is and will maintain himself in excellent physical condition. Player will undergo a complete physical examination by the Club physician upon Club request, during which physical examination Player agrees to make full and complete disclosure of any physical or mental condition known to him which might impair his performance under this contract, and to respond fully and in good faith when questioned by the Club physician about such condition. If Player fails to establish or maintain his excellent physical condition to the satisfaction of the Club physician, or make the required full and complete disclosure and good faith responses to the Club physician, then Club may terminate this contract.

9. **INJURY.** If Player is injured in the performance of his services under this contract and promptly reports such injury to the Club physician or trainer, then Player will receive such medical and hospital care during the term of this contract as the Club physician may deem necessary, and, in accordance with Club's practice, will continue to receive his yearly salary for so long, during the season of injury only and for no subsequent period, as Player is physically unable to perform the services required of him by this contract because of such injury. If Player's injury in the performance of his services under this contract results in his death, the unpaid balance of his yearly salary for the season of injury will be paid to his stated beneficiary, or in the absence of a stated beneficiary, to his estate.

10. **WORKMEN'S COMPENSATION.** Any compensation paid to Player under this contract or under any collective bargaining agreement in existence during the term of this contract for a period during which he is entitled to workmen's compensation benefits by reason of temporary total, permanent total, temporary partial, or permanent partial disability will be deemed an advance payment of workmen's compensation benefits due Player, and Club will be entitled to be reimbursed the amount of such payment out of any award of workmen's compensation.

11. **SKILL, PERFORMANCE AND CONDUCT.** Player understands that he is competing with other players for a position on Club's roster within the applicable player limits. If at any time, in the sole judgment of Club, Player's skill or performance has been unsatisfactory as compared with that of other players competing for positions on Club's roster, or if Player has engaged in personal conduct reasonably judged by Club to adversely affect or reflect on Club, then Club may terminate this contract.

12. **TERMINATION.** The rights of termination set forth in this contract will be in addition to any other rights of termination allowed either party by law. Termination will be effective upon the giving of written notice, except that Player's death, other than as a result of injury incurred in the performance of his services under this contract, will automatically terminate this contract. If this contract is terminated by Club and either Player or Club so request, Player will promptly undergo a complete physical examination by the Club physician.

13. **INJURY GRIEVANCE.** Unless a collective bargaining agreement in existence at the time of termination of this contract by Club provides otherwise, the following injury grievance procedure will apply: If Player believes that at the time of termination of this contract by Club he was physically unable to perform the services required of him by this contract because of any injury incurred in the performance of his services under this contract, Player may, within a reasonably brief time after examination by the Club physician, submit at his own expense to examination by a physician of his choice. If the opinion of Player's physician with respect to his physical ability to perform the services required of him by this contract is contrary to that of the Club's physician, the dispute will be submitted within a reasonable time to final and binding arbitration by an arbitrator selected by Club and Player, if they are unable to agree, the selection shall be made by the League Commissioner on application by either party.

14. **RULES.** Player will comply with and be bound by all reasonable Club rules and regulations in effect during the term of this contract which are not inconsistent with the provisions of this contract or of any collective bargaining agreement in existence during the term of this contract. Player's attention is also called to the fact that the League functions with certain rules and procedures expressive of its operation as a joint venture among its member clubs and that these rules and practices may affect Player's relationship to the League and its member clubs independently of the provisions of this contract.

15. **INTEGRITY OF GAME.** Player recognizes the detriment to the League and professional football that would result from impairment of public confidence in the honest and orderly conduct of NFL games or the integrity and good character of NFL players. Player therefore acknowledges his awareness that if he accepts a bribe or agrees to throw or fix an NFL game; bets on an NFL game; knowingly associates with gamblers or gambling activity; uses or

provides other players with stimulants or other drugs for the purpose of attempting to enhance on-field performance; or is guilty of any other form of conduct reasonably judged by the League Commission to be detrimental to the League or professional football, the Commissioner will have the right, but only after giving Player the opportunity for a hearing at which he may be represented by counsel of his choice, to fine Player in a reasonable amount; to suspend Player for a period certain or indefinitely; and/or to terminate this contract.

16. **EXTENSION.** If Player becomes a member of the Armed Forces of the United States or any other country, or retires from professional football as an active player, or otherwise fails or refuses to perform his services under this contract, then this contract will be tolled between the date of Player's induction into the Armed Forces, or his retirement, or his failure or refusal to perform, and the later date of his return to professional football. During the period this contract is tolled, Player will not be entitled to any compensation or benefits. On Player's return to professional football, the term of this contract will be extended for a period of time equal to the number of seasons (to the nearest multiple of one) remaining at the time the contract was tolled. The right of renewal, if any, contained in this contract will remain in effect until the end of any such extended term.

17. **RENEWAL.** Unless this contract specially provides otherwise, Club may, by sending written notice to Player on or before the February 1 expiration date referred to in Paragraph 1, renew this contract for a period of one year. The terms and conditions for the renewal year will be the same as those provided in this contract for the last preceding year, except that there will be no further right of renewal in Club and, unless this contract specially provides otherwise, the rate of compensation for the renewal year will be 110% of the rate of compensation provided in this contract for the last preceding year. The phrase "rate of compensation" as used above means yearly salary, including deferred compensation, and any performance bonus, but, excluding any signing or reporting bonus. In order for Player to receive 100% of any performance bonus under this contract he must meet the previously established conditions of that bonus during the renewal year.

18. **ASSIGNMENT.** Unless this contract specially provides otherwise, Club may assign this contract and Player's services under this contract to any successor to Club's franchise or to any other Club in the League. Player will report to the assignee club promptly upon

being informed of the assignment of his contract and will faithfully perform his services under this contract. The assignee club will pay Player's necessary traveling expenses in reporting to it and will faithfully perform this contract with Player.

19. **FILING.** This contract will be valid and binding upon Player and Club immediately upon execution. A copy of this contract, including any attachment to it, will be filed by Club with the League Commissioner within 10 days after execution. The Commissioner will have the right to disapprove this contract on reasonable grounds, including but not limited to an attempt by the parties to abridge or impair the rights of any other club, uncertainty or incompleteness in expression of the parties' respective rights and obligations, or conflict between the terms of this contract and any collective bargaining agreement then in existence. Approval will be automatic unless, within 10 days after receipt of this contract in his office, the Commissioner notifies the parties either of disapproval or of extension of this 10-day period for purposes of investigation or clarification pending his decision. On the receipt of notice of disapproval and termination, both parties will be relieved of their respective rights and obligations under this contract.

20. **DISPUTES.** Any dispute between Player and Club involving the interpretation or application of any provision of this contract will be submitted to final and binding arbitration in accordance with the procedure called for in any collective bargaining agreement in existence at the time the event giving rise to any such dispute occurs. If no collective bargaining agreement is in existence at such time, the dispute will be submitted within a reasonable time to the league Commissioner for final and binding arbitration by him, except as provided otherwise in Paragraph 13 of this contract.

21. **NOTICE.** Any notice, request, approval or consent under this contract will be sufficiently given if in writing and delivered in person or mailed (certified or first-class) by one party to the other at the address set forth in this contract or to such other address as the recipient may subsequently have furnished in writing to the sender.

22. **OTHER AGREEMENTS.** This contract, including any attachment to it, sets forth the entire agreement between Player and Club and cannot be modified or supplemented orally. Player and Club represent that no other agreement, oral or written, except as attached to or specifically incorporated in this contract, exists between them. The provisions of this contract will govern the relationship between Player and Club unless there are conflicting provisions in any collective bargaining agreement in existence during the term of this

contract, in which case the provisions of the collective bargaining agreement will take precedence over conflicting provisions of this contract relating to the rights or obligations of either party.

23. **LAW.** This contract is made under and shall be governed by the laws of the State of Maryland.

24. **SPECIAL PROVISIONS.**

   a. Club agrees to provide player with private lodging whenever the team travels to play an away game.

   b. Club agrees to provide player with five season tickets to each home game.

   THIS CONTRACT is executed in five (5) copies. Player acknowledges that before signing this contract he was given the opportunity to seek advice from or be represented by persons of his own selection.

Anthony Roberts   (SEAL)   *John Young*   (SEAL)

PLAYER   **THE STALLIONS**
                                     PRESIDENT

Name **Please Print Clearly**

1. Does the club have the authority to stop Tony from racing? What language in the document would support an injunction? Why would the NFL be able to regulate Tony's conduct when he's not playing football?

2. Is the NFL able to suspend Tony Roberts and may the league terminate the Stallion's football contract with the player? Does the Club have the power to punish Tony? If yes, what recourse is available to the football player to dispute any sanctions imposed by the Club? In other words, where should Tony go to challenge the Club's assertions concerning his alleged wrongdoings under the contract?

_____

_____

_____

_____

_____

_____

_____

3. May the Club terminate Tony's contract if he lies or misleads the team's orthopedic surgeon about a physical ailment? Can the club terminate Tony Roberts' contract even though the player believes he is in excellent physical condition but the Club thinks he is too out of shape to play football? Please cite to the relevant language in the contract that supports your answer.

_____

_____

_____

_____

_____

_____

_____

_____

SECTION 9.16
INTERNET REFERENCES

For more information about the topics in this chapter, see the following internet sites:

- **www.adr.org**
  The American Arbitration Association is the leading provider of arbitration services in a commercial setting.

- **cpradr.org**
  The mission for the Center for Public Resources is to promote public and private dispute resolution and to serve as multinational resource for resolution of business disputes.

- **www.iccwbo.org**
  The International Chamber of Commerce is the voice of world business promoting global economy and its services range from arbitration and dispute resolution to combating commercial crime.

- **jamsadr.com**
  Jams promotes itself as being instrumental in the evolution of alterative dispute resolution and claims to be the largest private ADR provider.

- **www.nasd.com**
  This organization helps investors resolve disputes with their brokers in a fair and efficient manner. It operates the largest dispute resolution forum in the securities industry.

- **www.arbitration-forum.com**
  The National Arbitration Forum is another company who helps to resolve disputes through ADR and is international in scope.

- **mediate.com**
  This is an on-line periodical that provides a good source of both current developments and background information regarding ADR.

- **adrworld.com**
  This is another on-line periodical that provides current developments in ADR nationwide. It is available by subscription; however, weekly headlines can be viewed without charge.

- **www.acrnet.org**
  The Association for Conflict Resolution is an organization whose website affords information on ADR generally.

- **crinfo.org**
  This address provides a resource concerning ADR that is funded by a large nonprofit foundation seeking to develop widespread acceptance of ADR.

KEYTERMS

Adjudicative Proceedings
Alternative Dispute Resolution
Arbitration
Caucuses
Litigation
Masters
Mediation

Minitrials
Negotiation
Non-Adjudicative Proceedings
Ombudsman
Settlement Conferences
Private Judges
Summary Jury Trial

CHAPTER 10

LIMITATIONS TO LAWSUITS

SECTION 10.1
RES JUDICATA

In a bizarre twist of fate, a convicted murderer who had bludgeoned his aunt to death and spent 10 years in a mental institution for sexually assaulting an 11-year-old girl was hired as a special police officer by the city of Scranton, Pennsylvania. Clothed with the official authority of a badge and gun, he sexually assaulted and killed two boys. Suit was filed against a variety of governmental entities for the deaths of the teenagers. This claim was dismissed on the basis that the government could not be sued for its actions. **Freach v. Commonwealth, 370 A.2d 1163 (Pa. 1997).**

Regardless of the merits of a claim, a limited number of defenses exist that will either bar or restrict lawsuits without considering the merits of the dispute. Certain entities such as the government, charities, diplomats, and parents, are often clothed with immunity and are not responsible for their actions. Claims must also be filed with the court within a finite period of time or be forever barred. This chapter will explore these technical defenses starting with **res judicata**.

Res judicata, an historical doctrine, is Latin for "the thing has been decided" and prevents a litigant from bringing the same lawsuit a second time. This principle forces the parties to use their best efforts at trial, insures that the controversy will be concluded at some point in time, and prevents inconsistent results. Res judicata saves time and expense for both the defendant and the court by avoiding redundant litigation even if new evidence is discovered after the first trial or the second claim is being advanced under a different theory of law.

Res judicata will bar a subsequent claim when: (1) the parties are the same as those who litigated the first case; (2) the issue is the same in both suits; (3) the first court had jurisdiction; and (4) the first action concluded with a final judgment on the merits.

This concept does not prohibit an appellate review of a court's decision, which is the normal process for an aggrieved party to challenge an unfavorable ruling.

This principle also applies in a criminal case to bar a subsequent prosecution involving the same crime. However, in criminal matters, this concept is called **double jeopardy.** This protection is contained in the Fifth Amendment to the United States Constitution and guarantees that no person may be tried twice for the same crime. More specifically, the Fifth Amendment provides "nor shall any person be subject for the same offense to be twice put in jeopardy of life or limb." While some may consider this rule harsh or a legal technicality, it serves a very legitimate purpose. Not only does it emotionally and financially safeguard a defendant from multiple trials but it is society's protection against an overzealous or harassing prosecutor who is dissatisfied with the original verdict and wishes to refile the criminal charges until a conviction is obtained. The Double Jeopardy Clause also protects against two other distinct abuses: a second prosecution for the same offense after conviction; and multiple punishments for the same offense. **United States v. Irwin Harper, 109 S. Ct. 1992 (1989).**

Suppose Joe Roberts is involved in an intersectional collision with Lori Brown on his way home from work. Both drivers claim that the other was responsible for the accident. Roberts sues Brown to recover the cost of repairs to his automobile and the court finds in Joe's favor since Ms. Brown was the cause of the accident. Subsequently, Ms. Brown sues Joe for personal injury. That suit will be barred by the doctrine of res judicata since the parties and the issue in both cases are the same.

Brinkman v. Brinkman
966 S.W. 2d 780 (Tex. App. 1998)

Leta and Lloyd Brinkman were married on May 29, 1993. On November 18, 1993, while the couple was on a trip, Mr. Brinkman physically assaulted Ms. Brinkman, causing permanent damage to two discs in her neck. On October 11, 1994, Mr. Brinkman sued Ms. Brinkman for divorce. Ms. Brinkman counter-sued, alleging cruel treatment by Mr. Brinkman as grounds for divorce. In support of her motion for spousal support, Ms. Brinkman testified that she needed continual medical and physical therapy treatment for the injuries she incurred on November 18, 1993.

On June 21, 1995, the parties filed a joint Motion informing the court that all matters in controversy had been settled. The parties then entered into an Agreed Decree of Divorce which resolved all issues in controversy.

On August 13, 1995, Ms. Brinkman filed suit against Mr. Brinkman for damages caused by the assault. The trial court granted summary judgment in favor of Mr. Brinkman, finding that the claims asserted by Ms. Brinkman are barred by the doctrine of res judicata and the Decree of Divorce entered in the previous action between the parties.

[The facts demonstrate that] Ms. Brinkman counter-sued Mr. Brinkman for divorce, alleging that the marriage was insupportable because of cruel treatment toward Ms. Brinkman by Mr. Brinkman. Ms. Brinkman requested a disproportionate share of the community property because of Mr. Brinkman's fault in the breakup of the marriage. Further, at a hearing on Ms. Brinkman's motion for support, the incident at issue was presented to the court.

When Ms. Brinkman chose to allege cruel treatment as grounds for divorce in order to receive a disproportionate share of community property, she was bound to assert all of her claims for cruel treatment arising out of the marriage. To hold otherwise would enable a spouse to use one instance of abuse as grounds for receiving a large amount of spousal support or a greater share of community property, and then another instance of abuse to obtain actual and punitive damages from the former spouse. The prevention of such a situation is one purpose of res judicata.

Because Ms. Brinkman knew about her personal injury claim against Mr. Brinkman and used it to her advantage in the divorce proceeding, the claim should have been joined with the divorce action. Accordingly, the trial court did not err in finding that Ms. Brinkman's personal injury claim is barred by res judicata.

SECTION 10.2
STATUTE OF LIMITATIONS

If a business associate fails to repay a loan or damages your car, how much time do you have to file a lawsuit? The **statute of limitations** refers to the time period within which an aggrieved party must institute suit or the claim will be barred. This rule is designed to force a claimant to act within a specified period of time so that the party being sued can take the necessary measures to properly defend the action. With the passage of time, people lose track of witnesses, misplace important evidence, and memories fade. By knowing that a lawsuit must be filed by a certain date, a party can safely assume that the matter is no longer of legal significance if the statute of limitations has expired and no suit has been instituted.

The statute of limitations has equal application in both criminal and civil cases. Even the Internal Revenue Service is mandated to act within a specified time if it wishes to pursue a tax claim. The IRS is generally required to reassess a tax within three years after the filing of a tax return. The Statute of Limitations, however, does not apply to a false or fraudulent return that has been filed with the intent to evade taxes.

Statute of limitations are established by the legislature and will vary from jurisdiction to jurisdiction and type of action. These time periods merely reflect an attempt by the legislature to establish a reasonable time frame within which a party must file suit. For instance, California requires a lawsuit for personal injury to be filed within two years of the date of the injury, or when a person discovers that an injury has occurred. Another state may require that the lawsuit be filed within one year. Is justice served, however, by the dismissal of a lawsuit because a claim for personal injury is filed one day after the two-year period? The statute of limitations provides ample time for the institution of suit so an aggrieved party should not wait until the last minute before seeking judicial relief. Therefore, a specific cutoff date will be enforced even if a party is late in filing the suit by one day.

When does the clock start to tick on the statute of limitations? A party is usually aware when an actionable wrong has occurred. Loans are to be repaid by a certain date and people know when they are involved in car accidents. The statute of limitations starts to run or "accrues," on the first day the loan is past due or when the collision occurs. If the statute of limitations for a car accident is two years and the incident occurred on August 1, 2006, the lawsuit must be filed no later than July 31, 2008.

There are a few exceptions to the statute of limitations. There is no bar to bringing criminal charges against a party for murder regardless of the time period that has elapsed. People with a legal disability, such as a child, also have extra time to bring a lawsuit since the statute of limitations is tolled or stopped during that period of disability. This is particularly true with minor children. For instance, the statute of limitations on a personal injury claim involving a child does not start to run until the minor has reached majority, since the child was previously under a legal disability.

Julie Bartlett v. J. Casey Elgin, D. O.
973 P.2d 694, Colo. App. (1998)

On November 2, 1990, defendant Harris-Dubose, a physician's assistant in the office of defendant Elgin, diagnosed plaintiff Heather Bartlett, who was then nine years old, as having the flu. Several days later, Heather underwent abdominal surgery after a diagnosis by hospital staff indicated a ruptured appendix and an abdominal infection.

Asserting claims which included loss of parental consortium, plaintiffs filed a complaint against defendant Elgin in July 1992. In April 1996, plaintiffs filed a motion to amend their complaint to include Harris-Dubose, the physician's assistant. That motion was granted.

Contending that the applicable statute of limitations had expired as to all claims brought against her, defendant Harris-Dubose filed a motion for summary judgment.

Actions against a health care professional must be instituted within two years after the cause of action accrues. A cause of action for personal injury accrues on the date both the alleged injury and its cause are known or should have been known through the exercise of reasonable diligence.

The two-year limitation of actions does not apply if the action is brought against a health care professional by or on behalf of:

> A person otherwise under disability which is defined as any person who is a minor under eighteen years of age, a mental incompetent, or a person under legal disability and who does not have a legal guardian.

"Legal representative" means a guardian, conservator, personal representative, executor, or administrator duly appointed by a court having jurisdiction of any person under a disability or his estate.

A legal representative of a person under a disability will be allowed not less than two years after appointment within which to take action on behalf of the disabled person. With certain exceptions, a person under a disability will be allowed to take action within two years after removal of the disability.

Prior to reaching the age of eighteen years, a minor is not competent to sue without a guardian or someone acting in his or her behalf. Here, the district court acknowledged that Heather "may be a person under disability by statutory definition," but found that definition inapplicable in this particular situation. Because Heather pursued this case against defendant Elgin through her parents as "next friends," which the trial court found to be the "functional equivalent" of a guardian, the trial court concluded that she was not under a disability that made it impossible for her to pursue litigation involving this incident.

However, Heather was unable to bring suit herself (while she was a minor). Because no legal representative had been appointed, and because she was nine years old at the time of her injury, Heather was clearly a "person under a disability" pursuant to the relevant statutory scheme.

Her parents, who knew in November 1990 of Heather's injury and its cause, chose to pursue her claim as next friends. Although their complaint against defendant Elgin was filed within two years, defendant Harris-Dubose was not named as a party until that initial complaint was amended in April 1996. Their knowledge and actions cannot be imputed to Heather.

Colorado does not impose upon a parent the responsibility to litigate a minor's personal injury claim. Contrary to the trial court's findings, we conclude that the statute of limitations as to Heather's claims against Harris-Dubose will not begin to run until Heather reaches her eighteenth birthday or until a legal representative is appointed for her. However, we agree with the district court that, because the parents are not similarly under a disability, their independent claims against defendant Harris-Dubose could have been brought within the time limits set by statute. Thus, we conclude that the two-year limitation period applies to the claims brought individually by Heather's parents (on their own behalf).

SECTION 10.3
ROBERTS v. JONES

PROBLEM TEN

PARK, BROWN & SMITH, P.C.
ATTORNEYS AT LAW
MEMORANDUM

To: All Law Clerks

From: Peter Smith, Esquire

Re: The Medical Malpractice Claim

Joe Roberts is the clear victim of medical malpractice. However, Joe's claim may be barred by the statute of limitations because there is a two-year time limitation for bringing this type of lawsuit. While Joe did not discover the malpractice until a few months ago, the surgeon's act of negligence actually occurred more than two years ago. Thus, we must ascertain when the statute of limitations begins to run. The following facts are provided to help you assess the situation.

Joe's problems stem back to the evening of December 31, 2003. Joe and Estelle were celebrating New Year's Eve with some friends. While eating dinner, a piece of food became lodged in Joe's throat. Luckily, Dr. Jones was at the gathering and quickly dislodged the food. The surgeon, however, was not convinced that Joe was out of danger since Joe's breathing was still labored. The doctor told Joe to go to the hospital. After some tests, Dr. Jones suggested exploratory surgery to determine the nature of the problem. As it turned out, a chicken bone was lodged in Joe's esophagus.

Joe's initial post-surgical recovery was uneventful. At his six-month check-up, Mr. Roberts appeared to be in perfect health. But in December of 2005, Joe began experiencing mild discomfort in his abdomen. At first, Dr. Jones wasn't concerned. This type of problem was common and represented the formation of scar tissue at the incision site. Joe's symptoms continued on a sporadic basis over the next six months. In June of 2006, Joe made another appointment with the surgeon who ordered x-rays that revealed a surgical sponge in the patient's stomach. Joe had to undergo additional surgery to remove the foreign object, which procedure was performed in July of 2006.

Our client wants to sue Dr. Jones for medical malpractice. Assume the current date is January of 2008. Please review **Bayless v. Philadelphia National League Club** in order to ascertain when the statute of limitations begins to run. Please let me know if we should take Joe's case, or does the two-year statute bar recovery?

Patrick Bayless v. Philadelphia National League Club a/k/a The Phillies
579 F.2d 37 (3rd Cir. 1978)

This diversity action presents the question whether the Pennsylvania two-year statute of limitations bars an action by one who did not discover the cause of his injury within the two-year period. Because there exist genuine issues of material fact as to when the limitations period began to run, we reverse the summary judgment granted the defendant.

The facts, considered in the light most favorable to the plaintiff, are as follows. Upon his graduation from high school in 1966, Patrick Bayless was hired as a baseball pitcher by the defendant Philadelphia National League Club, popularly known as the Philadelphia Phillies. In May of 1971, while playing on a Phillies' minor league team, Bayless began to experience severe pain in the lumbar-sacral area of his back and in his right leg. He complained to the team trainer and physician who treated him by administering massive doses of the pain-killing drugs, Decadron, Xylocaine, and Butazolidin. He claims to have been compelled to pitch while in a drug-induced stuporous condition. Bayless' pitching performance deteriorated. On August 12, 1971, the Phillies gave him his unconditional release.

Within thirty days, Bayless collapsed; an emergency laminectomy was performed. Nonetheless, he continued to suffer pain in his back. In September of 1971, Bayless began to exhibit erratic behavior and to suffer from severe depression. He was thereafter confined in state mental institutions on numerous occasions and has been diagnosed as a paranoid schizophrenic. He alleges that this condition was triggered by the drugs he was administered. He seeks damages from the Phillies for injuries associated with his back condition and for the mental illness he has suffered.

On October 15, 1976, more than five years after ingesting the drugs but, or so he claims, less than two years from the time that he discovered that it was the drugs that caused his mental illness, he filed this action. The defendant moved for summary judgment on the grounds that the action was barred by the Pennsylvania statute of limitations.

The district court ruled that Bayless's claims arising out of his back condition and those involving his mental illness were both governed by Pennsylvania's two-year limitations period for personal injuries, but it treated the two claims separately. It held that the cause of action based upon the back injuries arose no later than September 12, 1971, the date on which Bayless underwent the emergency laminectomy. It was then that Bayless knew of his back injury, and the district court held this was more than two years prior to filing the present suit.

Thus, the court held that this claim was time-barred. Bayless does not challenge this aspect of the trial court's ruling on appeal.

With respect to the claim for mental illness, the trial court ruled that the limitations period began to run "when plaintiff knew or reasonably should have discovered the extent of his mental illness." The court ruled that this occurred no later than January 23, 1973, the date on which Bayless was discharged from Napa State Hospital diagnosed, according to hospital records, as a paranoid schizophrenic. In other words, the court held that the limitations period began to run when Bayless learned that he suffered from a mental illness. Accordingly, the court held that this claim was barred as well.

The Pennsylvania statute of limitations for personal injuries reads, in relevant part:

> Every suit hereafter brought to recover damages for injury wrongfully done to the person, in case where the injury does not result in death, must be brought within two years from the time when the injury was done and not afterwards;

Our task is to decide when the limitations period commences to run. The court below held that it runs from the moment that the injury is known to the plaintiff, in this case, from the moment he knew of his mental illness. We hold that the rule in Pennsylvania is that the limitations period begins to run from the time that the plaintiff knows or reasonably should know the cause of his injury.

Analysis begins with the case of **Ayers v. Morgan, 397 Pa. 282, 154 A.2d 788 (1959).** Plaintiff Ayers underwent surgery for an ulcer in 1948. He was discharged within two weeks but he continued to suffer pains in his abdomen. In January of 1957, he returned to the hospital for tests. At that point it was determined that the surgeon who had performed surgery nine years earlier had left a sponge in his body. Defendant raised the statute of limitations as a bar; the trial court granted summary judgment in its favor. The Pennsylvania Supreme Court reversed, holding that the statue of limitations did not begin to run until Ayers knew, or by the exercise of reasonable diligence, could have learned of the presence of the foreign substance within his body. Because Ayers had averred that he did not become aware of the sponge until January 1957, and he had filed suit within two years of that date, the Court held that he was entitled to go to trial on his claims.

In **Irrera v. Southeastern Pennsylvania Transportation Authority, 231 Pa. Super. 508, 331 A.2d 705 (1974),** plaintiff suffered a fall due to a hole in a street surface. Pennsylvania law required that a notice of claim be filed within six months. Plaintiff gave notice more than six months after the accident, but within six months after ascertaining that the defendant was responsible for road maintenance. The court equated the notice statute with a statute of limitations. After discussing **Ayers** and **Daniels v. Beryllium Corp., 227 F. Supp. 591 (E.D. Pa. 1964),** it stated:

> From these cases it appears that the rule that best manifests the legislature's intent… is that time begins to run on the date of injury unless, because of fraud or concealment by the authority, or *in spite reasonable diligence by the claimant, knowledge of the negligence or its causes cannot be discovered until after the six month period.*

Because there was no evidence in the record to suggest that plaintiff could not have learned of the defendant's responsibility had she exercised reasonable diligence, summary judgment in defendant's favor was affirmed.

The *Daniels* case, which was cited with approval in *Irrera*, stands directly for the proposition that the statute of limitations does not begin to run until the plaintiff, in the exercise of reasonable diligence, could have discovered that his injury was caused by the defendant. In *Daniels*, plaintiff brought suit for beryllium poisoning caused by contamination of the atmosphere by defendant's manufacturing plant. Plaintiff first became ill in 1943, but her illness was not diagnosed as beryllium poisoning until 1953, and she did not bring suit until 1958. The court held that the statute began to run not when her symptoms first appeared, and not when the diagnosis was made, but rather when plaintiff should have known the causal connection between her illness and defendant's activities. This was deemed to be a jury question. Judge Higginbotham, now a member of this Court, had earlier interpreted Pennsylvania law in this matter in a wrongful death action. In **Gemignani v. Philadelphia Phillies National League Baseball Club, Inc., 287 F. Supp. 465 (E.D. Pa. 1967),** the deceased, like Bayless, played for the Phillies. In 1959, an examination by one of the Phillies' team physicians revealed a symptomatic blood condition. Nevertheless, the deceased was not treated, nor was he informed of his malady. In August 1960, he was hospitalized because of a serious kidney problem. He died as a result of uremic kidneys on September 3, 1960. On August 31, 1962, plaintiff instituted suit on the theory that the Phillies' failure to treat or to advise the deceased more than two years earlier permitted his condition to develop into one which was terminal.

Notwithstanding that the defendant's allegedly wrongful acts or omissions occurred in 1959, more than two years before suit was filed, the court ruled that the action was not time-barred. It framed the dispositive issue as follows; whether the statute of limitations begins to run from the date on which the plaintiff knows facts from which, through the exercise of reasonable diligence, he could learn the cause of the injury; or whether the statute begins to run from the time the plaintiff, through the exercise of reasonable diligence, should have learned both the facts in question and that those facts bore some causative relationship to the injury. The court opted for the later view:

> It is true that in **Byers v. Bacon, 250 Pa. 564, 95 A. 711 (1915); Smith v. Bell Telephone Co., 397 Pa. 134, 153 A.2d 477 (1959); Ayers v. Morgan, 397 Pa. 282, 154 A.2d 788 (1959),** the courts spoke in terms of discovery of facts. However, it is also clear from reading those cases that discovery of the causative facts necessarily gave us, simultaneously to discovery of the causative relationship. Moreover, it would require the most narrow reading of the language of those cases and the ignoring of the policy basis thereof to fail to recognize that "discovery of the cause of harm" must comprehend discovery of both the facts or occurrences and also discovery of reason to believe that those facts might bear a causative relationship to the harm.

Because the record was devoid of any evidence that prior to August 31, 1960, plaintiff reasonably suspected or should have reasonably suspected that the examination, the facts which it revealed, and the failure of the Phillies to either treat the condition or to inform the deceased's family about it were causally connected to the deceased's terminal illness, the suit was deemed timely.

We think that *Gemignani* accurately states the law of Pennsylvania. If common sense and reason dictate that the limitation period is not to run at least until a plaintiff knows that he has been hurt, then it should not run until he can reasonably determine what or who hurt him. Ordinarily, the two events will occur simultaneously, but this need not always be so. There are cases where one knows of an injury, but not its cause. This may be such a case.

The record here shows that Bayless began to develop symptoms of mental illness in September of 1971. His condition became so serious that he was institutionalized as early as 1972. According to the record, however, the first suggestion that Bayless's mental condition might have been caused by his ingestion of pain-killing drugs is a Neurology Clinic Consultation Report, dated January 15, 1973, prepared by a physician one week prior to Bayless's release from the Napa State Hospital in California. This report states in part, "One thought to keep in mind could be a toxic reaction to some of the drugs such as Butazolidin which does at times cause rather severe mental disturbances." The report, on its face, is titled, "Confidential Patient Information." There is nothing in the record to suggest that its contents were disclosed to the plaintiff or that the report was made available to him. In any event, under the circumstances of this case, the question when Bayless knew or should have known that his mental illness resulted from the Phillies' treatment of his back complaint is for the jury.

The order of the district court granting summary judgment to the defendant will therefore be reversed and the case will be remanded for further proceedings.

**ANSWER SHEET
PROBLEM TEN**

Name **Please Print Clearly**

1. According to **Bayless**, when does the statute of limitations begin to run?

_____

_____

_____

_____

_____

_____

_____

_____

_____

_____

_____

_____

_____

_____

_____

_____

_____

_____

_____

_____

_____

2. Should we take Joe's case, or does the two-year statute bar it?

_____

_____

_____

_____

_____

_____

_____

_____

_____

_____

_____

_____

_____

_____

_____

_____

_____

_____

_____

_____

_____

_____

SECTION 10.4
IMMUNITY FROM SUIT

Part of the fabric of our common law is the recognition that certain entities are immune from suit. Those who traditionally enjoy protection may be classified as follows:

1. sovereign or governmental authorities;
2. judges;
3. charities;
4. claims between certain family members;
5. parties who create immunity by contract; and
6. diplomats

Charitable immunity and intra-family immunity are outdated concepts, and the majority of jurisdictions have abolished these types of immunity or have severely limited their application. Sovereign immunity and immunity by contract are complex topics which are still recognized by the courts and warrant further discussion.

SECTION 10.5
SOVEREIGN IMMUNITY

Sovereign immunity essentially means "the king can do no wrong." In application, this ancient English concept prohibits suits against any governmental unit unless the sovereign gives its expressed consent to the litigation. As Justice Holmes stated: "A sovereign is exempt from suit... on the logical and practical ground that there can be no legal right as against the authority that makes the law on which the right depends." **Kawananakoa v. Polyblank, 205 U.S. 349 (1907).**

The justification for sovereign immunity is that:

1. such liability would open a floodgate of litigation;
2. governmental bodies have no available funds to pay damage awards; and
3. public policy favors the idea that it is better that one individual bear the burden of the loss rather than inconveniencing the public.

It is not hard to imagine the injustices suffered over the years by unsuspecting plaintiffs who are denied "a day in court" simply because the government happens to be the wrongdoer. While the courts are reluctant to bar an aggrieved party from pursuing a claim, sovereign immunity is constitutional and recognized by the courts.

So, has the government ever given its expressed consent to be sued? In 1946, Congress enacted the **Federal Tort Claims Act**, which requires that the federal government agree to be responsible for the wrongful conduct of its employees committed within the scope of their employment. Actions by federal employees that constitute intentional torts or discretionary acts are still exempt. As a United States Court of Appeals noted, the *Federal Tort Claims Act* is a general waiver of the immunity for the federal government. The legislation is designed to afford easy and simple access to the courts for persons injured by the activities of the federal government without having to ask the legislature for a special appropriation of funds for the sole purposes of providing compensation to an aggrieved party. The Act has also been expanded to allow claims when the wrongful conduct arises out of an assault, battery, false arrest, abuse of process, or malicious prosecution.

In those sectors of the government that have not passed legislation on the issue of immunity, the courts make a distinction between functions that are "governmental" and those which are "proprietary." **Governmental functions** are those tasks which can only be performed adequately by the governmental unit. In carrying out a governmental function, the political unit will retain its immunity from suit. Examples include the police department, fire department, and public schools. **Proprietary functions** are those activities which are performed by the government but can be delivered just as well by the private sector. These functions include rubbish collection or providing utilities. Suit against the governmental unit for these types of activities are allowed.

In those states or municipalities that have passed legislation on the topic, one must examine the terms of the law to see when suit has been authorized.

The following is a sample listing of areas in which governmental units will consider waiving their immunity for the torts of their officers and employees:

1. the negligent operation of a motor vehicle

2. improper custody or control of personal property;

3. dangerous conditions relating to government owned real estate, highways, and sidewalks;

4. dangerous conditions relating to utility services; and

5. the care, custody and control of animals.

Even though the government may waive its immunity defense, it will still impose a cap on the amount of recovery. For instance, the City of Philadelphia has imposed a $500,000 cap in the aggregate on any personal injury recovery against the municipality.

An exception to the immunity rule exists when the conduct of the state or local government employee is willful. In that situation, the immunity defense will not protect the governmental unit from tort liability.

For instance, Pennsylvania has waived its immunity defense if an employee engages in willful misconduct in carrying out the duties and functions of the job. In **Ramona Africa v. City of Philadelphia, 938 F. Supp. 1278 (E.D. Pa. 1996)**, the court discussed this concept in an action filed by MOVE members to recover damages for the bombing of their home by city officials in 1985. The court noted that the liability of a governmental unit for personal injury is limited to those situations involving injuries arising out of the operation or management of motor vehicles, streets, sidewalks, traffic control systems, reality, utilities, personality or animals, which are possessed or controlled by the municipality. However, in the case of egregious conduct, the city will remain responsible for the actions of its employees. This statutory waiver of immunity provides:

> In any action against a local agency or employee for damages on account of an injury caused by the act of an employee in which it is judicially determined that the employee caused the injury, and that such act constitutes a crime, actual fraud, actual malice, or willful misconduct, the defense of immunity shall not apply.

In those jurisdictions where the legislature has not clearly established the circumstances under which they will waive their immunity, courts frequently have to decide if a particular act constitutes a governmental function or a proprietary function. That is the issue in **Carter v. City of Norfolk** in which the plaintiff was injured when she stepped into a hole on a city street.

CARTER v. CITY OF NORFOLK
54 VA. CIR. 195 (VA. CIR. 2000)

On or about July 17, 1999, the plaintiff was walking along Ballantine Boulevard in Norfolk when she allegedly stepped into a hole and fell. The hole was located in a strip of grass abutting a sidewalk upon which the plaintiff was walking. She subsequently sued Norfolk, and the City filed a special plea in bar on the ground of sovereign immunity.

The parties agree that the hole was caused by a leak in a storm water drainage pipe buried beneath the grass. A seam in the pipe came apart, causing a cavern in the earth above, which eventually caved in, resulting in a visible hole at the surface. The City argues that the design and maintenance of the drainage pipe are governmental functions so the doctrine of sovereign immunity bars plaintiff's recovery for injuries. In Virginia, a municipality acts in a dual capacity, the one governmental and the other proprietary. It is immune from liability for negligence in performing or in failing to perform governmental functions. It is not so immune with respect to proprietary functions.

With respect to the issue of governmental functions, **Va. Code § 15.2-970** provides:

Any locality may construct a dam, levee, seawall, or other structure or device, hereinafter referred to as "works," the purpose of which is to prevent the tidal erosion, flooding or inundation of such locality. The design, maintenance and operation of any such works is a proper governmental function for a public purpose.

The plain language of the statute provides that the "maintenance" of "structures or devices" used to prevent flooding is a "governmental" function.

Several courts have determined that drainage pipes constitute "devices" to control flooding under **Va. Code §15.2-970**. In **Continental Casualty Co. v. Town of Blacksburg**, 846 F.Supp. 483 (W.D. Va.1993), the plaintiff sued for negligent maintenance of a storm water drainage system, much like the one at issue in this case. The court held that the system was a "structure" or "device" under §15.2-970, stating since Blacksburg's storm drainage system consists of structures, the purpose of which is to prevent flooding or inundation, it comes within the purview of Va. Code §15.2-970.

The question remains how the governmental function of storm drainage intersects with the proprietary function of sidewalk maintenance.

It is clear that a municipality may be held liable for negligently maintaining a public sidewalk. Therefore, if the hole were a defect in the sidewalk, the City would not be shielded by the doctrine of sovereign immunity.

When two functions of a municipality overlap, one being governmental and the other being proprietary, the governmental function prevails to shield the municipality from liability. In other words, where governmental and proprietary functions coincide, the governmental function is the overriding factor. In **Taylor v. City of Newport News, 197 S.E.2d 210**, the plaintiff slipped on a sidewalk due to grease spilled by a garbage truck. Although the maintenance of the sidewalk was a proprietary function for which the City could be sued, the collection of garbage was strictly governmental. In that case, the court ruled that the governmental function overrode the proprietary function.

The court finds that no defect existed in the sidewalk in this case. Therefore, no proprietary function by the city is involved. Even if, arguendo, there were a defect in the sidewalk, the court finds that such defect would have been caused by the leaking storm drainage pipe, thus resulting from a governmental function.

Accordingly, Norfolk's Special Plea in Bar is sustained, and the action is dismissed.

SECTION 10.6
JUDICIAL IMMUNITY

A judge has immunity from suit when he or she acts within the scope of judicial authority and in the discharge of official duties. The purpose of **judicial immunity** is to insure that a judge will be free to render a decision on the merits of a dispute without fear or influence of being sued by an aggrieved party. The concept, however, does have its limits. A judge remains liable for actions that are of a non-judicial nature, such as a charge of sexual harassment by a law clerk or improper disciplinary actions involving an employee.

Donald L. Meek v. County of Riverside
183 F. 3rd 96 (9ᵗʰ Cir. 1999)

Donald L. Meek brought an action against the County of Riverside and two municipal court judges alleging that his right to campaign for public office had been violated when he was fired in retaliation for his seeking election to a municipal court judgeship.

Meek was appointed a Commissioner of Municipal Court. In September of 1995, Meek learned that two vacancies on the Riverside Municipal Court would occur in March and April of 1996. One of the seats was to be filled by a non-partisan election and the other by a gubernatorial appointment. Meek approached then-Commissioner Albert J. Wojcik about an arrangement whereby Meek would support Wojcik in the March, 1996, non-partisan election for the first vacant seat and Wojcik would support Meek in his efforts to obtain a gubernatorial appointment to the second seat.

Shortly after his meeting with Wojcik, Meek concluded that Wojcik would not support him in his effort to obtain the gubernatorial appointment. He also learned that Municipal Judge Curtis R. Hinman had written a letter to Governor Wilson supporting Sherill Nielsen, a close friend of Municipal Judge Rodney Walker, for appointment to the municipal court. Deciding that he had little chance of obtaining the appointment, Meek chose to run against Wojcik in the March election. During the campaign, Judge Walker allegedly stated that he would fire Meek from his position of court commissioner if Meek lost the election and that he considered Meek his political enemy.

On March 26, 1996, Wojcik was elected judge and he took office on April 23, 1996. On April 4, 1996, then-Commissioner Wojcik, Judge Walker, and Judge Hinman held a vote on whether Meek should be terminated. Wojcik and Walker voted to fire Meek and Judge Hinman abstained.

Meek filed a suit against Wojcik, Walker, and the County of Riverside claiming that he had been fired in retaliation for exercising his right to run for office. Claiming judicial immunity, Wojcik and Walker moved to dismiss the complaint.

It is well settled that judges are generally immune from civil liability. Although unfairness and injustice to a litigant may result on occasion, it is a general principle of the highest importance to the proper administration of justice that a judicial officer, in exercising the authority vested in him, shall be free to act upon his own convictions, without apprehension of personal consequences to himself.

A judge is not deprived of immunity because he takes actions, which are in error, are done maliciously, or are in excess of his authority. The rationale for granting judges immunity from liability for even intentional and malicious conduct while acting in their judicial capacity is that judges should be free to make controversial decisions and act upon their convictions without fear of personal liability.

There are two situations in which judges are not absolutely immune from liability. First, a judge is not immune from liability for nonjudicial actions, i.e., actions not taken in the judge's judicial capacity. Second, a judge is not immune for actions, though judicial in nature, are taken in the complete absence of all jurisdiction.

A state court judge is generally not entitled to absolute immunity from liability arising out of a decision to fire a subordinate judicial employee because the decision is not a judicial or adjudicative act, but rather an administrative one. In determining the scope of judicial immunity, the Court stressed that the focus must be on the function that the immunity protects. Judges are granted absolute immunity for their judicial actions in order to safeguard independent and principled judicial decision-making. Although a judge's employment decisions "may be essential to the very functioning of the courts," they are not the type of decisions that traditionally have been regarded as judicial acts meriting absolute immunity.

Appellants' decision to fire a subordinate judicial employee is an administrative decision: the district court did not err in finding that the defendants are not entitled to judicial immunity for such actions.

SECTION 10.7
CHARITABLE IMMUNITY

Historically, charitable organizations, such as churches, hospitals and community organizations enjoyed immunity from claims for personal injury. This protection was based on the idea that charities should not be concerned about financial liability for their mistakes. Rather, they should focus their efforts on serving the public good. The law also wanted to guarantee that funds raised by the charities would not be depleted by civil judgments rendered against them. Most jurisdictions, however, have abolished **charitable immunity** as an obsolete doctrine or have curtailed its application since non-profit organizations may protect themselves through insurance. For example, Massachusetts allows suit against a charity but has placed a $20,000 cap on their liability if the cause of action arose out of a charitable purpose. This limitation of liability will not apply if the tort was committed in the course of activities that are primarily commercial in character.

The change in the laws of charitable immunity has partially accounted for the increased number of lawsuits filed against the clergy for sexual abuse. In fact, the religious organization itself has been named as a defendant in these claims and some of the cases have settled for millions of dollars. A number of lawsuits in 2005, however, were still pending against the Roman Catholic Archdiocese of Boston for the alleged sexual abuse by priests over the years. Whether the church will assert the statutory cap of liability of $20,000 remains to be seen because of the public relations implications of such a move. Nevertheless, charitable immunity is still a viable defense in Massachusetts.

Sink v. Vinton Wesleyan Church involves a claim for personal injury against a charity in one of the few states that still recognizes this outdated concept.

MERLIN S. SINK V. VINTON WESLEYAN CHURCH
50 VA. CIR. 361 (VA. CIR. 1999)

Merlin S. Sink arranged to use the chapel and social hall of Vinton Wesleyan Church for her daughter's wedding. Sink alleges that while at the social hall to decorate, she caught her shoe in a gap created by a detached carpet and was thrown into a brick fireplace, severely injuring herself. She has sued the church for negligence.

The church has filed a plea of charitable immunity claiming that it is a charitable organization. It alleges that Sink is a beneficiary of its charitable services.

Sink contends that the doctrine of charitable immunity is not applicable because, at the time of the accident, she was a business invitee. Her argument is based upon the facts that she was not baptized a member of the church and had paid a fee for the use of the social hall. She further relies upon the fact that the social hall was used by a fee-generating childcare center operated during the week by the pastor's wife and run separately from the church.

In Virginia, charitable institutions enjoy limited immunity from tort liability to their beneficiaries. While many jurisdictions have abandoned the concept of charitable immunity, the Supreme Court of Virginia has made it clear that the decision to abrogate the doctrine of charitable immunity rests with the General Assembly. The justification for the doctrine of charitable immunity rests on public policy grounds.

Charitable immunity does not extend to strangers or invitees who have no beneficial relationship to the charitable organization. To be considered a charitable beneficiary for the purpose of charitable immunity, a person must be a direct beneficiary through the receipt of money, goods, or services and not merely someone who indirectly received charitable benefits.

In the present case, Sink was utilizing the church's facilities for her daughter's wedding reception at the time that she fell. She was receiving a direct benefit of the church's charitable bounty. She had attended the church since the age of 16, considered the pastor to be her pastor, raised her children in the church, and even used the church's facilities previously for another daughter's wedding.

Nor does the payment of a fee bar Sink from being considered a beneficiary for the purposes of charitable immunity. Sink's testimony established that she paid approximately $25.00 for the use of the fellowship hall. The payment of this nominal amount does not remove her from being a beneficiary of the church's services and facilities.

Sink also advances the argument that the church's rental of the social hall during the week to a childcare center operated by the pastor's wife separate from the church should stop the church's claim of charitable immunity. There is no suggestion that the money gained by rental of the hall for the childcare center is inconsistent with the church's charitable purposes. Nor was Sink's use of the social hall in any way related to the childcare center. Rather, she was using the church's facilities to benefit herself and her family and friends.

Vinton Wesleyan is a charitable organization. Sink was a beneficiary of its charitable services at the time that she fell in the church's social hall. Accordingly, her claim for damages resulting from alleged negligence by the church is barred by the doctrine of charitable immunity.

**Section 10.8
Intra-Family Immunity**

Traditionally, spouses could not sue one another. **Spousal immunity** stemmed from the idea that a husband and wife became one legal entity upon marriage. Before states began passing Married Women's Property Acts, a wife had no standing to initiate legal action against her husband. These acts established a woman's right to property and the capacity to sue and be sued. However, spousal immunity continued to exist because courts feared that suits between spouses would be disruptive to the peace and harmony of the family unit. There was also concern that husbands and wives would fabricate fraudulent claims. Most recent decisions, however, have abolished spousal immunity and allow suits between married couples.

Immunity between children and parents did not exist at common law but was first recognized in 1891 in **Hewlett v. George**. This Mississippi decision established that minor children could not sue a parent because it would disrupt the peace and harmony of the family unit and deny parents the right to exercise discipline and parental control over their children. As the court noted, "So long as the parent is under an obligation to care for, guide and control, and the child is under a reciprocal obligation to aid, comfort and obey, no such action can be maintained."

Many jurisdictions now limit the application of parental immunity. The availability of insurance relieves parents of direct responsibility to their children in tort actions so these states allow suits between parents and children. To be more precise, eleven states have abrogated the concept, but at least thirty-two jurisdictions have limited its application to the negligent acts of a parent, which involve a reasonable exercise of parental authority or the exercise of ordinary parental discretion concerning the care and necessity of a child. Most of these jurisdictions, however, have determined that the granting of immunity does not protect a parent against intentional acts such as an assault of a child. As an example, Texas recognizes three exceptions to the parental immunity defense: (1) intentional or malicious acts; (2) acts committed by parents in an employer-employee relationship with their child; and (3) the negligent operation of a motor vehicle.

Immunity between family members has always been confined to spouses, or parents and their children. It has never extended to siblings suing each other.

Paula Bearden v. David Bearden
499 S.E. 2d 359 (Ga. App. 1998)

Paula Bearden was injured in an automobile accident while riding as a passenger in a car driven by her husband, David Bearden. She sued her husband, claiming her injuries were caused by his negligent operation of the car. The trial court granted summary judgment in favor of Mr. Bearden on the basis of the interspousal tort immunity doctrine. On appeal, Ms. Bearden claims the trial court erred in applying the doctrine because she alleges that the facts show she and her husband had not lived together for a long period of time and that no marital relationship existed between them. We agree that David Bearden was not entitled to be shielded by the doctrine of interspousal tort immunity as a matter of law, and reverse the trial court's decision.

Mr. Bearden stated that the parties married in November 1987 and separated in early 1989. He stated, however, that during the separation, he and his wife "were together frequently;...spent the night together at motels and other places,... and that, on the day of the accident, my wife and I had been together since the previous day." He stated they were returning from a swimming trip when the accident occurred.

Ms. Bearden stated that the parties have been separated since 1989 "because we could not get along with each other." She stated that during the separation, Mr. Bearden has lived with other women, and she has considered herself "unofficially divorced" from him with "no plan or hope for us getting back together." Ms. Bearden further stated "that there has not been any 'harmony' to preserve in our marriage since we separated in 1989." On the same day Ms. Bearden commenced the present action, she also filed an action seeking a divorce from Mr. Bearden.

The doctrine of interspousal immunity exists to (1) preserve the sanctity of marriage, and (2) to prevent the possibility of collusive lawsuits. This doctrine may be abrogated where there is no marital harmony or unity to preserve and where there is no possibility of collusion. Here, although Mr. and Ms. Bearden did occasionally spend the night together, such evidence without more, does not resolve the factual issue of whether there was a state of marital unity to be preserved. In light of Ms. Bearden's uncontroverted testimony that they had not lived together as husband and wife for more than six years, could not get along with each other, and had no hope or plan for reconciliation at the time of the accident, Mr. Bearden was not entitled to summary judgment as a matter of law. Our law does not presume that where there is some evidence of friendship, civility, or intimacy in a relationship, there exists as a matter of law, a de facto state of marital harmony.

Accordingly, the trial court's grant of summary judgment to Mr. Bearden on the basis of interspousal tort immunity is reversed.

SECTION 10.9
IMMUNITY BY CONTRACT

People are often cavalier in their conduct and take many risks unaware of the full consequences of their actions. We think nothing of leaving cars and other valuable possessions in the hands of strangers. Think about the last time that you parked your car in a garage. In exchange for your automobile, the attendant provided a ticket which probably contained phrases such as; "We assume no liability for loss or damage;" "Park at your own risk" or "We are not responsible..." These phrases provide immunity by contract and are known as **exculpatory clauses**.

The courts allow parties to allocate their risks by contract but will invalidate an exculpatory clause which results in unfair surprise to one party. The courts examine the subject matter of the contract, the relationship between the parties, the equality of bargaining power, and whether the agreement is against public policy. For instance, exculpatory clauses relieving a party from liability for intentional misconduct or for personal injury due to negligence are not favored. On the other hand, immunity from suit for property damage claims is not so easily challenged.

The following case involves a skiing accident and focuses on the criteria the court will use in deciding whether to enforce the exculpatory clause.

KARL KOTOVSKY v. SKI LIBERTY OPERATING CORPORATION
603 A.2D 663 (PA. SUPER. 1992)

WIEAND, Judge:

While participating in the second heat of a downhill ski race, Karl Kotovsky failed to negotiate a turn and collided with a wooden fence post. As a result of this accident, he received serious injuries. Alleging negligence in failing to pad the post, Kotovsky commenced an action for damages against Ski Liberty Operating Corporation (Ski Liberty), the owner of the slope. In its answer to the complaint, Ski Liberty pleaded two exculpatory agreements and releases which Kotovsky had executed prior to participating in the downhill ski race. By the terms of these agreements and releases, Kotovsky expressly assumed the "risks, condi-

tions and hazards which may occur whether they now be known or unknown." He also released the ski area, as well as the promoters, sponsors, organizers and others, "from any and all liability, whether known or unknown, even though the liability may arise out of negligence or carelessness on the part of persons or entities mentioned above."

Downhill skiing is a dangerous activity. Downhill racing is even more dangerous. In recognition of the hazardous nature of such activity, the legislature has expressly provided that assumption of the risk shall be a complete defense to actions for downhill skiing injuries. **42 Pa. C.S. Section 7102(c).**

In **Zimmer v. Mitchell and Ness, 385 A.2d 437 (1978),** the Superior Court laid down the following standards for a valid exculpatory agreement.

> The contract must not contravene any policy of the law. It must be a contract between individuals relating to their private affairs. Each party must be a free bargaining agent, not simply one drawn into an adhesion contract, with no recourse but to reject the entire transaction.

The agreement in the instant case was not one of adhesion. Appellant was not required to enter the contract, but did so voluntarily in order to participate in a downhill ski race. This activity was not essential to appellant's personal or economic well-being.

The releases also did not contravene public policy. They were contracts between private parties and pertained only to the parties' private rights.

The exculpatory agreement and release in this case demonstrated clearly and unequivocally the intent of the parties. Its purpose, as stated expressly therein, was to release the "ski area" from all liability for injury to appellant caused by natural or man made obstacles on the slope, including hazards resulting form negligence by the owner.

There was no compulsion for appellant to participate in the downhill ski race which caused his injuries. In order to participate in this hazardous event, he agreed to assume the risk of injury and released the owner of the slope, as well as others, from all liability for injuries resulting therefrom, including injuries caused by another's negligence. Appellant's exculpatory agreement and release bars the present action. Therefore, the trial court properly entered judgment on the pleadings for appellee.

Judgment affirmed.

SECTION 10.10
WORKERS COMPENSATION

Employees are frequently hurt on the job so remedial measures have been enacted to provide workers with a humanitarian, fast, and easy way to obtain compensation for those injuries. Dubbed **workers compensation,** employers are required to maintain a form of accident insurance that will provide employees with the prompt payment of medical bills and wages in the event a work-related injury. These benefits will be paid regardless of fault on the part of the employer or employee, and without the need to engage in time consuming litigation against the employer. In other words, even if the employee assumed the risk of the injury or if the employer is fault free, the benefits will be paid to the worker.

In exchange for these automatic benefits, the worker has surrendered his or her right to sue the employer for pain and suffering damages. As noted in **Kramer v. W.C.A.B., 883 A. 2d 518 (Pa. 2005),** this statutory scheme balances competing interests: while offering the prospect of specific recovery to employees regardless of fault on the part of their employers, the laws also provide employers relative cost-certainty in the form of limited exposure in the event of a work related injury.

The key to this compensation scheme, however, is that the aggrieved party must be an employee at the time of the injury and the injury must occur within the scope of the employment. An employee is one who performs services for another and whose employment is not casual or occasional. In determining whether a person is an employee as opposed to an independent contractor who would not be entitled to collect benefits from the employer, the critical factors are: (1) who controls the manner in which the work is performed, (2) which party supplies the equipment, (3) whether compensation is by the job or by time, and (4) whether the task is part of the regular work of the employer. For instance, a horse jockey who rides horses for a variety of owners, supplies the saddle, and controls the manner in which the horses are ridden during races, is an independent contractor and not an employee. On the other hand, a professor or instructor at a University is an employee of that institution.

The following case illustrates the difficulty in determining whether the employee's injury occurred within the scope of the employment.

Morris v. W.C.A.B
879 A.2d 869 (Pa. Cmwlth. 2005)

Claimant was employed at Walmart Stores, Inc. On the date of her injury, Morris' shift was to begin between 5:00 p.m. and 6:00 p.m. In the early afternoon, Claimant and her two daughters walked from their apartment to Employer's store to purchase school supplies, using Claimant's employee discount to do so. It was Claimant's intention that, after the shopping was completed, her daughters would return home and she would stay at the Employer's premises to begin her shift. While walking in the "big aisle" of the store, Morris slipped and fell, injuring her right knee.

Claimant asserts that she was within the course and scope of her employment at the time of the injury and, thus, it is compensable. An injury falls within the scope of employment under two possible situations. The first is where the employee, while injured, is actually engaged in

furtherance of the employer's business or affairs. Alternatively, an employee who is not actually engaged in the furtherance of her employer's business or affairs is eligible for workers' compensation benefits if: (1) she is on premises occupied or under the control of the employer, or upon which the employer's business or affairs are being carried on; (2) she is required by the nature of her employment to be on the premises; and (3) she sustains injuries caused by the condition of the premises or by operation of the employer's business or affairs thereon.

Claimant argues that she was actually engaged in the furtherance of the employer's affairs when she was injured. She relies on **Hoffman v. Workers' Comp. Appeal Bd., 741 A.2d 1286 (Pa. 1999)**. There, an employee was injured when she stopped at her employer's premises on her day off to pick up her paycheck. This method of collecting pay was one of three alternatives specifically approved by the employer. The Supreme Court, in concluding that the employee was acting within the course and scope of her employment, explained that receipt of wages is a "fundamental aspect of the employment relationship" and a "necessary affair" of the employer.

Claimant asserts that her employee discount was also a fundamental aspect of her employment. We disagree. Payment of salary is a legal obligation on the part of an employer. Providing an employee discount is not; rather, a discount is only a perquisite of employment. Therefore, an injury sustained by an employee collecting wages under an employer-designated method is distinguishable from an injury incurred by an employee who is using an employee discount while shopping during her non-work hours. We conclude that Claimant, while shopping, was not functioning as an employee who was furthering Employer's business; rather, she was only a member of the general public.

Employees still retain the right to sue any third party who causes the work related injury. For instance, an employee who is injured by a defective forklift will collect wages and medical expenses from his employer but will still be able to sue the defective product's manufacturer for such things as pain and suffering damages. Also, an injury sustained while the worker is traveling to and from work is generally not considered within the course of employment for purposes of workers compensation benefits nor is an injury incurred as the result of intoxication.

SECTION 10.11 DIPLOMATIC IMMUNITIES

Diplomats and their immediate families enjoy special privileges and immunities under the law because of the need to develop and maintain friendly relations between countries. This protection is firmly embedded in history and is known as **diplomatic immunity.** Simply put, a foreign dignitary is afforded immunity from suit or criminal prosecution while in the host country.

This principle was given uniform recognition around the world in 1961 through the **Vienna Convention on Diplomatic Relations** which noted that a diplomat shall not be subject to any form of arrest or detention. Also, the diplomat shall not be subject to service of process and shall be immune from suit in civil cases. These principles ensure the efficient performance of the functions of diplomatic missions and serve the needs of the foreign sovereign.

There are, however, three exceptions to this grant of immunity. The diplomat can be sued over a private real estate holding in the host country unless that property is being used as the diplomatic mission. Immunity is also waived when the diplomat acts as the personal representative of a decedent's estate or in an action relating to any commercial activity outside of his or her official functions.

The United States codified the requirements of the Vienna Convention in 1978 when Congress enacted the **Diplomatic Relations Act**. That legislation provides:

> Any action or proceeding brought against an individual who is entitled to immunity with respect to an action or proceeding under the Vienna Convention on Diplomatic Relations...or under any other law extending diplomatic privileges and immunities, shall be dismissed.

This grant of immunity can become controversial such as when a diplomat kills someone while driving under the influence of alcohol and is set free, when a diplomat's son, who was suspected of committing multiple rapes, is allowed to leave the county, or when millions of dollars in parking tickets go unpaid because the cars' operators are attached to a foreign embassy.

JAMES CRUM V. KINGDOM OF SAUDI ARABIA
2005 WL 3752271 E. D. VA. (2005)

This matter is before the court on Defendant's Motion for Judgment on the Pleadings.

James Crum began working as a limousine driver in the spring of 1986 for Defendants Royal Embassy of Saudi Arabia and the Kingdom of Saudi Arabia. During the time that Plaintiff worked for Defendants, he was well-qualified to do his job and fulfilled his employer's requirements for the position; he never had an accident or called in sick during sixteen years of service to the defendants.

According to Plaintiff's Complaint, after the attack on the World Trade Center Towers in New York City on September 11, 2001, Plaintiff alleges that his supervisor and other employees of the Embassy began making anti-American comments to Mr. Crum, including cursing at the plaintiff, calling him a "stupid American" and a "dumb-ass American." Drivers who were not American were not called these names.

Plaintiff's Complaint also alleges that in October 2001, Mr. Crum placed decals of the American flag on his personal automobile. Prince Bandar Bin Sultan's wife asked Mr. Crum questions about his patriotic feelings, including whether he knew anything about the individuals being held as prisoners in Guantanamo Bay, Cuba. Shortly thereafter, two other employees of the defendants told Mr. Crum that if he did not remove the American flag decals from his car, he would be fired. Mr. Crum did not remove the decals from his car and was fired on August 1, 2002. Other limousine drivers who were not American who placed American flag decals on their personal cars were not terminated by Defendants.

On November 12, 2003, Crum filed suit alleging national origin discrimination under **42 U.S.C. § 2000e**. Defendants filed a motion for judgment on the pleadings. In essence, Defendants argue that this Court has no jurisdiction to hear this claim of employment discrimination based on national origin because hiring a limousine driver does not constitute "commercial activity" within the meaning of the Immunity Act.

The Court holds that it does not have jurisdiction to decide this case under the Foreign Sovereign Immunities Act because the hiring of an individual to drive a limousine does not constitute a "commercial activity". The FSIA states that a foreign state shall be immune from the jurisdiction of the Courts of the United States and of States. However, one of the exceptions to the rule granting immunity is when a defendant engages in actions based on a "commercial activity." A "commercial activity" means either a regular course of commercial conduct or a particular commercial transaction or act. A foreign state engages in commercial activity where it exercises only those powers that can also be exercised by private citizens, as distinct from those powers peculiar to sovereigns.

Mr. Crum's case does not constitute an exception to the FSIA's grant of immunity because it does not pass the test for "commercial activity." Being employed as a chauffeur for the Saudi Arabian Embassy does not constitute a "commercial activity." The Fourth Circuit rejected a claim similar to Mr. Crum's in **Butters v. Vance International, Inc., 225 F.3d 462 (4th Cir.2000)**. In **Butters**, the plaintiff, a female security agent, argued that by hiring and firing employees, the Kingdom of Saudi Arabia engaged in the type of conduct ordinarily undertaken by any private company in commerce. The Fourth Circuit however determined "the relevant act" as the "foreign sovereign's decision as to how best to secure the safety of its leaders"-an "act peculiar to sovereigns." The Fourth Circuit concluded in **Butters** that the employment decision was "not a commercial act in which the state was acting in the manner of a private player within the market," and therefore could not trigger the FSIA's commercial activity exception.

Accordingly, the Court holds that it does not have jurisdiction to decide this case under the Foreign Sovereign Immunities Act because a foreign embassy hiring an individual to drive a limousine does not constitute "commercial activity" within the meaning of the Foreign Sovereign Immunities Act.

SECTION 10.12
OTHER IMMUNITIES

There are a number of other limited immunities afforded by the law as the result of special interest groups who have succeeded in having legislation enacted to protect a specific group from lawsuits. Other immunities have been granted as the result of society's desire to achieve a certain result such as the development of a vaccine when the drug manufacturer is afraid to become involved because of potential litigation if the product does not work or to encourage health care professionals to help people in an emergency situation without the fear of being sued.

The fast food industry received a jolt a few years ago when a class action lawsuit was filed against McDonald's because its food products allegedly caused obesity in children. That suit was largely unsuccessful but it prompted the enactment of legislation in a number of states to prohibit these types of claims. Known as the "Cheeseburger Bill," legislation has been introduced to limit the liability of food manufacturers, retailers and marketers for claims stemming from weight gain or other health problems as the result of fast food consumption. According to the National Restaurant Association, at least 25 states have enacted statutes limiting civil liability for obesity claims including Arizona, Colorado, Georgia, Florida, Idaho, Illinois, Louisiana, Michigan, Missouri, South Dakota, Tennessee, Utah and Washington.

The following is an example of the Cheeseburger Bill. This one was passed in Illinois, the national headquarters for McDonald's. The legislation is called the **Illinois Common Sense Consumption Act:**

> No person shall bring a civil liability action in state court against any seller of a qualified product which is defined as food under the Federal Food, Drug and Cosmetic Act.

> This immunity shall not extend to:

> (a) an action in which a seller of a qualified product knowingly and willfully violated a federal or State statute applicable to the marketing, distribution, advertisement, labeling, or sale of the product, and the violation was a proximate cause of the claim of injury resulting from a person's weight gain, obesity, or health condition related to weight gain or obesity; or (b) an action for breach of contract or express warranty in connection with the purchase of a qualified product.

Spectators at sporting events are routinely exposed to the risk of being hit by a foul ball or hockey puck that goes into the stands. The reader may even remember the child who was killed at a Columbus Yellow Jackets' hockey game when an errant puck struck her in the forehead. Most suits by injured spectators for damages, however, fail because of the doctrine of assumption of the risk. It is commonly assumed that people are aware of these types of dangers when attending a sporting event, and are barred from recovery if he or she is injured at the game. Stadium personnel also make periodic announcements that balls and pucks leave the playing field and people should be vigilant for these dangers.

This established defense was restricted in the following New Jersey case.

Louis Maisonave v. The Newark Bears
Professional Baseball Club, Inc.
185 N. J. 70 (2005)

Plaintiff suffered a facial injury when a foul ball struck him in the eye as he stood on the mezzanine at Riverfront Stadium, home field of minor league baseball team, the Newark Bears. The mezzanine is an open walking area exposed on one side to the baseball field. Vendors sell food and beverages on that level, and restrooms are located there. At the time of the incident, the stadium used movable vending carts for the sale of beverages because the built-in concession stands were not operational. The carts dotted the mezzanine along both the first and third base lines on the field-side of the mezzanine. The vendors stood with their backs to the diamond while the patrons faced it.

In **Hopkins v. Fox & Lazo Realtors**, we held that a landowner "owes a duty of reasonable care to guard against any dangerous conditions on his or her property that the owner either knows about or should have discovered." 132 N. J. 426 (1993). The operator of a commercial recreational facility, like the operator of any other business, has a general duty to exercise reasonable care for the safety of its patrons.

The (assumption of the risk rule) is a specialized negligence standard that has protected stadium owners and operators since the early days of modern baseball. Since the early twentieth century, courts have held that one of the natural risks assumed by spectators attending professional games is that of being struck by batted or thrown balls.

We now must decide whether the (assumption of the risk rule) should apply to areas other than the stands. We recognize that a different standard of care may be appropriate for areas of the stadium outside of the stands. Transformations in tort law and the game of baseball suggest boundaries to the (assumption of the risk rule).

Fans foreseeably and understandably let down their guard when they are in other areas of the stadium. Once the fan has disengaged him— or herself from the activity on the field and has left the stands, that individual is no longer trying to catch foul balls or even necessarily watching the game. It is all harmless fun— until that one foul ball comes screaming at the wrong time and in the wrong place.

Nothing about the game of baseball distinguishes it from other businesses in a way that justifies preferential treatment for stadium owners and operators for injuries that occur outside of the stands. Indeed, in areas outside of the stands, including concourses and mezzanines such as the one in this appeal, a commercial sports facility is no different than any other commercial establishment, and we do not hesitate to apply general negligence principles in virtually all other tort situations.

We conclude that the proper standard of care for all other areas of the stadium (outside of the stands) is the business invitee rule, which provides that a landowner owes a duty of reasonable care to guard against any dangerous conditions on his or her property that the owner either knows about or should have discovered.

The New Jersey legislature quickly responded to this change in the law by enacted legislation that provides baseball owners with immunity when a patron is struck by a ball anywhere in the stadium. Known as the **New Jersey Baseball and Spectator Safety Act of 2005**, the legislature noted that assumption of the risk is a complete bar to suit against a baseball team owner by a spectator who suffers an injury resulting from an inherent risk of attending a professional baseball game. The owner shall remain liable, however, if warning signs are not posted that contain the following notice:

WARNING

Under New Jersey law, a spectator of professional baseball assumes the risk of any injury to person or property resulting from any of the inherent dangers and risks of such activity and may not recover from an owner of a baseball team or an owner of a stadium where professional baseball is played for injury resulting from the inherent dangers and risks of observing professional baseball, including, but not limited to, being struck by a baseball or a baseball bat.

Does the law impose a duty upon a person to go to the aid of another in a position of danger? Examples have been well documented of those who turn their backs on victims of crimes, the injured and the sick. This conduct is ethically reprehensible but there is no legal duty to help another. The law, however, does require a person who harms a third person to go to that individual's assistance. Also, a legal duty is imposed to help in those situations where a special relationship exists between the parties such as in the case of a parent and child or an employer and employee.

Must a physician, however, stop and render emergency aid to the victim of a car accident? Despite the doctor's specialized training, the answer is no. Physicians are reluctant to become involved because of their fear of being sued for malpractice. To encourage healthcare professionals to render emergency help, many states have passed **Good Samaritan statutes,** which impose liability only in the event of gross misconduct.

The following is an example of one such law:

> Any physician or other practitioner of the healing arts or any registered nurse, who happens by chance upon the scene of an emergency or who is present when an emergency occurs and who, in good faith, renders emergency care at the scene of the emergency, shall not be liable for any civil damages as a result

of any acts or omissions by such physician or practitioner or registered nurse in rendering emergency care, except any acts or omissions intentionally designed to harm or any grossly negligent acts or omissions which result in harm to the person receiving emergency care.

This limited immunity also extends to a lay person offering emergency aid if that individual possesses a current certificate evidencing the successful completion of a course in first aid or basic life support sponsored by the American National Red Cross or a similar organization. A lay person will not enjoy the protections of the Good Samaritan statutes if the emergency aid extends beyond one's specialized training. For instance, a person trained in CPR cannot perform open-heart surgery or administer intravenous drugs to regulate the rhythm of the heart.

SECTION 10.13 PROBLEM CASES

1. Witte sold his beer distributorship in 1987. His accountant prepared Witte's tax returns. However, he did not include payments on Witte's individual income tax return for which the buyer of the business was making payment to an escrow account on Witte's behalf. Nevertheless, the bank reported the payments to the Internal Revenue Services; which audited the seller in 1994. As the result of the accountant's negligent actions in 1987, Witte had to pay approximately $325,000 in taxes, penalties, and interest. At the end of 1995, Witte sued the accountant for malpractice. The accountant argued the statute of limitations as a defense to his 1987 act of negligence. That statute of limitations in South Dakota provides that an action against an accountant for malpractice must be commenced within four years after the alleged occurrence in the absence of fraudulent concealment of the negligence advice. Is this claim for the account's malpractice barred by the statute of limitations? **Witte v. Goldey, 590 N.W. 2d 266 (S.D. 1999).**

2. A family court judge ordered Jamerson to provide child support and health insurance for his minor children. The father defaulted on this obligation, so the judge ordered Jamerson's wages attached. The father's employer sent a letter to the judge indicating that the employee had no health coverage available at work. The employer also told the judge to "get a real job" and to leave the employee "alone." The judge issued a contempt citation against the employer, which charges were subsequently dismissed. The employer then sued the judge for abuse of process. The employer claimed that the judge acted outside the scope of his jurisdiction in issuing a rule to hold the employer in contempt of court since he was not a party to the underlying litigation. Will the judge be protected by the doctrine of judicial immunity? **McEacheran v. Block, 496 S.E. 2d 659 (S.C. 1998).**

3. Mrs. Hack was injured in an automobile accident while she was a passenger in a car driven by her husband. She sued her husband to collect for personal injury. The negligent spouse claimed interspousal tort immunity. Will Mr. Hack be responsible to his wife for her injuries since Pennsylvania no longer recognized the doctrine of interspousal immunity? **Hack v. Hack, 433 A.2d 859 (Pa. 1981).**

4. A father opened a window in a second-story bedroom two inches in order to increase the air circulation in the room. He then left for work with the baby sitter asleep on the couch. The child awoke, opened the window, and fell out. The parents instituted suit against the owner of the building for negligent removal of the storm window and in failing to provide a guardrail to prevent the child's fall. In turn, the owner of the building sued the parents for contribution or indemnification in the action brought on behalf of the child. In New York, a parent cannot be liable for contribution or indemnification unless the act of the parent violates a duty owed to the "world at large," or unless a dangerous instrumentality was entrusted to the child, the use of which caused injury or harm. Will the parents be held liable for the injuries sustained by the child in the New York lawsuit? **McNamara v. Banney, 672 N.Y.S. 2d 569 (N.Y. App. 1998).**

SECTION 10.14
INTERNET REFERENCES

For more information on the materials contained in this chapter, see the following internet reference:

- **http://greatspirit.earth.com/taylor.html**
  This site provides a discussion of sovereign immunity.

KEY TERMS

Assumption of the Risk
Charitable Immunity
Diplomatic Immunity
Diplomatic Relations Act
Double Jeopardy
Exculpatory Clause
Federal Torts Claim Act
Good Samaritan Statute
Governmental Function
Immunity by Contract

Intra-Family Immunity
Judicial Immunity
Proprietary Functions
Res Judicata
Sovereign Immunity
Spousal Immunity
Statute of Limitations
Workers Compensation
Vienna Convention on
Diplomatic Relations

PART THREE

ETHICS

CHAPTER 11

ETHICS AND THE LAW
BY: TERRY ANN HALBERT, ESQ.

SECTION 11.1
AN OVERVIEW
OF ETHICS

Peter Christopher is walking through a park and is attracted to the sight of a pond where children are swimming. He notices that some of the children's cries sound more like desperation than enjoyment, and soon he realizes that a child is drowning. Christopher is a trained lifeguard. Since he is on the way to a concert, and not in the mood to get his clothes wet, Christopher turns and walks away from the pond. Would he be violating the law by failing to help?

Surprisingly, the answer is no. Our legal system, which was greatly influenced by the notions of individual freedom, will not force a person to help a stranger in an emergency unless that person has somehow caused the problem in the first place or there is a special relationship between the parties, such as a parent and child. If, as in this example, an individual just happens to discover a stranger in grave danger, that person is legally allowed to continue walking without stopping to help.

This principle is probably understandable in terms of the basic principles of our legal system, which generally finds a person liable for some wrong or careless action, not for inaction, not for something they failed to do. There are also practical reasons why the law backs away from demanding a rescue in these kinds of situations: Where is the line to be drawn? Who should rescue? Is everyone who hears the child screaming responsible for jumping in the pond to help? And how much help is enough? Suppose a person cannot swim, or suppose the pond is polluted?

But beyond the law is the concept of what is right, what is **ethical**. One might believe that there are ethical reasons for trying to help the drowning child, regardless of what the law expects. In fact, this is the major difference between law and ethics: the law is about what one must do to avoid liability, while ethics is about what one should do, about "doing the right thing."

Legal and ethical responsibilities do not necessarily overlap. The "No Duty To Rescue Rule" or "American Bystander Rule" demonstrates this point. Often the ethically right decision goes beyond the expectations of the law, sometimes far beyond. The gap between law and ethics is demonstrated in the following case involving the duty owed by a victim to her assailant when she injuries or kills him in self-defense. The case also provides an overview of the law involving the duty to rescue.

419

State of Montana v. Montana Thirteenth Judicial District Court
298 Mont. 146 (Mont. 2000)

Yellowstone County Sheriff's deputies were dispatched on April 19, 1998, to the home of Bonnie Kuntz and Warren Becker to investigate a reported stabbing. When the deputies arrived at the trailer house, Becker was dead from a single stab wound to the chest.

Kuntz told the deputies that she and Becker had argued the morning of April 18, 1998. At some point during the day, both parties left the trailer home. After Kuntz returned that evening, a physical altercation ensued. The alleged facts indicate that Kuntz and Becker, who had never married but had lived together for approximately six years, were in the process of ending a stormy relationship. When Kuntz arrived at the mobile home that night, she discovered that many of her personal belongings had been destroyed and the phone ripped from the wall. Kuntz told the deputies that she then went into the kitchen and Becker physically attacked her, and at one point grabbed her by the hair, shook her, and slammed her into the stove.

Kuntz told the deputies that she could not clearly remember what happened; only that she had pushed Becker away and had then gone outside by the kitchen door to "cool off." When she thought it was safe to go back inside, she returned to the kitchen. She discovered a trail of blood leading from the kitchen through the living room and out onto the front porch where she found Becker collapsed face-down on the porch. Kuntz does not allege that she personally contacted medical or law enforcement personnel; rather, authorities were summoned by Kuntz's sister-in-law.

Kuntz was charged with negligent homicide for causing the death of Becker by stabbing him in the chest. Kuntz entered a plea of not guilty

based on the defense of justifiable use of force. Shortly before trial, the State filed amended information alleging that Kuntz caused the death of Becker by stabbing him once in the chest with a knife *and* by failing to call for medical assistance.

For criminal liability to be based upon a failure to act, there must be a duty imposed by the law to act, and the person must be physically capable of performing the act. As a starting point in our analysis, the parties have identified what is referred to as *"the American bystander rule."* This rule imposes no legal duty on a person to rescue or summon aid for another person who is at risk or in danger, even though society recognizes that a moral obligation might exist. This is true even "when that aid can be rendered without danger or inconvenience to" the potential rescuer, **Pope v. State, 284 Md. 309.** Thus, an Olympic swimmer may be deemed by the community as a shameful coward, or worse, for not rescuing a drowning child in the neighbor's pool, but she is not a criminal.

But this rule is far from absolute. Professors La Fave and Scott have identified several common-law exceptions to the American bystander rule: 1) a duty based on a personal relationship, such as parent-child or husband-wife; 2) a duty based on statute; 3) a duty based upon voluntary assumption of care; and 4) a duty based on creation of the peril. Our review of the issues presented here can accordingly be narrowed to a duty based upon a personal relationship and a duty based on creation of the peril.

One of the lead authorities on the personal relationship duty arose in **State v. Mally, 139 Mont. 599 (1961).** This Court held that a husband has a duty to summon medical aid for his wife and a breach of that duty could render him criminally liable. The facts of the case described how Kay Mally, who was suffering from terminal kidney disease, fell and fractured her arms on a Tuesday evening. Her husband, Michael Mally, put her to bed and did not summon a doctor until Thursday morning. "During this period of time, she received but one glass of water." Although his wife ultimately died of kidney failure, Mally was found guilty of involuntary manslaughter.

As for a personal relationship other than husband and wife, a duty cannot be extended to a temporary, non-family relationship. For instance, a married defendant has no duty to summon medical help for his mistress, who was staying in his house for the weekend, after she took morphine following a bout of heavy drinking and fell into a "stupor."

When a person places another in a position of danger, and then fails to safeguard or rescue that person, and the person subsequently dies as a result of this omission, such an omission may be sufficient to support criminal liability. The legal duty based on creation of the peril has been extended in other jurisdictions to cases involving self-defense.

The legal duty imposed on personal relationships and those who create peril are not absolute; i.e., there are exceptions to these exceptions. The personal relationship legal duty, for example, does not require a person to jeopardize his own life. See **State v. Walden 306 N.C. 466** (stating that although a parent has a legal duty to prevent harm to his or her child, this is not to say that parents have the legal duty to

place themselves in danger of death or great bodily harm in coming to the aid of their children).

Similarly, the law does not require that a person, who places another person in a position of peril, risk bodily injury or death in the performance of the legally imposed duty to render assistance. Therefore, where self-preservation is at stake, the law does not require a person to save the other's life by sacrificing his own.

Does one who justifiably uses deadly force in defense of her person nevertheless have a legal duty to summon aid for the mortally wounded attacker? We hold that when a person justifiably uses force to fend off an aggressor, that person has no duty to assist her aggressor in any manner that may conceivably create a risk of bodily injury or death to herself, or other persons. This absence of a duty necessarily includes any conduct that would require the person to remain in, or return to, the zone of risk created by the original aggressor. We find no authority that suggests that the law should require a person, who is justified in her use of force, to subsequently check the pulse of her attacker, or immediately dial 911, before retreating to safety.

We conclude that the victim has but one duty after fending off an attack, and that is the duty owed to one's self-as a matter of self-preservation-to seek and secure safety away from the place the attack occurred. Thus, the person who justifiably acts in self-defense is temporarily afforded the same status as the innocent bystander.

Questions for Discussion:

1. Could there have been any circumstance in this case that would have resulted in liability against Bonnie Kuntz?

2. Should the duty of rescue when a special relationship exists between the parties be limited to those of spouses and parents and children?

3. Can you think of an example of a duty created by statute to help another?

4. France requires people to go to the aid of another. What country's law do you think is better?

The Hippocratic Oath, one of the oldest documents applicable to heath care professionals, requires physicians to use their best efforts to treat and cure patients. In fact, one of the tenets provides that a doctor shall remember that he or she is a member of society, with special obligations to fellow human beings, including those of sound mind and body as well as the infirm. Does this tenet change the "No Duty to Rescue Rule" and impose a legal obligation upon a physician to help another in need of medical care? Consider the following case:

WILSON V. ATHENS-LIMESTONE HOSP.
894 SO.2D 630 (ALA. 2004)

Ms. Wilson, as mother of Starsha L. Wilson, deceased, brought a medical-malpractice action against the hospital and Dr. Bibi Teng, who was a pediatrician, employed by the hospital, alleging that Dr. Teng wrongfully caused the death of her four-year-old daughter, Starsha Wilson, by not providing proper care while Starsha was a patient in the emergency room of the hospital.

The record reveals that Starsha was diagnosed with sickle-cell anemia and Dr. Teng became Starsha's regular pediatrician. Dr. Teng had instructed Wilson to take Starsha to the emergency room and to telephone Dr. Teng whenever Starsha had a fever of 101 degrees or higher.

On the morning of May 19, 1994, Starsha's temperature was 105 degrees, so Wilson rushed Starsha to the emergency room. The emergency room nurses checked Starsha's vital signs, and Dr. Patrick Tucker, an emergency room doctor, ordered medication for pain and fever, blood work, a renal profile, and a chest X-ray.

Dr. Teng testified that as she was leaving the hospital, she was informed that Starsha was in the emergency room, and she decided to stop by on the way out of the hospital. When Dr. Teng arrived at the emergency room, she briefly talked to both Wilson and Starsha and told Wilson that she would talk to Dr. Osborn, an emergency room physician, before she left the hospital.

After briefly discussing Starsha's case with Dr. Osborn, Dr. Teng returned and told Wilson that "everything looked good" and that Dr. Osborn would take good care of Starsha. Dr. Teng also told Wilson that Starsha had a mild infection.

Dr. Osborn discharged Starsha from the hospital but Starsha returned to the emergency room in cardiac arrest. Dr. Teng returned to the emergency room and attempted to resuscitate Starsha, but was unsuccessful, and Starsha died. The cause of death was an infection, a complication of sickle-cell anemia.

Dr. Teng testified that on Starsha's first visit to the emergency room, Dr. Teng did not have a physician-patient relationship with Starsha. Dr. Teng further testified that it would have been improper for her to take over Starsha's care because Starsha was an emergency room patient and Dr. Osborn was the emergency room physician when Starsha was admitted. Dr. Osborn testified that she was Starsha's doctor on that morning and that all decisions concerning Starsha's care, including the decision to discharge Starsha, were made by her.

Liability for medical malpractice depends, first, on the existence of a duty to the patient, which, in turn depends on the existence of a physician-patient relationship creating the duty. The following is the general rule concerning the creation of a physician-patient relationship:

> A physician is under no obligation to engage in practice or to accept professional employment, but when the professional services of a physician are accepted by another person for the purposes of medical or surgical treatment, the relation of physician and patient is created. The relationship between a physician and patient may result from an express or implied contract, and the rights and liabilities of the parties

thereto are governed by the general law of contract, although the existence of the relation does not need to rest on any express contract between the physician and the person treated.

Wilson argues that Dr. Teng owed Starsha a duty to intervene in Dr. Osborn's treatment of Starsha.

In **Dodd-Anderson v. Stevens, 905 F.Supp. 937 (D. Kan.1995),** the court, under similar circumstances, held that a duty did not exist. We find the following rationale from **Dodd-Anderson** persuasive:

> This court is not persuaded by the expert's opinion that defendant had a duty to assume control of the patient's care and order her immediate transfer. The court finds that no reasonable person, applying contemporary standards, would recognize and agree that a physician has, or should have, a legal duty to unilaterally and perhaps forcibly override the medical judgment of another physician, particularly a treating physician. The list of adverse consequences to the medical community and to patients is obvious and endless and need not be elaborated upon. The result would be medical, and ultimately legal, chaos.

While there are possible factual scenarios where such a duty may exist, the specific facts of this case do not create such a duty. The undisputed facts show that Dr. Teng did not treat or diagnose Starsha during Starsha's first visit to the emergency room on the day Starsha died and did not prescribe any medication or give any medical advice on that first visit. The emergency-room doctors, Dr. Osborn and Dr. Tucker, retained control over Starsha's course of treatment at all times during that first visit. There is no evidence showing that their medical treatment of Starsha was such that Dr. Teng had a duty to override their independent medical judgment. Under these facts, we hold that as a matter of law Dr. Teng did not have a duty to intervene in Starsha's treatment by Dr. Osborn.

QUESTIONS FOR DISCUSSION:

1. Should people who are trained to rescue or assist others in emergency situations be held to a higher standard of care?

2. The Hippocratic Oath, which outlines the ethical goals of doctors, contains the following promise: "According to my power and judgment to use the medical knowledge for the benefit of those who suffer, as judged by myself to be fair, and to avoid from doing any harm or injustice." Did Dr. Teng violate the Hippocratic Oath?

All states contain Good Samaritan statutes that protect people who are medically trained from being held liable in an emergency rescue should they decide to help. These laws, however, do not demand that the medically-trained offer assistance in these situations. Today a doctor may decide to "walk on by," unless she or he is already treating the patient, or is on duty in a medical facility offering treatment.

Over the years, a few exceptions to the "No Duty to Rescue Rule" have developed. There is the "Special Relationship" exception: between members of a family, between employers and employees, between providers of public transportation and passengers, or between owners of business and their customers, for instance, the law insists on a reasonable attempt at assistance in an emergency. So, if the person in the park was a father who was hearing his own drowning daughter's screams, he would have a duty to take reasonable steps to help her.

SECTION 11.2
ETHICAL THEORIES

If ethics is about choosing the right behavior, the moral way to live one's life, how does society achieve this goal? There are many different ethical beliefs individuals can hold. Abortion is just one example of an issue that separates people who have very strong but completely opposite ethical beliefs. And in a multicultural society, doesn't it become even more difficult to decide on one single ethically correct position? Who is to say which personal or cultural ethical standard is correct or is there a universal ethic?

For centuries, human beings have struggled to determine the answers to these types of questions. Within Western civilization, two major philosophical theories about ethics have evolved:

1. **Utilitarian Theory:** Focuses on the consequences—both short and long term—of any particular action for all individuals affected. Benefits and harms are balanced against one another, to determine which action produces the most happiness for the greatest number of people.

2. **Rights Theory:** Concerned with the reasons for action, not just the results. People have certain basic rights—the right to life, freedom of expression, privacy, for instance—that are of value in themselves and must be protected. This theory also includes the notion of "Universality:" Whatever we choose to do must be behavior we would be willing to have done to everyone, including to ourselves—a version of the Golden Rule.

Sometimes these two theories serve the same purpose. For example, a student who sees another student cheating on an exam employs her freedom of expression to alert the professor. Not only has she acted for ethical reasons — the Rights Theory — but she has come to the aid of the rest of the class, who benefit by having their grades accurately measured. Thus, she has also acted in accordance with the Utilitarian Theory, the greatest good (better grades) for the greatest number (the rest of the class).

Occasionally, however, the two theories are diametrically opposed to each other. The classic example is slavery, where a minority of the population is enslaved, but the rest of society benefited economically. Before the Civil War, the economy of the Southern states prospered, providing the greatest good to the greatest number and satisfying the Utilitarian Theory. But the Rights Theory suffered, since human beings were enslaved, prevented from enjoying the same rights as the other members of society.

Can you think of other examples where the two philosophies go hand-in-hand? How about situations where they diverge? Consider these examples when you work on the following problem.

PARK, BROWN & SMITH, P.C.
ATTORNEYS AT LAW
M E M O R A N D U M

TO: All Law Clerks

FROM: Peter Smith, Esquire

RE: Kathy Roberts and Eastcoast Airlines

Kathy Roberts decided to obtain a job in order to prove that she has finally grown up. To her credit, she landed a position in the real estate department of Eastcoast Airlines.

Eastcoast has tried to diversify by acquiring a number of properties in Florida. Eastcoast Airlines, like so many of its competitors, has been suffering substantial losses in the years since airline deregulation, and has a negative cash flow. Unless the company could control its high labor costs and increase its popularity with the flying public, bankruptcy is a possibility. Kathy's boss, Robert Stingle sees selling off the Florida properties, as an important way of alleviating the company's financial crisis.

Kathy contacted Silvertooth, Inc., a developer of nursing homes, about the Florida properties and found an interested buyer. The corporation thought that one of the parcels would be perfect for a retirement villa and would feature elaborate walking trails and outdoor recreational facilities.

Eastcoast had conducted a full environmental audit of the property six months earlier, and no problems were revealed. A copy of the report was given to a Silvertooth representative who also examined the property and discovered no problems.

As negotiations progressed with Silvertooth, Kathy was approached by one of her friends at Eastcoast, Steve Flame. He told Kathy that there is highly toxic waste on the property that she is attempting to transfer to Silvertooth, Inc. The person who told Steve about the situation was recently in Florida at the site, and had found several buried metal containers marked "Danger! Biohazard. Radioactive medical waste." The containers were cracked and liquid was seeping out onto the ground. Steve said he wanted Kathy to know about the dangerous condition because he is concerned that innocent people could be harmed if the sale goes through.

Kathy contacted her boss, but before she could mention the containers, Stingle told her it is vital that the sale be closed quickly, and that their jobs depend on it. Kathy consulted with a lawyer who explained that Florida law does not require disclosure of hazardous substances on commercial property so long as there hasn't been a fraudulent misstatement about the condition of the property.

Kathy is very upset. She knows that Silvertooth is considering other similar properties, and if she mentions the toxic spill problem to the potential buyer, they will back out of the sale. Kathy also realizes that she will never deal with Silvertooth again since Eastcoast didn't own any other property that is suitable for a retirement community.

Although there appears to be no legal consequences if Kathy says nothing, and allows the sale to go through, from an ethical perspective the situation might be different. Write an advisory memo to Kathy on the ethics of the choice she must make, "To Disclose or Not To Disclose?"

1. First apply the Utilitarian Theory. Who are the people affected by Kathy's decision? What choice would result in "the greatest good for the greatest number?"

2. Now do the analysis from the Rights Theory perspective. What rights do the various affected individuals and groups have in this situation? How do they weigh against one another? What would be the result if Kathy thinks about the Golden Rule?

3. Finally, summarize your own ethical opinion: If you were in Kathy's shoes, what would you do, and why?

ANSWER SHEET
PROBLEM ELEVEN—A

Name   **Please Print Clearly**

1. First apply the Utilitarian Theory. Who are the people affected by Kathy's decision? What choice would probably result in "the greatest good for the greatest number?"

_____

_____

_____

_____

_____

_____

_____

_____

2. Now do the analysis from the Rights Theory perspective. What rights do the various affected individuals and groups have in this situation? How do they weigh against one another? What would be the result if Kathy thinks about the Golden Rule?

_____

_____

_____

_____

_____

_____

_____

_____

3. Finally, summarize your own ethical opinion: If you were in Kathy's shoes, what would you do, and why?

_____

_____

_____

_____

_____

_____

_____

_____

_____

_____

_____

_____

_____

_____

_____

_____

_____

_____

_____

_____

_____

SECTION 11.4
THE WHISTLEBLOWER

Suppose Kathy decides to warn Silvertooth about the hazardous waste and the deal falls through. Kathy feels good about this outcome, but not so good when she discovers that she has been fired. Since all her other work for Eastcoast has been highly commended, Ms. Roberts believes she was fired in retaliation for letting the toxic cat out of the bag. (Under the federal "Superfund" law, Eastcoast as owner of the property will be responsible for paying for the clean up of the site.)

Kathy is a **whistleblower,** a person who feels compelled to get certain information into the hands of the people who can act to correct a problem, when it seems that the problem won't be corrected otherwise. When employees "blow the whistle," they might tell a superior, or they might go outside their company and tell government authorities, or even the media.

There is no one exact definition of a whistleblower. As the court noted in **Winters v. Houston Chronicle Pub. Co., 795 S.W.2d 723 (Tex. 1990),** a whistleblower is the person who sounds the alarm "when wrongdoing occurs on his or her beat, which is usually within a large organization." Another definition is set forth in a report co-edited by Ralph Nader in which it was said that whistleblowing is "the act of a man or woman who, believing that the public interest overrides the interest of the organization he serves, publicly blows the whistle if the organization is involved in corrupt, illegal, fraudulent, or harmful activity." *Whistle Blowing: The Report of the Conference on Professional Responsibility*, R. Nader, P. Petkas & K. Blackwell, eds. 1972.

What are Kathy's legal rights in this situation? She may have none. Unless she has an employment contract with Eastcoast for a certain stated time period, she is an **employee at will**. (Most employees fall into this category.) Generally speaking, an employer can fire at-will employees at any time for any reason, or for no reason at all, unless the reason violates a statute, such as a law against discrimination on the basis of race, gender, age, or handicap. Kathy might also be protected if she was part of the 14 percent of American workers who belong to a union. She could then argue she was fired in violation of a collective bargaining agreement between her union and her employer. (A union contract generally provides that workers cannot be fired unless for "just cause.)" Finally, some state and federal laws protect whistleblow-ers who report violations of those laws to the government. For instance, Congress passed the **Whistleblower Protection Act of 1989** in order to strengthen and improve the protections of federal employees who report fraud, waste, abuse and unnecessary expenditures within the government. The Act, however, does not allow an employee to file a lawsuit for retaliation by a supervisor. Instead, the worker must pursue an administrative remedy that is usually administered by the U. S. Department of Labor. A number of states have also passed laws protecting the whistleblower. For instance, Pennsylvania has enacted the **Whistleblower's Law** which provides that no employer may discharge, or otherwise retaliate against an employee because the employee makes a good faith report or is about to report to the employer or appropriate authority, an instance of wrongdoing or waste. A person who alleges a violation of this Act may bring a civil action within 180 days after the occurrence of the alleged violation. **43 P. S. §1421.** The Superfund law, for example, would protect Kathy if she had gone straight to the Environmental Protection Agency with news about the spill. Since she told Silvertooth, she may not be protected.

Why does the law give so much freedom to employers to hire and fire workers as they see fit? Is "employment at will" a fair rule? How should society strike a balance between an employer's right to control and an employee's right to bring ethical concerns forward without fear of retaliation? Consider these issues as you read **Geary v. United States Steel Corporation.** In it, the Pennsylvania Supreme Court deals with the tort of "wrongful discharge," which would hold an employer responsible for firing an employee in a way that violates public policy. The case is one of first impression.

George Geary v. United States Steel Corporation
319 A.2d 174 (Pa. Super. 1974)

The complaint avers that appellant, George Geary, was continuously employed by appellee, United States Steel Corporation from 1953 until July 13, 1967, when he was dismissed from his position. Geary's duties involved the sale of tubular products to the oil and gas industry. His employment was at will. The dismissal is said to have stemmed from a disagreement concerning one of the company's new products, a tubular casing designed for use under high pressure. Geary alleges that he believed the product had not been adequately tested and constituted a serious danger to anyone who used it; that he voiced his misgivings to his superiors and was ordered to "follow directions," which he agreed to do; that he nevertheless continued to express his reservations, taking his case to a vice-president in charge of sale of the product; that as a result of his efforts the prod-

uct was reevaluated and withdrawn from the market; that he at all times performed his duties to the best of his ability and always acted with the best interests of the company and the general public in mind; and that because of these events he was summarily discharged without notice. Geary asserts that the company's conduct in so acting was "wrongful, malicious and abusive."

[Geary] candidly admits that he is beckoning us into uncharted territory. No court in this Commonwealth has ever recognized a nonstatutory cause of action for an employer's termination of an at-will employment relationship. Pennsylvania law is in accordance with the weight of authority elsewhere. Absent a statutory or contractual provision to the contrary, the law has taken for granted the power of either party to terminate an employment relationship for any or no reason.

We recognize that economic conditions have changed radically since [the turn of the century, when employment at will was first established.] The huge corporate enterprises which have emerged in this century wield an awesome power over their employees.

Against the background of these changes, the broad question to which [Geary] invites our attention is whether the time has come to impose judicial restrictions on an employer's power of discharge. [His] argument is an appeal to considerations of public policy. Geary asserts in his complaint that he was acting in the best interests of the general public as well as of his employer in opposing the marketing of a product which he believed to be defective. Certainly, the potential for abuse of an employer's power of dismissal is particularly serious where an employee must exercise independent, expert judgment in matters of product safety, but Geary does not hold himself out as this sort of employee. So far as the complaint shows, he was involved only in the sale of company products. There is no suggestion that he possessed any expert qualifications, or that his duties extended to making judgments in matters of product safety. In essence, Geary argues that his conduct should be protected because his intentions were good. No doubt most employees who are dismissed from their posts can make the same claim. We doubt that establishing a right to litigate every such case as it arises would operate either in the best interest of the parties or of the public.

Given the rapidity of change in corporate personnel in the areas of employment not covered by labor agreements, suits like the one at bar could well be expected to place a heavy burden on our judicial system in terms of both an increased case load. Of greater concern is the possible impact of such suits on the legitimate interest of employers in hiring and retaining the best personnel available. The ever-present threat of suit might well inhibit the making of critical judgments by employers concerning employee qualifications.

The problem extends beyond the question of individual competence, for even an unusually gifted person may be of no use to his employer if he cannot work effectively with fellow employees. Here, for example, Geary's complaint shows that he by-passed his immediate superiors and pressed his views on higher officers, utilizing his close contacts with a company vice president. The praiseworthiness of Geary's motives does not detract from the company's legitimate interest in preserving its normal operational procedures from disruption. In sum, while we agree that employees should be encouraged to express their educated views on the quality of their employer's products, we are not persuaded that creating a new non-statutory cause of action of the sort proposed by appellant is the best way to achieve this result. On balance, whatever public policy imperatives can be discerning here seem to militate against such a course.

It may be granted that there are areas of an employee's life in which his employer has no legitimate interest. An intrusion into one of these areas by virtue of the employer's power of discharge might plausibly give rise to a cause of action, particularly where some recognized facet of public policy is threatened. But this case does not require us to define in comprehensive fashion the perimeters of this privilege, and we decline to do so. We hold only that where the complaint itself discloses a plausible and legitimate reason for terminating an at-will employment relationship and no clear mandate of public policy is violated thereby, an employee at will has no right of action against his employer for wrongful discharge.

Questions for Discussion:

1. What are the reasons for the court's decision?

2. Would the case have turned out differently if the tubular casings Geary was worried about were being manufactured in violation of federal safety regulations?

3. Do you agree with the court's decision?

Partly in response to this case, the Pennsylvania legislature passed the following law on whistle-blowing:

> No employer may discharge, threaten or otherwise discriminate or retaliate against an employee regarding the employee's compensation, terms, conditions, location of privileges of employment because the employee...makes a good faith report or is about to report, verbally or in writing, to the employer or appropriate authority an instance of wrongdoing or waste.

> It shall be a defense to an action under this section if the defendant proves...that the action taken by the employer occurred for separate and legitimate reasons, which are not merely pretextual.

Here are some of the definitions of terms used in Pennsylvania's whistleblower law:

Appropriate authority: A federal, state or local government body, agency or organization.

Employee: A person who performs a service for wages or other remuneration under a contract of hire, written oral, for a public body.

Good faith report: A report of conduct defined in this act as wrongdoing or waste which is made without malice or consideration of personal benefit and which the person making the report has reasonable cause to believe is true.

Waste: An employer's conduct or omissions which result in substantial abuse, misuse, destruction or loss of funds or resources belonging to or derived from Commonwealth or political subdivision sources.

Wrongdoing: A violation that is not of a merely technical or minimal nature of a federal or state statute or regulation or of a code of conduct or ethics designed to protect the interest of the public or the employer.

Questions for Discussion:

1. Considering the definitions as well as the body of the law, would Kathy Roberts be protected for telling Silvertooth about the toxic spill? Why or why not? Would George Geary be protected?

2. Write your own version of a whistleblower law.

**SECTION 11.5
ETHICS, LAW
AND PRIVACY**

It may be granted that there are areas of an employee's life in which his employer has no legitimate interest. An intrusion into one of these areas by virtue of the employer's power of discharge might plausibly give rise to a cause of action, particularly where some recognized facet of public policy is threatened.

—**Pennsylvania Supreme Court**
Geary v. U.S. Steel

As the Court in **Geary** suggests, there are times when an employer's power to control its employees is in danger of stretching too far. For instance, should an employer have the right to insist that none of its employees smoke cigarettes? Consider the following statistics. The Centers for Disease Control and Prevention estimates that 44.5 million people in this country smoke cigarettes even though this habit will result in the death or disability of half of all continuing smokers. In fact, the economic burden of tobacco use is staggering with more than $75 billion per year being spent in medical care and another $92 billion per year resulting from lost productivity. As for secondhand smoke exposure, it causes heart disease and lung cancer in non-smoking adults and non-smokers who are exposed to smoke at work or at home increase their risk of heart disease by at least 25%. Research also shows that smokers have a 50 percent greater absentee rate and produce 50 percent higher medical costs. But does this mean that an employer should be able to screen out and refuse to hire smokers, or fire them if they refuse to stop? And if these practices are allowed, what is to stop employers from insisting that employees change other expensive, unhealthy personal habits? What if a worker has a high cholesterol count, or is obese? Assuming that people who get regular exercise and eat sensibly are healthy and will produce fewer medical expenses, should an employer be able to insist that its workers eat salads for lunch and use a gym three times a week?

These are some of the questions raised by the conflict between employee privacy rights and an employer's interest in controlling its operations. There is also the question of testing. Workers with AIDS will end up with horrendous medical and insurance expenses: Therefore should employers be allowed to test their workers for the AIDS virus? (This is illegal under the Americans with Disabilities Act of 1990.) These types of issues were put to the test when Weyco, Inc, a Michigan firm specializing in employee benefit plans, informed their workers that as of January 1, 2005 anyone testing positive on nicotine testing would be fired. Not only would an employee be discharged if he or she was caught smoking at work, but the no-smoking policy also applied to employees who smoked while off of the job. While it is true that an employer may pay higher insurance costs because of the adverse consequences of smoking, should an employer be allowed to regulate what a worker does while home? According to the American Civil Liberties Union of Michigan, this practice is lawful since the state has no law barring employers from regulating employee practices outside of the office. As reported by *The Detroit News,* state and federal civil rights laws prohibit job action based upon color, age, gender, national origin and religion. Smoking, however, does not fall within one of these protected classes so an employer can enforce what it considers to be desirable traits and skills in the work place.

At the current time, a small group of states, including Florida, California, Massachusetts, Delaware and New York have enacted legislation banning smoking in the work place.

SECTION 11.6
DRUG TESTING

Illegal drug use is tremendously expensive. In 1988, the government estimated it to be a $100 billion drain on our economy, and employers can expect that drug use cost them plenty in terms of absenteeism, lower productivity, injuries and theft. Yet does this mean employers should be allowed to force their workers to undergo urinalysis testing for illegal drugs?

Drug testing in the workplace had its inception in 1986 when President Regan initiated such a program among federal employees. The President stated that the Federal government, as the largest employer in the Nation, is concerned with the well-being of its employees, the successful accomplishment of agency missions, and the need to maintain employee productivity. The Executive Order also required that federal employees refrain from the use of illegal drugs whether on or off duty and provided that the head of each Executive agency shall establish a program to test for the use of illegal drugs by employees in sensitive positions. Since this initiative, drug testing has become firmly embedded in the work place both inside and outside of the government and three types of programs have emerged: pre-employment screening, random drug testing and post-incident drug testing. The following materials highlight some of the issues with drug testing in the work place.

PAUL LUEDTKE V. NABORS ALASKA DRILLING, INC.
834 P.2D 1220 (ALASKA 1992)

COMPTON, Justice

This case addresses one aspect of drug testing by employers. A private employer, Nabors Alaska Drilling, Inc. [Nabors], established a drug testing program for its employees. Paul Luedtke worked on drilling rigs on the North Slope [and] refused to submit to urinalysis screening for drug use as required by Nabors. As a result [he was] fired.

Luedtke began working for Nabors, which operates drilling rigs on Alaska's North Slope, in February 1978. [He] began as a "floorman" and was eventually promoted to "driller." A driller oversees the work of an entire drilling crew. Luedtke started work with Nabors as a union member, initially being hired from the union hall. During his tenure, however, Nabors "broke" the union. Luedtke continued to work without a union contract. He had no written contract with Nabors at the time of his discharge.

During his employment with Nabors, Luedtke was accused twice of violating the company's drug and alcohol policies. Once he was suspended for 90 days for taking alcohol to the North Slope. The other incident involved a search of the rig on which Luedtke worked. Aided by dogs trained to sniff out marijuana, the searchers found traces of marijuana on Luedtke's suitcase. Luedtke was allowed to continue working on the rig only after assuring his supervisors he did not use marijuana.

In October 1982, Luedtke scheduled a two-week vacation. Because his normal work schedule was two weeks of work on the North Slope followed by a week off, a two-week vacation amounted to 28 consecutive days away from

work. Just prior to his vacation, he was instructed to arrange for a physical examination in Anchorage. He arranged for it to take place on October 19, during his vacation. It was at this examination that Nabors first tested Paul's urine for signs of drug use. The purpose of the physical, as understood by Luedtke, was to enable him to work on offshore rigs should Nabors receive such contracts. Although Luedtke was told it would be a comprehensive physical he had no idea that a urinalysis screening test for drug use would be performed. He did voluntarily give a urine sample but assumed it would be tested only for "blood sugar, any kind of kidney failure [and] problems with bleeding." Nabors' policy of testing for drug use was not announced until November 1, 1982, almost two weeks after Luedtke's examination.

[On] November 16, Luedtke received a letter informing him that his urine had tested positive for cannabinoids. The letter informed him that he would be required to pass two subsequent urinalysis tests, one on November 30 and the other on December 30, before he would be allowed to return to work. In response Luedtke hand delivered a letter drafted by his attorney to the Manager of Employee Relations for Nabors, explaining why he felt the testing and suspension were unfair. Luedtke did not take the urinalysis test on November 30 as requested by Nabors. On December 14, Nabors sent Luedtke a letter informing him that he was discharged for refusing to take the test on November 30.

The right to privacy is a recent creation of American law. The inception of this right is generally credited to a law review article published in 1890 by Louis Brandeis and his law partner, Samuel Warren. They wrote:

Recent inventions...call attention to the next step which must be taken for the protection of the person, and for securing to the individual ...the right "to be let alone." Instantaneous photographs and newspaper enterprise have invaded the sacred precincts of private and domestic life; and numerous mechanical devices threaten to make good the prediction that "what is whispered in the closet shall be proclaimed from the housetops."

While the legal grounds of this right were somewhat tenuous in the 1890's, American jurists found the logic of Brandeis and Warren's arguments compelling. By 1960, Professor Prosser could write that "the right of privacy, in one form or another, is declared to exist by the overwhelming majority of the American courts." He cited cases in which private parties had been held liable in tort for eavesdropping on private conversations by means of wiretapping and microphones, or for peering into the windows of homes. Eventually the right to privacy attained sufficient recognition to be incorporated in several state constitutions.

Interpreting the Constitution of the United States, the United States Supreme Court in 1965 held that a Connecticut statute banning the use of birth control devices by married couples was "repulsive to the notions of privacy surrounding the marriage relationship." **Griswold v. Connecticut, 381 U.S. 479, 486 (1965).** The Supreme Court wrote that "specific guarantees in the Bill of Rights have penumbras, formed by emanations from those guarantees that help give them life and substance. Various guarantees create zones of privacy..." Since Griswold the Supreme Court has found the federal constitutional right of privacy to apply a number of other situations. **Roe v. Wade, 410 U.S. 113 (1973)** (right of privacy broad enough to encompass a woman's decision whether or not to terminate her pregnancy); **Eisenstadt v. Baird, 405 U.S. 438 (1972)** (regulation which made contraceptives less available to unmarried than married couples invalidated). But see **Bowers v. Hardwick, 478 U.S. 186 (1986)** (due process clause of Fourteenth Amendment does not confer any fundamental right on homosexuals to engage in acts of consensual sodomy).

Thus, the concept of privacy has become pervasive in modern legal thought. But a clear definition of this right...has eluded both courts and legal scholars. It is the fundamental nature of the concept that leads to such great difficulty in application.

The next question we address is whether a public policy exists protecting an employee's right to withhold certain "private" information from his employer.

We believe such a policy does exist, and is evidenced in the common law, statutes and constitution of this state. Alaska law clearly evidences strong support for the public interest in employee privacy. First, state statutes support the policy that there are private sectors of employee's lives not subject to direct scrutiny by their employers. For example, employers may not require employees to take polygraph tests as a condition of employment. In addition, Alaska Statute 18.80.200(a) provides:

> It is determined and declared as a matter of legislative finding that discrimination against an inhabitant of the state because of race, religion, color, national origin, age, sex, marital status, changes in marital status, pregnancy, or parenthood is a matter of public concern and that this discrimination not only threatens the rights and privileges of the inhabitants of the state but also menaces the institutions of the state and threatens peace, order, health, safety and general welfare of the state and its in-

habitants. [It is] unlawful for employers to inquire into such topics in connection with prospective employment. Second, as previously noted, Alaska's constitution contains a right to privacy clause. Third, there exists a common law right to privacy.

[T]here is a sphere of activity in every person's life that is closed to scrutiny by others. The boundaries of that sphere are determined by balancing a person's right to privacy against other public policies, such as "the health, safety, rights and privileges of others." Luedtke claim[s] that whether or not [he] use[s] marijuana is information within that protected sphere into which his employer, Nabors, may not intrude. We disagree. As we have previously observed, marijuana can impair a person's ability to function normally.

We also observe that work on an oil rig can be very dangerous. We have determined numerous cases involving serious injury or death resulting from accidents on oil drilling rigs. In addition, the trial court expressly considered the dangers of work on oil rigs.

Where the public policy supporting Luedtke's privacy in off-duty activities conflicts with the public policy supporting the protection of the health and safety of other workers, and even Luedtke himself, the health and safety concerns are paramount. As a result, Nabors is justified in determining whether Luedtke is possibly impaired on the job by drug usage off the job.

We observe, however, that the employer's prerogative does have limitations. First, the drug test must be conducted at a time reasonably contemporaneous with the employee's work time. The employer's interest is in monitoring drug use that may directly affect employee performance. The employer's interest is not in the broader police function of discovering and con-

trolling the use of illicit drugs in general society. In the context of this case, Nabors could have tested Luedtke immediately prior to [his] departure for the North Slope, or immediately upon his return from the North Slope when the test could be reasonably certain of detecting drugs consumed there. Further, given Nabors' need to control the oil rig community, Nabors could have tested him at any time he was on the North Slope.

Second, an employee must receive notice of the adoption of a drug testing program. By requiring a test, an employer introduces an additional term of employment. An employee should have notice of the additional term so that he may contest it, refuse to accept it and quit, seek to negotiate its conditions, or prepare for the test so that he will not fail it and thereby suffer sanctions.

These considerations do not apply with regard to the tests Luedtke refused to take. Luedtke was given notice of the future tests. He did not take the test on November 30. As a result, Nabors was justified in discharging him.

The Problem of the False Positive

Both employers and employees share at least one concern: whether or not urinalysis is a reliable means of uncovering drug use. Employees are concerned over the accuracy of drug testing since they may be hired or fired on the basis of results. Employers are interested because they don't want to waste time and money ferreting out innocent workers, only to spend more time and money replacing them.

There are many serious reliability problems. Certain over-the-counter drugs may register as illegal ones. Test results on people using the familiar cold remedies Contac or Sudafed have (wrongly) indicated that they were on amphetamines. The pain relievers Datril and Advil have shown up as marijuana, and cough syrups containing dextromethorphan may register as opiate traces. False positives can be produced in the oddest ways: A person with the disease lupus (in remission) might appear to be taking amphetamines. A person who had ingested poppy seeds just before urinalysis might seem to have opium in his system. Research indicates that "passive inhalation" can also cause positive results. In other words, a person could test as a marijuana user, not because of actually smoking the drug, but because of being at a concert, a party, or on a bus where it was smoked.

How often are these mistakes made? The testing laboratories assert that the most commonly used procedures are 95-99 percent accurate. At best, then, the industry itself claims an inaccuracy rate of 1 percent. But since 4 to 5 million people are tested annually, 40,000 to 50,000 people must be falsely accused each year.

Perhaps most telling are the results of a 1987 study performed by the National Institute on Drug Abuse, which found that 20 percent of the 50 laboratories tested reported the presence of drugs in urine specimens when no drugs were present. These mistakes were made even though each laboratory had been warned in advance that its competence was about to be evaluated by the federal government.[1]

TEST REVELATIONS

Urinalysis picks up traces of certain substances in the blood. Although drug testing cannot tell an employer whether an employee was "high" while at work (it measures the presence of a substance, not the time it was ingested), it can reveal that the employee had used marijuana sometime during the past few weeks. Some substances linger in the body longer than others: drug tests can reveal that the subject smoked one marijuana cigarette as many as 81 days earlier, while cocaine traces will be undetectable after 2-3 days, and evidence of alcohol will be flushed from the body within a half day.

Urine tests can also reveal extraneous information—whether a worker is pregnant, or is taking medication for a heart condition, asthma, epilepsy, diabetes, or manic depression, for example.

CONTROL OF PERSONAL INFORMATION

Privacy is not just a matter of minimizing the amount of information known about a person. It also involves control over that information. Employees worry that the confidentiality of test results is not guaranteed. Will they become part of a permanent, computerized file, accessible to any number of people? Will a worker be blacklisted because of a false positive, and never know why his or her career was stagnating?

SECTION 11.7
THE DRUG TESTING
OF TONY ROBERTS

PROBLEM ELEVEN—B

PARK, BROWN & SMITH, P.C.
ATTORNEYS AT LAW
M E M O R A N D U M

To: All Law Clerks

FROM: Peter Smith, Esquire

RE: Tony's Drug Testing Problem

In the middle of the season with the Stallions, Tony Roberts took a short vacation during the team's off week and returned to Philadelphia. He spent Saturday night with an old girlfriend. They had dinner and went dancing at the Aztec Club on the waterfront. One thing led to another, and he spent the night at her apartment. The next day, it all seemed like a dream. Tony had spent much of the previous night high on something that she had given him to smoke. But it was Sunday, and he had to return to the Stallions.

The player arrived at practice on Monday, and the coach greeted the team with a stack of small, plastic specimen cups. "I hate to surprise you guys," said the coach, "But life can be surprising." Tony realized that he and his teammates were expected to produce a urine sample while the assistant coaches looked on. Tony felt embarrassed—but he also felt scared. Therefore, he refused the test and the team suspended him. Read **"Luedtke v. Nabors Alaska Drilling Company"** and the materials about drug testing and answer the following questions:

1. What are the chances that Tony will show "positive" results from the urinalysis test?

2. If Tony does test positive and is fired from the team, would he win a lawsuit for wrongful discharge?

3. What ethical issues are raised here and what do you think is fair in this situation?

ANSWER SHEET
PROBLEM ELEVEN—B

Name   **Please Print Clearly**

1. What are the chances that Tony will show "positive" results from the urinalysis test?

2. If Tony does test positive and is fired from the team, would he win a lawsuit for wrongful discharge?

3. What ethical issues are raised here and what do you think is fair in this situation?

_____

_____

_____

_____

_____

_____

_____

_____

_____

_____

_____

_____

_____

_____

_____

_____

_____

_____

_____

_____

SECTION 11.8
SEXUAL HARASSMENT

In 1964 Congress passed comprehensive Civil Rights legislation including this excerpt, known as **Title VII**:

a. It shall be an unlawful employment practice for an employer:

1. to fail or refuse to hire or to discharge any individual, or otherwise to discriminate against any individual with respect to his compensation, terms, conditions, or privileges of employment because of such individual's race, color, religion, sex, or national origin.

The statute itself outlaws discrimination in broad, general language. The job of clarifying the statute by providing detailed examples of illegal discrimination is left to an administrative agency. In the case of Title VII, that government agency is the **Equal Employment Opportunity Commission** (EEOC), created by Congress to interpret and enforce the employment provisions of the Civil Rights Law.

In 1980, the EEOC adopted the following guidelines:

a. Harassment on the basis of sex consists of unwelcome sexual advances, requests for sexual favors, and other verbal or physical conduct of a sexual nature and will constitute sexual harassment when:

1. submission to such conduct is made either explicitly or implicitly a term or condition of an individual's employment,

2. submission to or rejection of such conduct by an individual is used as the basis for employment decisions affecting such individual, or

3. such conduct has the purpose or effect of unreasonably interfering with an individual's work performance or creating an intimidating, hostile, or offensive working environment.

b. In determining whether alleged conduct constitutes sexual harassment, the Commission will look at the record as a whole and at the totality of the circumstances, such as the nature of the sexual advances and the context in which the alleged incidents occurred. The determination of the legality of a particular action will be made from the facts, on a case by case basis.

c. An employer is responsible for its acts and those of its agents and supervisory employees with respect to sexual harassment regardless of whether the specific acts complained of were authorized or even forbidden by the employer and regardless of whether the employer knew or should have known of their occurrence. (In its first sexual harassment case, the Supreme Court in 1986 made it clear that in cases of "hostile environment" sexual harassment an employer would only be held responsible if he knew or should have known about the harassment.)

d. With respect to conduct between fellow employees, an employer is responsible for acts of sexual harassment in the workplace where the employer (or its agents or supervisory employees) knows or should have known of the conduct, unless it can show that it took immediate and appropriate corrective action.

e. Prevention is the best tool for the elimination of sexual harassment. An employer should take all steps necessary to prevent sexual harassment from occurring, such as affirmatively raising the subject, expressing strong disapproval, developing appropriate sanctions informing employees of their right to raise and how to raise the issue of harassment under Title VII, and developing methods to sensitize all concerned.

TYPES OF SEXUAL HARASSMENT

Courts have identified two kinds of sexual harassment. The first, called **quid pro quo** (or "tangible benefit loss") happens when an employee is expected to give into sexual demands or suffer the loss of some specific job benefit: a raise, a promotion, or even the job itself. Quid pro quo harassment would exist where a woman is fired for refusing to go on a date with her supervisor, for example.

The other kind of harassment, labelled **hostile environment**, involves less specific consequences. It occurs, for example, when a woman is constantly subjected to sexual harangues and obscenities in her workplace, or when she must repeatedly refuse unwanted sexual advances from her supervisor. Although she suffers no economic loss, she is a victim of discrimination because she must put up with a down-graded work atmosphere, pervaded with unpleasantness.

This second type of harassment has proved to be complicated: How offensive must the environment be to justify a complaint of sexual harassment? What factors should a court take into account in considering whether or not a particular workplace is so hostile to women that it discriminates against them? The next case provides contrasting views on hostile environment sexual harassment.

Vivienne Rabidue v. Osceola Refining Co.
805 F.2d 611 (6th Cir. 1986)

KRUPANSKY, Circuit Judge

The plaintiff was a capable, independent, ambitious, aggressive, intractable, and opinionated individual. The plaintiff's supervisors and co-employees with whom plaintiff interacted almost uniformly found her to be an abrasive, rude, antagonistic, extremely willful, uncooperative, and irascible personality. She consistently argued with co-workers and company customers in defiance of supervisory direction and jeopardized Osceola's business relationships with major oil companies. She disregarded supervisory instruction and company policy whenever such direction conflicted with her personal reasoning and conclusions. In sum, the plaintiff was a troublesome employee.

The plaintiff's charged sexual harassment arose primarily as a result of her unfortunate acrimonious working relationship with Douglas Henry. Henry was a supervisor of the company's key punch and computer section. Occasionally, the plaintiff's duties required coordination with Henry's department and personnel, although Henry exercised no supervisory authority over the plaintiff nor the plaintiff over him. Henry was an extremely vulgar and crude individual who customarily made obscene comments about women generally, and on occasion, directed such obscenities to the plaintiff. Management was aware of Henry's vulgarity but had been unsuccessful in curbing his offensive personality traits during the time encompassed by this controversy. The plaintiff and Henry, on the occasions when their duties exposed them to each other, were constantly in a confrontational posture. The plaintiff, as well as other female employees, were annoyed by Henry's vulgarity. In addi-

tion to Henry's obscenities, other male employees from time to time displayed pictures of nude or scantily clad women in their offices and/or work areas, to which the plaintiff and other women employees were exposed.

[T]o prove a claim of abusive work environment premised upon sexual harassment, a plaintiff must demonstrate that she would not have been the object of harassment but for her sex. It is of significance to note that instances of complained sexual conduct that prove equally offensive to male and female workers would not support a Title VII sexual harassment charge because both men and women were accorded like treatment.

[S]exually hostile or intimidating environments are characterized by multiple and varied combinations and frequencies of offensive exposures which require the plaintiff to demonstrate that injury resulted not from a single or isolated offensive incident, comment, or conduct, but from incidents, comments or conduct which occurred with some frequency. To accord appropriate protection to both plaintiffs and defendants in a hostile and/or abusive work environment sexual harassment case, the trier of fact, when judging the totality of the circumstances impacting upon the asserted abusive and hostile environment must adopt the perspective of a reasonable person's reaction to a similar environment under essentially like or similar circumstances. Thus, in the absence of conduct which would interfere with that hypothetical reasonable individual's work performance and affect seriously the psychological well-being of that reasonable person under like circumstances, a plaintiff may not prevail. The plaintiff must also demonstrate that she was actually offended by the defendant's conduct and that she suffered some degree of injury as a result of the abusive and hostile work environment.

The trier of fact should also consider such objective and subjective factors as the nature of the alleged harassment, the background and experience of the plaintiff, her co-workers and supervisors, the totality of the physical environment of the workplace both before and after the plaintiff's introduction into its environs, coupled with the reasonable expectation of the plaintiff upon voluntarily entering that environment. As Judge Newblatt aptly stated in his opinion in the district court:

> Indeed, it cannot seriously be disputed that in some work environments, humor and language are rough hewn and vulgar. Sexual jokes, sexual conversation and girlie magazines may abound. Title VII was not meant to—or can—change this. It must never be forgotten that Title VII is the federal court mainstay in the struggle for equal employment opportunity for the female workers of America. But it is quite different to claim that Title VII was designed to bring about a magical transformation in the social mores of American workers.

In the case at bar, Henry's obscenities, although annoying, were not so startling as to have affected seriously the psyches of the plaintiff or other female employees. The evidence did not demonstrate that this single employee's vulgarity substantially affected the totality of the workplace. The sexually oriented poster displays had a de minimis effect on the plaintiff's work environment when considered in the context of a society that condones and publicly features and commercially exploits open displays of written and pictorial erotica at the newsstands, on prime-time television, at the cinema, and in other public places. In sum,

Henry's vulgar language, coupled with the sexually oriented posters, did not result in a working environment that could be considered intimidating, hostile or offensive. It necessarily follows that the plaintiff failed to sustain her burden of proof that she was the victim of a Title VII sexual harassment violation.

KEITH, Circuit Judge, dissenting in part:

For seven years plaintiff worked at Osceola as the sole woman in a salaried management position. In common work areas plaintiff and other female employees were exposed daily to displays of nude or partially clad women belonging to a number of male employees at Osceola. One poster, which remained on the wall for eight years, showed a prone woman who had a golf ball on her breasts with a man standing over her, golf club in hand, yelling "Fore." And one desk plaque declared, "Even male chauvinist pigs need love..."

In addition, Computer Division Supervisor Doug Henry regularly spewed anti-female obscenity. Of plaintiff, Henry specifically remarked "All that bitch needs is a good lay" and called her "fat ass." Plaintiff arranged at least one meeting of female employees to discuss Henry and repeatedly filed written complaints on behalf of her herself and other female employees who feared losing their jobs if they complained directly. Osceola Vice President Charles Muetzel stated he knew that employees were "greatly disturbed" by Henry's language. However, because Osceola needed Henry's computer expertise, Muetzel did not reprimand or fire Henry. In response to subsequent complaints about Henry, a later supervisor, Charles Shoemaker, testified that he gave Henry "a little fatherly advice" about Henry's prospects if he learned to become "an executive type person."

In my view, Title VII's precise purpose is to prevent such behavior and attitudes from poisoning the work environment of classes protected under the Act. To condone the majority's notion of the "prevailing workplace" I would also have to agree that if an employer maintains an anti-Sematic workforce and tolerates a workplace in which "kike" jokes, displays of Nazi literature and anti-Jewish conversation "may abound," a Jewish employee assumes the risk of working there, and a court must consider such a work environment as "prevailing." I cannot. As I see it, job relatedness is the only additional factor which legitimately bears on the inquiry of plaintiff's reasonableness in finding her work environment offensive. In other words, the only additional question I would find relevant is whether the behavior complained of is required to perform the work.

QUESTIONS FOR DISCUSSION:

1. According to one survey, when people were asked how they would feel about having a co-worker express romantic interest in them when they didn't want to respond, two-thirds of the women said they would feel insulted, and two-thirds of the men said they would be flattered. This is one of many indicators that men and women view the same behavior in very different ways. What are the implications of this?

2. Remember the two ethical theories: Utilitarian, focusing on consequences for all concerned, and Rights-based, focusing on the competing rights of all concerned. How does each theory guide us in looking at sexual harassment?

3. What do you think should be done about sexual harassment?

SECTION 11.9
SHARON ROCK
v. JOSEPH ROBERTS

PROBLEM ELEVEN—C

PARK, BROWN & SMITH, P.C.
ATTORNEYS AT LAW
MEMORANDUM

To: All Law Clerks

From: Peter Smith, Esquire

Re: Sexual Harassment

Joe Roberts' construction firm is mostly male. Over the years, the only women in the company were those who worked in the office: the receptionist, secretaries, and the bookkeeper. But last year, Joe decided to hire a woman, Theresa Rock, for one of his crews. She was a certified electrician. Joe also liked her looks, especially since she was shapely, even in work clothes.

Things seemed to be going well with Ms. Rock. After about a month though, Joe saw something that made him wonder. On one of the stalls in the bathroom, he noticed lewd comments about Theresa. On a job site about a week later, he overheard some of his men laughing together about something. As he walked over to listen, he noticed Theresa pushing through the knot of men. She seemed upset. Joe asked what was going on. "It's Mizz Sensitive," said the foreman. "What's that about?" asked Joe. "Nothing. It's about nothing, but she wants it to be something." Joe changed the subject, and began talking about the job at hand.

Several weeks later, Theresa told Joe she had to talk to him. He was busy, but she seemed upset. Theresa explained that she felt she was being picked on by her co-workers. "Maybe they're jealous of me because I am a really good electrician, but I think they just hate me because I'm a woman. They think it's their kingdom or something." When Joe asked who was doing what, she was unsure. "Someone's been taking my equipment. I'll be missing a tool, or my hard-hat, things like that. And when I don't have the hat, the foreman sends me home." Joe asked her if she'd talked to the foreman. "I went to Bill right away, but he just said I was paranoid."

Joe spoke to Bill, after his interview with Theresa, and got nowhere. It seemed that she was imagining things, and she couldn't take a joke. "It's rough out here," said the foreman. "Maybe she can't take it."

The next time Joe saw Theresa they were both in the parking area. It was early in the morning and no one else was around. Joe thought Theresa seemed a little depressed. He said, "Theresa, what about having dinner tonight?" She looked up at him, squinted, paused and said, "Okay."

But there would be no chance to find out why Theresa seemed depressed. Later that day, Joe's secretary told him that Theresa had quit and gone home. Supposedly, the crane operator had dropped a stack of pallets from a height of about two stories onto the ground in front of Theresa. She had left the site in tears, telling the foreman she would never be back.

And a few weeks later, Joe received papers in a sexual harassment lawsuit that Theresa brought against him, his workers and his company. She alleged that the atmosphere at work had been filled with tension from the minute she arrived, that she was belittled by sexual jokes and graffiti, constant teasing, and other harassing behavior—all of which, she alleged was due to the fact that she was a woman. She even accused Joe of sexual harassment for asking her out. The implication was that Joe would use his power over her as the boss if she refused to go out with him.

Joe was shocked, and nervous about the probable reaction to the news by his wife. Based upon the materials in this section on Sexual Harassment, and **Rabidue v. Osceola Refining Company**, answer the following questions:

1. What are the types of sexual harassment, and which one(s) might apply to whom in this situation?

2. What is the likely outcome if a judge follows the reasoning of Judge Krupansky in the **Rabidue** case?

3. What is the likely outcome if a judge follows the reasoning of Judge Keith in **Rabidue**?

4. Assume Joe is not liable for merely asking Theresa out on a date. Is he still liable for his behavior of his men?

ANSWER SHEET
PROBLEM ELEVEN—C

Name   **Please Print Clearly**

1. What are the two types of sexual harassment, and which one(s) might apply to whom in this situation?

_____

_____

_____

_____

_____

_____

_____

_____

_____

2. What is the likely outcome if a judge follows the reasoning of Judge Krupansky in the **Rabidue** case?

_____

_____

_____

_____

_____

_____

_____

_____

3. What is the likely outcome if a judge follows the reasoning of Judge Keith in **Rabidue**?

_____

_____

_____

_____

_____

_____

_____

_____

4. Assume Joe is not liable for merely asking Theresa out on a date. Is he still liable for the behavior of his men?

_____

_____

_____

_____

_____

_____

_____

_____

_____

_____

SECTION 11.10
PROBLEM CASES

1. Butler was shopping at an Acme market when she walked towards her car in the parking lot. Suddenly, she was assaulted and her pocketbook was stolen. An investigation showed that over a period of one year, there had been seven attacks on the Acme market premises. Five of these attacks, occurred in the parking lot during the four month period immediately preceding the assault on Butler. The supermarket had hired off-duty police officers to act as security guards during the evening hours. However, there was only one security guard on duty at the time of the attack. Does the supermarket owe a duty of care to safeguard its patrons when they are in parking lot of their store? **Helen Butler v. Acme Markets, Inc., 426 A.2d 522 (N.J. App. 1981).**

2. The car being driven by Wagner collided with a bicycle on which a ten year old boy was riding. The child's father, thinking that his son was dying, ran from the house, jumped from the porch, over the steps and onto the ground thereby fracturing his leg. The father sued the driver of the automobile on the basis that the father owed a duty to rescue his son and his injury was a natural consequence of the car driver's negligence. Wagner argued that the father rashly and unnecessarily exposed himself to danger and should be barred from recovery. Should the driver of the automobile be responsible for the father's broken leg? **Mark v. Wagner, 307 N.E. 2d 480 (Oh. App. 1977).**

3. Saltsman went to an entertainment complex in order to use the batting cage. The manager noticed a patron carrying alcoholic beverages and asked that individual to leave. In response, the patron slammed the cup of beer into the manager's face. Saltsman followed the assailant to the parking lot in order to obtain a license plate number from the assailant's vehicle. This led to a physical encounter in which Saltsman was attacked by the assailant with a golf club. Saltsman sued the entertainment complex for his injuries. An investigation showed that there had been no similar criminal activity on the premises in the past. Is the sporting complex responsible for the injuries to Saltsman? **Doug Saltsman v. Michael Corazo, 721 A.2d 1000 (N.J. Super. 1998).**

4. Estella brought a sexual harassment suit against his employer, Garage Management Corporation, for sexual harassment by a person of the same sex. The employer argued that same sex harassment does not rise to the level of a hostile work environment because the aggrieved party cannot prove that the harassment complained of

was based upon his sex. Does sexual harassment of an individual by a person of the same sex, give rise to a viable cause of action? **Estella v. Garage Management Corporation, 2000 W.L. 1228968 (S.D. N.Y. 2000).**

5. A high school student was engaged in a sexual relationship with one of her teachers. She did not report that relationship to school officials. After the couple was discovered having sex, the teacher was arrested and terminated from his employment. The school district had not distributed any type of official grievance policy for lodging sexual harassment complaints as required by Federal regulations. The high school student then filed suit against the school district claiming a violation of Title IX which provides in pertinent part, "that a person cannot be subjected to discrimination under any educational program or activity which receives Federal financial assistance." An investigation into the incident revealed that no one in a supervisory power over the high school teacher knew of the affair with the student. Can the student recover damages for teacher-student sexual harassment because they failed to have a sexual harassment policy in place even though the school district officials were unaware of the teacher's misconduct? **Alida Gebser v. Lago Vista, Independent School District, 524 U.S. 274 (1998).**

SECTION 11.11
INTERNET REFERENCES

For a discussion of some of the topics contained in this chapter, see the following internet sites:

A. Drug Testing

- **www.mrinc.com/**
  A drug testing company maintains this site and provides news on drug testing, and provides answers to frequently asked questions about drug testing in the workplace.

B. Sexual Harassment

- **www.capstn.com/quiz.html**
  This site offers a quiz about sexual harassment.

- **www.EEOC.gov/facts/fs-sex.html**
  The Equal Employment Opportunity Commission may be found at this address and internet users may obtain information about sexual harassment, as well as the text of Title VII of the Civil Rights Act of 1964.

- **www.feminist.org/911/harass.html**
  This site lists various national hotlines for sexual harassment, including information on what to do if you or someone you know is sexually harassed.

C. Ethics

- **www.legalethics.com/ethics.law**
  This site provides ethics information in each state involving, lawyer ethics, confidentiality, and advertising.

- **www.usoge.gov/**
  The United States Office of Government Ethics Home Page is maintained at this location.

Footnote: 1. "Labs Err on Drug Test, Study Finds," *The Philadelphia Inquirer*, April 8, 1987, at A3, col. 1.

KEY TERMS

Drug Testing
EEOC
Employee at Will
Ethics
Good Faith Report
Hostile Work Environment
Quid Pro Quo

Rights Theory
Sexual Harassment
Special Relationship
Title VII
Utilitarian Theory
Waste
Whistleblower

APPENDIX

During your tenure with the firm, your input and advice will be sought on a number of issues. Several matters will require a written response in the nature of a legal memorandum. As law clerks, your answers must conform to the format as established by this office.

I am providing you with a sample memo and answer that was written by James Jones, a former associate. The matter deals with a lawsuit filed against Joseph Roberts for palimony that was brought to a successful conclusion. In the instant case, the associate was provided with a case involving a suit for palimony against rock star, Peter Frampton. He merely had to read the case and provide a written answer to the problem presented.

PARK, BROWN AND SMITH, P.C.
ATTORNEYS AT LAW
S A M P L E M E M O R A N D U M

TO: James Jones

FROM: Gregory Olan Dodge

RE: Mary Smith v. Joe Roberts Palimony Suit

In the past, Joe Roberts has had some momentary lapses in judgment. There was a time when he drank too much. As a result, his work suffered and so did his marriage. During this difficult period, he and the bartender became quite friendly. Now that Joe is a millionaire, this old pal, Mary has resurfaced, demanding half of Joe's new-found wealth. She claims that Joe promised to support her if she would leave her husband and four children to live with him in a "love nest" above the bar. Mary further claims to have complied with Joe's request, thereby accepting his offer. Joe, of course, denies all of the bartender's allegations. He does admit that they were friends.

I do not think that Mary has a good case for breach of contract even if her allegations are true. Please read **McCall v. Frampton** and assess this situation. Your memorandum should address the following questions:

1. Is this alleged contract enforceable?
2. Why might this contract be against public policy?
3. Does it matter whether Joe actually made these promises to Mary?

McCall v. Frampton
415 New York Supplement, 2d 754 (1979)

GAGLIARDI, Joseph F., Justice

This is an action brought by plaintiff to recover damages for breach of an oral contract allegedly made between plaintiff and defendant in 1973. The complaint alleges that in and prior to 1972 plaintiff had expertise and was engaged in the business of promotion and management of musicians involved in "Rock and Roll" or "Rock" and, during that period, besides doing so for compensation engaged in those activities without compensation for others; that plaintiff met defendant in 1972 when defendant was a member of the musical group known as "Humble Pie" and when plaintiff was married to the group's manager (a Mr. Brigden); that in 1973 defendant "requested that McCall leave her then husband and her then employment… and that she become associated with and work with Frampton in the promotion of Frampton as a musician representing to McCall that if she did so they would be equal partners in all proceeds from his employment in that field" (Emphasis supplied); that in reliance upon these representations plaintiff left her husband and her employment and went to live with defendant, "thereafter devoting all her resources, time and effort to the promotion and success of Frampton in his endeavors;" that beginning in 1973 plaintiff, at defendant's request, used all of her financial resources to support herself and defendant, and engaged in performing various services for defendant "including, but not limited to, public relations and promotion work; aiding in costuming of Frampton and his associates; managing Frampton's personal finances and traveling with Frampton during tours conducted by him;" that at various times from 1973 to 1978, defendant acknowledged plaintiff's

efforts both in public and in private and shared his receipts from his business with plaintiff, as well as bank accounts and other credit sources, and that both charged expenses incurred for the benefit of each to accounts maintained for that purpose "in accordance with their prior agreement;" in sum, that the parties were equal partners from 1973 through July, 1978.

The complaint requests an accounting of defendant's earnings from 1973 to date and a judgment equally dividing those earnings between the parties.

In support of her argument that the complaint should not be dismissed, plaintiff relies principally upon the following cases: **Marvin v. Marvin,** 18 Cal.3d 660, 134 Cal. Rptr. 815, 557 P.2d 106; **Dosek v. Dosek** (Conn.Sup.Ct., decided October 4, 1978, reported in 4 Family Law Reporter, October 31, 1978, p. 2828); **McCullon v. McCullon,** 96 Misc.2d 962, 410 N.Y.S.2d 226 [Sup.Ct., Erie County 1978]; **Hewitt v. Hewitt,** 62 Ill. App.3d 861, 20 Ill.Dec. 476 380 N.E.2d 454; **Carlson v. Olson,** 256 N.W.2d 249 [Minn. 1977]. These cases are all distinguishable for there is no allegation herein that plaintiff and defendant ever intended to marry each other, that they held themselves out to the public as husband and wife, or that the plaintiff and defendant were ever free to marry each other. There is no allegation that plaintiff ever changed her surname to that of defendant. (Apparently no children were born as a result of the sexual relationship between the parties.)

This court holds that the contract between the plaintiff and defendant is void and unenforceable as a matter of public policy. Plaintiff pleads as the consideration for this agreement the commission of adultery on her part; that she leave her husband and live with defendant and become associated with him. This contract was, therefore, in derogation of her existing marriage and prohibited by section 255-17 of the Penal Law: "A person is guilty of adultery when he engages in sexual intercourse with another person at a time when he has a living spouse, or the other person has a living spouse." (The papers submitted leave no doubt that there was an illicit sexual relationship between the parties. There is no indication that plaintiff has ever been divorced from her husband. Apparently, defendant was divorced from his wife during the time when the parties lived together.)

It is settled that agreements against public policy are unlawful and void. This rule is not based on a desire to benefit the party who breaches an illegal contract, but on a desire to protect the common wealth, the general welfare of society being damaged by the very making of such a contract. By refusing to enforce such a contract and leaving the parties without a legal remedy for breach, society is protected by discouraging the making of contracts contrary to the common good.

To define public policy is often difficult, for it is a concept which is flexible. The Court has recently addressed this point:

"Controversies involving questions of public policy can rarely, if ever, be resolved by the blind application of sedentary legal principles. The very nature of the concept of public policy itself militates against an attempt to define its ingredients in a manner which would allow one to become complacent in the thought that these precepts which society so steadfastly embraces today will continue to serve as the foundation upon which society will function tomorrow. Public policy, like society, is continually evolving and those entrusted with its implementation must respond to its ever-changing demands."

It is the opinion of this court that the contract, as alleged by plaintiff, is clearly subject to the defense of illegality. It is contrary to the public policy of this state, which recognizes the state of marriage and the protection thereof as essential to the welfare of our society. It requires, in its performance, the commission of adultery which remains a crime in this state. The plaintiff's Complaint is therefore dismissed.

SAMPLE ANSWER

James Jones

Name: **James Jones**	**Please Print Clearly**

According to **McCall v. Frampton,** the alleged contract between Joe and Mary to engage in an adulteress relationship is unenforceable because it is against public policy. As the court noted, "It is settled that agreements against public policy are unlawful and void." **Frampton**, at 755. The court goes on to explain that these types of contracts are harmful to the welfare of society. "By refusing to enforce such a contract and leaving the parties without a legal remedy for breach, society is protected by discouraging the making of contracts contrary to the public good." **Frampton**, at 755. Thus, it is clear that once this contract is classified as being against public policy, Mary has no legal remedy regardless of the truthfulness of her allegations.

Although the **Frampton** court does explain the difficulties involved in determining which agreements are unenforceable, Joe and Mary's alleged contract is strikingly similar to the one made in **Frampton**. That court explained that "…the public policy of this state…recognizes the state of marriage and the protection thereof as essential to the welfare of society." **Frampton**, at 756. A contract in which Mary agrees to leave her husband and children in return for Joe's support would clearly undermine marriage and the family unit. While the **Frampton** court didn't discuss family life, we may assume that the state is as interested in promoting a stable family relationship as it is in marriage. After all, part of the reason our society protects marriage is because of it's effect on American family life.

Whether or not Joe actually made these promises to Mary is irrelevant. Even if he did, the contract is unenforceable because it violates public policy. Furthermore, an agreement to create an adulteress relationship is illegal and illegal contracts are not enforced by the courts. Like the complaint in **Frampton**, this action should be dismissed.

SECTION A.2 CONSTITUTION

THE CONSTITUTION OF THE UNITED STATES

We the people of the United States, in order to form a more perfect union, establish justice, insure domestic tranquility, provide for the common defense, promote the general welfare, and secure the blessings of liberty to ourselves and our posterity, do ordain and establish this Constitution for the United States of America.

ARTICLE I

SECTION 1

All legislative powers herein granted shall be vested in a Congress of the United States, which shall consist of a Senate and House of Representatives.

SECTION 2

1. The House of Representatives shall be composed of members chosen every second year by the people of the several States, and the electors in each State shall have the qualifications requisite for electors of the most numerous branch of the State legislature.

2. No person shall be a representative who shall not have attained to the age of twenty-five years, and been seven years a citizen of the United States, and who shall not, when elected, be an inhabitant of that State in which he shall be chosen.

3. Representatives and direct taxes[1] shall be apportioned among the several States which may be included within this Union, accord-

ing to their respective numbers, which shall be determined by adding to the whole number of free persons, including those bound to service for a term of years, and excluding Indians not taxed, three fifths of all other persons.[2] The actual enumeration shall be made within three years after the first meeting of the Congress of the United States, and within every subsequent term of ten years, in such manner as they shall by law direct. The number of representatives shall not exceed one for every thirty thousand, but each State shall have at least one representative; and until such enumeration shall be made, the State of New Hampshire shall be entitled to choose three, Massachusetts eight, Rhode Island and Providence Plantations one, Connecticut five, New York six, New Jersey four, Pennsylvania eight, Delaware one, Maryland six, Virginia ten, North Carolina five, South Carolina five, and Georgia three.

4. When vacancies happen in the representation from any State, the executive authority thereof shall issue writs of election to fill such vacancies.

5. The House of Representatives shall choose their speaker and other officers; and shall have the sole power of impeachment.

Section 3

1. The Senate of the United States shall be composed of two senators from each State, chosen by the legislature thereof,[3] for six years; and each senator shall have one vote.

2. Immediately after they shall be assembled in consequence of the first election, they shall be divided as equally as may be into three classes. The seats of the senators of the first class shall be vacated at the expiration of the second year, of the second class at the expiration of the fourth year and of the third class at the expiration of the sixth year, so that one third may be chosen every second year; and if vacancies happen by resignation, or otherwise, during the recess of the legislature of any State, the executive thereof may make temporary appointments until the next meeting of the legislature, which shall then fill such vacancies.[4]

3. No person shall be a senator who shall not have attained to the age of thirty years, and been nine years a citizen of the United States, and who shall not, when elected, be an inhabitant of that State for which he shall be chosen.

4. The Vice President of the United States shall be President of the Senate, but shall have no vote, unless they be equally divided.

5. The Senate shall choose their other officers, and also a president pro tempore, in the absence of the Vice President, or when he shall exercise the office of the President of the United States.

6. The Senate shall have the sole power to try all impeachments. When sitting for that purpose, they shall be on oath or affirmation. When the President of the United States is tried, the chief justice shall preside: and no person shall be convicted without the concurrence of two thirds of the members present.

7. Judgment in cases of impeachment shall not extend further than to removal from office, and disqualifications to hold and enjoy any office of honor, trust or profit under the United States: but the party convicted shall nevertheless be liable and subject to indictment, trial, judgment and punishment, according to law.

SECTION 4

1. The times, places, and manner of holding elections for senators and representatives, shall be prescribed in each State by the legislature thereof: but the Congress may at any time by law make or alter such regulations, except as to the places of choosing senators.

2. The Congress shall assemble at least once in every year, and such meeting shall be on the first Monday in December, unless they shall by law appoint a different day.

SECTION 5

1. Each House shall be the judge of the elections, returns and qualifications of its own members, and a majority of each shall constitute a quorum to do business; but a smaller number may adjourn from day to day, and may be authorized to compel the attendance of absent members, in such manner, and under such penalties as each House may provide.

2. Each House may determine the rules of its proceedings, punish its members for disorderly behavior, and, with the concurrence of two thirds, expel a member.

3. Each House shall keep a journal of its proceedings, and from time to time punish the same, excepting such parts as may in their judgment require secrecy; and the yeas and nays of the members of either House on any question shall, at the desire of one fifth of those present, be entered on the journal.

4. Neither House, during the session of Congress, shall, without the consent of the other, adjourn for more than three days, nor to any other place than that in which the two Houses shall be sitting.

SECTION 6

1. The senators and representatives shall receive a compensation for their services, to be ascertained by law, and paid out of the Treasury of the United States. They shall in all cases, except treason,

felony, and breach of the peace, be privileged from arrest during their attendance at the session of their respective Houses, and in going to and returning from the same; and for any speech or debate in either House, they shall not be questioned in any other place.

2. No senator or representative shall, during the time for which he was elected, be appointed to any civil office under the authority of the United States, which shall have been created, or the emoluments whereof shall have been increased, during such time; and no person holding any office under the United States shall be a member of either House during his continuance in office.

Section 7

1. All bills for raising revenue shall originate in the House of Representatives; but the Senate may propose or concur with amendments as on other bills.

2. Every bill which shall have passed the House of Representatives and the Senate, shall, before it become a law, be presented to the President of the United States; If he approves he shall sign it, but if not he shall return it, with his objections, to that House in which it shall have originated, who shall enter the objections at large on their journal, and proceed to reconsider it. If after such reconsideration two thirds of that House shall agree to pass the bill, it shall be sent, together with the objections, to the other House, by which it shall likewise be reconsidered, and if approved by two thirds of that House, it shall become a law. But in all such cases the votes of both Houses shall be determined by yeas and nays, and the names of the persons voting for and against the bill shall be entered on the journal of each House respectively. If any bill shall not be returned by the President within ten days (Sundays excepted) after it shall have been presented to him, the same shall be a law, in like manner as if he had signed it, unless the Congress by their adjournment prevent its return, in which case it shall not be a law.

Every order, resolution, or vote to which the concurrence of the Senate and the House of Representatives may be necessary (except on a question of adjournment) shall be presented to the President of the United States; and before the same shall take effect, shall be approved by him, or being disapproved by him, shall be repassed by two thirds of the Senate and House of Representatives, according to the rules and limitations prescribed in the case of a bill.

SECTION 8

THE CONGRESS SHALL HAVE THE POWER

1. To lay and collect taxes, duties, imposts, and excises, to pay the debts and provide for the common defense and general welfare of the United States; but all duties, imposts, and excises shall be uniform throughout the United States;

2. To borrow money on the credit of the United States;

3. To regulate commerce with foreign nations, and among the several States, and with the Indian tribes;

4. To establish an uniform rule of naturalization, and uniform laws on the subject of bankruptcies throughout the Untied States;

5. To coin money, regulate the value thereof, and of foreign coin, and fix the standard of weights and measures;

6. To provide for the punishment of counterfeiting the securities and current coin of the United States;

7. To establish post offices and post roads;

8. To promote the progress of science and useful arts, by securing for limited times to authors and inventors the exclusive right to their respective writings and discoveries;

9. To constitute tribunals inferior to the Supreme Court;

10. To define and punish piracies and felonies committed on the high seas, and offenses against the law of nations;

11. To declare war, grant letters of marque and reprisal, and make rules concerning captures on land and water;

12. To raise and support armies, but no appropriations of money to that use shall be for a longer term than two years;

13. To provide and maintain a navy;

14. To make rules for the government and regulation of the land and naval forces;

15. To provide for calling forth the militia to execute the laws of the Union, suppress insurrections and repel invasions;

16. To provide for organizing, arming, and disciplining the militia, and for governing such part of them as may be employed in the service of the United States, reserving to the States respectively, the appointment of the officers, and the authority of training the militia according to the discipline prescribed by Congress;

17. To exercise exclusive legislation in all cases whatsoever, over such district (not exceeding ten miles square) as may, by cession of particular States and the acceptance of Congress, become the seat of

the government of the United States, and to exercise like authority over all places purchased by the consent of the legislature of the State in which the same shall be, for the erection of forts, magazines, arsenals, dockyards, and other needful buildings; and

18. To make all laws which shall be necessary and proper for carrying into execution the foregoing powers, and all other powers vested by this Constitution in the government of the United States, or any department or officer thereof.

Section 9

1. The migration or importation of such persons as any of the States now existing shall think proper to admit, shall not be prohibited by the Congress prior to the year one thousand eight hundred and eight, but a tax or duty may be imposed on such importation, not exceeding ten dollars for each person.

2. The privilege of the writ of hàbeas corpus shall not be suspended, unless when in cases of rebellion or invasion the public safety may require it.

3. No bill of attainder or ex post facto law shall be passed.

4. No capitation, or other direct, tax shall be laid, unless in proportion to the census or enumeration hereinbefore directed to be taken.[5]

5. No tax or duty shall be laid on articles exported from any State.

6. No preference shall be given by any regulation of commerce or revenue to the ports of one State over those of another: nor shall vessels bound to, or from, one State be obliged to enter, clear, or pay duties in another.

7. No money shall be drawn from the treasury, but in consequence of appropriations made by law; and a regular statement and account of the receipts and expenditures of all public money shall be published from time to time.

8. No title of nobility shall be granted by the United States: and no person holding any office of profit or trust under them, shall, without the consent of the Congress, accept of any present, emolument, office, or title, of any kind whatever, from any king, prince, or foreign State.

Section 10

1. No State shall enter into any treaty, alliance, or confederation; grant letters of marque and reprisal; coin money; emit bills of credit; make any thing but gold and silver coin a tender in payment of debts; pass any bill of attainder, ex post facto law, or law impairing the obligation of contracts, or grant any title of nobility.

2. No State shall, without the consent of the Congress, lay any imposts or duties on imports or exports, except what may be absolutely necessary for executing its inspection laws: and the net produce of all duties and imposts laid by any State on imports or exports, shall be for the use of the treasury of the United States; and all such laws shall be subject to the revision and control of the Congress.

3. No State shall, without the consent of the Congress, lay any duty of tonnage, keep troops, or ships of war in time of peace, enter into any agreement or compact with another State, or with a foreign power, or engage in war, unless actually invaded, or in such imminent danger as will not admit of delay.

ARTICLE II   SECTION 1

1. The executive power shall be vested in a President of the United States of America. He shall hold his office during the term of four years, and, together with the Vice President, chosen for the same term, be elected, as follows:

2. Each State shall appoint, in such manner as the legislature thereof may direct, a number of electors, equal to the whole number of senators and representatives to which the State may be entitled in the Congress: but no senator or representative, or person holding an office of trust or profit under the United States, shall be appointed an elector.

The electors shall meet in their respective States, and vote by ballot for two persons, of whom one at least shall not be an inhabitant of the same State with themselves. And they shall make a list of all the persons voted for, and of the number of votes for each; which list they shall sign and certify, and transmit sealed to the seat of the government of the United States, directed to the president of the Senate. The president of the Senate shall, in the presence of the Senate and House of Representatives, open all the certificates, and the votes shall then be counted. The person having the greatest number of votes shall be the President, if such number be a majority of the whole number of electors appointed; and if there be more than one who have such majority, and have an equal number of votes, then the House of Representatives shall immediately choose by ballot one of them for President; and if no person have a majority, then from the five highest on the list the said House shall in like manner choose the President. But in choosing the President, the votes shall be taken by States, the representation from each State having one vote; a quorum for this purpose shall consist of a member or members from two thirds of the States, and a majority of all the States shall be necessary to a choice. In every case, after the choice of the President, the person having the greatest number of votes of the electors shall be the Vice President. But if there should remain two or more who have equal votes, the Senate shall choose from them by ballot the Vice President.[6]

3. The Congress may determine the time of choosing the electors, and the day on which they shall give their votes; which day shall be the same throughout the United States.

4. No person except a natural born citizen, or a citizen of the United States, at the time of the adoption of this Constitution, shall be eligible to the office of President; neither shall any person be eligible to that office who shall not have attained to the age of thirty-five years, and been fourteen years a resident within the United States.

5. In case of the removal of the President from office, or his death, resignation, or inability to discharge the powers and duties of the said office, the same shall devolve on the Vice President, and the Congress may be law provide for the case of removal, death, resignation or inability, both of the President and Vice President, declaring what officer shall then act as President, and such officer shall act accordingly, until the disability be removed, or a President shall be elected.

6. The President shall, at stated times, receive for his services a compensation, which shall neither be increased nor diminished during the period for which he shall have been elected, and he shall not receive within that period any other emolument from the United States, or any of them.

7. Before he enter on the execution of his office, he shall take the following oath or affirmation: "I do solemnly swear (or affirm) that I will faithfully execute the office of President of the Untied States, and will to the best of my ability, preserve, protect, and defend the Constitution of the United States."

SECTION 2

1. The President shall be commander in chief of the army and navy of the United States, and of the militia of the several States, when called into the actual service of the United States; he may require the opinion, in writing, of the principal officer in each of the executive departments, upon any subject relating to the duties of their respective offices, and he shall have power to grant reprieves and pardons for offenses against the United States, except in cases of impeachment.

2. He shall have power, by and with the advice and consent of the Senate, to make treaties, provided two thirds of the senators present concur; and he shall nominate, and by and with the advice and consent of the Senate, shall appoint ambassadors, other public ministers and consuls, judges of the Supreme Court, and all other officers of the United States, whose appointment are not herein otherwise provided for, and which shall be established by law: but the Congress may by law vest the appointment of such inferior officers, as they think proper, in the President alone, in the courts of law, or in the heads of departments.

3. The President shall have power to fill up all vacancies that may happen during the recess of the Senate, by granting commissions which shall expire at the end of their next session.

SECTION 3

He shall from time to time give to the Congress information of the state of the Union, and recommend to their considerations such measures as he shall judge necessary and expedient; he may, on extraordinary occasions, convene both Houses, or either of them, and in case of disagreement between them with respect to the time of adjournment, he may adjourn them to such time as he shall think proper; he shall receive ambassadors and other public ministers; he shall take care that the laws be faithfully executed, and shall commission all the officers of the United States.

SECTION 4

The President, Vice President, and all civil officers of the United States, shall be removed from office on impeachment for, and conviction of, treason, bribery, or other high crimes and misdemeanors.

ARTICLE III   SECTION 1

The judicial power of the United States shall be vested in one Supreme Court, and in such inferior courts as the Congress may from time to time ordain and establish. The judges, both of the Supreme and inferior courts, shall hold their offices during good behavior, and shall, at stated times, receive for their services, a compensation, which shall not be diminished during their continuance in office.

SECTION 2

1. The judicial power shall extend to all cases, in law and equity, arising under this Constitution, the laws of the United States, and treaties made, or which shall be made, under their authority;—to all cases affecting ambassadors, other public ministers and con-

suls;—to all cases of admiralty and maritime jurisdiction;—to controversies to which the United States shall be a party;[7]—to controversies between two or more States;—between a State and citizens of another State;—between citizens of different States;—between citizens of the same State claiming lands under grants of different States, and between a State, or the citizens thereof, and foreign States, citizens or subjects.

2. In all cases affecting ambassadors, other public ministers and consuls, and those in which a State shall be party, the Supreme Court shall have original jurisdiction. In all the other cases before mentioned, the Supreme Court shall have appellate jurisdiction, both as to law and fact, with such exceptions, and under such regulations as the Congress shall make.

3. The trial of all crimes, except in cases of impeachment, shall be by jury; and such trial shall be held in the State where the said crimes shall have been committed; but when not committed within any State, the trial shall be at such place or places as the Congress may by law have directed.

Section 3

1. Treason against the United States shall consist only in levying war against them, or in adhering to their enemies, giving them aid and comfort. No person shall be convicted of treason unless on the testimony of two witnesses to save overt act, or on confession in open court.

2. The Congress shall have power to declare the punishment of treason, but no attainder of treason shall work corruption of blood, or forfeiture except during the life of the person attained.

Article IV   ### Section 1

Full faith and credit shall be given in each State to the public acts, records, and judicial proceedings of every other State. And the Congress may by general laws prescribe the manner in which such acts, records and proceedings shall be proved, and the effect thereof.

Section 2

1. The citizens of each State shall be entitled to all privileges and immunities of citizens in the several States.[8]

2. A person charged in any State with treason, felony, or other crime, who shall flee from justice, and be found in another State, shall on demand of the executive authority of the State from which he fled, be delivered up to be removed to the State having jurisdiction of the crime.

3. No person held to service or labor in one State under the laws thereof, escaping into another, shall in consequence of any law or regulation therein, be discharged from such service or labor, but shall be delivered up on claim of the party to whom such service or labor may be due.[9]

Section 3

1. New States may be admitted by the Congress into this Union; but no new State shall be formed or erected within the jurisdiction of any other State; nor any State be formed by the junction of two or more States, or parts of States, without the consent of the legislatures of the States concerned as well as the Congress.

2. The Congress shall have power to dispose of and make all needful rules and regulations respecting the territory or other property belonging to the United States; and nothing in this Constitution shall be so construed as to prejudice any claims of the United States, or of any particular State.

Section 4

The United States shall guarantee to every State in this Union a republican form of government, and shall protect each of them against invasion; and on application of the legislature, or of the executive (when the legislature cannot be convened) against domestic violence.

Article V The Congress, whenever two thirds of both Houses shall deem it necessary, shall propose amendments to this Constitution, or, on the application of the legislatures of two thirds of the several States, shall call a convention for proposing amendments, which in either case shall be valid to all intents and purposes, as part of this Constitution, when ratified by the legislatures of three fourths of the several States, or by conventions in three fourths thereof, as the one or the other mode of ratification may be proposed by the Congress; Provided that no amendment which may be made prior to the year one thousand eight hundred and eight shall in any manner affect the first and fourth clauses in the ninth section of the first article; and that no State, without its consent, shall be deprived of its equal suffrage in the Senate.

Article VI 1. All debts contracted and engagements entered into, before the adoption of this Constitution, shall be as valid against the United States under this Constitution, as under the Confederation.

2. This Constitution, and the laws of the United States which shall be made in pursuance thereof; and all treaties made, or which shall be made, under the authority of the United States, shall be supreme

law of the land; and the Judges in every State shall be bound thereby, any thing in the Constitution or laws of any State to the contrary notwithstanding.

3. The senators and representatives before mentioned, and the members of the several State legislatures, and all executive and judicial officers, both of the United States and of the several States, shall be bound by oath or affirmation to support this Constitution; but no religious test shall ever be required as a qualification to any office or public trust under the United States.

ARTICLE VII The ratification of the conventions of nine States shall be sufficient for the establishment of this Constitution between the States so ratifying the same.

Done in Convention by the unanimous consent of the States present the seventeenth day of September in the year of our Lord one thousand seven hundred and eighty-seven, and of the independence of the United States of America the twelfth. In witness whereof we have hereunto subscribed our names.

AMENDMENT I [FIRST TEN AMENDMENTS RATIFIED IN 1791]

Congress shall make no law respecting an establishment of religion, or prohibiting the free exercise thereof; or abridging the freedom of speech, or the press; or the right of the people peaceably to assemble, and to petition the government for a redress of grievances.

AMENDMENT II

A well regulated militia, being necessary to the security of a free State, the right of the people to keep and bear arms, shall not be infringed.

AMENDMENT III

No soldier shall, in the time of peace be quartered in any house, without the consent of the owner, nor in time of war, but in a manner to be prescribed by law.

AMENDMENT IV

The right of the people to be secure in their persons, houses, papers, and effects, against unreasonable searches and seizures, shall not be violated, and no warrants shall issue, but upon probable cause, supported by oath or affirmation, and particularly describing the place to be searched, and the persons or things to be seized.

Amendment V

No person shall be held to answer for a capital, or otherwise infamous crime, unless on a presentment or indictment of a grand jury, except in cases arising in the land or naval forces, or in the militia, when in actual service in time of war or public danger; nor shall any person be subject for the same offense to be twice put in jeopardy of life or limb; nor shall be compelled in any criminal case to be a witness against himself; nor be deprived of life, liberty, or property, without due process of law; nor shall private property be taken for public use, without just compensation.

Amendment VI

In all criminal prosecutions, the accused shall enjoy the right to a speedy and public trial, by an impartial jury of the State and district wherein the crime shall have been committed, which district shall have been previously ascertained by law, and to be informed of the nature and cause of the accusation; to be confronted with the witnesses against him; to have compulsory process for obtaining witnesses in his favor, and to have the assistance of the counsel for his defense.

Amendment VII

In suits at common law, where the value in controversy shall exceed twenty dollars, the right of trial by jury shall be preserved, and no fact tried by a jury shall be otherwise reëxamined in any court of the United States, than according to the rules of the common law.

Amendment VIII

Excessive bail shall not be required, nor excessive fines imposed, nor cruel and unusual punishments inflicted.

Amendment IX

The enumeration in the Constitution of certain rights shall not be construed to deny or disparage others retained by the people.

Amendment X

The powers not delegated to the United States by the Constitution, nor prohibited by it to the States, are reserved to the States respectively, or to the people.

Amendment XI [Ratified in 1798]

The judicial power of the United States shall not be construed to extend to any suit in law or equity, commenced or prosecuted against one of the United States by citizens of another State, or by citizens or subjects of any foreign State.

AMENDMENT XII [RATIFIED IN 1804]

The electors shall meet in their respective States, and vote by ballot for President and Vice President, one of whom, at least, shall not be an inhabitant of the same State with themselves; they shall name in their ballots the person voted for as President, and in distinct ballots, the person voted for as Vice President, and they shall make distinct lists of all persons voted for as President and of all persons voted for as Vice President, and of the number of votes for each, which lists they shall sign and certify, and transmit sealed to the seat of the government of the Untied States, directed to the President of the Senate;—The President of the Senate shall, in the presence of the Senate and House of Representatives, open all the certificates and the votes shall then be counted;—The person having the greatest number of votes for President, shall be the President, if such number be a majority of the whole number of electors appointed; and if no person have such majority, then form the persons having the highest numbers not exceeding three on the list of those voted for as President, the House of Representatives shall choose immediately, by ballot, the President. But in choosing the President, the votes shall be taken by States, the representation from each State having one vote; a quorum for this purpose shall consist of a member or members from two thirds of the States, and a majority of all the States shall be necessary to a choice. And if the House of Representatives shall not choose a President whenever the right of choice shall devolve upon them, before the fourth day of March next following, then the Vice President shall act as President, as in the case of the death or other constitutional disability of the President. The person having the greatest number of votes as Vice President shall be the Vice President, if such number be a majority of the whole number of electors appointed, and if no person have a majority, then from the two highest numbers on the list, the Senate shall choose the Vice President; a quorum for the purpose shall consist of two thirds of the whole number of Senators, and a majority of the whole number shall be necessary to a choice. But no person constitutionally ineligible to the office of President shall be eligible to that of Vice President of the United States.

AMENDMENT XIII [RATIFIED IN 1865]

SECTION 1

Neither slavery nor involuntary servitude, except as a punishment for crime whereof the party shall have been duly convicted, shall exist within the United States, or any place subject to their jurisdiction.

SECTION 2

Congress shall have power to enforce this article by appropriate legislation.

AMENDMENT XIV [RATIFIED IN 1868]

SECTION 1

All persons born or naturalized in the United States, and subject to the jurisdiction thereof, are citizens of the United States and of the State wherein they reside. No State shall make or enforce any law which shall abridge the privileges or immunities of citizens of the United States; nor shall any State deprive any person of life, liberty, or property, without due process of law; nor deny to any person within its jurisdiction the equal protection of the laws.

SECTION 2

Representatives shall be apportioned among the several States according to their respective numbers, counting the whole number of persons in each State, excluding Indians not taxed. But when the right to vote at any election for the choice of electors for President and Vice President of the United States, representatives in Congress, the executive and judicial officers of a State, or the members of the legislature thereof, is denied to any of the male inhabitants of such State, being twenty-one years of age, and citizens of the United States, or in any way abridge, except for participating in rebellion, or other crime, the basis or representation therein shall be reduced in the proportion which the number of such male citizens shall bear to the whole number of male citizens twenty-one years of age in such State.

SECTION 3

No person shall be a senator or representative in Congress, or elector of President and Vice President, or hold any office, civil or military under the United States, or under any State, who having previously taken an oath, as a member of Congress, or as an officer of the United States, or as a member of any State legislature, or as an executive or judicial officer of any State, to support the Constitution of the United States, shall have engaged in insurrection or rebellion against the same, or given aid or comfort to the enemies thereof. But Congress may by a vote of two thirds of each House, remove such disability.

SECTION 4

The validity of the public debt of the United States, authorized by law, including the debts incurred for payment of pensions and bounties for services in suppressing insurrection or rebellion, shall not be questioned. But neither the United States nor any State shall assume or pay any debt or obligation incurred in aid of insurrection or rebellion against the United States, or any claim for the loss or emancipation of any slave; but all such debts, obligations, and claims shall be held illegal and void.

SECTION 5

The Congress shall have power to enforce, by appropriate legislation, the provisions of this article.

AMENDMENT XV [RATIFIED IN 1870]

SECTION 1

The right of citizens of the United States to vote shall not be denied or abridged by the United States or by any State on account of race, color, or previous condition of servitude.

SECTION 2

The Congress shall have power to enforce this article by appropriate legislation.

AMENDMENT XVI [RATIFIED IN 1913]

The Congress shall have power to lay and collect taxes on incomes, from whatever source derived, without apportionment among the several States, and without regard to any census or enumeration.

AMENDMENT XVII [RATIFIED IN 1913]

The Senate of the United States shall be composed of two senators from each State, elected by the people thereof, for six years; and each senator shall have one vote. The electors in each State shall have the qualifications requisite for electors of the most numerous branch of the State legislature.

When vacancies happen in the representation of any State in the Senate, the executive authority of such State shall issue writs of election to fill such vacancies: *Provided*, That the legislature of any State may empower the executive thereof to make temporary appointments until the people fill the vacancies by election as the legislature may direct.

This amendment shall not be so construed as to affect the election or term of any senator chosen before it becomes valid as part of the Constitution.

AMENDMENT XVIII[10] [RATIFIED IN 1919]

After one year from the ratification of this article, the manufacture, sale, or transportation of intoxicating liquors within, the importation thereof into, or the exportation thereof from the United States and all territory subject to the jurisdiction thereof for beverage purposes is thereby prohibited.

The Congress and the several States shall have concurrent power to enforce this article by appropriate legislation.

This article shall be inoperative unless it shall have been ratified as an amendment to the Constitution by the legislature of the several States, as provided in the Constitution, within seven years from the date of the submission hereof to the States by Congress.

AMENDMENT XIX [RATIFIED IN 1920]

The right of citizens of the United States to vote shall not be denied or abridged by the United States or by any State on account of sex.

Congress shall have the power to enforce this article by appropriate legislation.

AMENDMENT XX [RATIFIED IN 1933]

SECTION 1

The terms of the President and Vice President shall end at noon on the 20th day of January, and the terms of Senators and Representatives at noon on the 3rd day of January, of the years in which such terms would have ended if this article had not been ratified; and the terms of their successors shall then begin.

SECTION 2

The Congress shall assemble at least once in every year, and such meeting shall begin at noon on the 3d day of January, unless they shall by law appoint a different day.

SECTION 3

If, at the time fixed for the beginning of the term of President, the President-elect shall have died, the Vice President-elect shall become President. If a President shall not have been chosen before the time fixed for the beginning of his term, or if the President-elect shall have failed to qualify, then the Vice President-elect shall act as President until a President shall have qualified; and the Congress may by law provide for the case wherein neither a President-elect nor a Vice President-elect shall have qualified, declaring who shall then act as President, or the manner in which one who is to act shall be selected, and such person shall act accordingly until a President or Vice President shall have qualified.

SECTION 4

The Congress may by law provide for the case of the death of any of the persons from whom the House of Representatives may choose a President whenever the right of choice shall have devolved upon them, and for the case of the death of any of the persons from whom the Senate may choose a Vice President whenever the right of choice shall have devolved upon them.

SECTION 5

Sections 1 and 2 shall take effect on the 15th day of October following the ratification of this article.

SECTION 6

This article shall be inoperative unless it shall have been ratified as an amendment to the Constitution by the legislatures of three-fourths of the several States within seven years from the date of its submission.

AMENDMENT XXI [RATIFIED IN 1933]

SECTION 1

The Eighteenth Article of amendment to the Constitution of the United States is hereby repealed.

SECTION 2

The transportation or importation into any State, Territory, or possession of the United States for delivery or use therein of intoxicating liquors in violation of the laws thereof, is hereby prohibited.

SECTION 3

This article shall be inoperative unless it shall have been ratified as an amendment to the Constitution by conventions in the several States as provided in the Constitution, within seven years from the date of the submission thereof to the States by the Congress.

AMENDMENT XXII [RATIFIED IN 1951]

No person shall be elected to the office of the President more than twice, and no person who has held the office of President, or acted as President, for more than two years of a term to which some other person was elected President shall be elected to the office of President more than once.

But this article shall not apply to any person holding the office of President when this article was proposed by the Congress, and shall not prevent any person who may be holding the office of President, or acting as President, during the term within which this article becomes operative from holding the office of President or acting as President during the remainder of such term.

This article shall be inoperative unless it shall have been ratified as an amendment to the Constitution by the legislatures of three-fourths of the several States within seven years from the date of its submission to the States by the Congress.

AMENDMENT XXIII [RATIFIED IN 1961]

SECTION 1

The District constituting the seat of Government of the United States shall appoint in such manner as the Congress may direct:

A number of electors of President and Vice President equal to the whole number of Senators and Representatives in Congress to which the District would be entitled if it were a State, but in no event more than the least populous State; they shall be in addition to those appointed by the States, but they shall be considered, for the purposes of the election of President and Vice President, to be electors appointed by a State; and they shall meet in the District and perform such duties as provided by the twelfth article of amendment.

SECTION 2

The Congress shall have power to enforce this article by appropriate legislation.

AMENDMENT XXIV [RATIFIED IN 1964]

SECTION 1

The right of citizens of the United States to vote in any primary or other election for President or Vice President, for electors for President or Vice President, or for Senator or Representative in Congress, shall not be denied or abridged by the United States or any State by reason of failure to pay any poll tax or other tax.

SECTION 2

The Congress shall power to enforce this article by appropriate legislation.

Amendment XXV [Ratified in 1967]

Section 1

In case of the removal of the President from office or his death or resignation, the Vice President shall become President.

Section 2

Whenever there is a vacancy in the office of the Vice President, the President shall nominate a Vice President who shall take office upon confirmation by a majority vote of both Houses of Congress.

Section 3

Whenever the President transmits to the President pro tempore of the Senate and the Speaker of the House of Representatives his written declaration that he is unable to discharge the powers and duties of his office, and until he transmits to them a written declaration to the contrary, such powers and duties shall be discharged by the Vice President as Acting President.

Section 4

Whenever the Vice President and a majority of either the principal officers of the executive departments or of such other body as Congress may by law provide, transmit to the President pro tempore of the Senate and the Speaker of the House of Representatives their written declaration that the President is unable to discharge the powers and duties of his office, the Vice President shall immediately assume the powers and duties of the office as Acting President.

Thereafter, when the President transmits to the President pro tempore of the Senate and the Speaker of the House of Representatives his written declaration that no inability exists, he shall resume the powers and duties of his office unless the Vice President and a majority of either the principal officers of the executive departments or of such other body as Congress may by law provide, transmit within four days to the President pro tempore of the Senate and the Speaker of the House of Representatives their written declaration that the President is unable to discharge the powers and duties of his office. Thereupon Congress shall decide the issue, assembling within forty-eight hours for that purpose if not in session. If the Congress, within twenty-one days after receipt of the latter written declaration, or, if Congress is not in session, within twenty-one days after Congress is required to assemble, determines by two-thirds vote of both Houses that the President is unable to discharge the powers and duties of his office, the Vice President shall continue to discharge the same as Acting President; otherwise, the President shall resume the powers and duties of his office.

Amendment XXVI [Ratified in 1971]

Section 1

The right of citizens of the United States, who are eighteen years of age or older, to vote shall not be denied nor abridged by the United States or by any State on account of age.

Section 2

The Congress shall have power to enforce this article by appropriate legislation.

Amendment XXVII [Ratified in 1992]

No law, varying the compensation for the services of the Senators and Representatives, shall take effect, until an election of Representatives shall have intervened.

Footnotes:
1. Altered by the 16th Amendment.
2. Altered by the 14th Amendment
3. Superseded by the 17th Amendment.
4. Altered by the 17th Amendment.
5. Superseded by the 16th Amendment.
6. Superseded by the 12th Amendment.
7. Cf. the 11th Amendment.
8. Superseded by the 14th Amendment, Sec. 1
9. Voided by the 13th Amendment.
10. Repealed by the 21st Amendment.

Section A.3

Administrative Agency–a governmental body charged with administering and implementing particular legislation; administrative agencies have legislative, executive, and judicial powers.

Affirm–when a decision is affirmed, the appellate court determines that the lower court reached the correct decision.

Appellee–party against whom the appeal is filed.

Appellant–person who appeals the lower court's decision.

Arbitration- a form of alternate disputed resolution often used in a commercial setting where both parties agree to have a third party or arbitrator resolve a controversy.

Assault–the intentional tort consisting of an act intended to put another in fear of an immediate battery.

Assumption of the Risk–a defense to a negligence action asserting that when the plaintiff knows of the danger but voluntarily exposes himself to the harm, the plaintiff will be barred from recovery.

Battery–the intentional tort consisting of an intentional touching of the body of another or an object closely associated with the body in an offensive or harmful manner.

Bench Trial–a trial with no jury where the judge decides both factual and legal questions.

Bill–the form used for the introduction of proposed legislation.

Business Visitor–one who enters the premises for a business purpose.

Caption–part of a case that identifies the parties to the lawsuit.

Charging the Jury–the situation where the judge explains what law the jury must consider in reaching a verdict.

Closing Speech–a speech given by each side after the evidence has been heard arguing to the jury how and why the evidence supports their view or theory of the case.

Comity–the principle that allows the recognition of the rules and laws of a foreign jurisdiction in this country.

Comparative Negligence–a defense to a negligence action that as long as the plaintiff's negligence is not greater than the defendant's, the plaintiff may recover damages, but the verdict will be reduced by the percentage of the plaintiff's negligence.

Compensatory Damages–a sum of money that will return an aggrieved party to the status quo as though nothing ever happened.

Compurgation–one of the three English pre-jury methods of trial that was necessary when a person's oath was questioned; compurgation required the accused person to bring forward 11 supporters, called compurgators, making 12 people in all who would be willing to take an oath on behalf of the accused.

Compurgators–the 11 persons who would swear on behalf of the accused in a compurgation; they did not swear that what the accused said was true but served more as character witnesses.

Concurring Opinion–an opinion written by a judge who agrees with the outcome of the case but wants to note a difference in logic for reaching the decision.

Constitutional Relativity–the concept that the constitution was intentionally written in broad vague terms to ensure that the constitution could adapt to changing times.

Continuance–a situation in which a case is postponed until a later date.

Contract–the exchange of promises voluntarily made by those whose agreement is enforceable in court; the five essential elements of a contract are offer, acceptance, consideration, capacity, and legality.

Contributory Negligence–a defense to a negligence action asserting the failure of the plaintiff to act as a reasonable person under the circumstances.

Crime–a violation of those duties which an individual owes to the community and for breach of which the law requires that the offender make satisfaction to the public; an offense against society or the state that violates a penal law and carries a possible punishment of imprisonment.

Criminal Complaint–a statement of facts about a crime which later becomes the basis for formal charges against the accused.

Criminal Homicide–a unlawful killing of another; includes murder and manslaughter.

Defamation–a statement that is false and tends to harm the reputation of another or to lower him in the estimation of the community.

Defendant–party who is being sued.

Derivative Suit–litigation brought by a minority shareholder on behalf of the corporation to contest the illegal or improper acts of the majority.

Dissenting Opinion–a judge writes a dissent when he or she disagrees with the result reached by the majority; the dissent has no value as precedent.

Double Jeopardy–the right guaranteed by the Fifth Amendment of the United States Constitution that no person shall be tried twice for the same offense.

Duty of Care–establishes the type of behavior a person must exhibit in a given situation; the basic rule is that a person must conform to the standard of care of a "reasonable person under the circumstances."

Excusable Homicide–a killing by accident or mistake where the wrongdoer does not have criminal culpability.

Fair Use–an exception to the Copyright Act which permits the utilization of copyrighted work for the restricted purpose of criticism, comment, news reporting, teaching, scholarship or research.

False Imprisonment–the unlawful detention of a person against his or her will.

Felony Murder–an unintentional killing of another committed during the commission of a felony; also called "second degree murder."

First Degree Murder–an unlawful killing of another with malice aforethought and the specific intent to kill.

Forum non-conveniens–means that the place of the trial is inconvenient for the parties and the witnesses involved in the trial.

Gift–a transfer of title to property without payment or compensation.

Good–personal property that is both tangible and movable.

Homicide–the killing of another human.

Hostile Environment–a type of sexual harassment that does not involve specific consequences like economic loss, but under which a victim suffers a down-graded work atmosphere, pervaded with unpleasantness.

Imputed Negligence–the concept that because of a special relationship that exists between the parties, one person can be held liable for the negligence of the other; also called vicarious liability.

Injunction–an equitable order issued by a court that directs a person to do something (mandatory injunction) or not to do something (prohibitory injunction).

Insanity–a defense to a crime based on the criminal's failure to appreciate what he or she did is wrong or the person did not know the difference between right and wrong because of some mental disease or defect.

Intangible Property–property that is not a physical object, e.g. a patent or trademark.

Intentional Tort–when a wrongdoer purposely sets out to harm another.

Intoxication–not a defense to a criminal act unless it negates a specific mental state.

Invasion of Privacy–the intentional tort consisting of an unwarranted intrusion upon a person's right to be left alone.

Involuntary Manslaughter–an unintentional killing of another which is the result of outrageous conduct or gross negligence.

Joint Ownership–a term used when ownership to property is shared and title is held by two or more people (see also "concurrent ownership").

Joint Tenancy with the Right of Survivorship–a form of concurrent or joint ownership in which the co-owners have essentially equal rights to the property; if one co-owner dies, her share will pass to the surviving co-owner.

Judge–the person who presides over the trial and decides questions of law.

Judgment on the Verdict–the final pronouncement by the court of a defendant's guilt or innocence after the verdict has been announced.

Judicial Immunity–a judge has immunity from suit when he or she acts within the scope of judicial authority and in the discharge of official duties.

Jurisdiction–refers to the power of a court to determine the merits of a dispute and to grant an aggrieved party relief.

Jury–the individuals who decide questions of fact.

Justifiable Homicide–a killing in self-defense or an execution carried out by court order.

Larceny–the taking and carrying away of property of another without consent and with the intention of depriving the other of the goods permanently.

Lease–an encumbrance upon property where a landlord holds property as a fee simple absolute but has given a tenant the rights to possess and use the property exclusively.

Legal Capacity–the capacity of the organization to sue and be sued in its own name.

Lessee–a tenant who is given the rights to possess and use the property exclusively by a landlord who holds property as a fee simple absolute.

Lessor–a landlord who holds property as a fee simple absolute but has given a tenant the rights to possess and use the property exclusively.

Libel–the publication of defamatory matter by written or printed words.

Liquidated Damages–a sum of money agreed upon by contracting parties that will be paid in the event of a default or breach of contract.

Majority Opinion–a decision reached by more than half of the judges of an appellate court panel; a decision rendered by the majority of the court which is the law.

Malice Aforethought–describes the conduct that exhibits a wanton disregard for the safety of others.

Mediation–a form of alternate dispute resolution used primarily in disputes between labor and management; mediation is advisory in nature.

Mens Rea–the necessary state of mind that a perpetrator must have to be found guilty of committing a particular crime; criminal intent.

Mini-trial–a form or alternate dispute resolution where the parties submit their case to a panel of experts or neutral advisor who suggest the likely outcome if the case were to go to court.

Negligence–the failure to do what a reasonable person would do under the circumstances; the three elements of negligence are 1) a duty, 2) breach of duty, and 3) the negligence must be the proximate cause of the harm.

Neighborhood Justice Centers–programs where local cases, usually neighborhood or family disputes, are decided by a panel of local residents.

No Duty to Rescue Rule–the rule under which the law does not force a person to help a stranger in an emergency unless that person has somehow caused the problem or has a special relationship to the party.

Nominal Damages–provide a remedy where a technical wrong has been committed but no actual harm has resulted.

Non-binding Trial–see "mini-trial."

Opening Statement–a speech given by each side at the beginning of the case describing what the evidence will prove.

Permanent Injunction–a final resolution of a dispute issued after a full hearing of all relevant factors.

Personal Property–consists of all property that is not land or attached to land; the two kinds of personal property are tangible and intangible; includes such things as a car, book, clothes, and furniture as well as bank accounts, stocks, bonds, patents and copyrights.

Plaintiff–party who initiates the case.

Precedent–the process whereby judges apply the decision and rules or prior cases to the present case over which they are presiding; see also "*stare decisis.*"

Preliminary Injunction–an order granted as an emergency measure before a full hearing on the merits can be held.

Private Judging–a form of alternate dispute resolution used when parties are constrained by time and can afford to hire a private judge; private judging proceeds as a normal trial would be conducted.

Private Law–involves matters between individuals; most common forms are contract, tort, and property law.

Procedural Law–the way that substantive law is made, enforced, and administered.

Products Liability–the concept of holding sellers of defective products liable for harm caused to the user, consumer, or his property even though the seller has exercised all possible care in the preparation and sale of the product; also called strict liability.

Property–everything that may be owned, either as real property or personal property.

Property Law–deals with the rights and duties that arise out of the ownership or possession of real or personal property; defines and enforces the rights and responsibilities that accompany ownership.

Proximate Cause–requires that there be a reasonable connection between the negligence of the defendant and the harm suffered by the plaintiff.

Public Law–involves the rights of society as a whole, and those interests are usually handle by a government agency; most common forms are criminal, constitutional, and administrative law.

Punitive Damages–a sum of money awarded to punish the tort-feasor for his or her misconduct so that the type of incident in question will never occur again.

Quid Pro Quo–a type of sexual harassment where an employee is expected to give in to sexual demands or suffer the loss of some specific job or benefit.

Rape–the unlawful carnal knowledge of a person another through force or the threat of force and without consent.

Real Property–land and everything attached to the land.

Receiving Stolen Property–intentionally obtaining property of another that has been stolen, or believed to be stolen.

Reformation–a remedy that allows modification of a contract that does not reflect the true intention of the parties.

Remand–the appellate court remands—or sends back—a case to the trial court when the appellate court finds that the trial judge committed an error in deciding the case or additional evidence must be obtained.

Res Judicata–"the thing has been decided."

Rescission–the voiding of a contract for some reason such as misrepresentation, fraud, duress, undue influence or impossibility, under which each party must return the property they received from the other.

Restitution–a remedy to prevent one party from unfairly benefiting at the expense of another.

Reverse–the appellate court reverses a decision when it finds that the lower court's decision was incorrect.

Rights Theory–the ethical theory that focuses on the reasons for actions.

Robbery–larceny with the additional requirement that the taking be accomplished by force or threat of force.

Second Degree Murder–an unintentional killing of another committed during the commission of a felony; also called felony murder.

Self-defense–the right of a person unlawfully attacked to use reasonable force to protect himself.

Slander–a defamatory statement that is verbal or oral in nature.

Sovereign Immunity–the concept that prohibits suits against any level of the government unless the sovereign gives its expressed consent to the litigation.

Standing–the concept that a plaintiff in a lawsuit must have a direct and substantial interest in the outcome of the case that he or she intends to bring.

Stare Decisis–the process whereby judges apply the decision and rules or prior cases to the present case over which they are presiding; (see also "precedent").

Statute of Frauds–requirement that certain agreements be in writing in order to enforceable by the court.

Statute of Limitations–the time period within which an aggrieved party must institute suit or the claim will be forever barred.

Statutory Rape–generally occurs when a man over the age of 16 has sexual relations with the consent of a girl under sixteen; her consent is presumed meaningless because of her young age.

Strict Liability–see "products liability."

Substantive Due Process–the requirement that the law be fundamentally fair; legislation must be capable of serving a legitimate public interest, and the law cannot be vague.

Substantive Law–the "actual law" which defines the duties and rights of members of society.

Tangible Property–a physical object.

Tenancy by the Entirety–a special form of co-ownership for married couples which carries the right of survivorship; however, neither spouse can convey his or her interest in the property since each spouse owns a 100 percent interest in the property.

Tenancy in Common–a form of concurrent or joint ownership in which the co-owners have essentially equal rights to the property; if one co-owner dies, his share will pass to his heirs.

Third Degree Murder–a killing of another with malice aforethought but with no specific intent to kill and not occurring during the commission of a felony.

Title–the right of ownership.

Trespasser–one who comes upon the premises of another without consent and with no legal right to be on the property.

TRO–(temporary restraining order) an injunction granted without notice to the defendant.

Tort–a private or civil wrong against an individual for which the court will award money damages; torts are classified into the categories of negligence or intentional torts.

Tort Damages–a sum of money that should place the injured party in as substantially a good position as she occupied before the injury.

Trial by Cold Water–a form of trial by ordeal where the accused was bound and placed in a body of water that had been purified by prayer. If he sank, he was considered innocent because the water would "accept" one who was pure; floating indicated that the accused's body was polluted by sin by rejecting it.

Trial by Fire–a form of trial by ordeal where the accused was tested with some type of fire, for example holding a hot iron or walking across hot coals. The accused was guilty if burned or innocent if not burned; sometimes the test was not whether the person was burned but how well the burn healed.

Trial by Hot Water–a form of trial by ordeal where the accused would remove a ring from a cauldron of boiling water after being cleansed by prayer; if he was burned he was considered guilty, and if he was unharmed he was considered innocent.

Trial by Ordeal–an old fashioned method of determining justice where the accused was subject to some sort of physical test, the results of which were supposed to indicate guilt or innocence; e.g. trial by hot water, trial by cold water, trial by fire.

United States Constitution–the legal document which establishes the fundamental rights of United States citizens and protects them from unlawful governmental interference.

Utilitarian Theory–the theory of ethics that focuses on the consequences of actions.

Venue–the place where a case should be heard.

Verdict–the decision regarding a defendant's guilt or innocence made by either a judge or jury.

Vicarious Liability–see "imputed negligence."

Voir Dire–process for selecting a jury by which members of the jury are questioned by the judge or attorneys to ascertain whether they are suitable to serve at trial; issue of prejudice, conflicts of interest, and philosophies of life are explored.

Wager of Law–one of the three English pre-jury methods of trial that simply required the accused person to take an oath, swearing to a fact.

Whistleblower–a person who feels compelled to get certain information into the hands of people who can act to correct a problem when it seems that the problem cannot be corrected otherwise.

STUDENT NOTES

STUDENT NOTES